CASE CLOSED
VOLUME 69

Gosho Aoyama

Case Briefing:

Subject:
Occupation:
Special Skills:
Equipment:

Jimmy Kudo, a.k.a. Conan Edogawa
High School Student/Detective
Analytical thinking and deductive reasoning, Soccer
Bow Tie Voice Transmitter, Super Sneakers,
Homing Glasses, Stretchy Suspenders

The subject is hot on the trail of a pair of suspicious men in black when he is attacked from behind and administered a strange substance which physically transforms him into a first grader. When the subject confides in the eccentric inventor Dr. Agasa, they decide to keep the subject's true identity a secret for the safety of everyone around him. Assuming the new identity of first-grader Conan Edogawa, the subject continues to assist the police force on their most baffling cases. The only problem is that most crime-solving professionals won't take a little kid's advice!

Table of Contents

CASE CLOSED

CONFIDEN

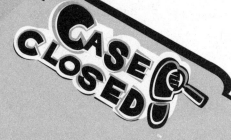

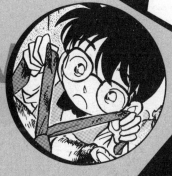

CASE CLOSED

Volume 69
Shonen Sunday Edition

Story and Art by GOSHO AOYAMA

MEITANTEI CONAN Vol. 69
by Gosho AOYAMA
© 1994 Gosho AOYAMA
All rights reserved.
Original Japanese edition published by SHOGAKUKAN.
English translation rights in the United States of America, Canada,
the United Kingdom and Ireland arranged with SHOGAKUKAN.

Translation
Tetsuichiro Miyaki

Touch-up & Lettering
Freeman Wong

Cover & Graphic Design
Andrea Rice

Editor
Shaenon K. Garrity

Printed in the U.S.A.

Published by VIZ Media, LLC
P.O. Box 77010
San Francisco, CA 94107

10 9 8 7 6 5 4 3 2 1
First printing, January 2019

FILE 1: THE CLIENT FROM THE DEEP

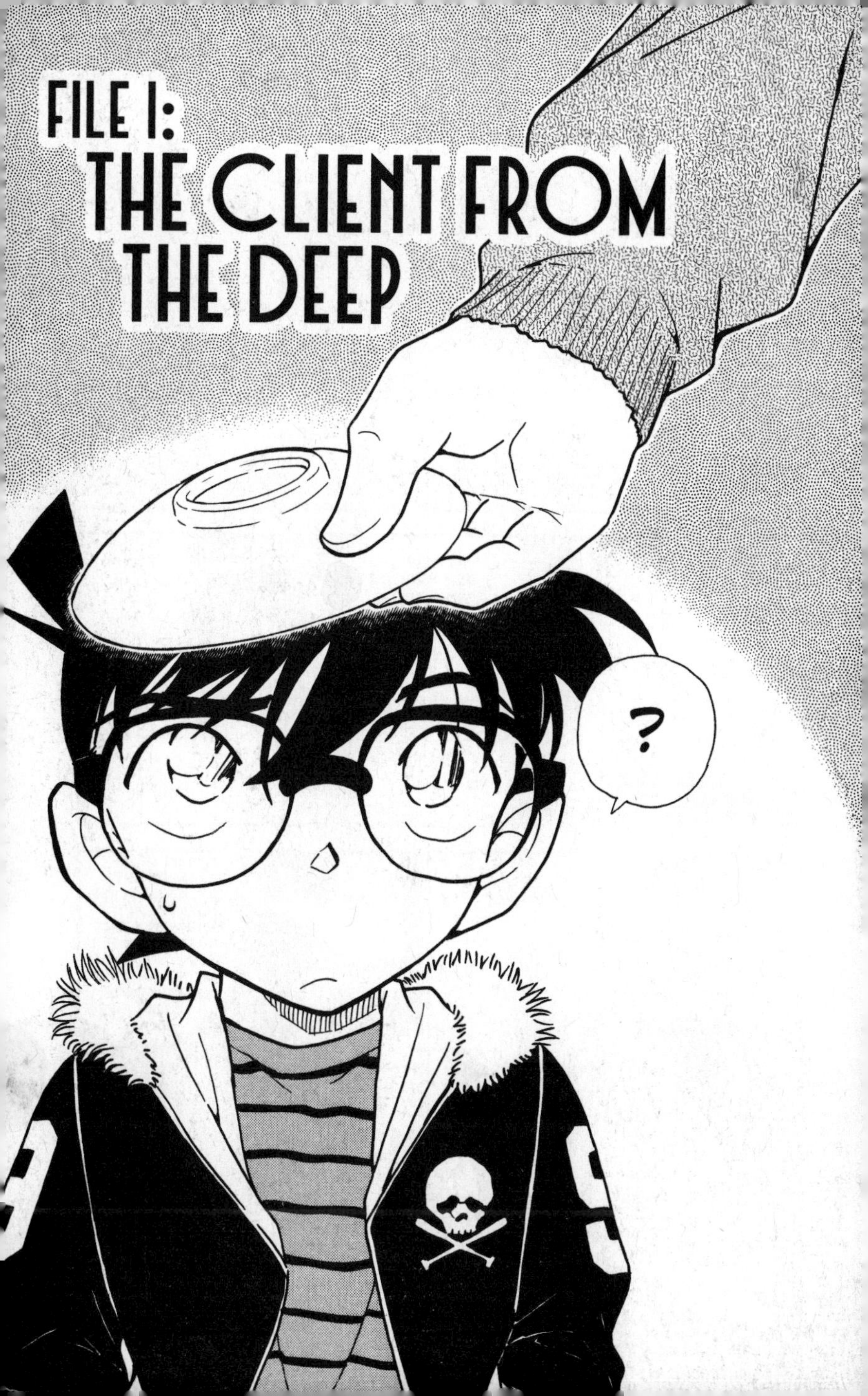
?

"...I AM WRITING TO YOU BECAUSE YOU ARE A RENOWNED DETECTIVE."

VROOM

"DEAR MR. MOORE..."

"PLEASE USE YOUR REMARKABLE DEDUCTION SKILLS TO CLEAR MY NAME."

"ELEVEN YEARS AGO, I WAS ACCUSED OF MURDER."

YEAH... ...MAYBE.

WAIT A SEC! ARE WE MEETING WITH A MURDERER ON THE RUN?

"MIKA TATEZATO."

"MEET ME ON THE MORNING OF JANUARY 24 AT THE KORA INN, IN THE VILLAGE OF KUCHIBASHI IN GUNMA, AND I'LL EXPLAIN ALL THE DETAILS. IT'S NEAR THE SCENE OF THE CRIME."

Dear Mr. Moore,

I am writing to you because you are a renowned detective. Eleven years ago, I was accused... Please use your remarkable deduction skills to clear...

Meet me on the morning of January 24 at the Kora Inn, in the village of Kuchibashi in Gunma, and I'll explain all the details. It's near the scene of the crime.

Mika Tatezato

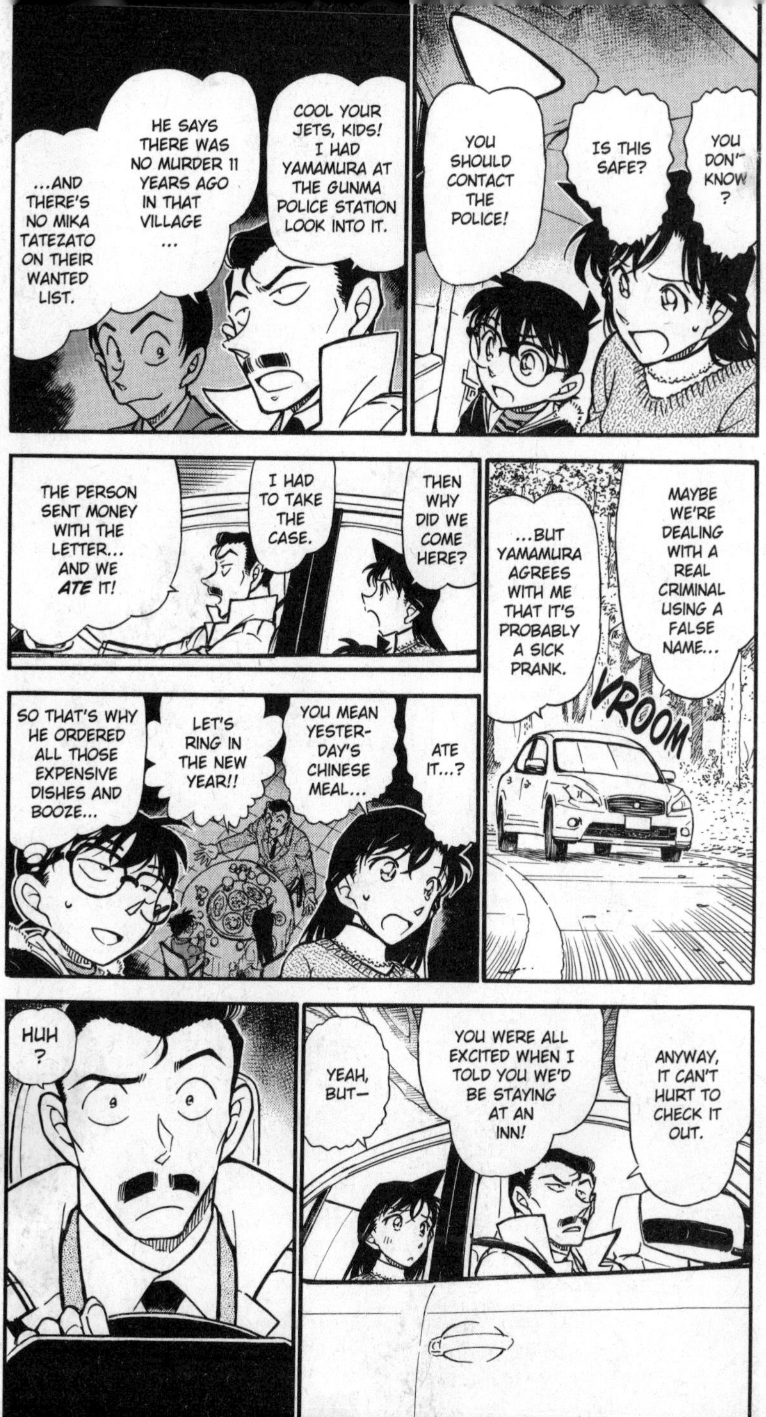
YOU DON'T KNOW?
IS THIS SAFE?
YOU SHOULD CONTACT THE POLICE!
COOL YOUR JETS, KIDS! I HAD YAMAMURA AT THE GUNMA POLICE STATION LOOK INTO IT.
HE SAYS THERE WAS NO MURDER 11 YEARS AGO IN THAT VILLAGE...
...AND THERE'S NO MIKA TATEZATO ON THEIR WANTED LIST.
MAYBE WE'RE DEALING WITH A REAL CRIMINAL USING A FALSE NAME...
...BUT YAMAMURA AGREES WITH ME THAT IT'S PROBABLY A SICK PRANK.
VROOM
THEN WHY DID WE COME HERE?
I HAD TO TAKE THE CASE.
THE PERSON SENT MONEY WITH THE LETTER... AND WE *ATE* IT!
ATE IT...?
YOU MEAN YESTERDAY'S CHINESE MEAL...
LET'S RING IN THE NEW YEAR!!
SO THAT'S WHY HE ORDERED ALL THOSE EXPENSIVE DISHES AND BOOZE...
ANYWAY, IT CAN'T HURT TO CHECK IT OUT.
YOU WERE ALL EXCITED WHEN I TOLD YOU WE'D BE STAYING AT AN INN!
YEAH, BUT—
HUH?

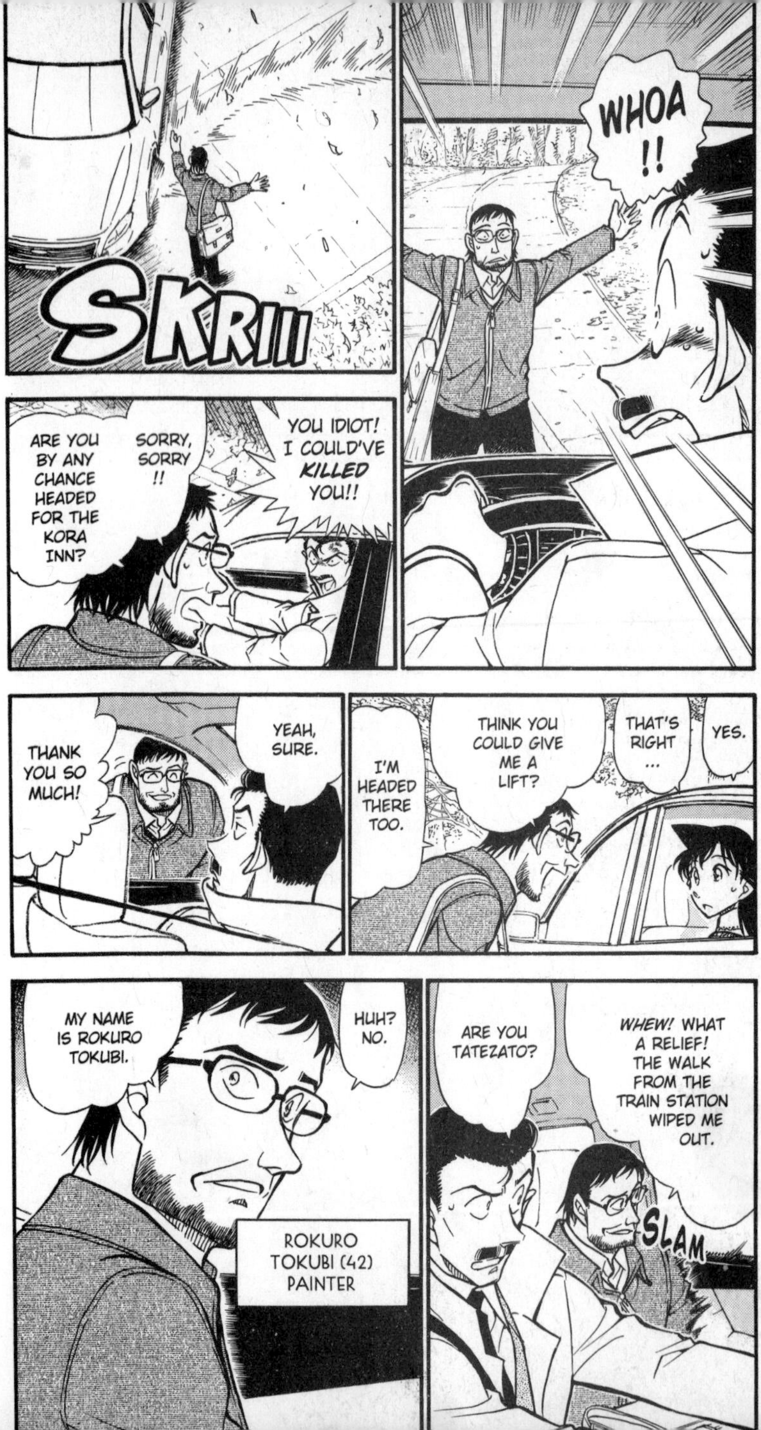
WHOA !!
SKRIII
YOU IDIOT! I COULD'VE KILLED YOU!!
SORRY, SORRY !!
ARE YOU BY ANY CHANCE HEADED FOR THE KORA INN?
YES.
THAT'S RIGHT ...
THINK YOU COULD GIVE ME A LIFT?
I'M HEADED THERE TOO.
YEAH, SURE.
THANK YOU SO MUCH!
WHEW! WHAT A RELIEF! THE WALK FROM THE TRAIN STATION WIPED ME OUT.
SLAM
ARE YOU TATEZATO?
HUH? NO.
MY NAME IS ROKURO TOKUBI.
ROKURO TOKUBI (42) PAINTER

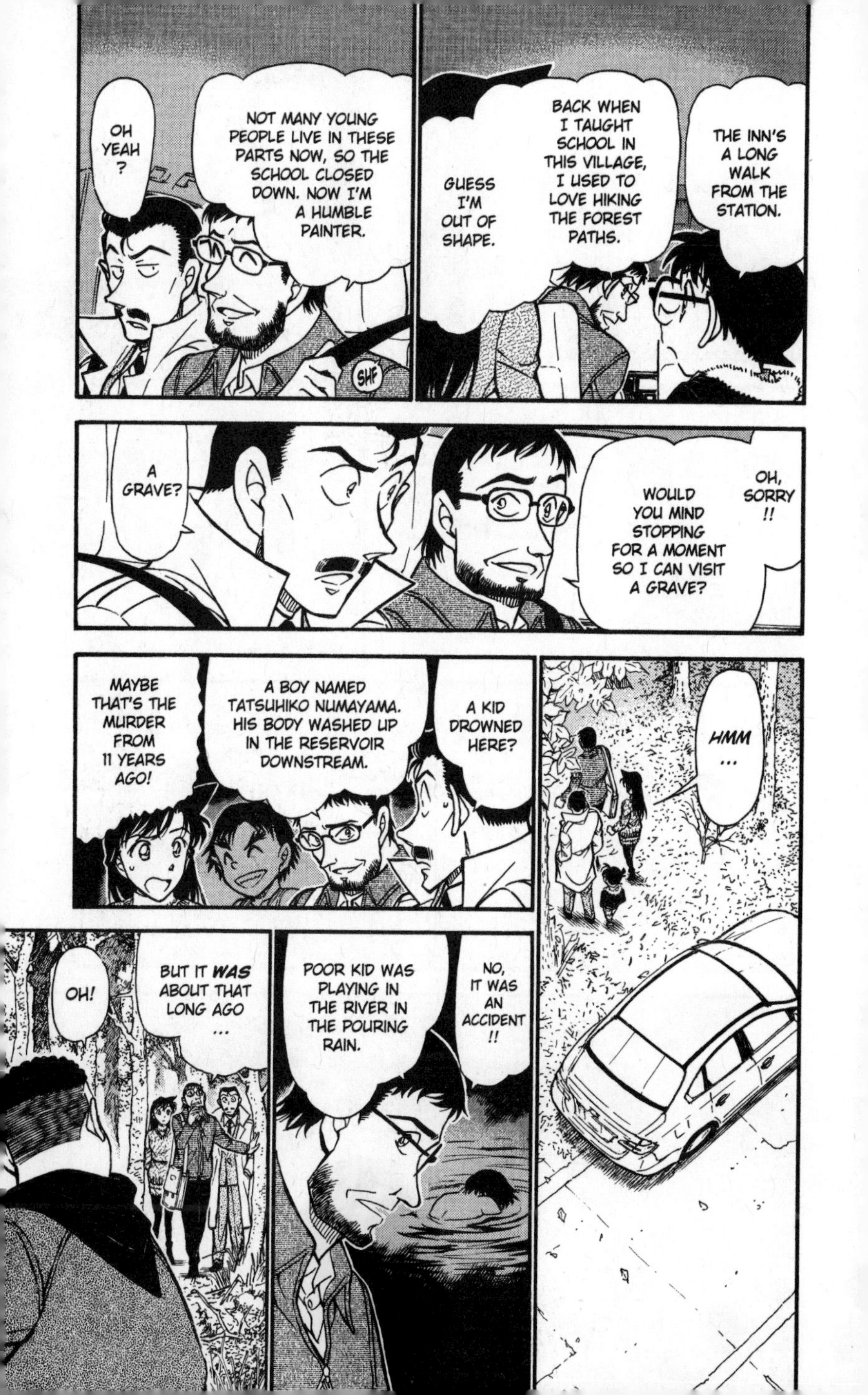
THE INN'S A LONG WALK FROM THE STATION.
BACK WHEN I TAUGHT SCHOOL IN THIS VILLAGE, I USED TO LOVE HIKING THE FOREST PATHS.
GUESS I'M OUT OF SHAPE.
NOT MANY YOUNG PEOPLE LIVE IN THESE PARTS NOW, SO THE SCHOOL CLOSED DOWN. NOW I'M A HUMBLE PAINTER.
SHF
OH YEAH?
OH, SORRY!!
WOULD YOU MIND STOPPING FOR A MOMENT SO I CAN VISIT A GRAVE?
A GRAVE?
HMM...
A KID DROWNED HERE?
A BOY NAMED TATSUHIKO NUMAYAMA. HIS BODY WASHED UP IN THE RESERVOIR DOWNSTREAM.
MAYBE THAT'S THE MURDER FROM 11 YEARS AGO!
NO, IT WAS AN ACCIDENT!!
POOR KID WAS PLAYING IN THE RIVER IN THE POURING RAIN.
BUT IT *WAS* ABOUT THAT LONG AGO...
OH!

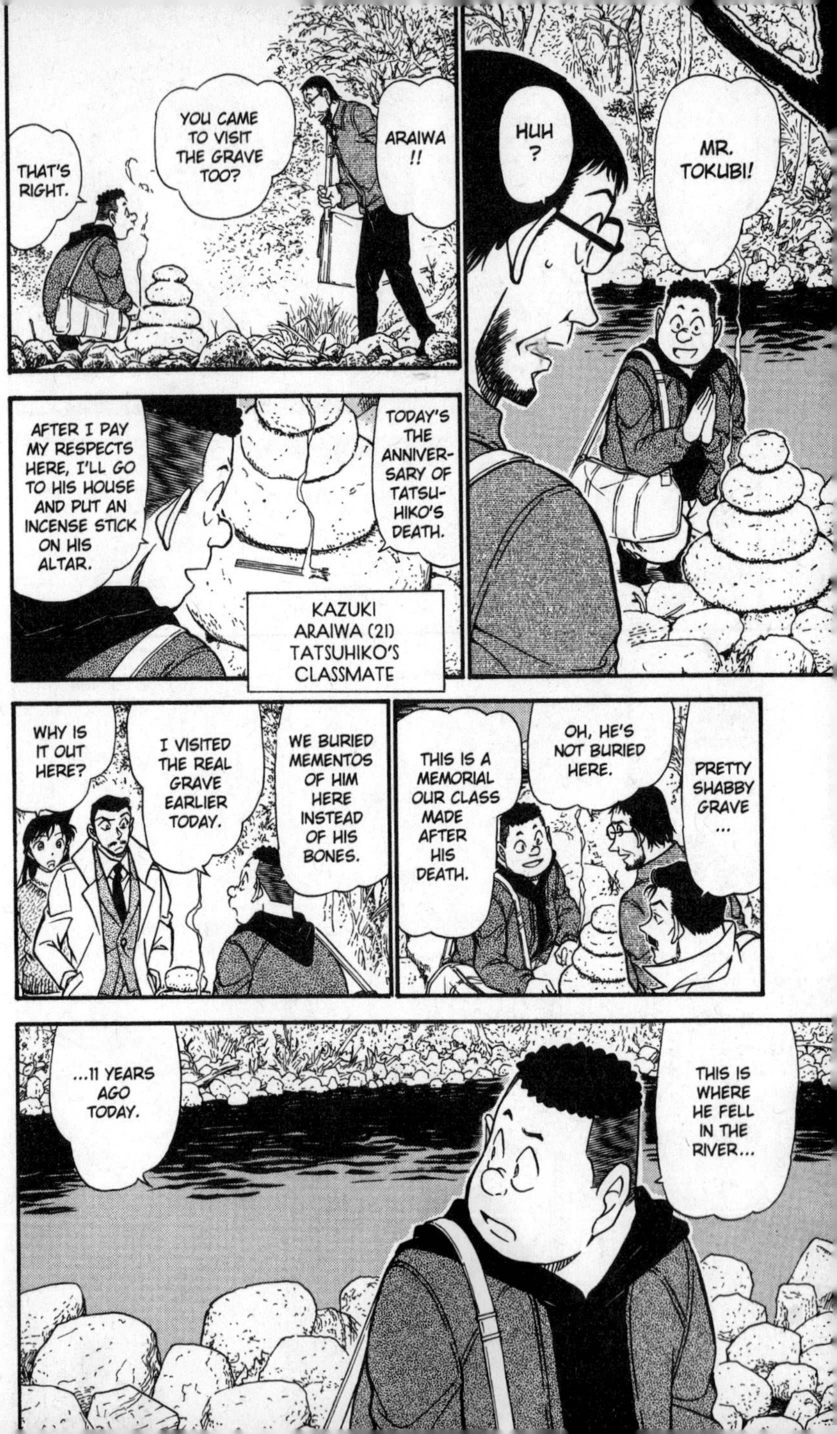
MR. TOKUBI!
HUH ?
ARAIWA !!
YOU CAME TO VISIT THE GRAVE TOO?
THAT'S RIGHT.
TODAY'S THE ANNIVERSARY OF TATSUHIKO'S DEATH.
AFTER I PAY MY RESPECTS HERE, I'LL GO TO HIS HOUSE AND PUT AN INCENSE STICK ON HIS ALTAR.
KAZUKI ARAIWA (21) TATSUHIKO'S CLASSMATE
PRETTY SHABBY GRAVE ...
OH, HE'S NOT BURIED HERE.
THIS IS A MEMORIAL OUR CLASS MADE AFTER HIS DEATH.
WE BURIED MEMENTOS OF HIM HERE INSTEAD OF HIS BONES.
I VISITED THE REAL GRAVE EARLIER TODAY.
WHY IS IT OUT HERE?
THIS IS WHERE HE FELL IN THE RIVER...
...11 YEARS AGO TODAY.

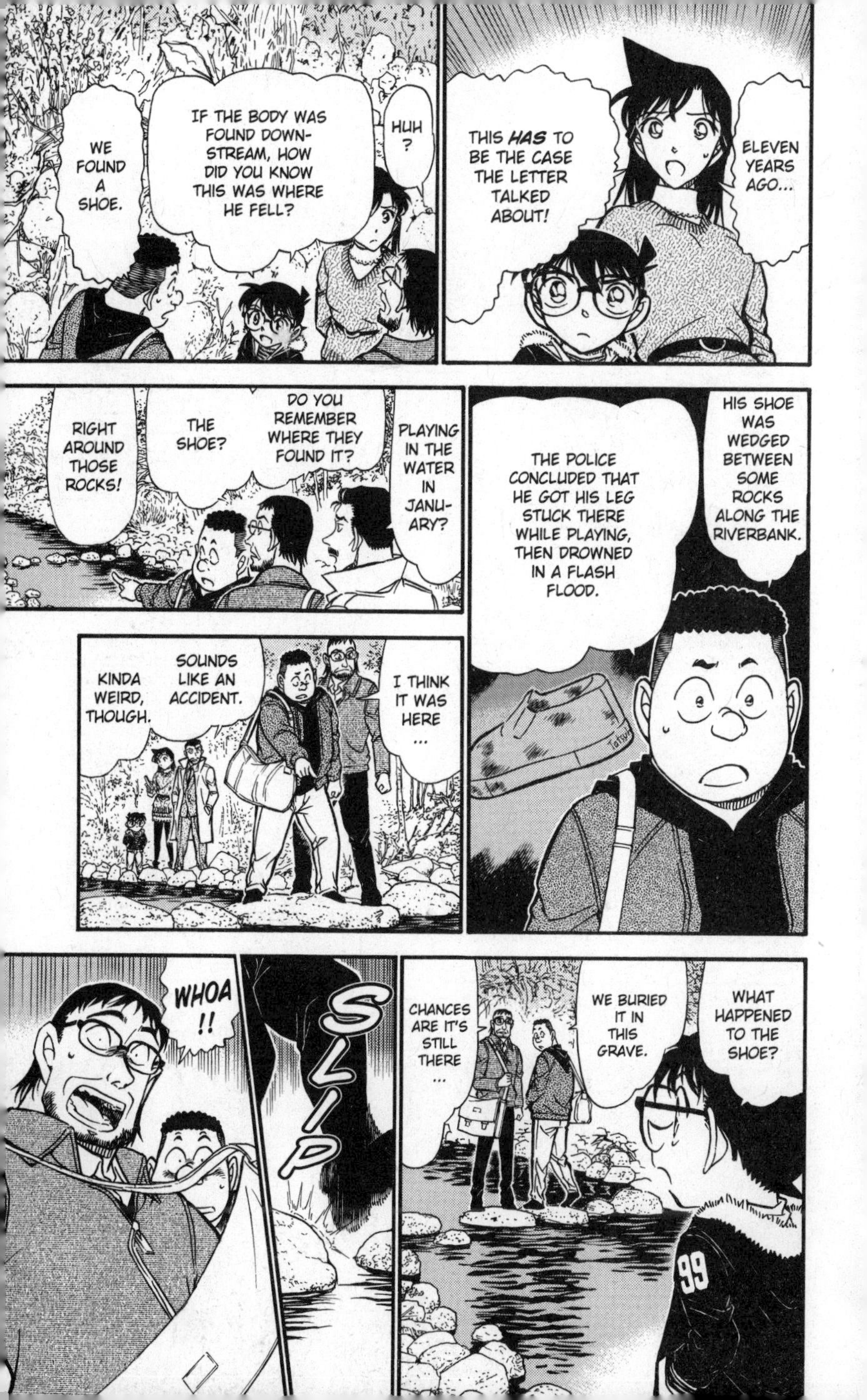
ELEVEN YEARS AGO...
THIS ***HAS*** TO BE THE CASE THE LETTER TALKED ABOUT!
HUH?
IF THE BODY WAS FOUND DOWN-STREAM, HOW DID YOU KNOW THIS WAS WHERE HE FELL?
WE FOUND A SHOE.
HIS SHOE WAS WEDGED BETWEEN SOME ROCKS ALONG THE RIVERBANK.
THE POLICE CONCLUDED THAT HE GOT HIS LEG STUCK THERE WHILE PLAYING, THEN DROWNED IN A FLASH FLOOD.
PLAYING IN THE WATER IN JANU-ARY?
DO YOU REMEMBER WHERE THEY FOUND IT?
THE SHOE?
RIGHT AROUND THOSE ROCKS!
I THINK IT WAS HERE ...
SOUNDS LIKE AN ACCIDENT.
KINDA WEIRD, THOUGH.
WHAT HAPPENED TO THE SHOE?
WE BURIED IT IN THIS GRAVE.
CHANCES ARE IT'S STILL THERE ...
SLIP
WHOA !!

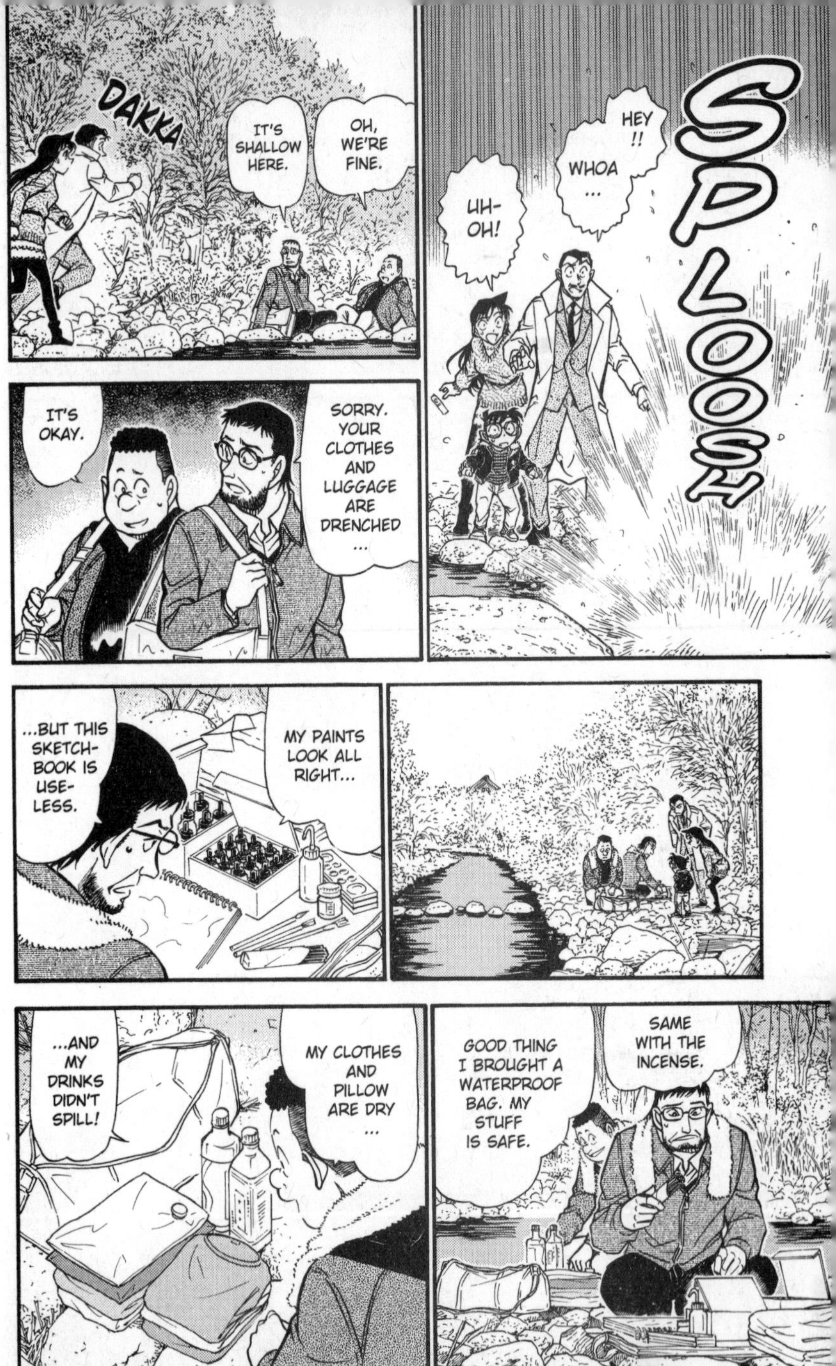

SPLOOSH
HEY !!
WHOA ...
UH-OH!
OH, WE'RE FINE.
IT'S SHALLOW HERE.
DAKKA
SORRY. YOUR CLOTHES AND LUGGAGE ARE DRENCHED ...
IT'S OKAY.
MY PAINTS LOOK ALL RIGHT...
...BUT THIS SKETCH-BOOK IS USE-LESS.
SAME WITH THE INCENSE.
GOOD THING I BROUGHT A WATERPROOF BAG. MY STUFF IS SAFE.
MY CLOTHES AND PILLOW ARE DRY ...
...AND MY DRINKS DIDN'T SPILL!

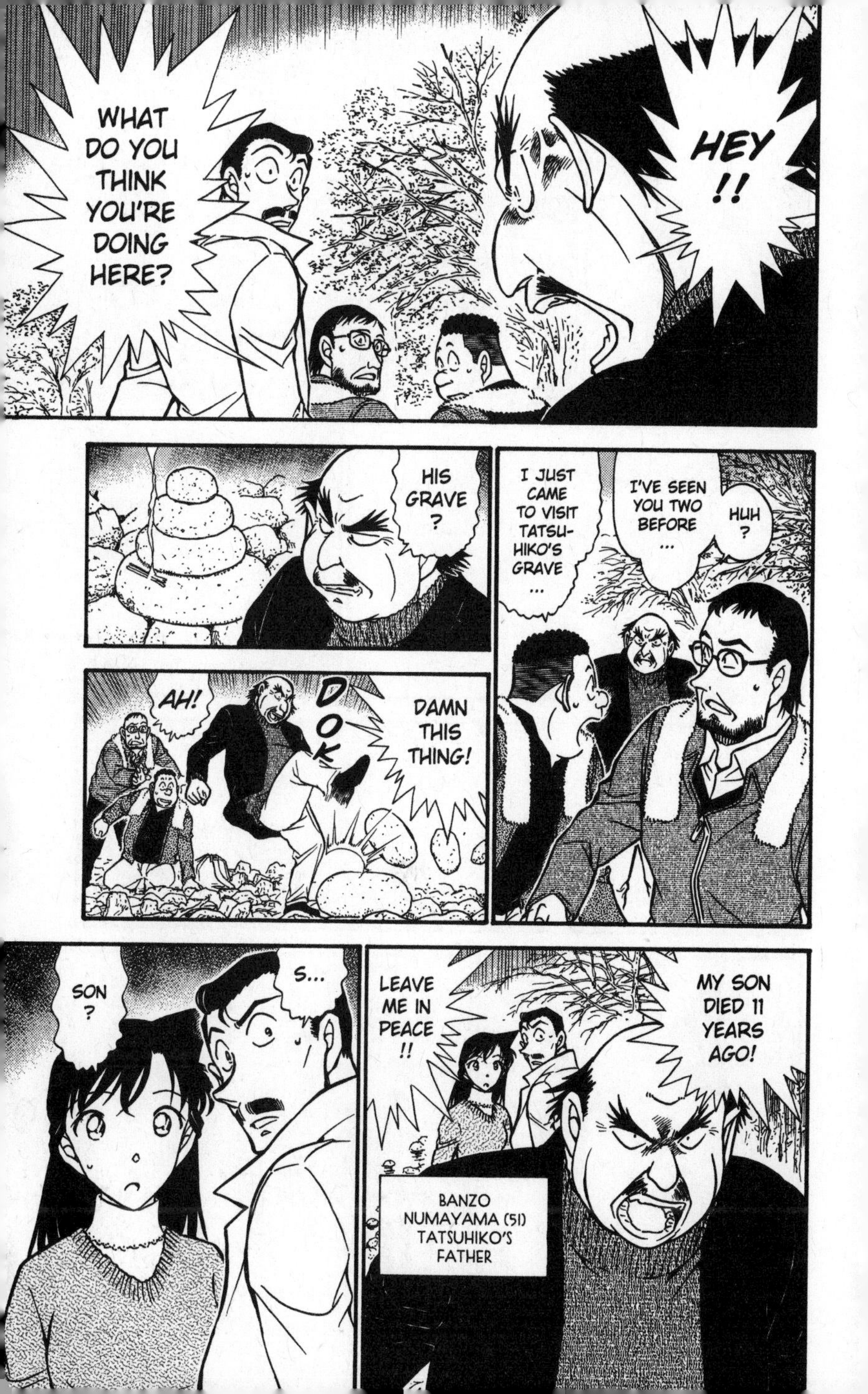
HEY!!
WHAT DO YOU THINK YOU'RE DOING HERE?
HUH?
I'VE SEEN YOU TWO BEFORE...
I JUST CAME TO VISIT TATSUHIKO'S GRAVE...
HIS GRAVE?
DOK
DAMN THIS THING!
AH!
MY SON DIED 11 YEARS AGO!
LEAVE ME IN PEACE!!
BANZO NUMAYAMA (51) TATSUHIKO'S FATHER
S...
SON?

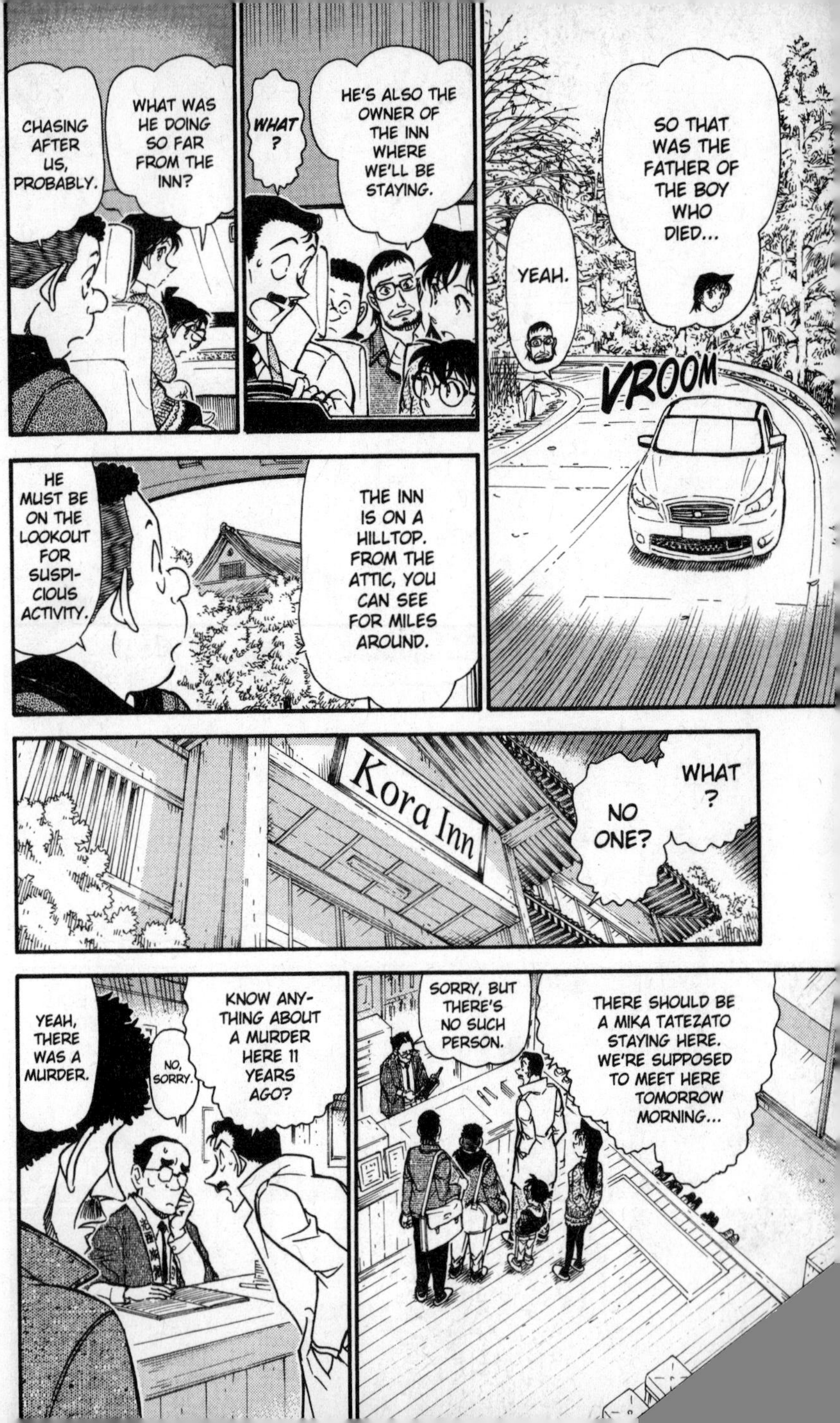
SO THAT WAS THE FATHER OF THE BOY WHO DIED...
YEAH.
VROOM
HE'S ALSO THE OWNER OF THE INN WHERE WE'LL BE STAYING.
WHAT?
WHAT WAS HE DOING SO FAR FROM THE INN?
CHASING AFTER US, PROBABLY.
THE INN IS ON A HILLTOP. FROM THE ATTIC, YOU CAN SEE FOR MILES AROUND.
HE MUST BE ON THE LOOKOUT FOR SUSPICIOUS ACTIVITY.
Kora Inn
WHAT?
NO ONE?
THERE SHOULD BE A MIKA TATEZATO STAYING HERE. WE'RE SUPPOSED TO MEET HERE TOMORROW MORNING...
SORRY, BUT THERE'S NO SUCH PERSON.
KNOW ANYTHING ABOUT A MURDER HERE 11 YEARS AGO?
NO, SORRY.
YEAH, THERE WAS A MURDER.

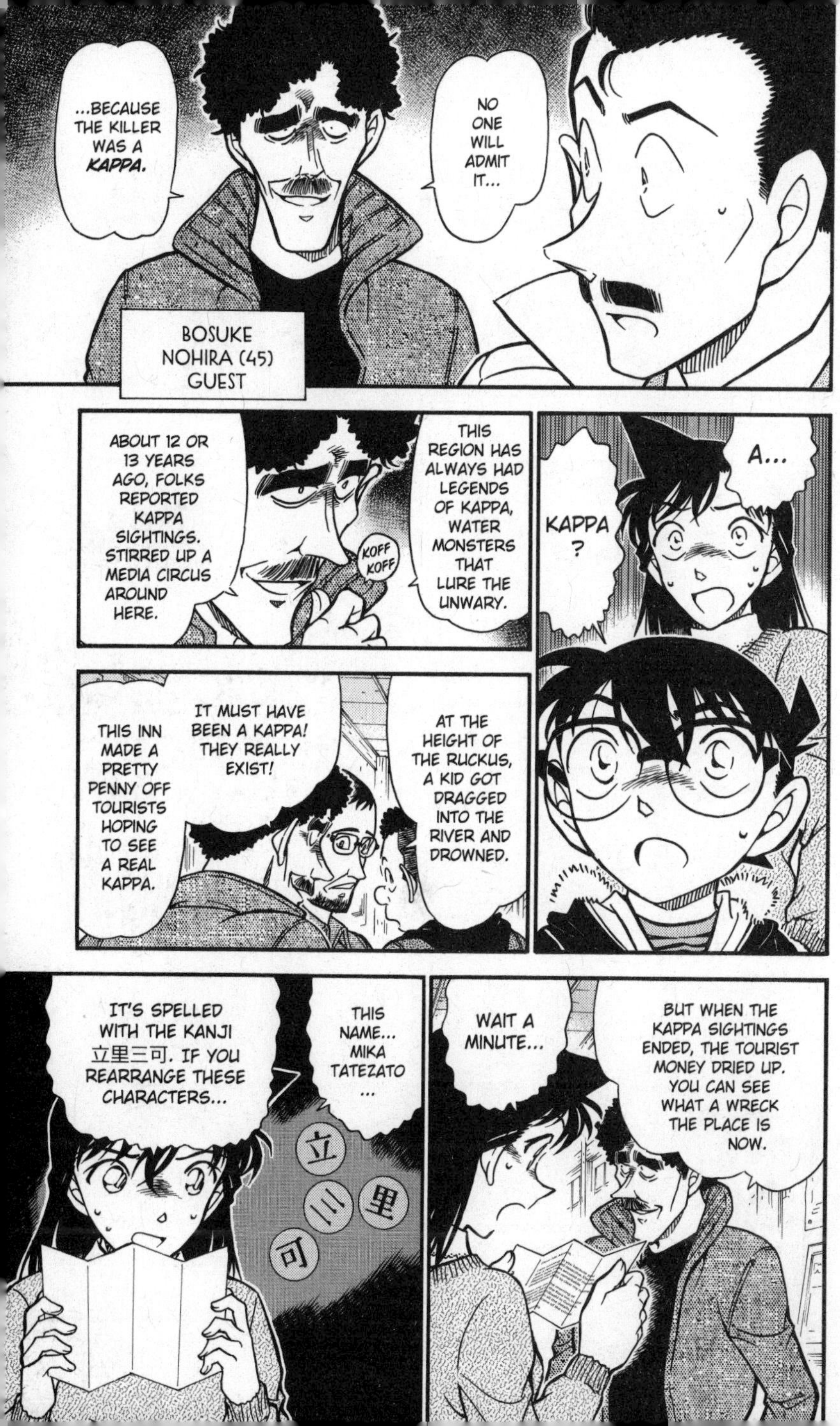
NO ONE WILL ADMIT IT...
...BECAUSE THE KILLER WAS A *KAPPA.*
BOSUKE NOHIRA (45) GUEST
A... KAPPA?
THIS REGION HAS ALWAYS HAD LEGENDS OF KAPPA, WATER MONSTERS THAT LURE THE UNWARY.
KOFF KOFF
ABOUT 12 OR 13 YEARS AGO, FOLKS REPORTED KAPPA SIGHTINGS. STIRRED UP A MEDIA CIRCUS AROUND HERE.
AT THE HEIGHT OF THE RUCKUS, A KID GOT DRAGGED INTO THE RIVER AND DROWNED.
IT MUST HAVE BEEN A KAPPA! THEY REALLY EXIST!
THIS INN MADE A PRETTY PENNY OFF TOURISTS HOPING TO SEE A REAL KAPPA.
BUT WHEN THE KAPPA SIGHTINGS ENDED, THE TOURIST MONEY DRIED UP. YOU CAN SEE WHAT A WRECK THE PLACE IS NOW.
WAIT A MINUTE...
THIS NAME... MIKA TATEZATO ...
IT'S SPELLED WITH THE KANJI 立里三可. IF YOU REARRANGE THESE CHARACTERS...
立
里
三
可

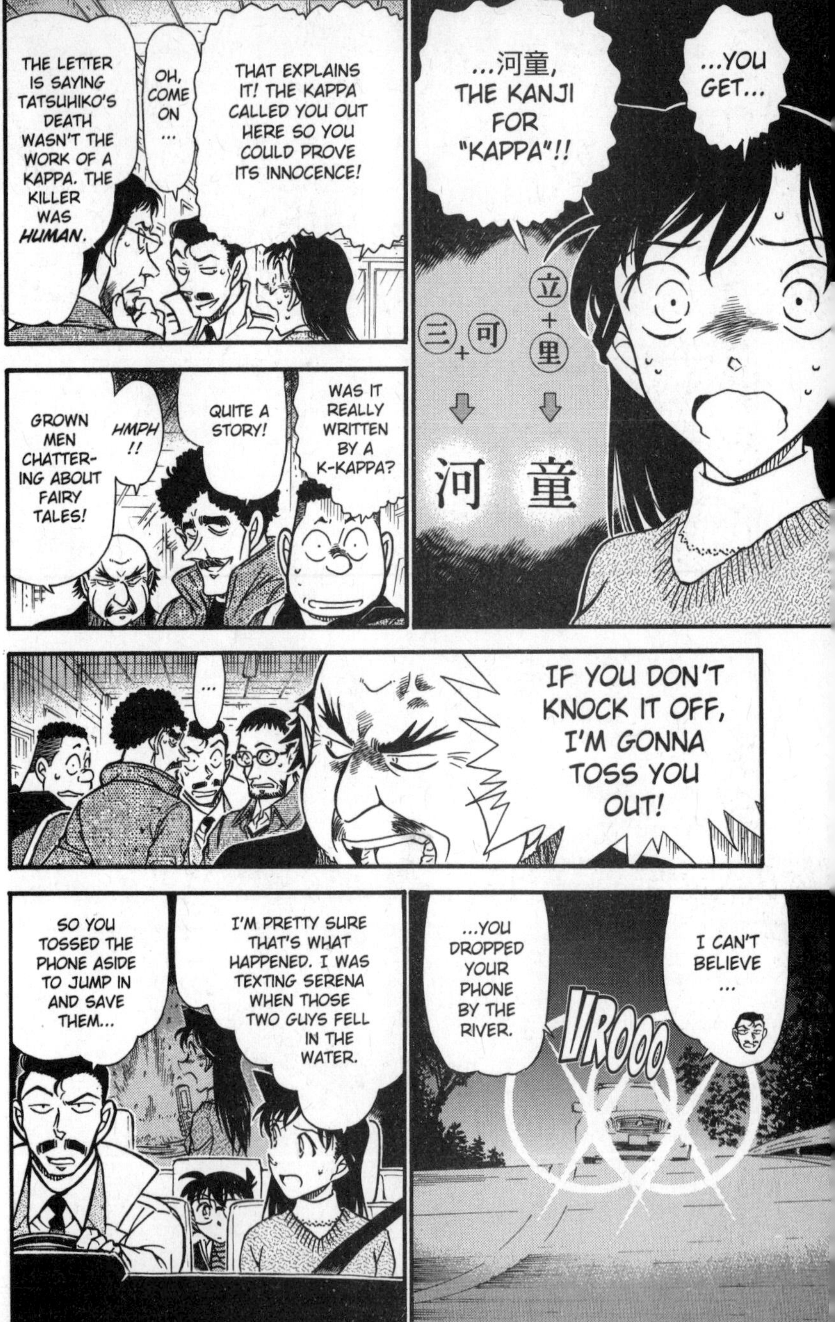
...YOU GET...
...河童, THE KANJI FOR "KAPPA"!!
立 + 里
童
三 + 可
河
THAT EXPLAINS IT! THE KAPPA CALLED YOU OUT HERE SO YOU COULD PROVE ITS INNOCENCE!
OH, COME ON ...
THE LETTER IS SAYING TATSUHIKO'S DEATH WASN'T THE WORK OF A KAPPA. THE KILLER WAS HUMAN.
WAS IT REALLY WRITTEN BY A K-KAPPA?
QUITE A STORY!
HMPH!!
GROWN MEN CHATTERING ABOUT FAIRY TALES!
IF YOU DON'T KNOCK IT OFF, I'M GONNA TOSS YOU OUT!
...
I CAN'T BELIEVE ...
...YOU DROPPED YOUR PHONE BY THE RIVER.
VROOO
I'M PRETTY SURE THAT'S WHAT HAPPENED. I WAS TEXTING SERENA WHEN THOSE TWO GUYS FELL IN THE WATER.
SO YOU TOSSED THE PHONE ASIDE TO JUMP IN AND SAVE THEM...

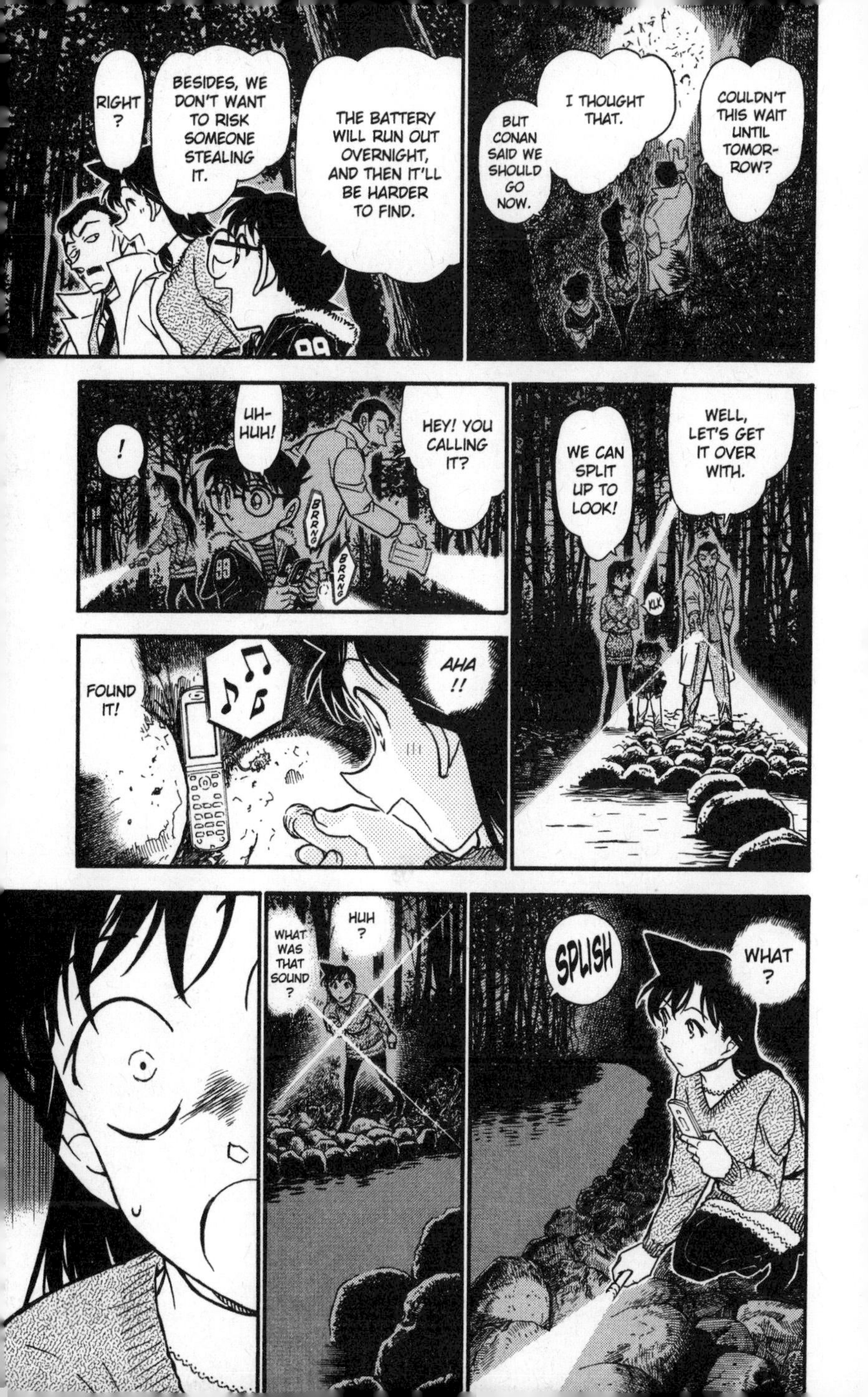
COULDN'T THIS WAIT UNTIL TOMORROW?
I THOUGHT THAT.
BUT CONAN SAID WE SHOULD GO NOW.
THE BATTERY WILL RUN OUT OVERNIGHT, AND THEN IT'LL BE HARDER TO FIND.
BESIDES, WE DON'T WANT TO RISK SOMEONE STEALING IT.
RIGHT?
WELL, LET'S GET IT OVER WITH.
WE CAN SPLIT UP TO LOOK!
KLIK
HEY! YOU CALLING IT?
UH-HUH!
BRRNG
BRRNG
!
AHA!!
FOUND IT!
WHAT?
SPLISH
HUH?
WHAT WAS THAT SOUND?

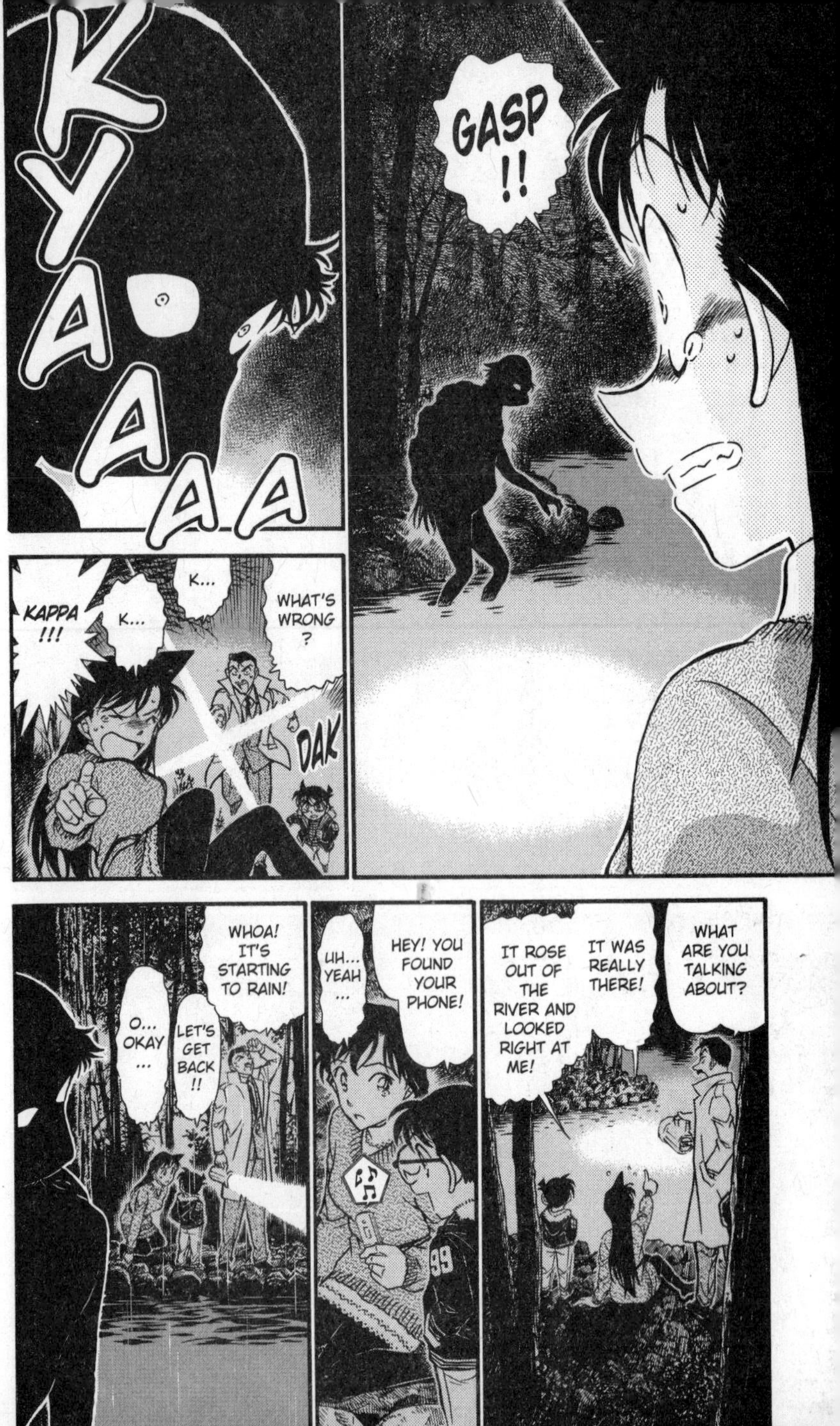
GASP !!
KYAAAAA
WHAT'S WRONG ?
K...
K...
KAPPA !!!
DAK
WHAT ARE YOU TALKING ABOUT?
IT WAS REALLY THERE!
IT ROSE OUT OF THE RIVER AND LOOKED RIGHT AT ME!
HEY! YOU FOUND YOUR PHONE!
UH... YEAH ...
WHOA! IT'S STARTING TO RAIN!
LET'S GET BACK !!
O... OKAY ...

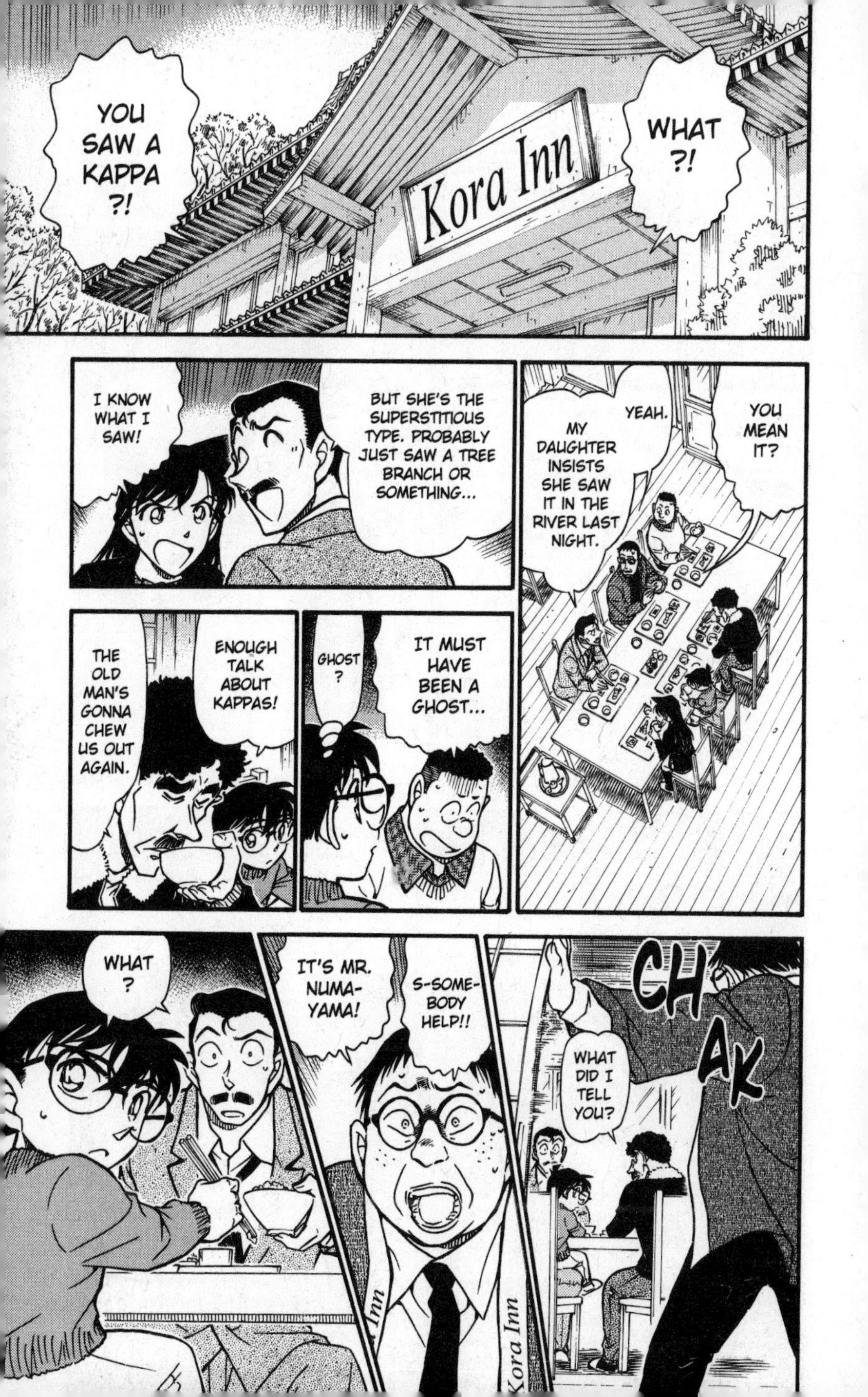
WHAT ?!
Kora Inn
YOU SAW A KAPPA ?!
YOU MEAN IT?
YEAH.
MY DAUGHTER INSISTS SHE SAW IT IN THE RIVER LAST NIGHT.
BUT SHE'S THE SUPERSTITIOUS TYPE. PROBABLY JUST SAW A TREE BRANCH OR SOMETHING...
I KNOW WHAT I SAW!
IT MUST HAVE BEEN A GHOST...
GHOST ?
ENOUGH TALK ABOUT KAPPAS!
THE OLD MAN'S GONNA CHEW US OUT AGAIN.
CHAK
WHAT DID I TELL YOU?
Kora Inn
S-SOMEBODY HELP!!
IT'S MR. NUMA-YAMA!
WHAT ?

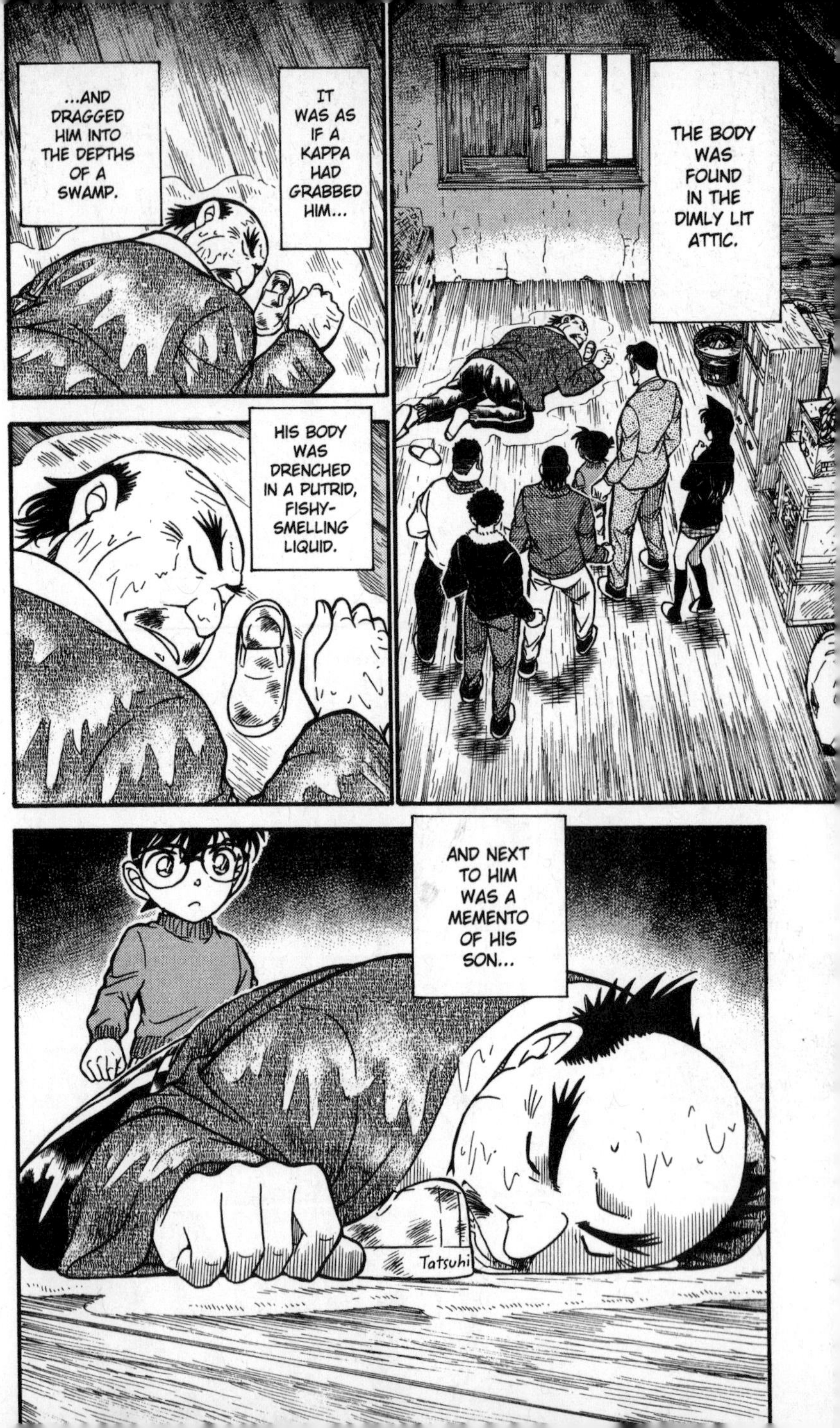
THE BODY WAS FOUND IN THE DIMLY LIT ATTIC.
IT WAS AS IF A KAPPA HAD GRABBED HIM...
...AND DRAGGED HIM INTO THE DEPTHS OF A SWAMP.
HIS BODY WAS DRENCHED IN A PUTRID, FISHY-SMELLING LIQUID.
AND NEXT TO HIM WAS A MEMENTO OF HIS SON...
Tatsuhi

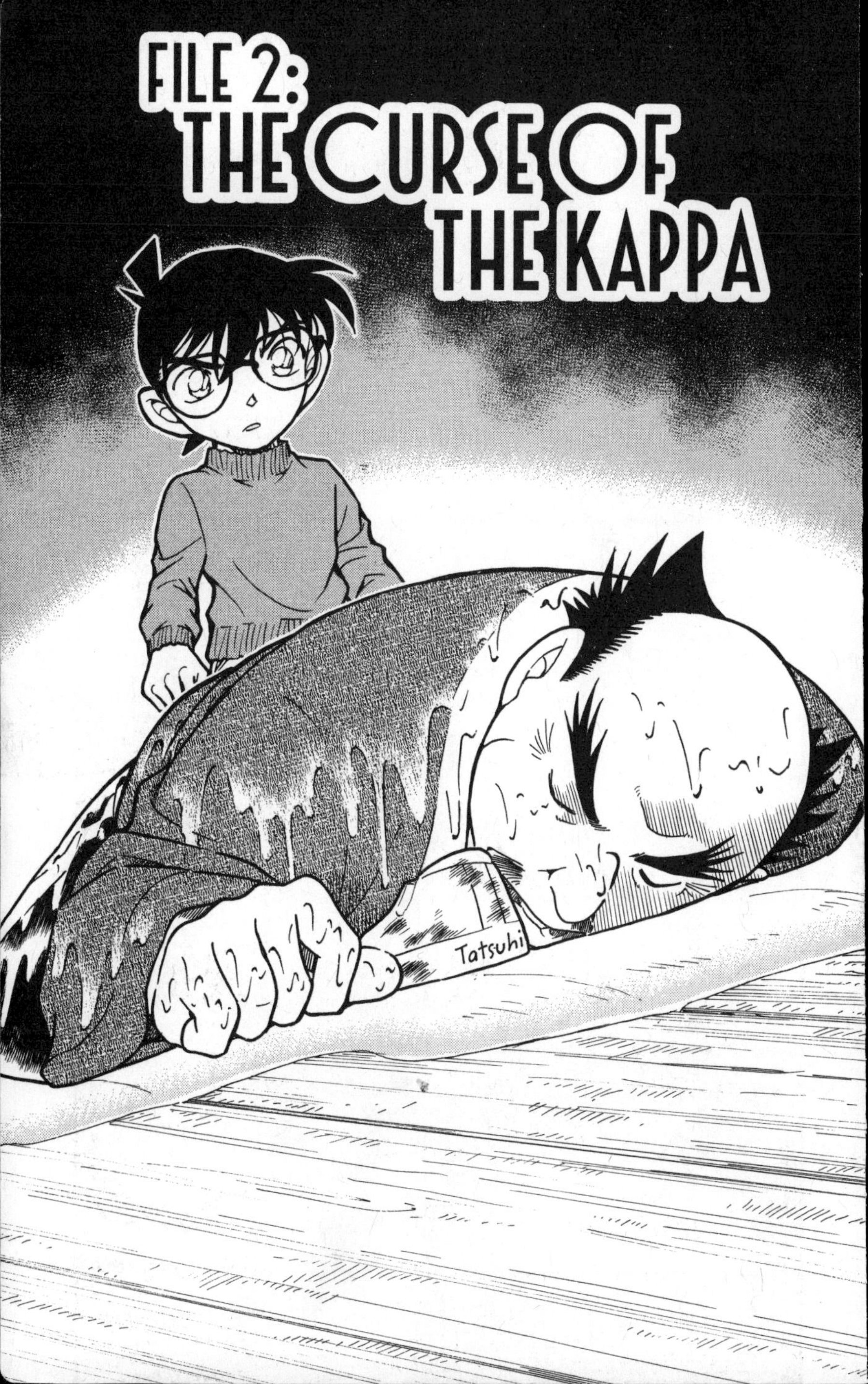
FILE 2:
THE CURSE OF THE KAPPA
Tatsuhi

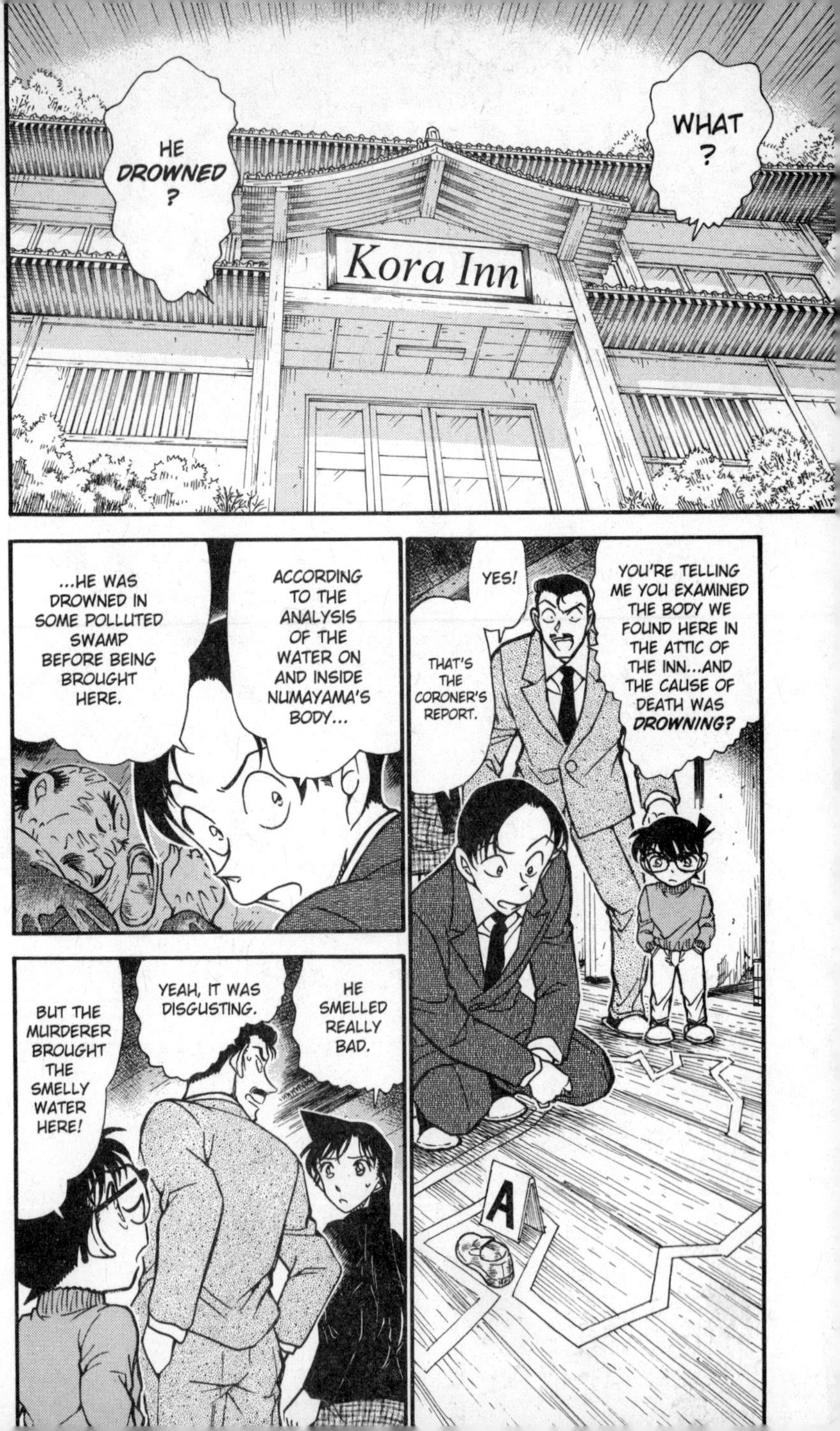
WHAT?
HE DROWNED?
Kora Inn
YOU'RE TELLING ME YOU EXAMINED THE BODY WE FOUND HERE IN THE ATTIC OF THE INN...AND THE CAUSE OF DEATH WAS DROWNING?
YES!
THAT'S THE CORONER'S REPORT.
A
ACCORDING TO THE ANALYSIS OF THE WATER ON AND INSIDE NUMAYAMA'S BODY...
...HE WAS DROWNED IN SOME POLLUTED SWAMP BEFORE BEING BROUGHT HERE.
HE SMELLED REALLY BAD.
YEAH, IT WAS DISGUSTING.
BUT THE MURDERER BROUGHT THE SMELLY WATER HERE!

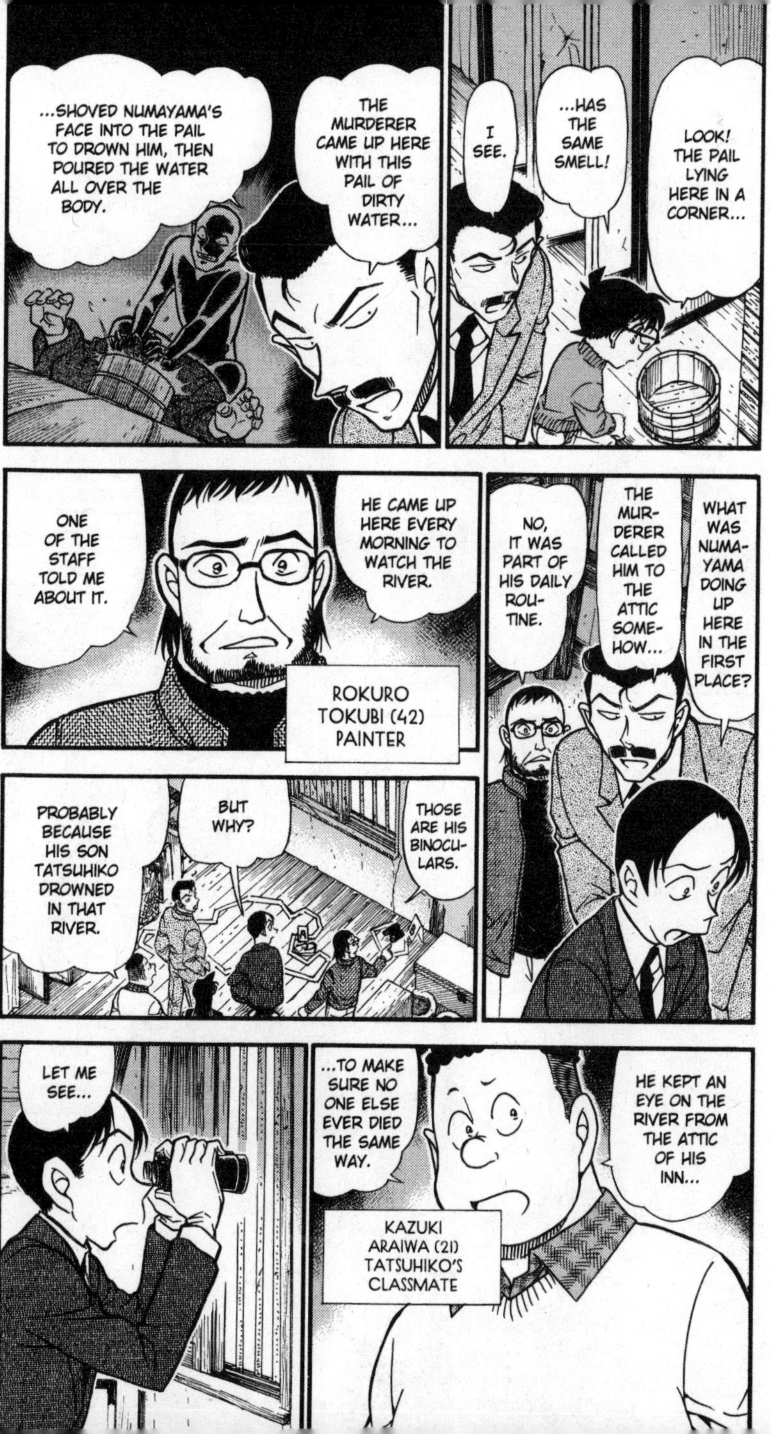
LOOK! THE PAIL LYING HERE IN A CORNER...
...HAS THE SAME SMELL!
I SEE.
THE MURDERER CAME UP HERE WITH THIS PAIL OF DIRTY WATER...
...SHOVED NUMAYAMA'S FACE INTO THE PAIL TO DROWN HIM, THEN POURED THE WATER ALL OVER THE BODY.
WHAT WAS NUMAYAMA DOING UP HERE IN THE FIRST PLACE?
THE MURDERER CALLED HIM TO THE ATTIC SOMEHOW...
NO, IT WAS PART OF HIS DAILY ROUTINE.
HE CAME UP HERE EVERY MORNING TO WATCH THE RIVER.
ONE OF THE STAFF TOLD ME ABOUT IT.
ROKURO TOKUBI (42) PAINTER
THOSE ARE HIS BINOCULARS.
BUT WHY?
PROBABLY BECAUSE HIS SON TATSUHIKO DROWNED IN THAT RIVER.
HE KEPT AN EYE ON THE RIVER FROM THE ATTIC OF HIS INN...
...TO MAKE SURE NO ONE ELSE EVER DIED THE SAME WAY.
KAZUKI ARAIWA (21) TATSUHIKO'S CLASSMATE
LET ME SEE...

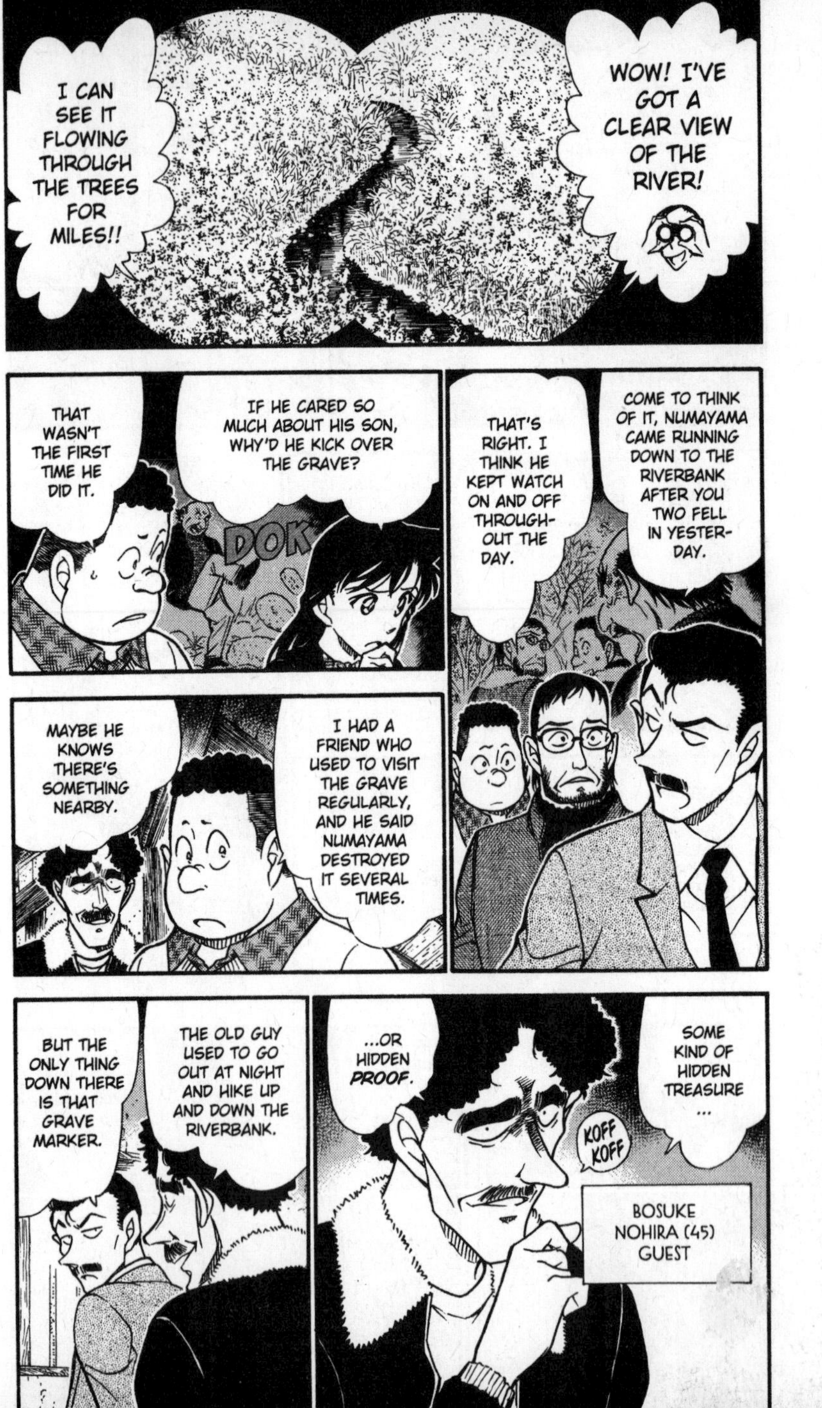
WOW! I'VE GOT A CLEAR VIEW OF THE RIVER!
I CAN SEE IT FLOWING THROUGH THE TREES FOR MILES!!
COME TO THINK OF IT, NUMAYAMA CAME RUNNING DOWN TO THE RIVERBANK AFTER YOU TWO FELL IN YESTER-DAY.
THAT'S RIGHT. I THINK HE KEPT WATCH ON AND OFF THROUGH-OUT THE DAY.
IF HE CARED SO MUCH ABOUT HIS SON, WHY'D HE KICK OVER THE GRAVE?
DOK
THAT WASN'T THE FIRST TIME HE DID IT.
I HAD A FRIEND WHO USED TO VISIT THE GRAVE REGULARLY, AND HE SAID NUMAYAMA DESTROYED IT SEVERAL TIMES.
MAYBE HE KNOWS THERE'S SOMETHING NEARBY.
SOME KIND OF HIDDEN TREASURE ...
KOFF KOFF
...OR HIDDEN *PROOF*.
BOSUKE NOHIRA (45) GUEST
THE OLD GUY USED TO GO OUT AT NIGHT AND HIKE UP AND DOWN THE RIVERBANK.
BUT THE ONLY THING DOWN THERE IS THAT GRAVE MARKER.

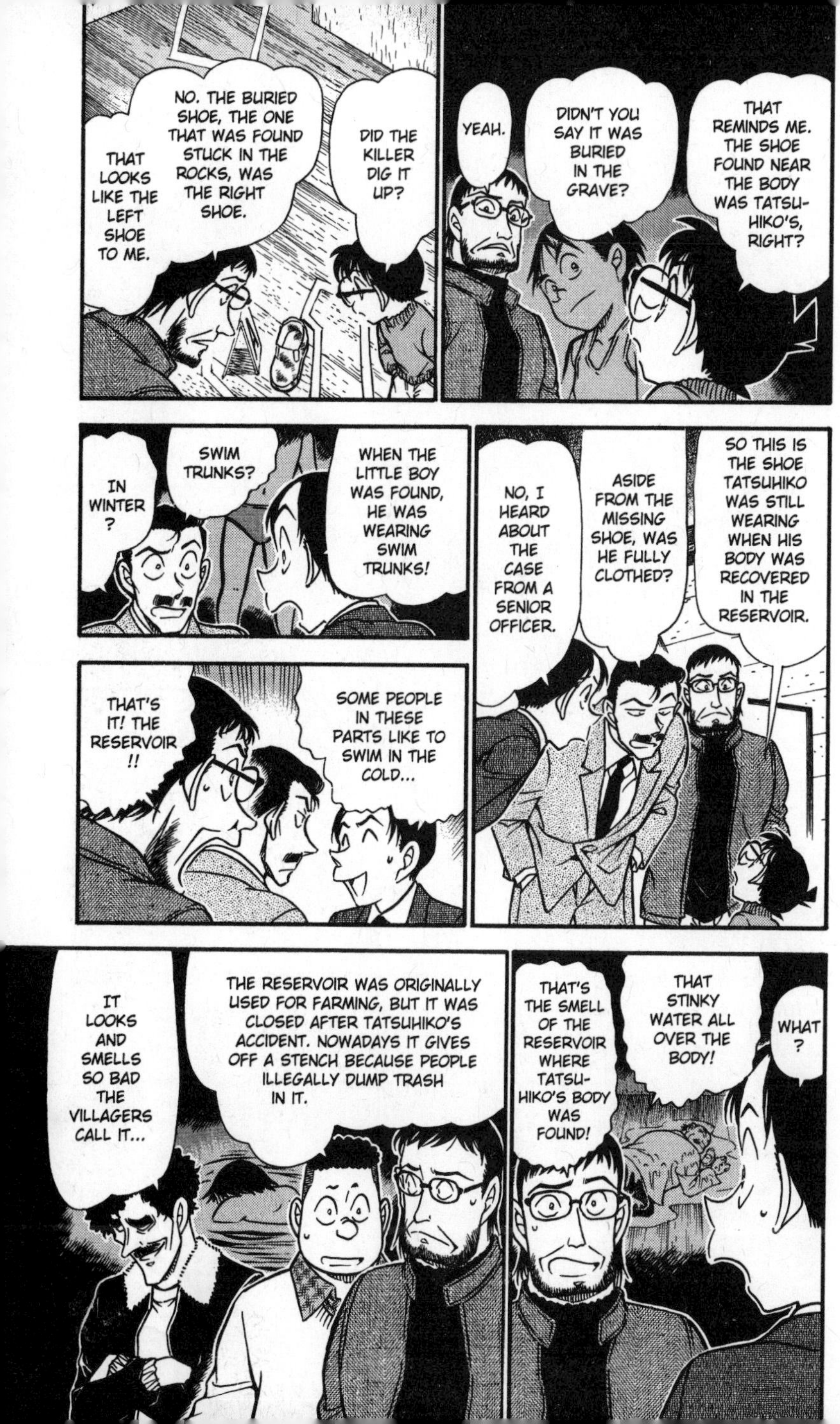
THAT REMINDS ME. THE SHOE FOUND NEAR THE BODY WAS TATSUHIKO'S, RIGHT?
DIDN'T YOU SAY IT WAS BURIED IN THE GRAVE?
YEAH.
DID THE KILLER DIG IT UP?
NO. THE BURIED SHOE, THE ONE THAT WAS FOUND STUCK IN THE ROCKS, WAS THE RIGHT SHOE.
THAT LOOKS LIKE THE LEFT SHOE TO ME.
SO THIS IS THE SHOE TATSUHIKO WAS STILL WEARING WHEN HIS BODY WAS RECOVERED IN THE RESERVOIR.
ASIDE FROM THE MISSING SHOE, WAS HE FULLY CLOTHED?
NO, I HEARD ABOUT THE CASE FROM A SENIOR OFFICER.
WHEN THE LITTLE BOY WAS FOUND, HE WAS WEARING SWIM TRUNKS!
SWIM TRUNKS?
IN WINTER?
SOME PEOPLE IN THESE PARTS LIKE TO SWIM IN THE COLD...
THAT'S IT! THE RESERVOIR!!
WHAT?
THAT STINKY WATER ALL OVER THE BODY!
THAT'S THE SMELL OF THE RESERVOIR WHERE TATSUHIKO'S BODY WAS FOUND!
THE RESERVOIR WAS ORIGINALLY USED FOR FARMING, BUT IT WAS CLOSED AFTER TATSUHIKO'S ACCIDENT. NOWADAYS IT GIVES OFF A STENCH BECAUSE PEOPLE ILLEGALLY DUMP TRASH IN IT.
IT LOOKS AND SMELLS SO BAD THE VILLAGERS CALL IT...

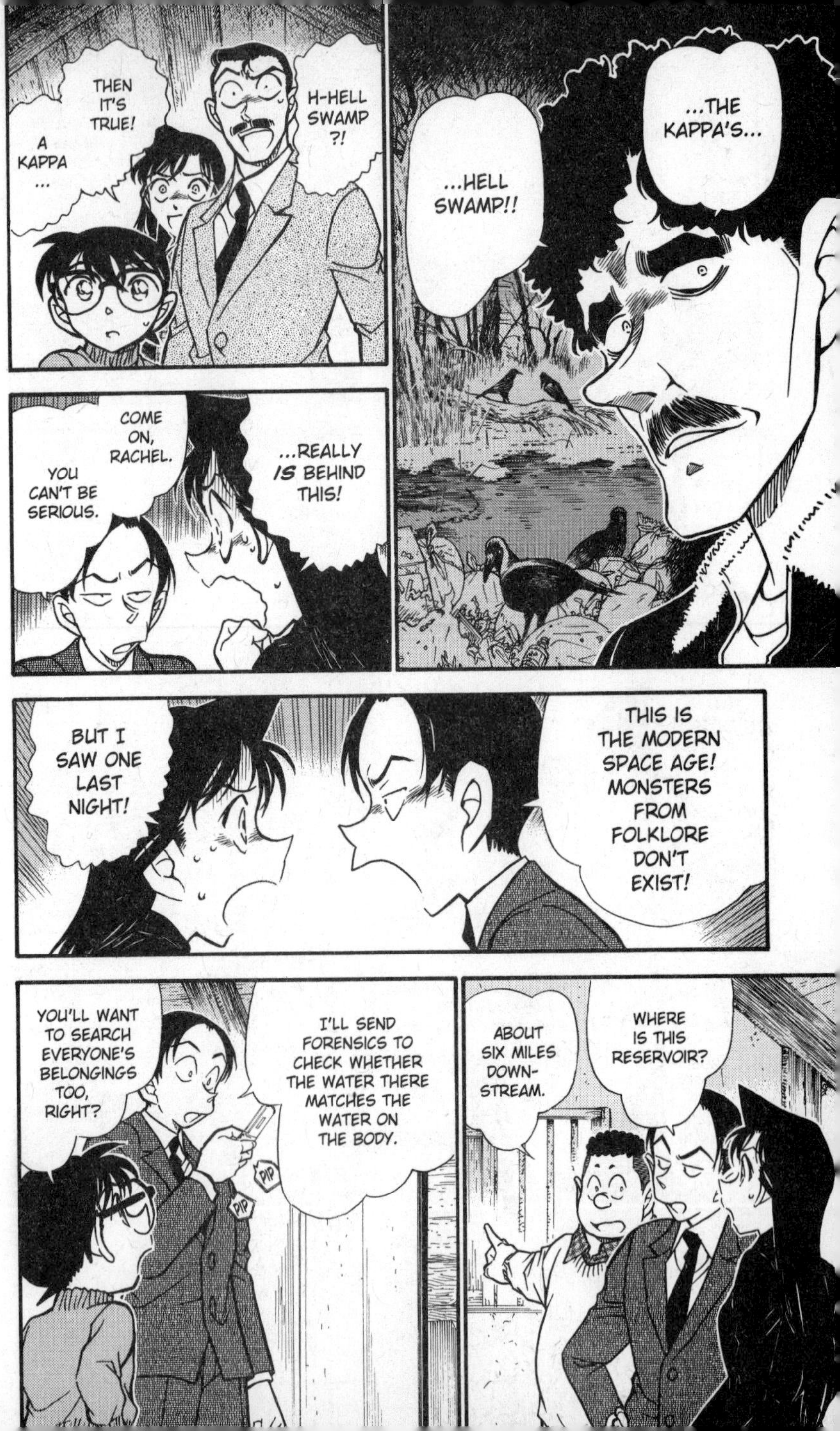
...THE KAPPA'S...
...HELL SWAMP!!
H-HELL SWAMP?!
THEN IT'S TRUE!
A KAPPA ...
...REALLY *IS* BEHIND THIS!
COME ON, RACHEL.
YOU CAN'T BE SERIOUS.
THIS IS THE MODERN SPACE AGE! MONSTERS FROM FOLKLORE DON'T EXIST!
BUT I SAW ONE LAST NIGHT!
WHERE IS THIS RESERVOIR?
ABOUT SIX MILES DOWN-STREAM.
I'LL SEND FORENSICS TO CHECK WHETHER THE WATER THERE MATCHES THE WATER ON THE BODY.
PIP
PIP
YOU'LL WANT TO SEARCH EVERYONE'S BELONGINGS TOO, RIGHT?

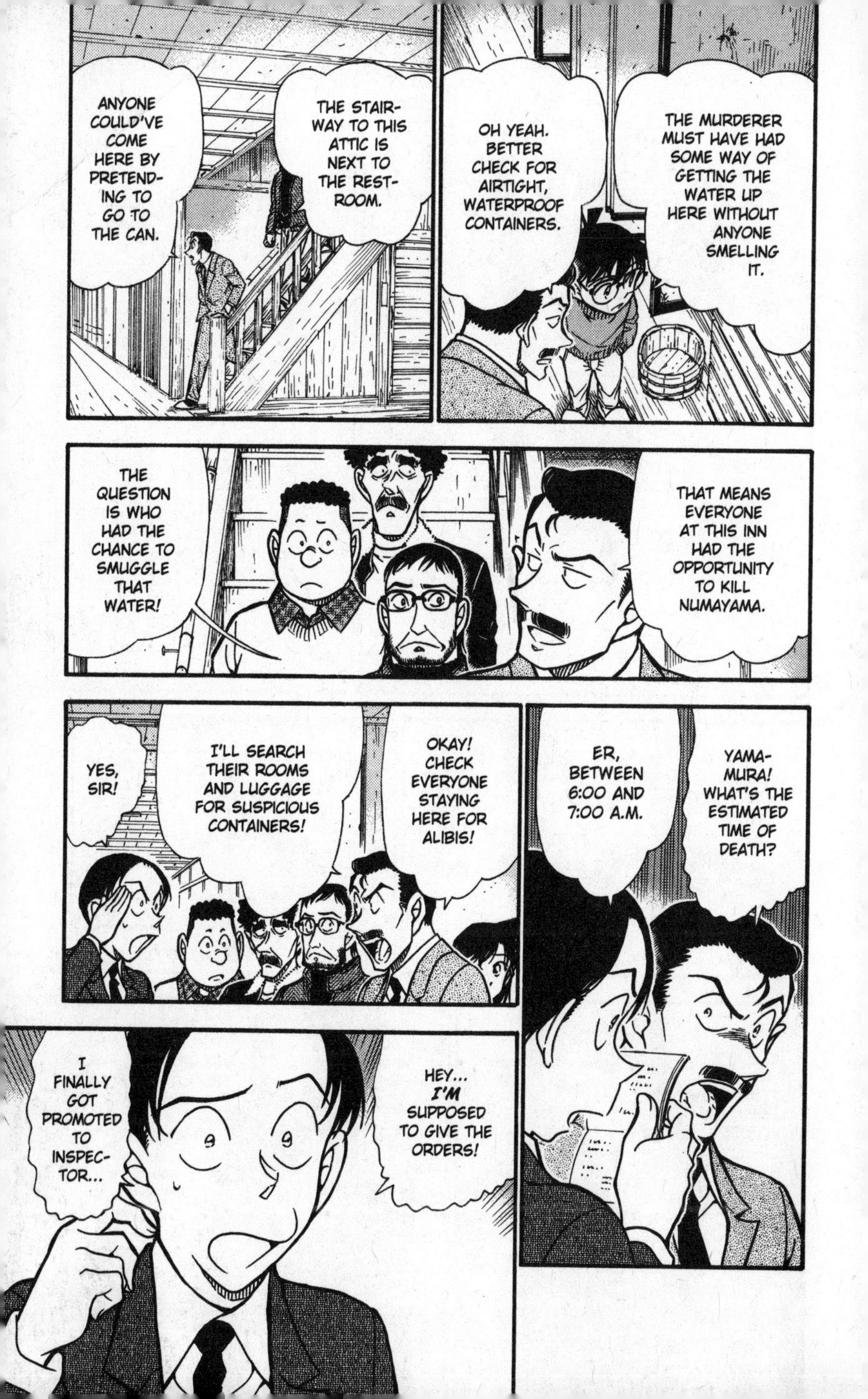
THE MURDERER MUST HAVE HAD SOME WAY OF GETTING THE WATER UP HERE WITHOUT ANYONE SMELLING IT.
OH YEAH. BETTER CHECK FOR AIRTIGHT, WATERPROOF CONTAINERS.
THE STAIRWAY TO THIS ATTIC IS NEXT TO THE RESTROOM.
ANYONE COULD'VE COME HERE BY PRETENDING TO GO TO THE CAN.
THAT MEANS EVERYONE AT THIS INN HAD THE OPPORTUNITY TO KILL NUMAYAMA.
THE QUESTION IS WHO HAD THE CHANCE TO SMUGGLE THAT WATER!
YAMAMURA! WHAT'S THE ESTIMATED TIME OF DEATH?
ER, BETWEEN 6:00 AND 7:00 A.M.
OKAY! CHECK EVERYONE STAYING HERE FOR ALIBIS!
I'LL SEARCH THEIR ROOMS AND LUGGAGE FOR SUSPICIOUS CONTAINERS!
YES, SIR!
HEY... ***I'M*** SUPPOSED TO GIVE THE ORDERS!
I FINALLY GOT PROMOTED TO INSPECTOR...

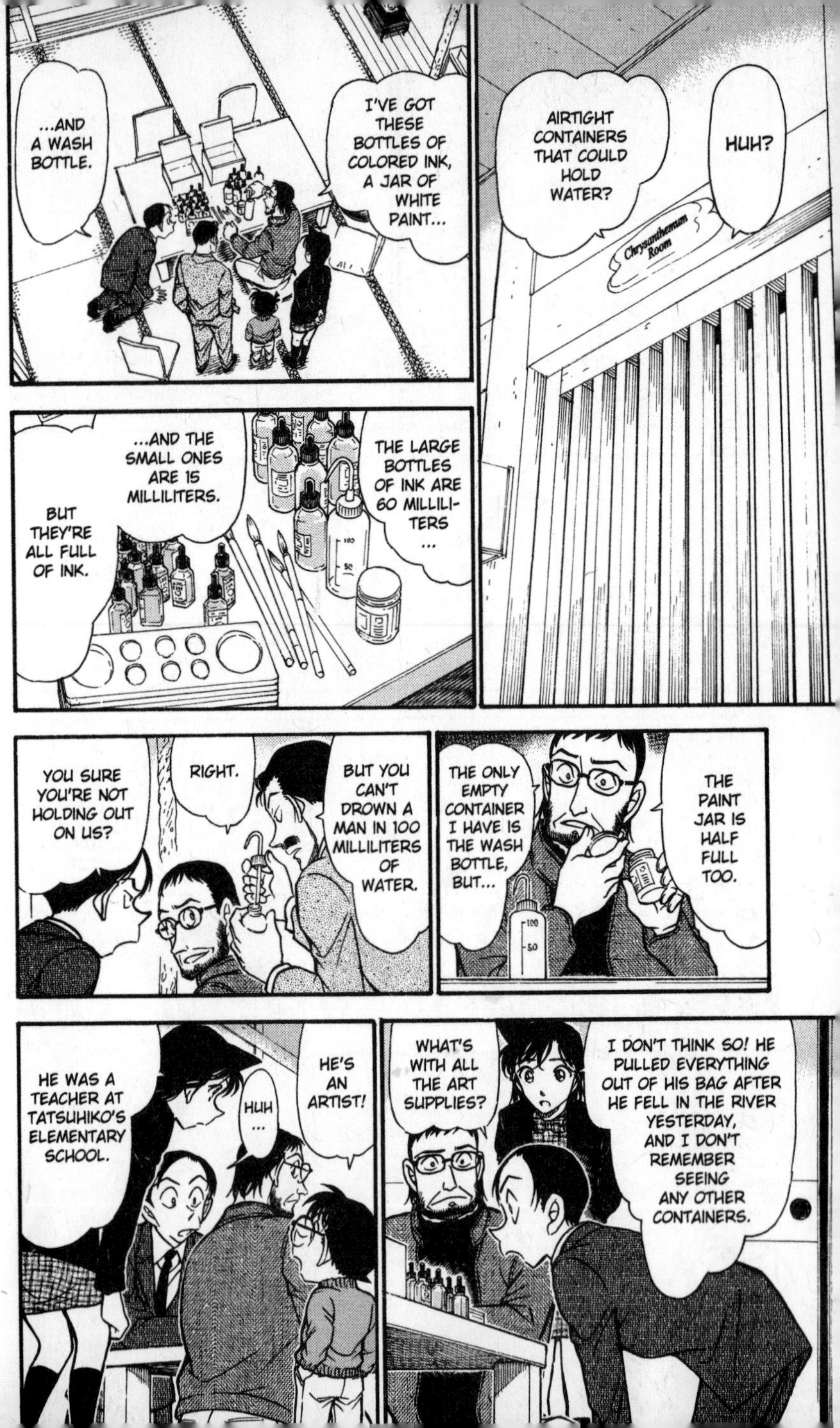
HUH?
AIRTIGHT CONTAINERS THAT COULD HOLD WATER?
Chrysanthemum Room
I'VE GOT THESE BOTTLES OF COLORED INK, A JAR OF WHITE PAINT...
...AND A WASH BOTTLE.
THE LARGE BOTTLES OF INK ARE 60 MILLILITERS...
...AND THE SMALL ONES ARE 15 MILLILITERS.
BUT THEY'RE ALL FULL OF INK.
THE PAINT JAR IS HALF FULL TOO.
THE ONLY EMPTY CONTAINER I HAVE IS THE WASH BOTTLE, BUT...
BUT YOU CAN'T DROWN A MAN IN 100 MILLILITERS OF WATER.
RIGHT.
YOU SURE YOU'RE NOT HOLDING OUT ON US?
I DON'T THINK SO! HE PULLED EVERYTHING OUT OF HIS BAG AFTER HE FELL IN THE RIVER YESTERDAY, AND I DON'T REMEMBER SEEING ANY OTHER CONTAINERS.
WHAT'S WITH ALL THE ART SUPPLIES?
HE'S AN ARTIST!
HUH...
HE WAS A TEACHER AT TATSUHIKO'S ELEMENTARY SCHOOL.

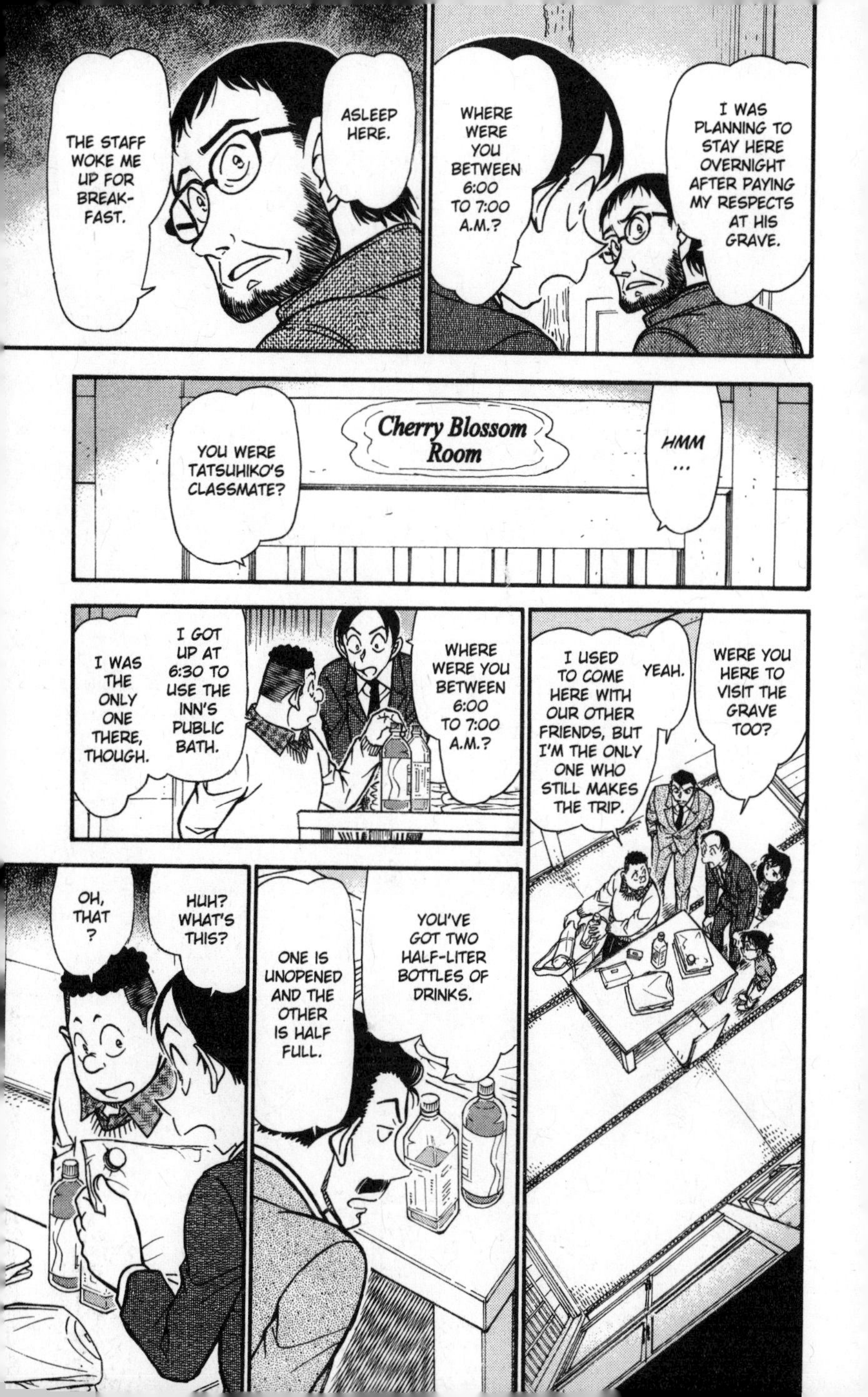
I WAS PLANNING TO STAY HERE OVERNIGHT AFTER PAYING MY RESPECTS AT HIS GRAVE.
WHERE WERE YOU BETWEEN 6:00 TO 7:00 A.M.?
ASLEEP HERE.
THE STAFF WOKE ME UP FOR BREAK-FAST.
HMM ...
Cherry Blossom Room
YOU WERE TATSUHIKO'S CLASSMATE?
WERE YOU HERE TO VISIT THE GRAVE TOO?
YEAH.
I USED TO COME HERE WITH OUR OTHER FRIENDS, BUT I'M THE ONLY ONE WHO STILL MAKES THE TRIP.
WHERE WERE YOU BETWEEN 6:00 TO 7:00 A.M.?
I GOT UP AT 6:30 TO USE THE INN'S PUBLIC BATH.
I WAS THE ONLY ONE THERE, THOUGH.
YOU'VE GOT TWO HALF-LITER BOTTLES OF DRINKS.
ONE IS UNOPENED AND THE OTHER IS HALF FULL.
HUH? WHAT'S THIS?
OH, THAT ?

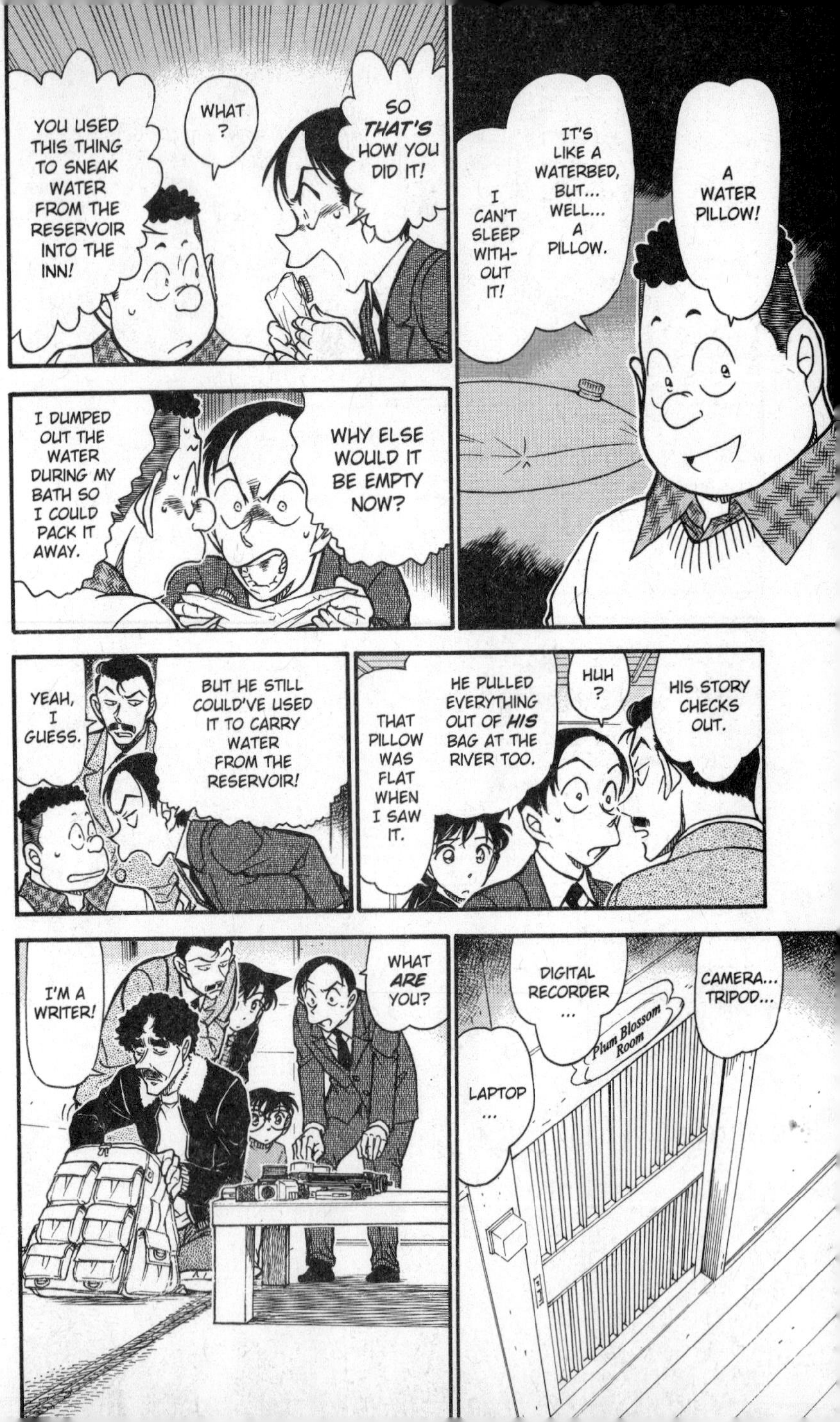
A WATER PILLOW!
IT'S LIKE A WATERBED, BUT... WELL... A PILLOW.
I CAN'T SLEEP WITHOUT IT!
SO *THAT'S* HOW YOU DID IT!
WHAT?
YOU USED THIS THING TO SNEAK WATER FROM THE RESERVOIR INTO THE INN!
WHY ELSE WOULD IT BE EMPTY NOW?
I DUMPED OUT THE WATER DURING MY BATH SO I COULD PACK IT AWAY.
HIS STORY CHECKS OUT.
HUH?
HE PULLED EVERYTHING OUT OF *HIS* BAG AT THE RIVER TOO.
THAT PILLOW WAS FLAT WHEN I SAW IT.
BUT HE STILL COULD'VE USED IT TO CARRY WATER FROM THE RESERVOIR!
YEAH, I GUESS.
CAMERA... TRIPOD...
Plum Blossom Room
DIGITAL RECORDER ...
LAPTOP ...
WHAT *ARE* YOU?
I'M A WRITER!

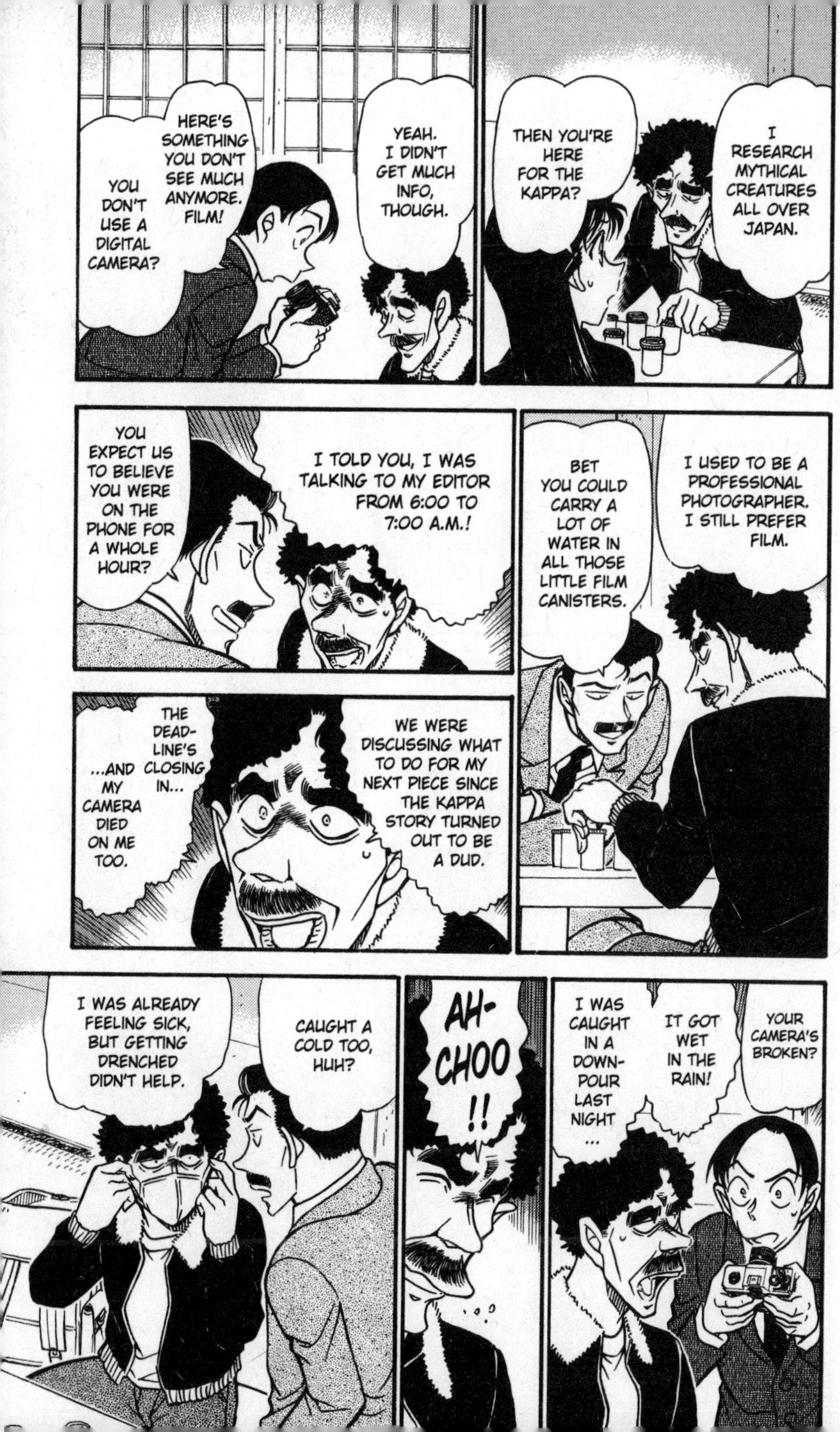
I RESEARCH MYTHICAL CREATURES ALL OVER JAPAN.
THEN YOU'RE HERE FOR THE KAPPA?
YEAH. I DIDN'T GET MUCH INFO, THOUGH.
HERE'S SOMETHING YOU DON'T SEE MUCH ANYMORE. FILM!
YOU DON'T USE A DIGITAL CAMERA?
I USED TO BE A PROFESSIONAL PHOTOGRAPHER. I STILL PREFER FILM.
BET YOU COULD CARRY A LOT OF WATER IN ALL THOSE LITTLE FILM CANISTERS.
I TOLD YOU, I WAS TALKING TO MY EDITOR FROM 6:00 TO 7:00 A.M.!
YOU EXPECT US TO BELIEVE YOU WERE ON THE PHONE FOR A WHOLE HOUR?
WE WERE DISCUSSING WHAT TO DO FOR MY NEXT PIECE SINCE THE KAPPA STORY TURNED OUT TO BE A DUD.
THE DEAD-LINE'S CLOSING IN...
...AND MY CAMERA DIED ON ME TOO.
YOUR CAMERA'S BROKEN?
IT GOT WET IN THE RAIN!
I WAS CAUGHT IN A DOWN-POUR LAST NIGHT...
AH-CHOO!!
CAUGHT A COLD TOO, HUH?
I WAS ALREADY FEELING SICK, BUT GETTING DRENCHED DIDN'T HELP.

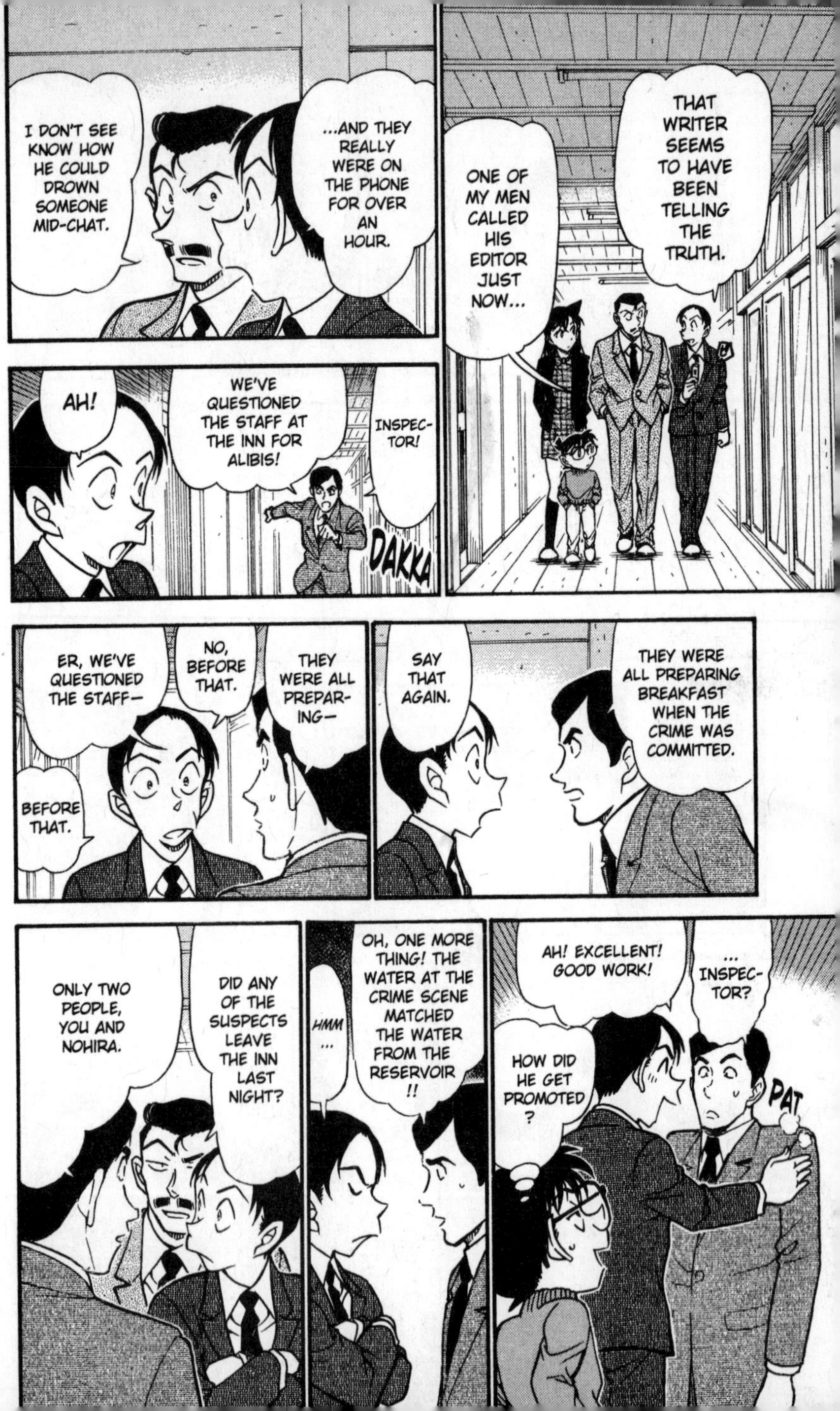
THAT WRITER SEEMS TO HAVE BEEN TELLING THE TRUTH.
ONE OF MY MEN CALLED HIS EDITOR JUST NOW...
...AND THEY REALLY WERE ON THE PHONE FOR OVER AN HOUR.
I DON'T SEE KNOW HOW HE COULD DROWN SOMEONE MID-CHAT.
INSPECTOR!
WE'VE QUESTIONED THE STAFF AT THE INN FOR ALIBIS!
AH!
DAKKA
THEY WERE ALL PREPARING BREAKFAST WHEN THE CRIME WAS COMMITTED.
SAY THAT AGAIN.
THEY WERE ALL PREPARING—
NO, BEFORE THAT.
ER, WE'VE QUESTIONED THE STAFF—
BEFORE THAT.
...INSPECTOR?
AH! EXCELLENT! GOOD WORK!
HOW DID HE GET PROMOTED?
PAT
OH, ONE MORE THING! THE WATER AT THE CRIME SCENE MATCHED THE WATER FROM THE RESERVOIR!!
HMM...
DID ANY OF THE SUSPECTS LEAVE THE INN LAST NIGHT?
ONLY TWO PEOPLE, YOU AND NOHIRA.

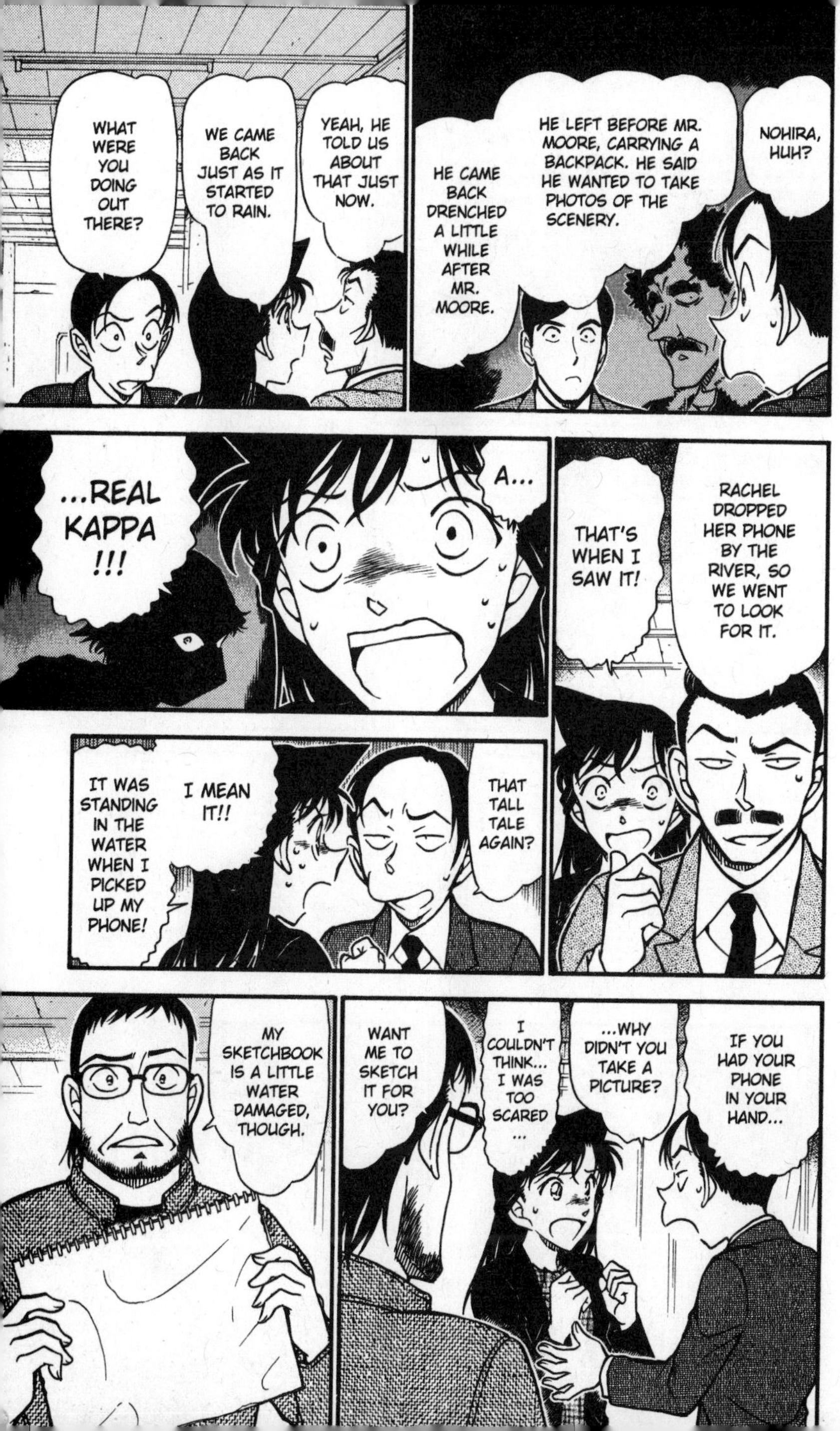
NOHIRA, HUH?
HE LEFT BEFORE MR. MOORE, CARRYING A BACKPACK. HE SAID HE WANTED TO TAKE PHOTOS OF THE SCENERY.
HE CAME BACK DRENCHED A LITTLE WHILE AFTER MR. MOORE.
YEAH, HE TOLD US ABOUT THAT JUST NOW.
WE CAME BACK JUST AS IT STARTED TO RAIN.
WHAT WERE YOU DOING OUT THERE?
RACHEL DROPPED HER PHONE BY THE RIVER, SO WE WENT TO LOOK FOR IT.
THAT'S WHEN I SAW IT!
A...
...REAL KAPPA!!!
THAT TALL TALE AGAIN?
I MEAN IT!!
IT WAS STANDING IN THE WATER WHEN I PICKED UP MY PHONE!
IF YOU HAD YOUR PHONE IN YOUR HAND...
...WHY DIDN'T YOU TAKE A PICTURE?
I COULDN'T THINK... I WAS TOO SCARED ...
WANT ME TO SKETCH IT FOR YOU?
MY SKETCHBOOK IS A LITTLE WATER DAMAGED, THOUGH.

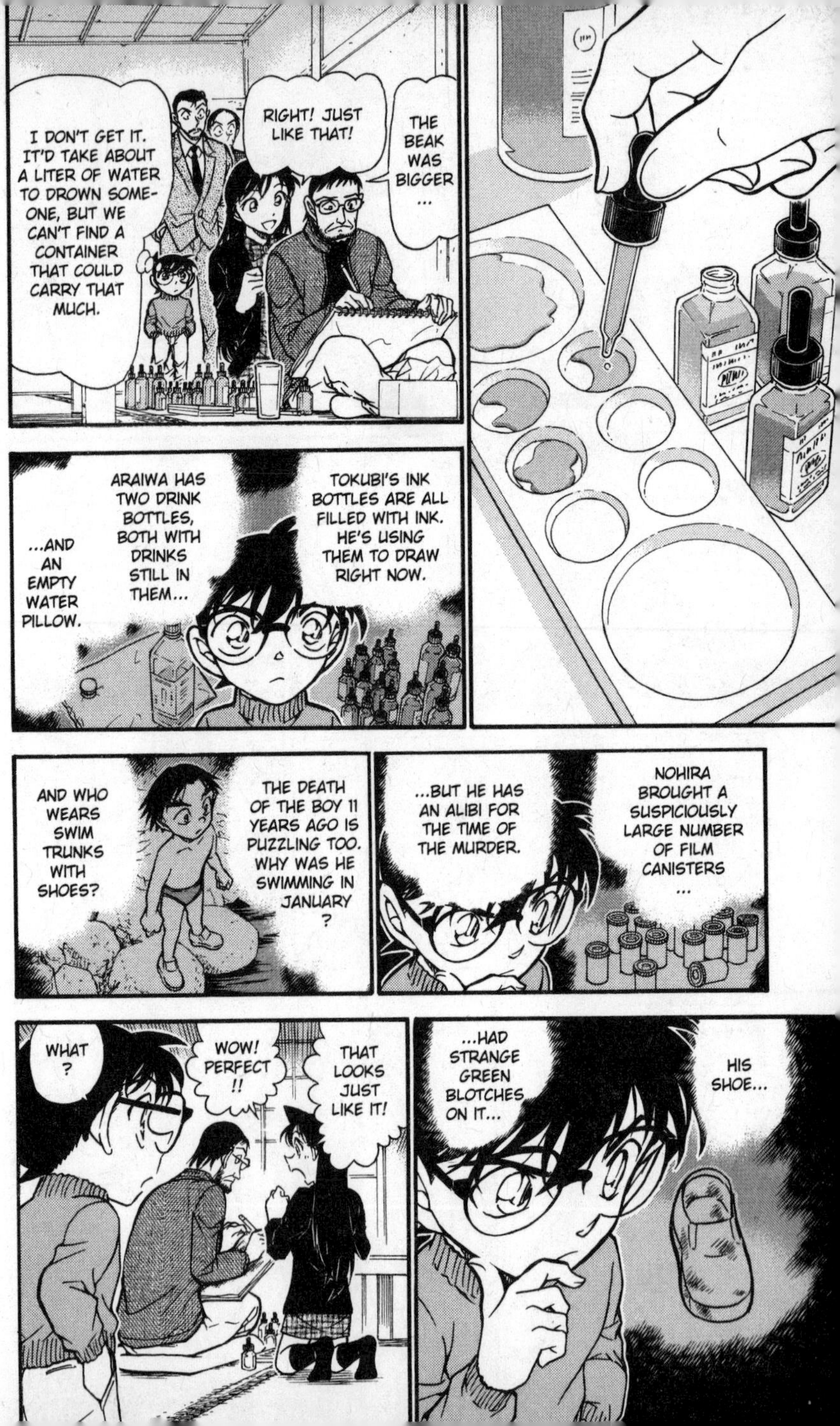
THE BEAK WAS BIGGER...
RIGHT! JUST LIKE THAT!
I DON'T GET IT. IT'D TAKE ABOUT A LITER OF WATER TO DROWN SOMEONE, BUT WE CAN'T FIND A CONTAINER THAT COULD CARRY THAT MUCH.
TOKUBI'S INK BOTTLES ARE ALL FILLED WITH INK. HE'S USING THEM TO DRAW RIGHT NOW.
ARAIWA HAS TWO DRINK BOTTLES, BOTH WITH DRINKS STILL IN THEM...
...AND AN EMPTY WATER PILLOW.
NOHIRA BROUGHT A SUSPICIOUSLY LARGE NUMBER OF FILM CANISTERS...
...BUT HE HAS AN ALIBI FOR THE TIME OF THE MURDER.
THE DEATH OF THE BOY 11 YEARS AGO IS PUZZLING TOO. WHY WAS HE SWIMMING IN JANUARY?
AND WHO WEARS SWIM TRUNKS WITH SHOES?
HIS SHOE...
...HAD STRANGE GREEN BLOTCHES ON IT...
THAT LOOKS JUST LIKE IT!
WOW! PERFECT!!
WHAT?

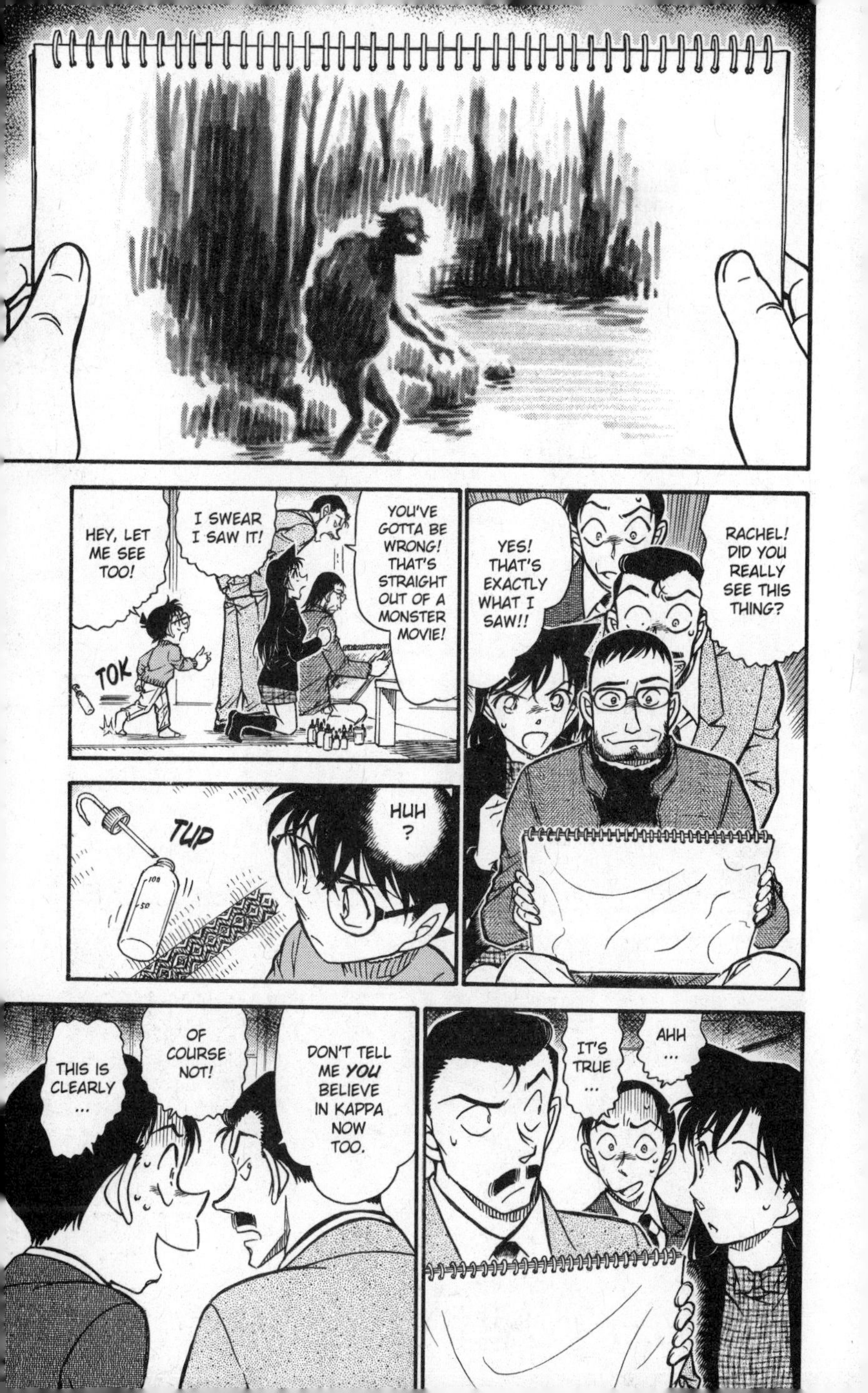
RACHEL! DID YOU REALLY SEE THIS THING?
YES! THAT'S EXACTLY WHAT I SAW!!
YOU'VE GOTTA BE WRONG! THAT'S STRAIGHT OUT OF A MONSTER MOVIE!
I SWEAR I SAW IT!
HEY, LET ME SEE TOO!
TOK
HUH?
TUP
AHH...
IT'S TRUE...
DON'T TELL ME *YOU* BELIEVE IN KAPPA NOW TOO.
OF COURSE NOT!
THIS IS CLEARLY...

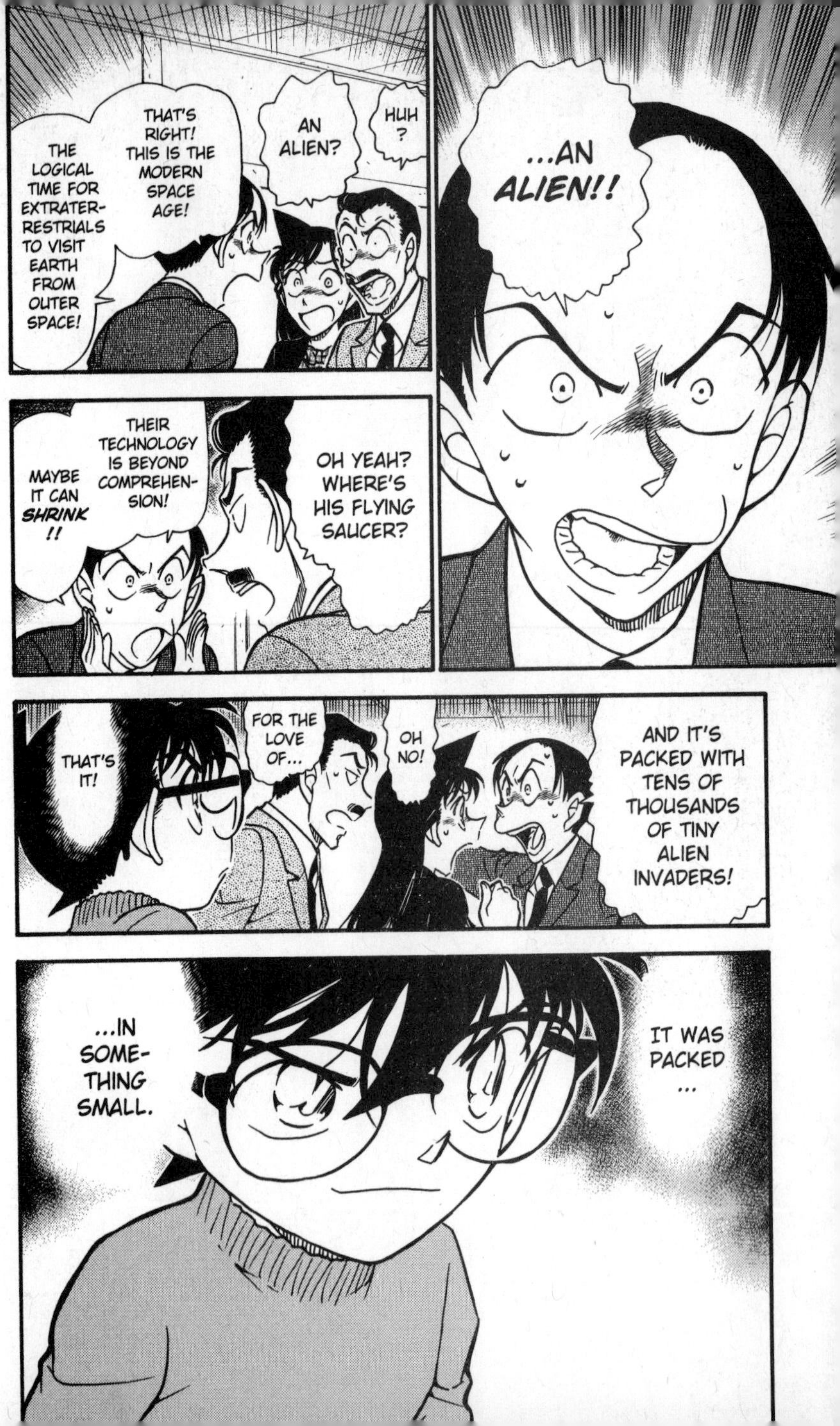
...AN ALIEN!!
HUH?
AN ALIEN?
THAT'S RIGHT! THIS IS THE MODERN SPACE AGE!
THE LOGICAL TIME FOR EXTRATERRESTRIALS TO VISIT EARTH FROM OUTER SPACE!
OH YEAH? WHERE'S HIS FLYING SAUCER?
THEIR TECHNOLOGY IS BEYOND COMPREHENSION!
MAYBE IT CAN SHRINK!!
AND IT'S PACKED WITH TENS OF THOUSANDS OF TINY ALIEN INVADERS!
OH NO!
FOR THE LOVE OF...
THAT'S IT!
IT WAS PACKED...
...IN SOMETHING SMALL.

FILE 3: THE IDENTITY OF THE KAPPA

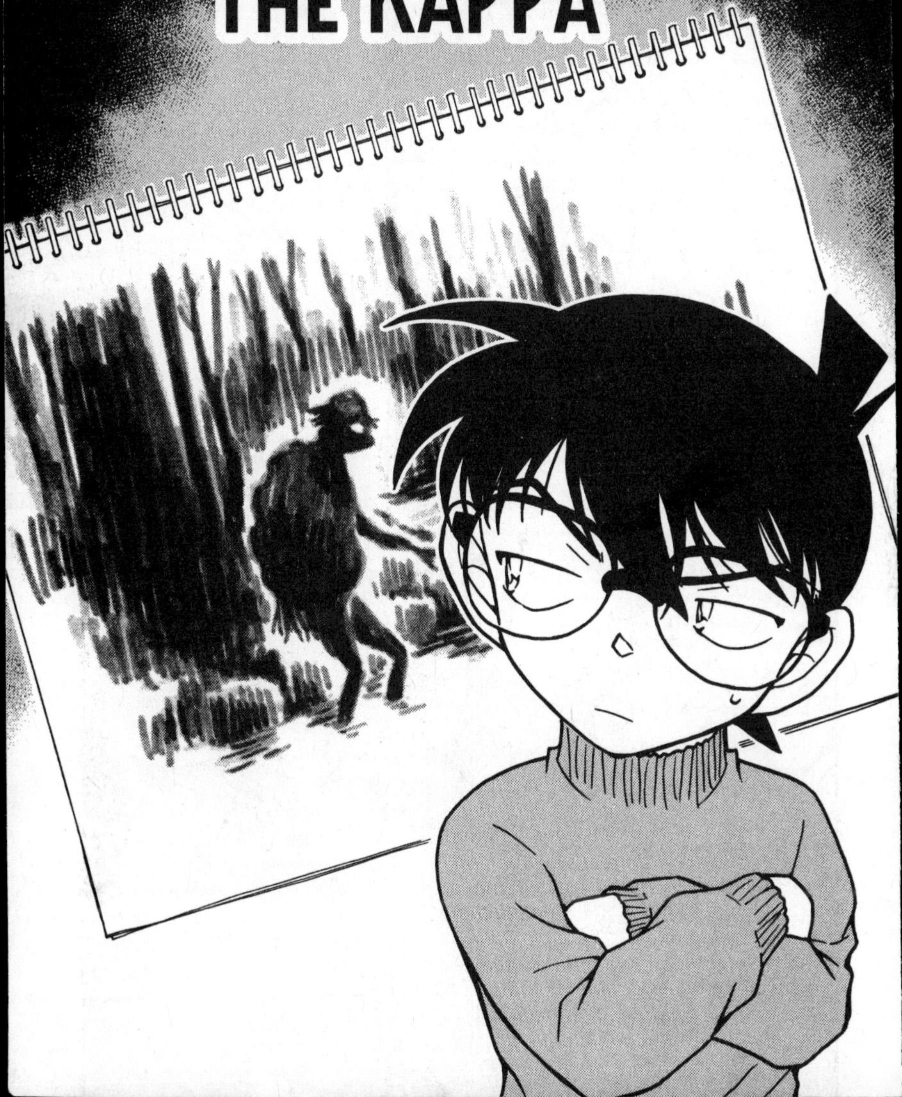

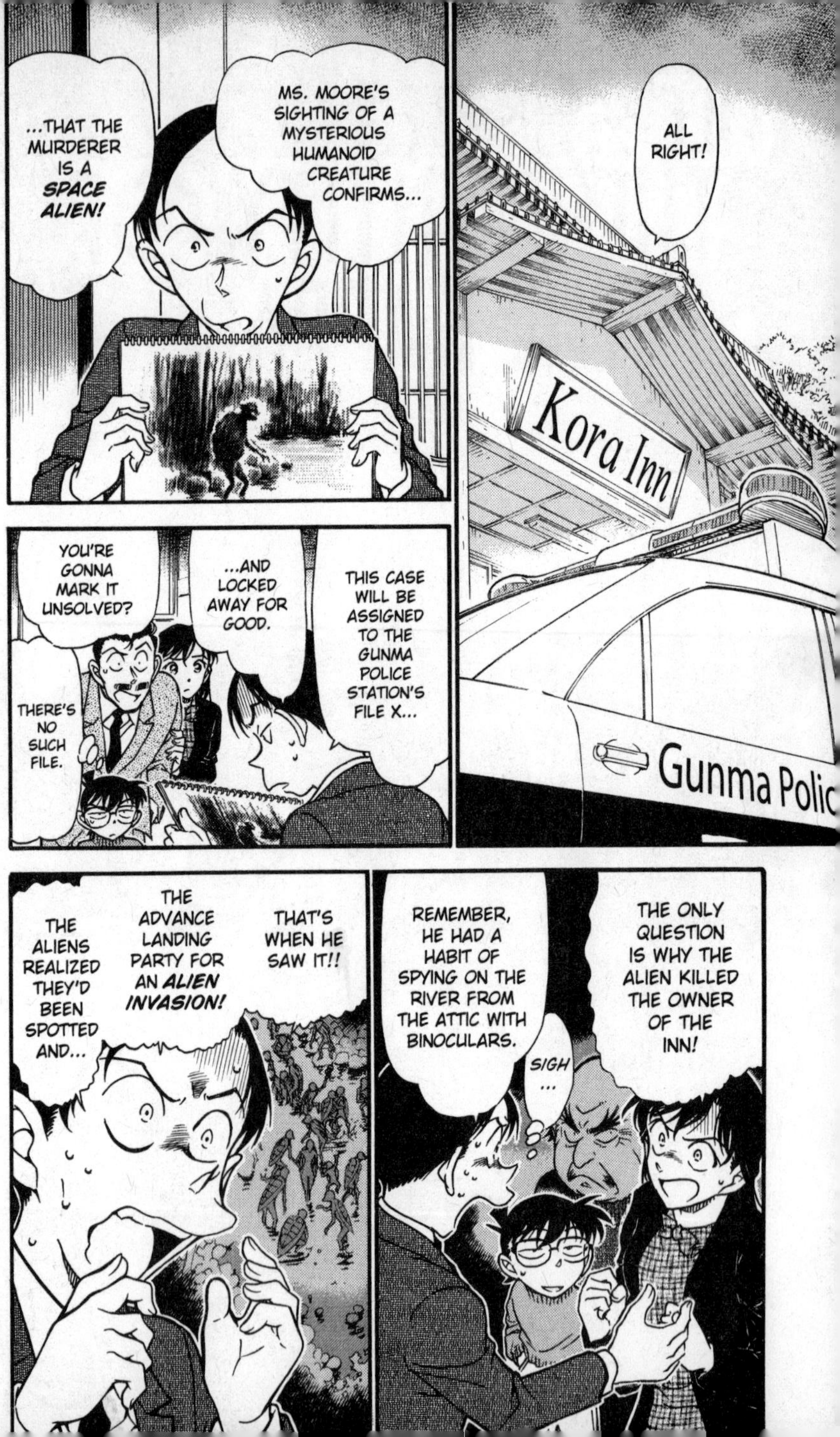
ALL RIGHT!
Kora Inn
Gunma Polic
MS. MOORE'S SIGHTING OF A MYSTERIOUS HUMANOID CREATURE CONFIRMS...
...THAT THE MURDERER IS A *SPACE ALIEN!*
THIS CASE WILL BE ASSIGNED TO THE GUNMA POLICE STATION'S FILE X...
...AND LOCKED AWAY FOR GOOD.
YOU'RE GONNA MARK IT UNSOLVED?
THERE'S NO SUCH FILE.
THE ONLY QUESTION IS WHY THE ALIEN KILLED THE OWNER OF THE INN!
REMEMBER, HE HAD A HABIT OF SPYING ON THE RIVER FROM THE ATTIC WITH BINOCULARS.
SIGH...
THAT'S WHEN HE SAW IT!!
THE ADVANCE LANDING PARTY FOR AN *ALIEN INVASION!*
THE ALIENS REALIZED THEY'D BEEN SPOTTED AND...

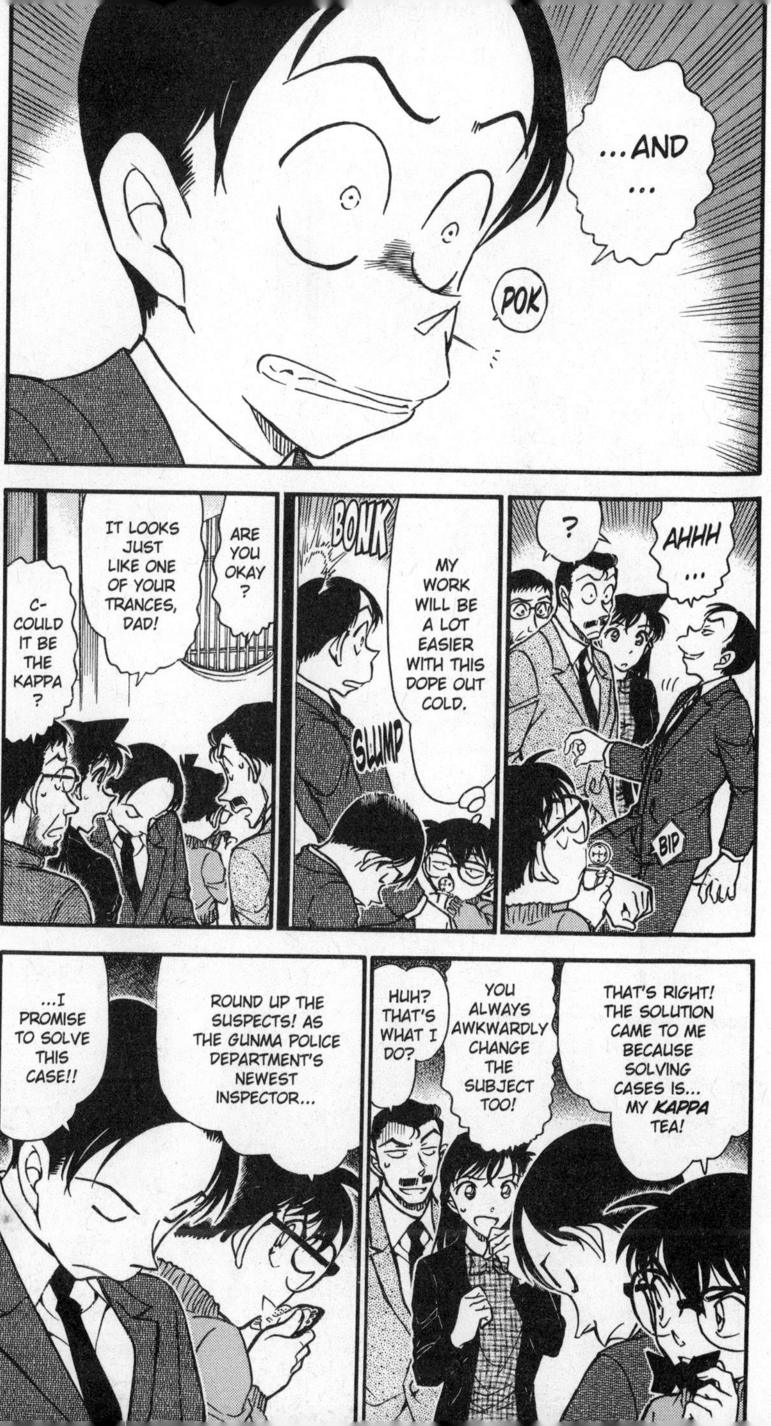
...AND ...
POK
AHHH ...
?
BIP
BONK
MY WORK WILL BE A LOT EASIER WITH THIS DOPE OUT COLD.
SLUMP
ARE YOU OKAY?
IT LOOKS JUST LIKE ONE OF YOUR TRANCES, DAD!
C-COULD IT BE THE KAPPA?
THAT'S RIGHT! THE SOLUTION CAME TO ME BECAUSE SOLVING CASES IS... MY *KAPPA* TEA!
YOU ALWAYS AWKWARDLY CHANGE THE SUBJECT TOO!
HUH? THAT'S WHAT I DO?
ROUND UP THE SUSPECTS! AS THE GUNMA POLICE DEPARTMENT'S NEWEST INSPECTOR...
...I PROMISE TO SOLVE THIS CASE!!

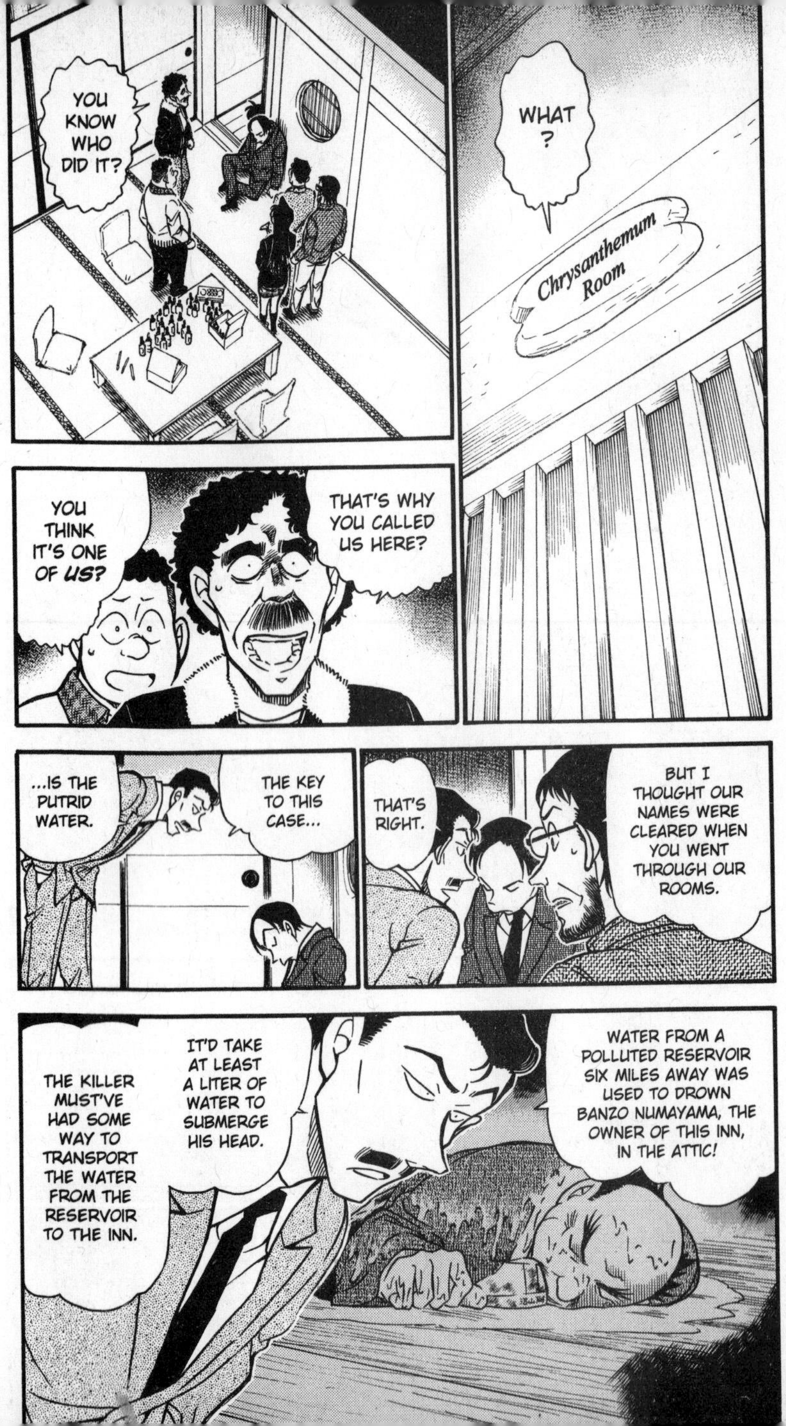
WHAT?
Chrysanthemum Room
YOU KNOW WHO DID IT?
THAT'S WHY YOU CALLED US HERE?
YOU THINK IT'S ONE OF *US*?
BUT I THOUGHT OUR NAMES WERE CLEARED WHEN YOU WENT THROUGH OUR ROOMS.
THAT'S RIGHT.
THE KEY TO THIS CASE...
...IS THE PUTRID WATER.
WATER FROM A POLLUTED RESERVOIR SIX MILES AWAY WAS USED TO DROWN BANZO NUMAYAMA, THE OWNER OF THIS INN, IN THE ATTIC!
IT'D TAKE AT LEAST A LITER OF WATER TO SUBMERGE HIS HEAD.
THE KILLER MUST'VE HAD SOME WAY TO TRANSPORT THE WATER FROM THE RESERVOIR TO THE INN.

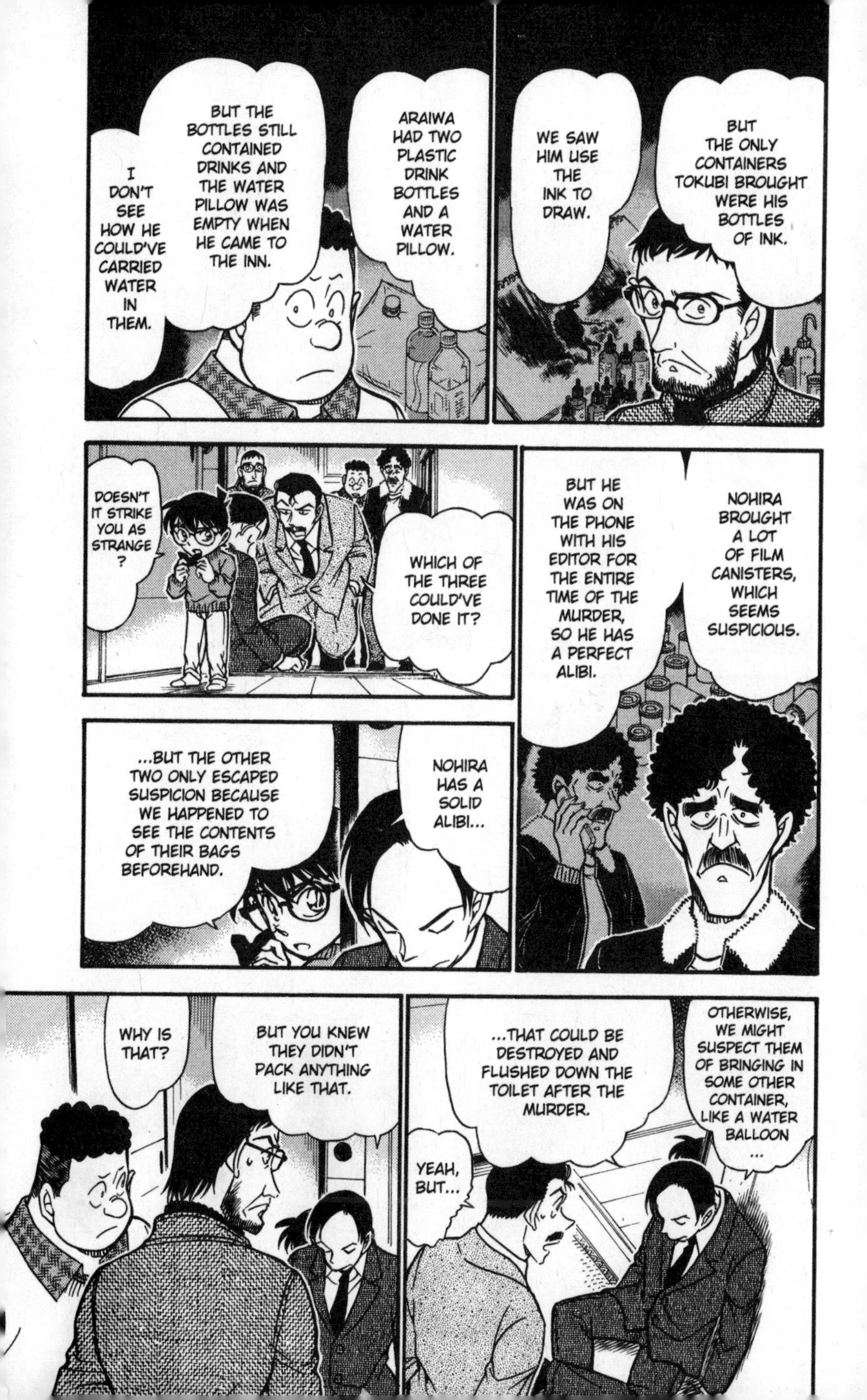
BUT THE ONLY CONTAINERS TOKUBI BROUGHT WERE HIS BOTTLES OF INK.
WE SAW HIM USE THE INK TO DRAW.
ARAIWA HAD TWO PLASTIC DRINK BOTTLES AND A WATER PILLOW.
BUT THE BOTTLES STILL CONTAINED DRINKS AND THE WATER PILLOW WAS EMPTY WHEN HE CAME TO THE INN.
I DON'T SEE HOW HE COULD'VE CARRIED WATER IN THEM.
NOHIRA BROUGHT A LOT OF FILM CANISTERS, WHICH SEEMS SUSPICIOUS.
BUT HE WAS ON THE PHONE WITH HIS EDITOR FOR THE ENTIRE TIME OF THE MURDER, SO HE HAS A PERFECT ALIBI.
WHICH OF THE THREE COULD'VE DONE IT?
DOESN'T IT STRIKE YOU AS STRANGE?
NOHIRA HAS A SOLID ALIBI...
...BUT THE OTHER TWO ONLY ESCAPED SUSPICION BECAUSE WE HAPPENED TO SEE THE CONTENTS OF THEIR BAGS BEFOREHAND.
OTHERWISE, WE MIGHT SUSPECT THEM OF BRINGING IN SOME OTHER CONTAINER, LIKE A WATER BALLOON ...
...THAT COULD BE DESTROYED AND FLUSHED DOWN THE TOILET AFTER THE MURDER.
YEAH, BUT...
BUT YOU KNEW THEY DIDN'T PACK ANYTHING LIKE THAT.
WHY IS THAT?

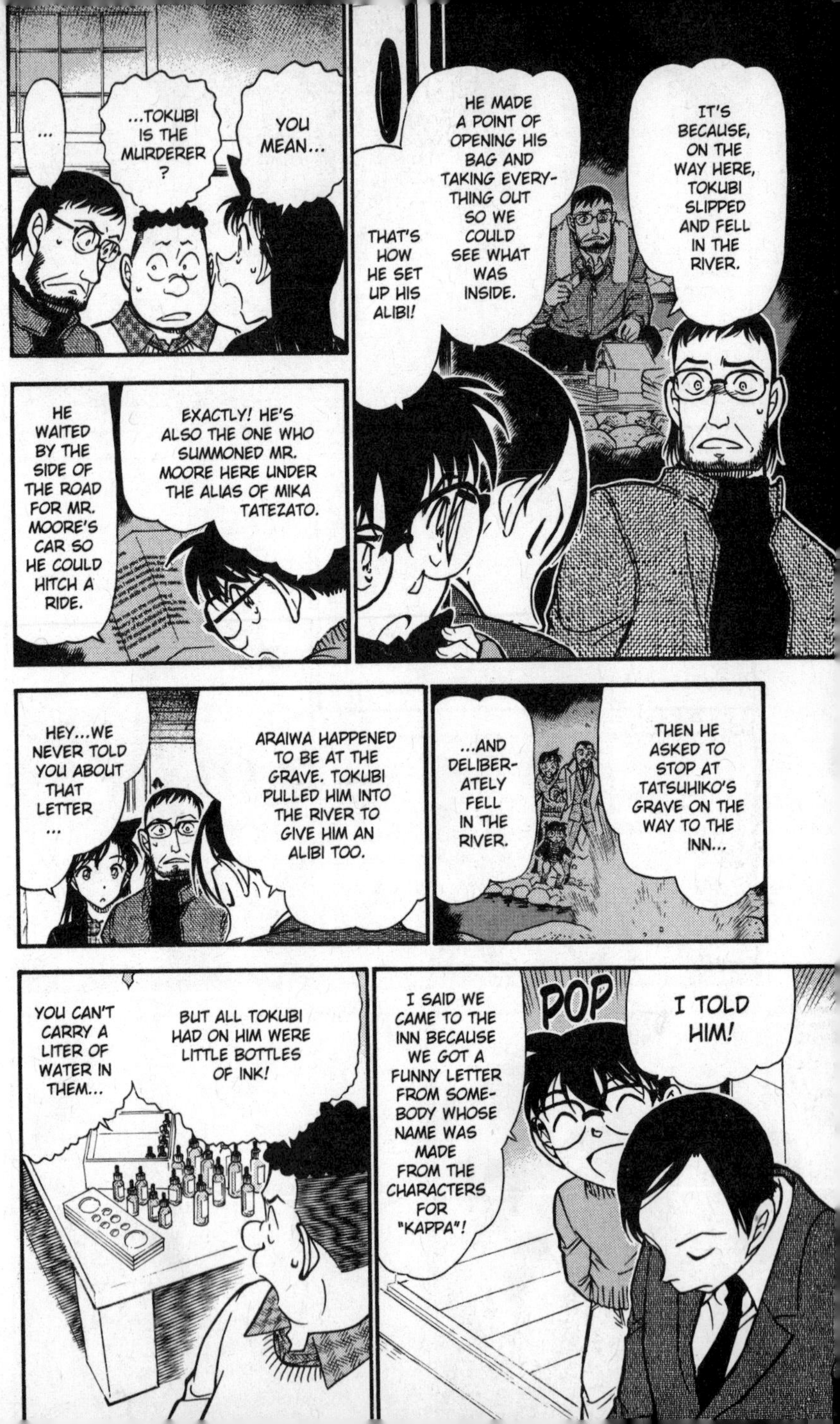
IT'S BECAUSE, ON THE WAY HERE, TOKUBI SLIPPED AND FELL IN THE RIVER.
HE MADE A POINT OF OPENING HIS BAG AND TAKING EVERYTHING OUT SO WE COULD SEE WHAT WAS INSIDE.
THAT'S HOW HE SET UP HIS ALIBI!
YOU MEAN...
...TOKUBI IS THE MURDERER?
...
EXACTLY! HE'S ALSO THE ONE WHO SUMMONED MR. MOORE HERE UNDER THE ALIAS OF MIKA TATEZATO.
HE WAITED BY THE SIDE OF THE ROAD FOR MR. MOORE'S CAR SO HE COULD HITCH A RIDE.
THEN HE ASKED TO STOP AT TATSUHIKO'S GRAVE ON THE WAY TO THE INN...
...AND DELIBERATELY FELL IN THE RIVER.
ARAIWA HAPPENED TO BE AT THE GRAVE. TOKUBI PULLED HIM INTO THE RIVER TO GIVE HIM AN ALIBI TOO.
HEY...WE NEVER TOLD YOU ABOUT THAT LETTER...
I TOLD HIM!
POP
I SAID WE CAME TO THE INN BECAUSE WE GOT A FUNNY LETTER FROM SOMEBODY WHOSE NAME WAS MADE FROM THE CHARACTERS FOR "KAPPA"!
BUT ALL TOKUBI HAD ON HIM WERE LITTLE BOTTLES OF INK!
YOU CAN'T CARRY A LITER OF WATER IN THEM...

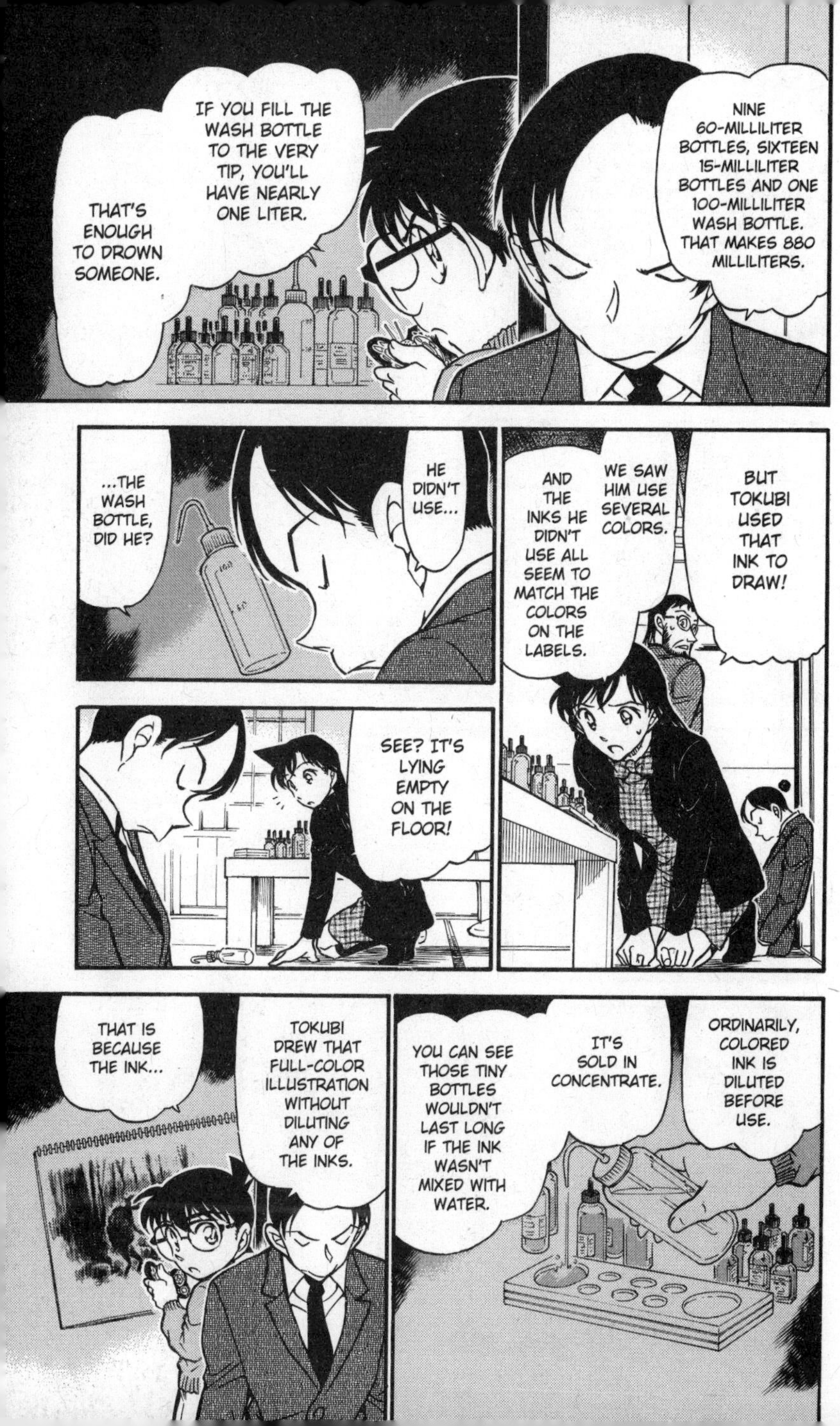
NINE 60-MILLILITER BOTTLES, SIXTEEN 15-MILLILITER BOTTLES AND ONE 100-MILLILITER WASH BOTTLE. THAT MAKES 880 MILLILITERS.
IF YOU FILL THE WASH BOTTLE TO THE VERY TIP, YOU'LL HAVE NEARLY ONE LITER.
THAT'S ENOUGH TO DROWN SOMEONE.
BUT TOKUBI USED THAT INK TO DRAW!
WE SAW HIM USE SEVERAL COLORS.
AND THE INKS HE DIDN'T USE ALL SEEM TO MATCH THE COLORS ON THE LABELS.
HE DIDN'T USE...
...THE WASH BOTTLE, DID HE?
SEE? IT'S LYING EMPTY ON THE FLOOR!
ORDINARILY, COLORED INK IS DILUTED BEFORE USE.
IT'S SOLD IN CONCENTRATE.
YOU CAN SEE THOSE TINY BOTTLES WOULDN'T LAST LONG IF THE INK WASN'T MIXED WITH WATER.
TOKUBI DREW THAT FULL-COLOR ILLUSTRATION WITHOUT DILUTING ANY OF THE INKS.
THAT IS BECAUSE THE INK...

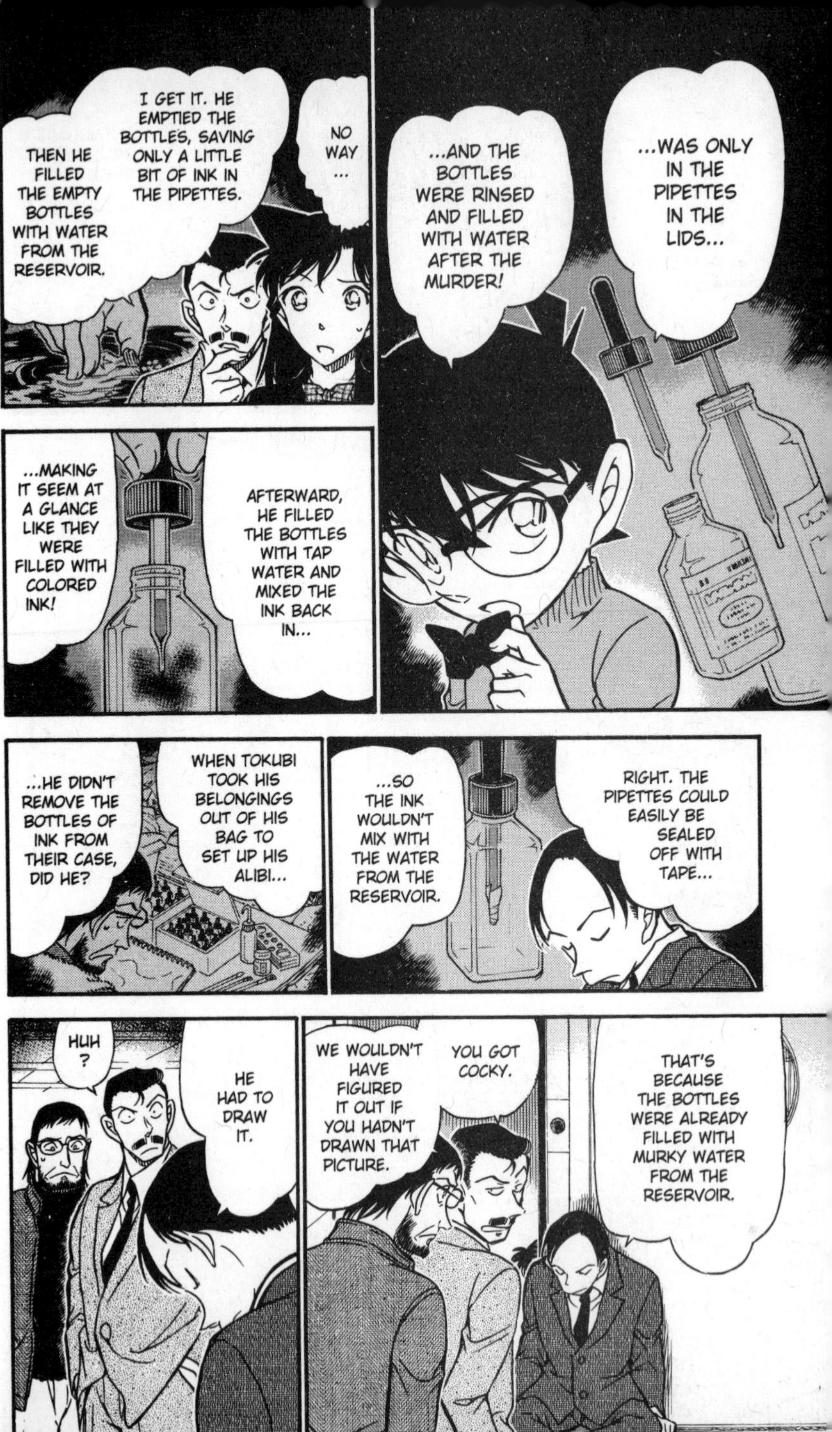
...WAS ONLY IN THE PIPETTES IN THE LIDS...
...AND THE BOTTLES WERE RINSED AND FILLED WITH WATER AFTER THE MURDER!
NO WAY ...
I GET IT. HE EMPTIED THE BOTTLES, SAVING ONLY A LITTLE BIT OF INK IN THE PIPETTES.
THEN HE FILLED THE EMPTY BOTTLES WITH WATER FROM THE RESERVOIR.
AFTERWARD, HE FILLED THE BOTTLES WITH TAP WATER AND MIXED THE INK BACK IN...
...MAKING IT SEEM AT A GLANCE LIKE THEY WERE FILLED WITH COLORED INK!
RIGHT. THE PIPETTES COULD EASILY BE SEALED OFF WITH TAPE...
...SO THE INK WOULDN'T MIX WITH THE WATER FROM THE RESERVOIR.
WHEN TOKUBI TOOK HIS BELONGINGS OUT OF HIS BAG TO SET UP HIS ALIBI...
...HE DIDN'T REMOVE THE BOTTLES OF INK FROM THEIR CASE, DID HE?
THAT'S BECAUSE THE BOTTLES WERE ALREADY FILLED WITH MURKY WATER FROM THE RESERVOIR.
YOU GOT COCKY.
WE WOULDN'T HAVE FIGURED IT OUT IF YOU HADN'T DRAWN THAT PICTURE.
HE HAD TO DRAW IT.
HUH ?

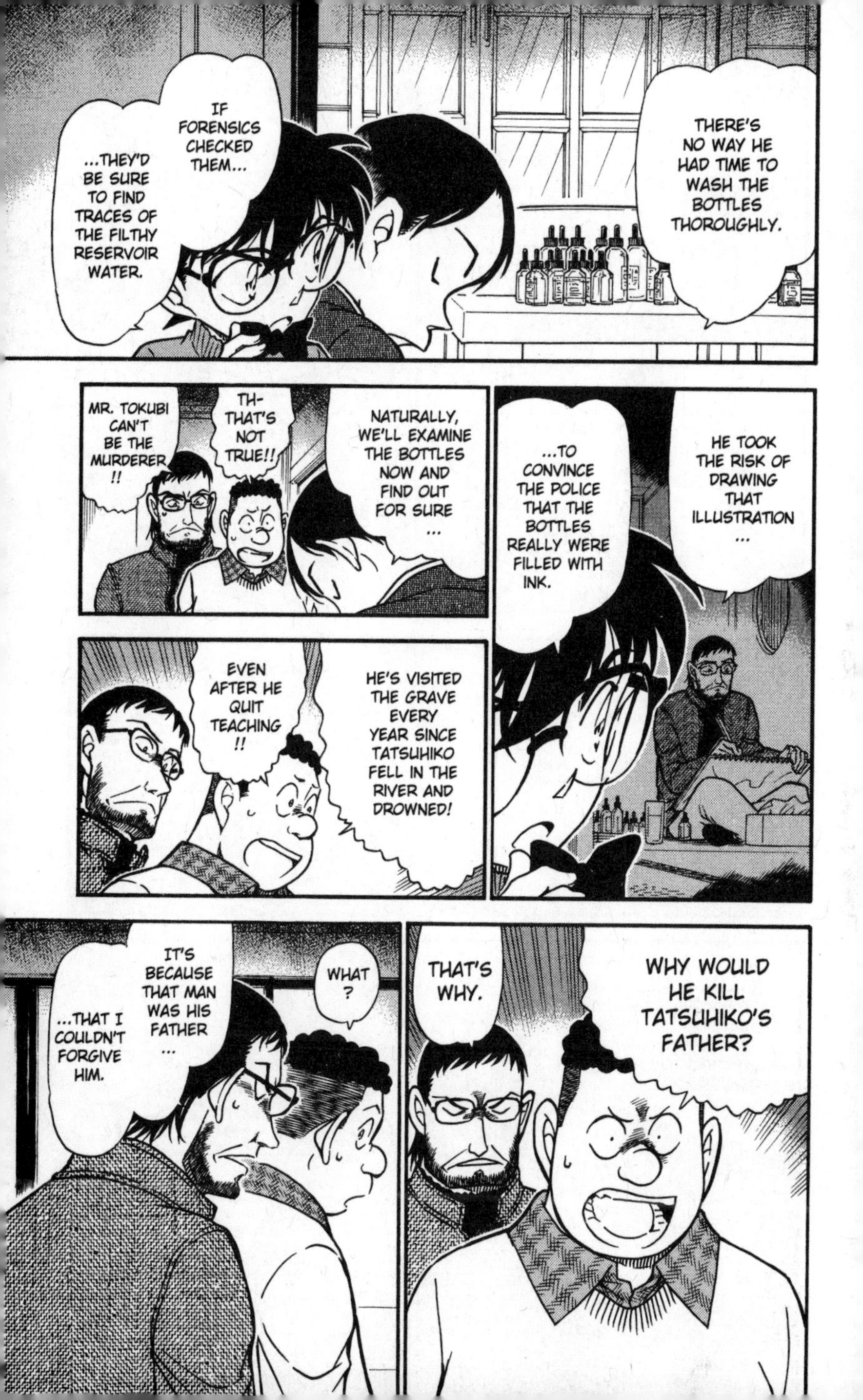
THERE'S NO WAY HE HAD TIME TO WASH THE BOTTLES THOROUGHLY.
IF FORENSICS CHECKED THEM...
...THEY'D BE SURE TO FIND TRACES OF THE FILTHY RESERVOIR WATER.
HE TOOK THE RISK OF DRAWING THAT ILLUSTRATION ...
...TO CONVINCE THE POLICE THAT THE BOTTLES REALLY WERE FILLED WITH INK.
NATURALLY, WE'LL EXAMINE THE BOTTLES NOW AND FIND OUT FOR SURE ...
TH- THAT'S NOT TRUE!!
MR. TOKUBI CAN'T BE THE MURDERER !!
HE'S VISITED THE GRAVE EVERY YEAR SINCE TATSUHIKO FELL IN THE RIVER AND DROWNED!
EVEN AFTER HE QUIT TEACHING !!
WHY WOULD HE KILL TATSUHIKO'S FATHER?
THAT'S WHY.
WHAT ?
IT'S BECAUSE THAT MAN WAS HIS FATHER ...
...THAT I COULDN'T FORGIVE HIM.

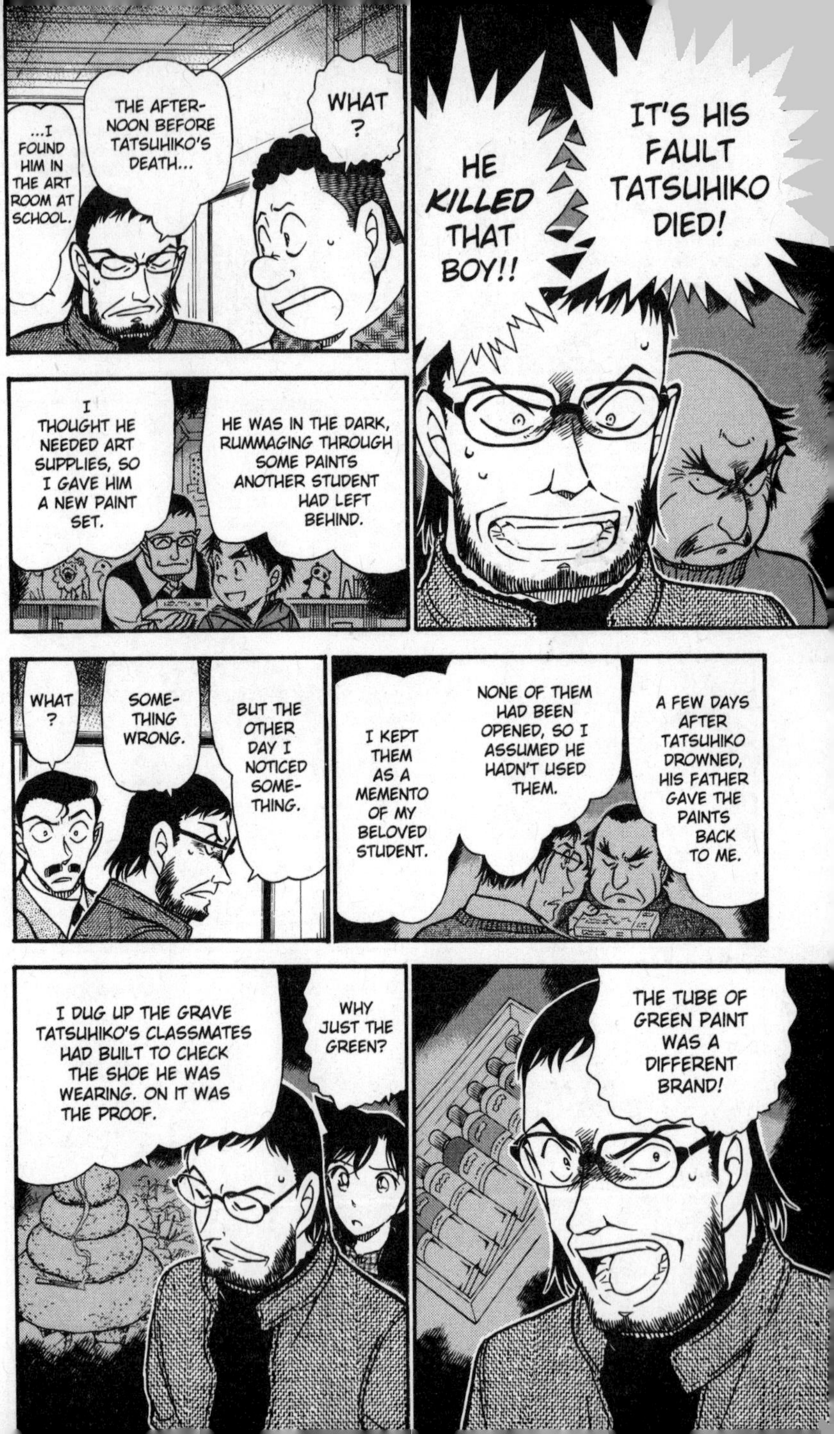
IT'S HIS FAULT TATSUHIKO DIED!
HE *KILLED* THAT BOY!!
WHAT?
THE AFTER-NOON BEFORE TATSUHIKO'S DEATH...
...I FOUND HIM IN THE ART ROOM AT SCHOOL.
HE WAS IN THE DARK, RUMMAGING THROUGH SOME PAINTS ANOTHER STUDENT HAD LEFT BEHIND.
I THOUGHT HE NEEDED ART SUPPLIES, SO I GAVE HIM A NEW PAINT SET.
A FEW DAYS AFTER TATSUHIKO DROWNED, HIS FATHER GAVE THE PAINTS BACK TO ME.
NONE OF THEM HAD BEEN OPENED, SO I ASSUMED HE HADN'T USED THEM.
I KEPT THEM AS A MEMENTO OF MY BELOVED STUDENT.
BUT THE OTHER DAY I NOTICED SOME-THING.
SOME-THING WRONG.
WHAT?
THE TUBE OF GREEN PAINT WAS A DIFFERENT BRAND!
WHY JUST THE GREEN?
I DUG UP THE GRAVE TATSUHIKO'S CLASSMATES HAD BUILT TO CHECK THE SHOE HE WAS WEARING. ON IT WAS THE PROOF.

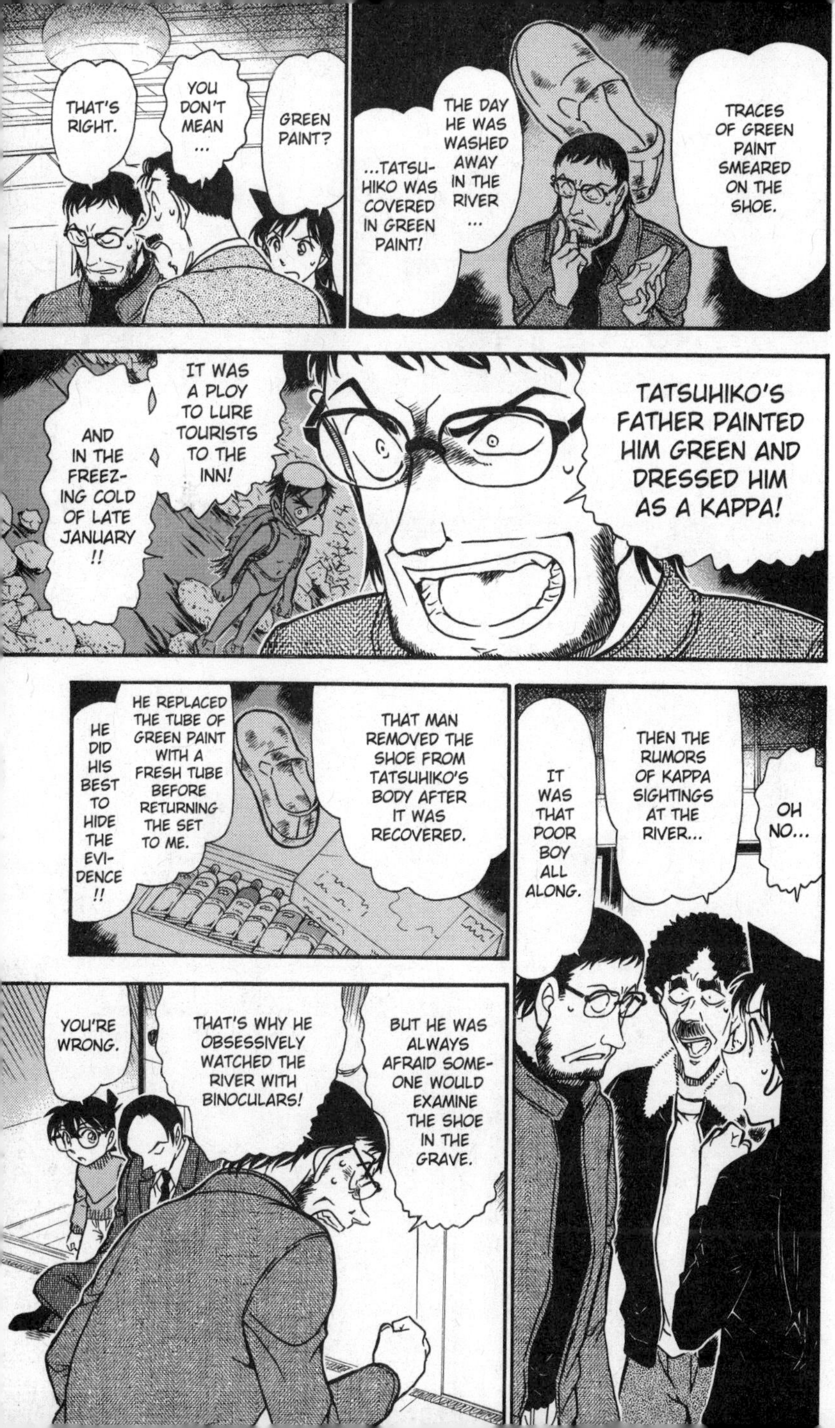
TRACES OF GREEN PAINT SMEARED ON THE SHOE.
THE DAY HE WAS WASHED AWAY IN THE RIVER ...
...TATSUHIKO WAS COVERED IN GREEN PAINT!
GREEN PAINT?
YOU DON'T MEAN ...
THAT'S RIGHT.
TATSUHIKO'S FATHER PAINTED HIM GREEN AND DRESSED HIM AS A KAPPA!
IT WAS A PLOY TO LURE TOURISTS TO THE INN!
AND IN THE FREEZING COLD OF LATE JANUARY!!
OH NO...
THEN THE RUMORS OF KAPPA SIGHTINGS AT THE RIVER...
IT WAS THAT POOR BOY ALL ALONG.
THAT MAN REMOVED THE SHOE FROM TATSUHIKO'S BODY AFTER IT WAS RECOVERED.
HE REPLACED THE TUBE OF GREEN PAINT WITH A FRESH TUBE BEFORE RETURNING THE SET TO ME.
HE DID HIS BEST TO HIDE THE EVIDENCE!!
BUT HE WAS ALWAYS AFRAID SOMEONE WOULD EXAMINE THE SHOE IN THE GRAVE.
THAT'S WHY HE OBSESSIVELY WATCHED THE RIVER WITH BINOCULARS!
YOU'RE WRONG.

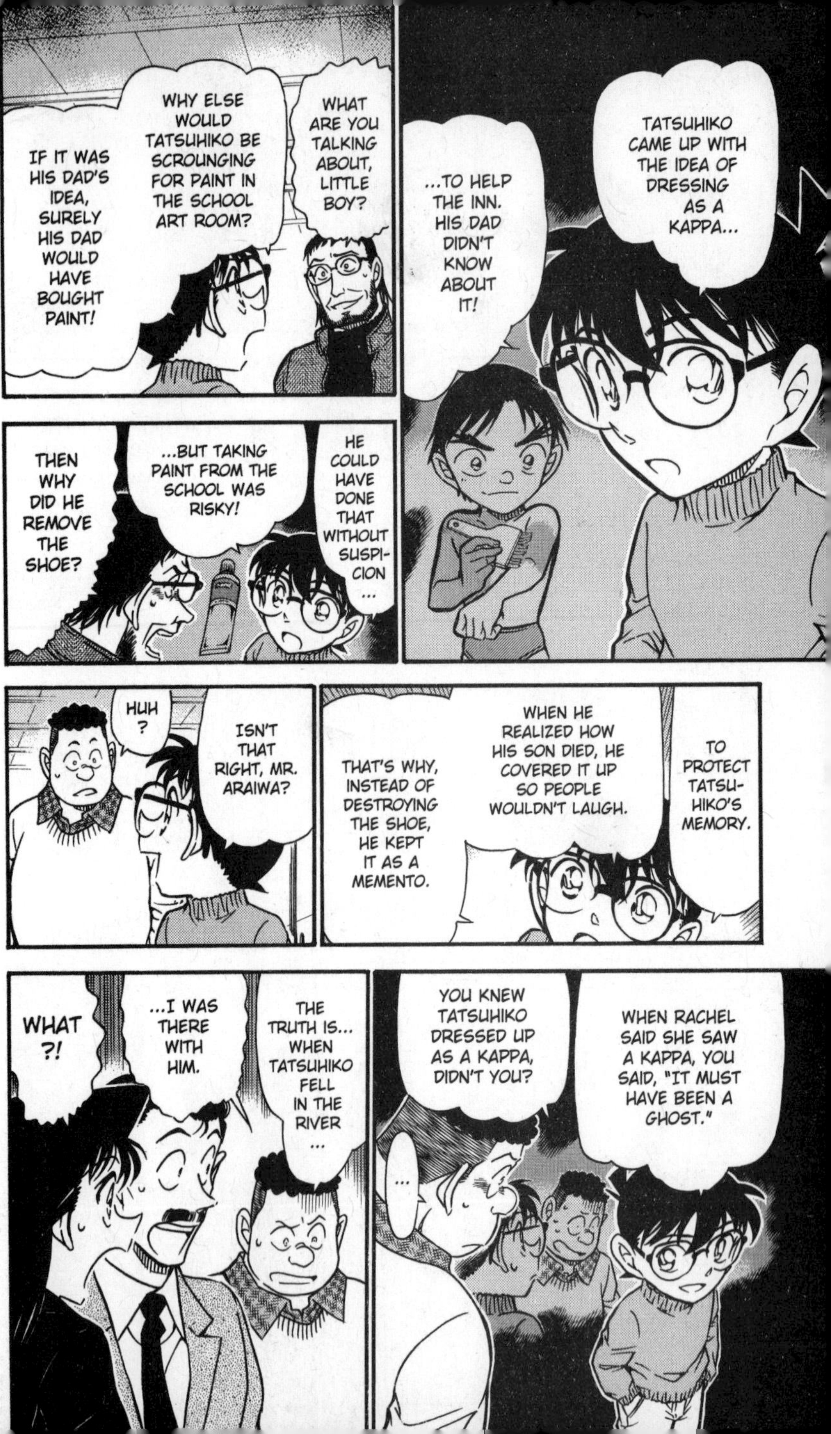
TATSUHIKO CAME UP WITH THE IDEA OF DRESSING AS A KAPPA...
...TO HELP THE INN. HIS DAD DIDN'T KNOW ABOUT IT!
WHAT ARE YOU TALKING ABOUT, LITTLE BOY?
WHY ELSE WOULD TATSUHIKO BE SCROUNGING FOR PAINT IN THE SCHOOL ART ROOM?
IF IT WAS HIS DAD'S IDEA, SURELY HIS DAD WOULD HAVE BOUGHT PAINT!
HE COULD HAVE DONE THAT WITHOUT SUSPICION...
...BUT TAKING PAINT FROM THE SCHOOL WAS RISKY!
THEN WHY DID HE REMOVE THE SHOE?
TO PROTECT TATSUHIKO'S MEMORY.
WHEN HE REALIZED HOW HIS SON DIED, HE COVERED IT UP SO PEOPLE WOULDN'T LAUGH.
THAT'S WHY, INSTEAD OF DESTROYING THE SHOE, HE KEPT IT AS A MEMENTO.
ISN'T THAT RIGHT, MR. ARAIWA?
HUH?
WHEN RACHEL SAID SHE SAW A KAPPA, YOU SAID, "IT MUST HAVE BEEN A GHOST."
YOU KNEW TATSUHIKO DRESSED UP AS A KAPPA, DIDN'T YOU?
...
THE TRUTH IS... WHEN TATSUHIKO FELL IN THE RIVER...
...I WAS THERE WITH HIM.
WHAT?!

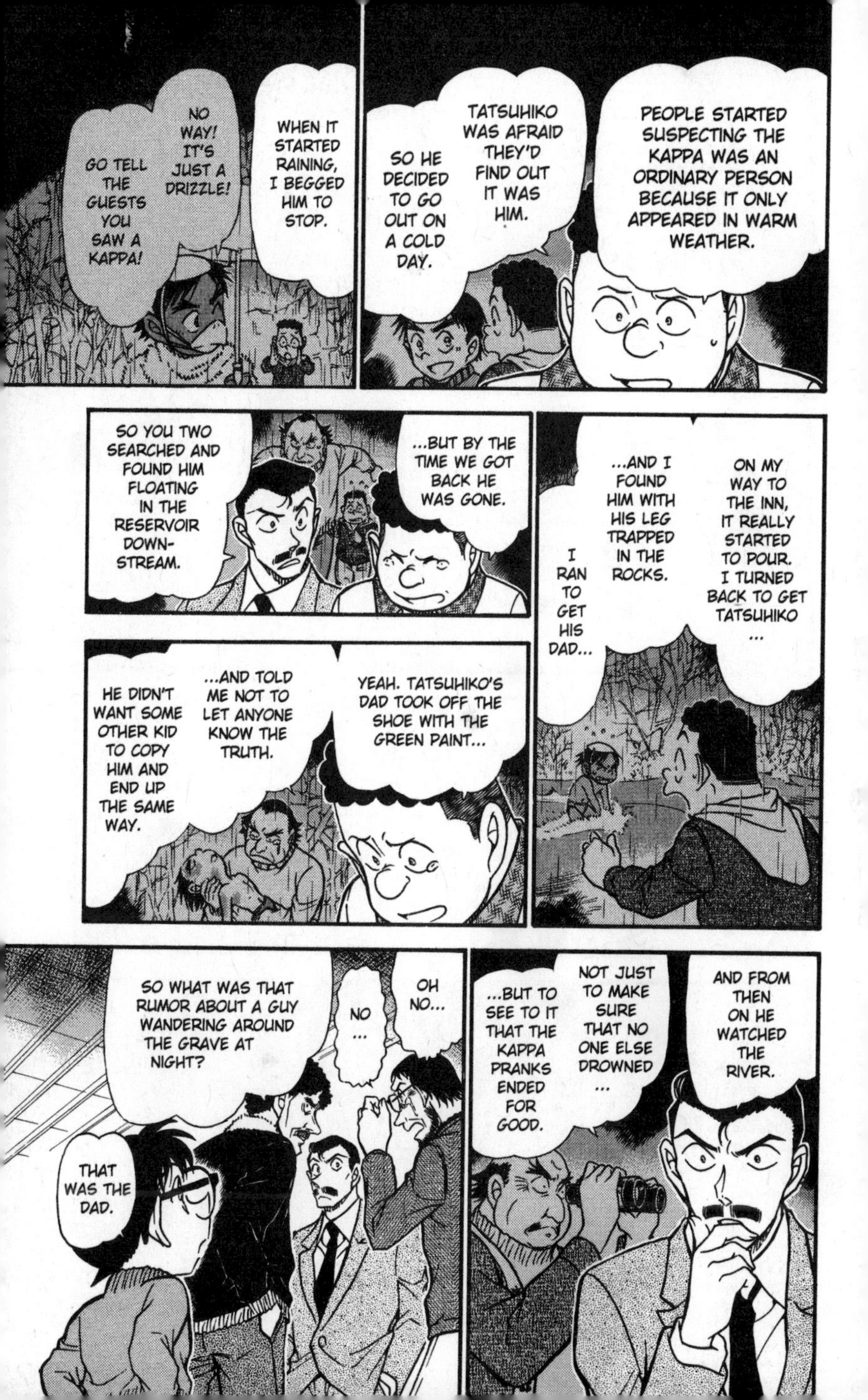
PEOPLE STARTED SUSPECTING THE KAPPA WAS AN ORDINARY PERSON BECAUSE IT ONLY APPEARED IN WARM WEATHER.
TATSUHIKO WAS AFRAID THEY'D FIND OUT IT WAS HIM.
SO HE DECIDED TO GO OUT ON A COLD DAY.
WHEN IT STARTED RAINING, I BEGGED HIM TO STOP.
NO WAY! IT'S JUST A DRIZZLE!
GO TELL THE GUESTS YOU SAW A KAPPA!
ON MY WAY TO THE INN, IT REALLY STARTED TO POUR. I TURNED BACK TO GET TATSUHIKO...
...AND I FOUND HIM WITH HIS LEG TRAPPED IN THE ROCKS.
I RAN TO GET HIS DAD...
...BUT BY THE TIME WE GOT BACK HE WAS GONE.
SO YOU TWO SEARCHED AND FOUND HIM FLOATING IN THE RESERVOIR DOWN-STREAM.
YEAH. TATSUHIKO'S DAD TOOK OFF THE SHOE WITH THE GREEN PAINT...
...AND TOLD ME NOT TO LET ANYONE KNOW THE TRUTH.
HE DIDN'T WANT SOME OTHER KID TO COPY HIM AND END UP THE SAME WAY.
AND FROM THEN ON HE WATCHED THE RIVER.
NOT JUST TO MAKE SURE THAT NO ONE ELSE DROWNED...
...BUT TO SEE TO IT THAT THE KAPPA PRANKS ENDED FOR GOOD.
OH NO...
NO...
SO WHAT WAS THAT RUMOR ABOUT A GUY WANDERING AROUND THE GRAVE AT NIGHT?
THAT WAS THE DAD.

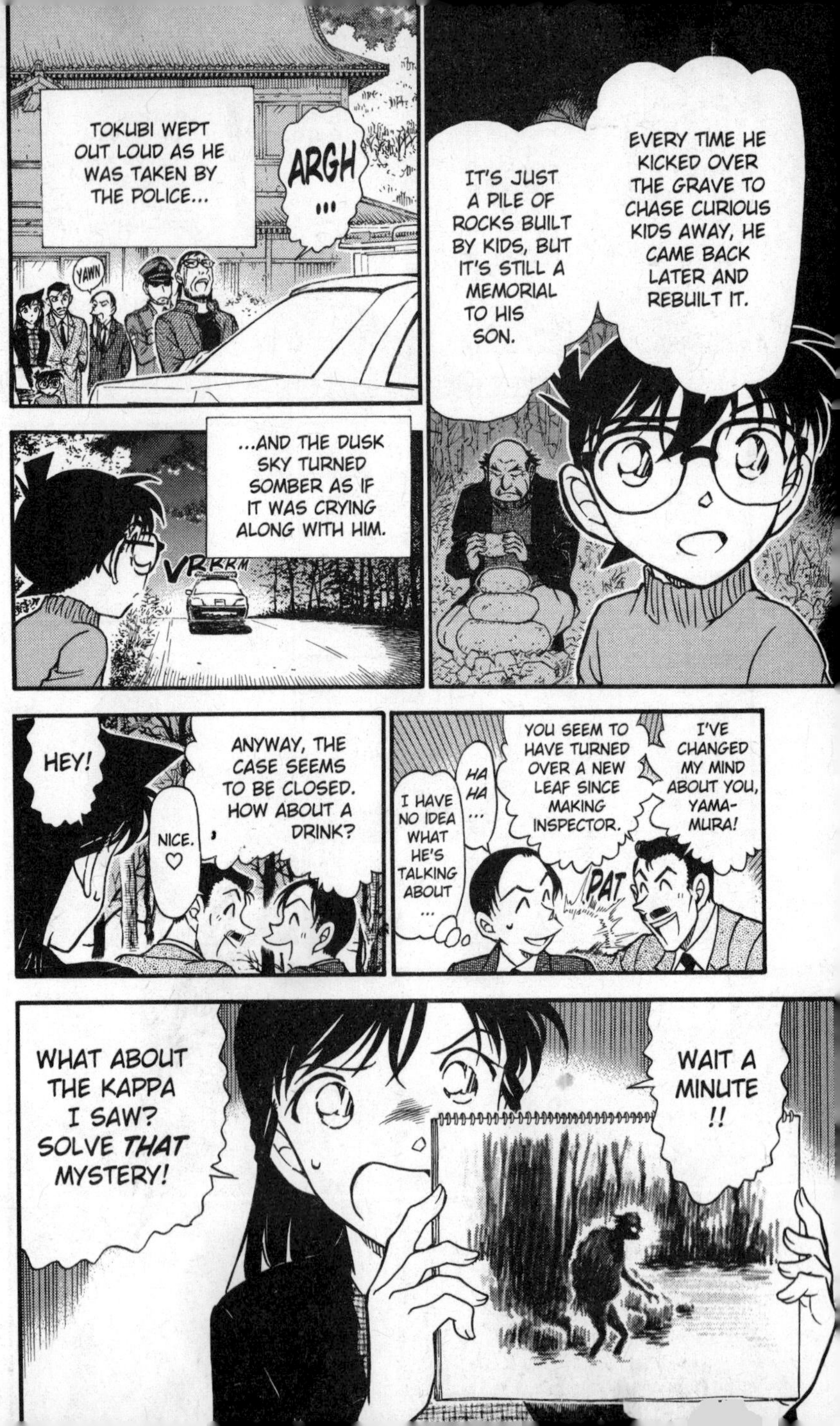
EVERY TIME HE KICKED OVER THE GRAVE TO CHASE CURIOUS KIDS AWAY, HE CAME BACK LATER AND REBUILT IT.
IT'S JUST A PILE OF ROCKS BUILT BY KIDS, BUT IT'S STILL A MEMORIAL TO HIS SON.
TOKUBI WEPT OUT LOUD AS HE WAS TAKEN BY THE POLICE...
ARGH ...
YAWN
...AND THE DUSK SKY TURNED SOMBER AS IF IT WAS CRYING ALONG WITH HIM.
VRRRM
I'VE CHANGED MY MIND ABOUT YOU, YAMA-MURA!
YOU SEEM TO HAVE TURNED OVER A NEW LEAF SINCE MAKING INSPECTOR.
PAT
HA HA ...
I HAVE NO IDEA WHAT HE'S TALKING ABOUT ...
ANYWAY, THE CASE SEEMS TO BE CLOSED. HOW ABOUT A DRINK?
NICE. ♡
HEY!
WAIT A MINUTE !!
WHAT ABOUT THE KAPPA I SAW? SOLVE *THAT* MYSTERY!

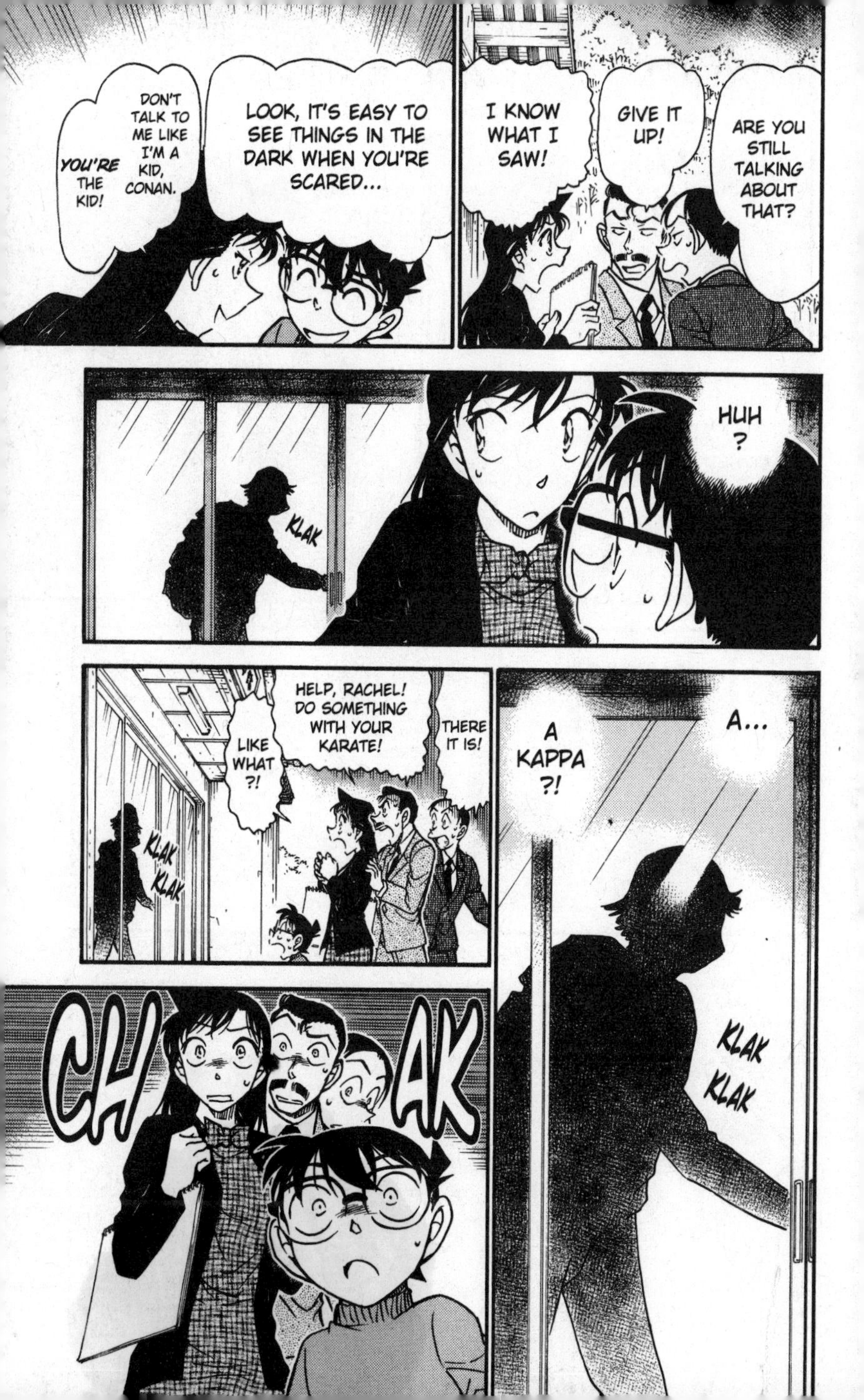
ARE YOU STILL TALKING ABOUT THAT?
GIVE IT UP!
I KNOW WHAT I SAW!
LOOK, IT'S EASY TO SEE THINGS IN THE DARK WHEN YOU'RE SCARED...
DON'T TALK TO ME LIKE I'M A KID, CONAN.
YOU'RE THE KID!
HUH?
KLAK
A...
A KAPPA?!
KLAK KLAK
THERE IT IS!
HELP, RACHEL! DO SOMETHING WITH YOUR KARATE!
LIKE WHAT?!
KLAK KLAK
CH AK

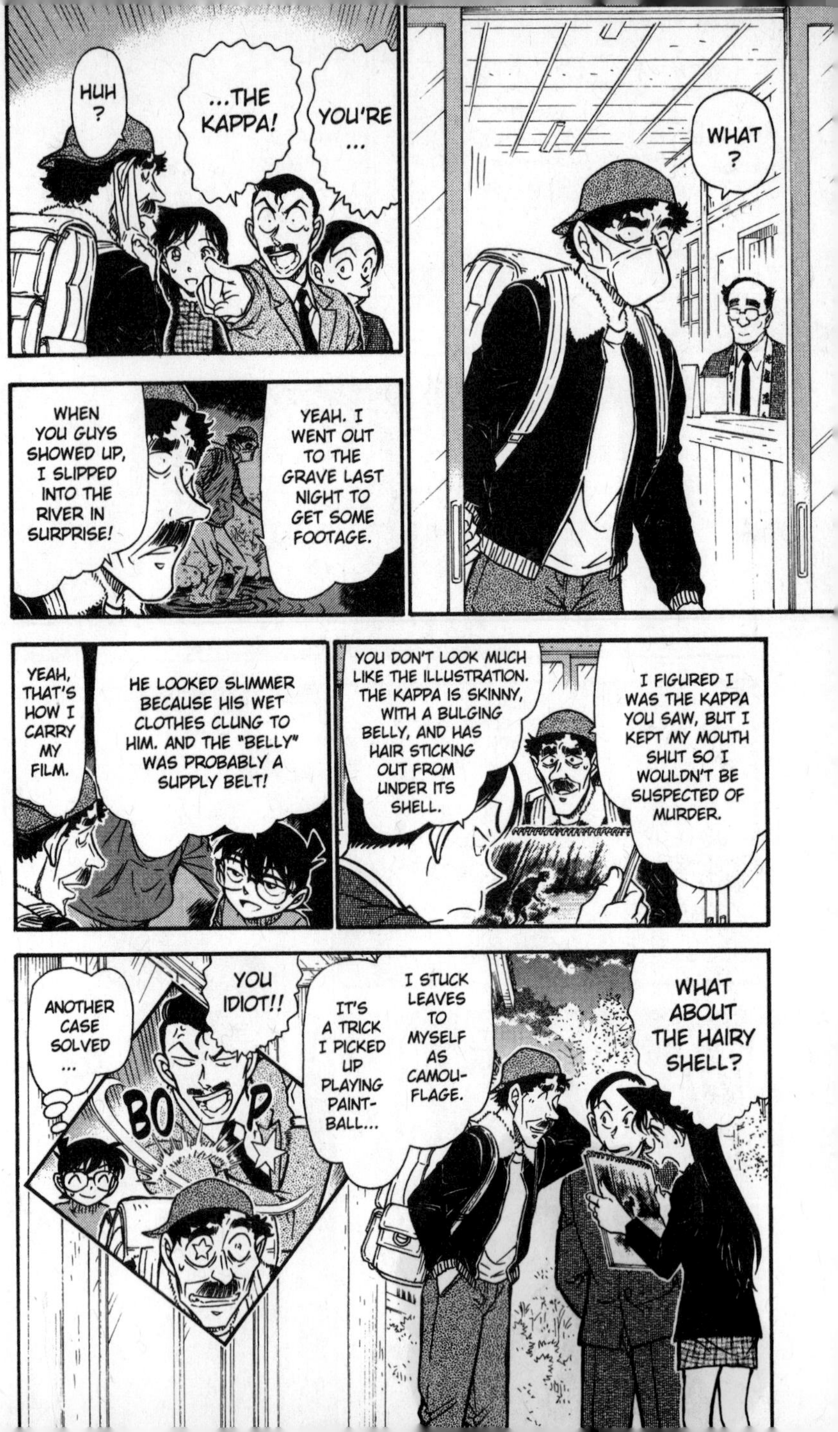
WHAT ?
YOU'RE ...
...THE KAPPA!
HUH ?
YEAH. I WENT OUT TO THE GRAVE LAST NIGHT TO GET SOME FOOTAGE.
WHEN YOU GUYS SHOWED UP, I SLIPPED INTO THE RIVER IN SURPRISE!
I FIGURED I WAS THE KAPPA YOU SAW, BUT I KEPT MY MOUTH SHUT SO I WOULDN'T BE SUSPECTED OF MURDER.
YOU DON'T LOOK MUCH LIKE THE ILLUSTRATION. THE KAPPA IS SKINNY, WITH A BULGING BELLY, AND HAS HAIR STICKING OUT FROM UNDER ITS SHELL.
HE LOOKED SLIMMER BECAUSE HIS WET CLOTHES CLUNG TO HIM. AND THE "BELLY" WAS PROBABLY A SUPPLY BELT!
YEAH, THAT'S HOW I CARRY MY FILM.
WHAT ABOUT THE HAIRY SHELL?
I STUCK LEAVES TO MYSELF AS CAMOU-FLAGE.
IT'S A TRICK I PICKED UP PLAYING PAINT-BALL...
YOU IDIOT!!
BOP
ANOTHER CASE SOLVED ...

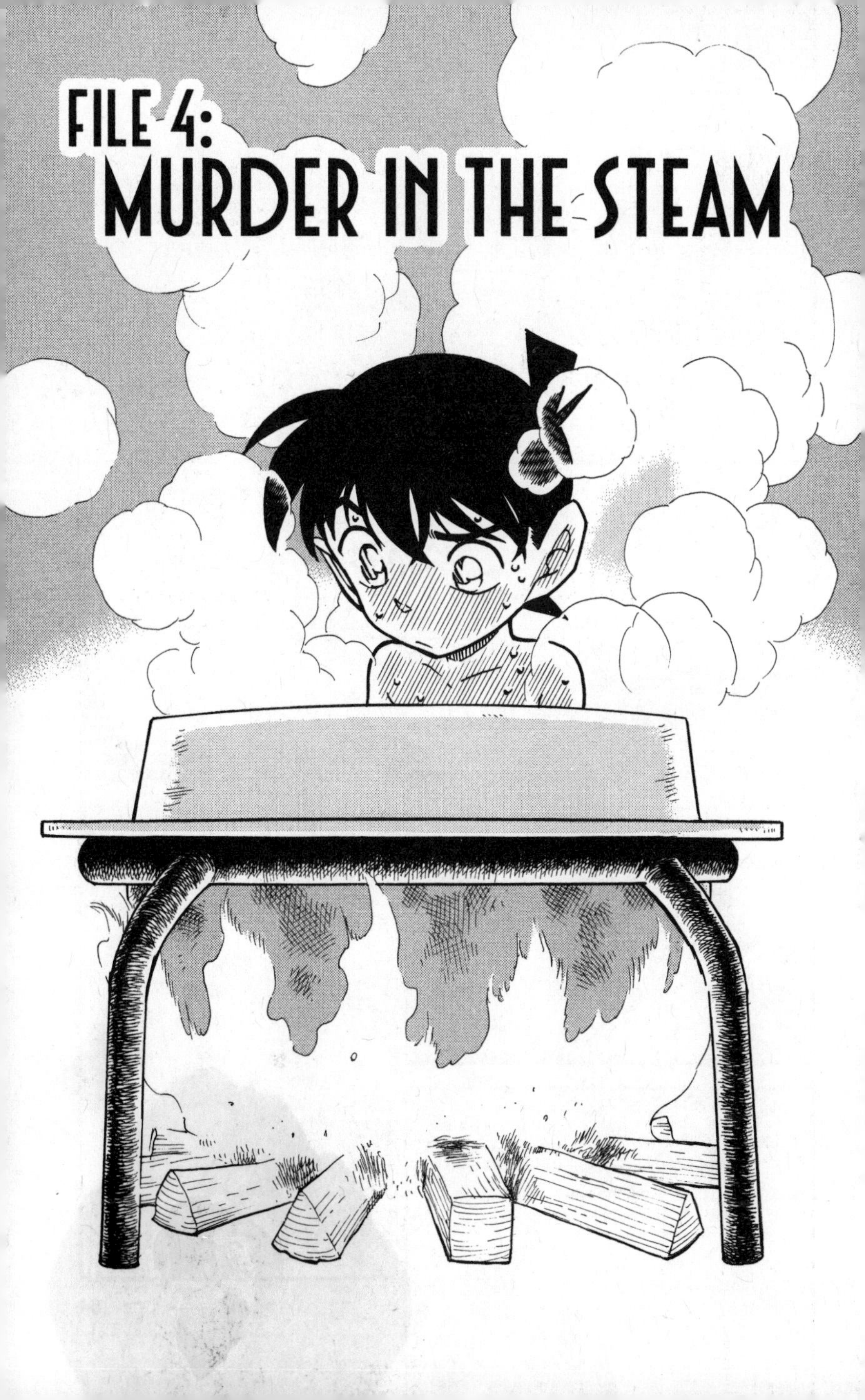
FILE 4:
MURDER IN THE STEAM

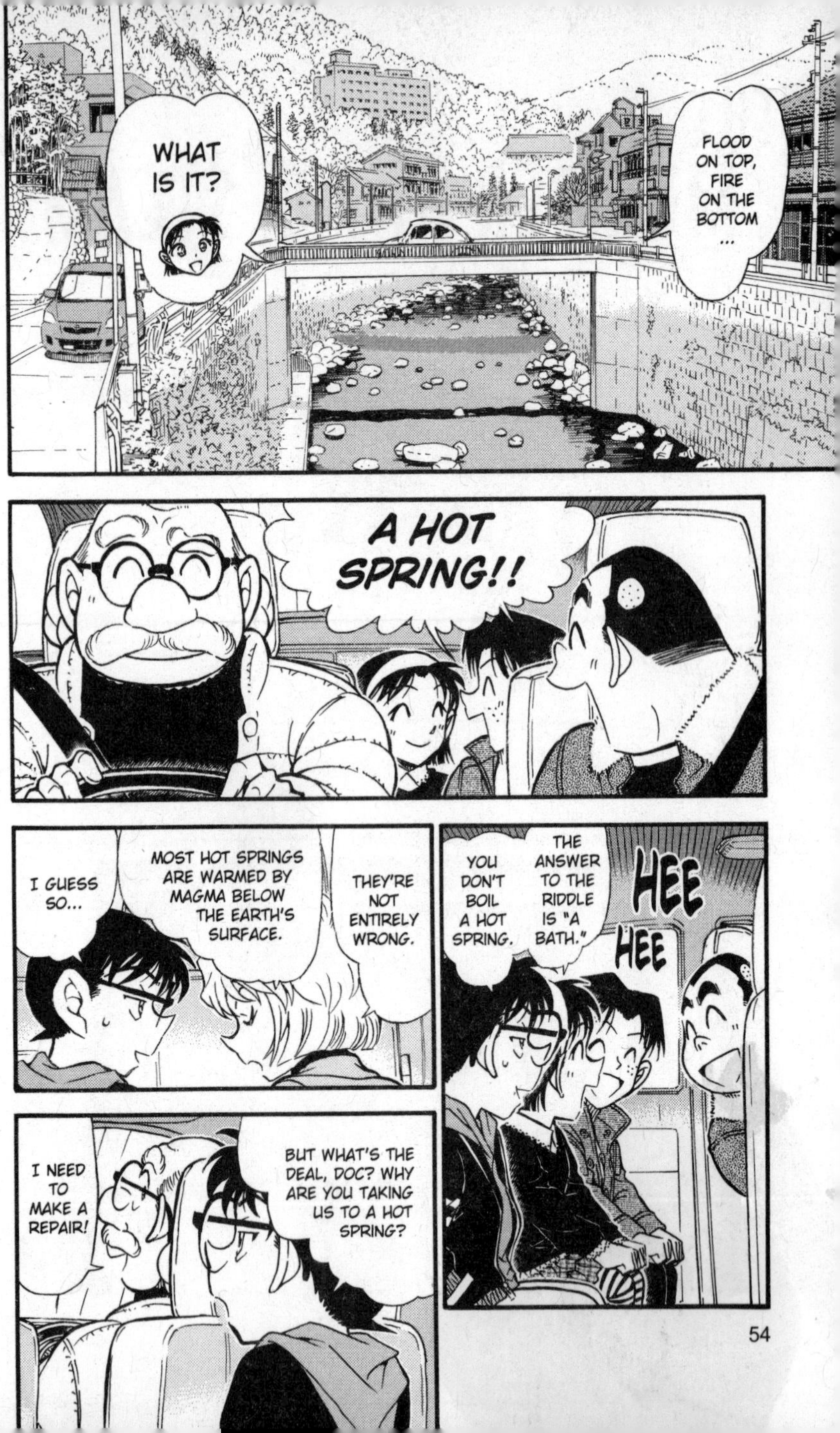
FLOOD ON TOP, FIRE ON THE BOTTOM...
WHAT IS IT?
A HOT SPRING!!
THE ANSWER TO THE RIDDLE IS "A BATH."
YOU DON'T BOIL A HOT SPRING.
HEE HEE
THEY'RE NOT ENTIRELY WRONG.
MOST HOT SPRINGS ARE WARMED BY MAGMA BELOW THE EARTH'S SURFACE.
I GUESS SO...
BUT WHAT'S THE DEAL, DOC? WHY ARE YOU TAKING US TO A HOT SPRING?
I NEED TO MAKE A REPAIR!

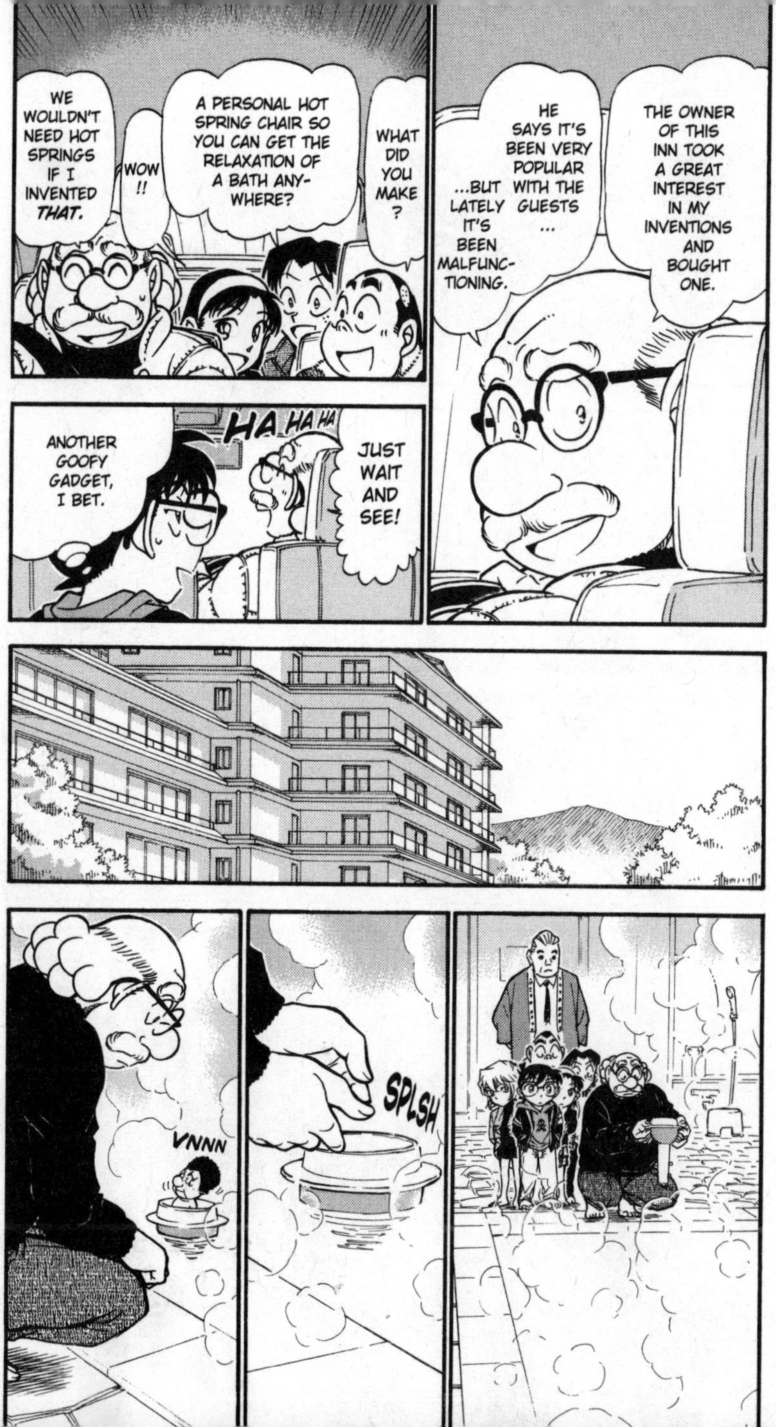
THE OWNER OF THIS INN TOOK A GREAT INTEREST IN MY INVENTIONS AND BOUGHT ONE.
HE SAYS IT'S BEEN VERY POPULAR WITH THE GUESTS ...
...BUT LATELY IT'S BEEN MALFUNCTIONING.
WHAT DID YOU MAKE?
A PERSONAL HOT SPRING CHAIR SO YOU CAN GET THE RELAXATION OF A BATH ANYWHERE?
WOW!!
WE WOULDN'T NEED HOT SPRINGS IF I INVENTED *THAT.*
HA HA HA
JUST WAIT AND SEE!
ANOTHER GOOFY GADGET, I BET.
SPLSH
VNNN

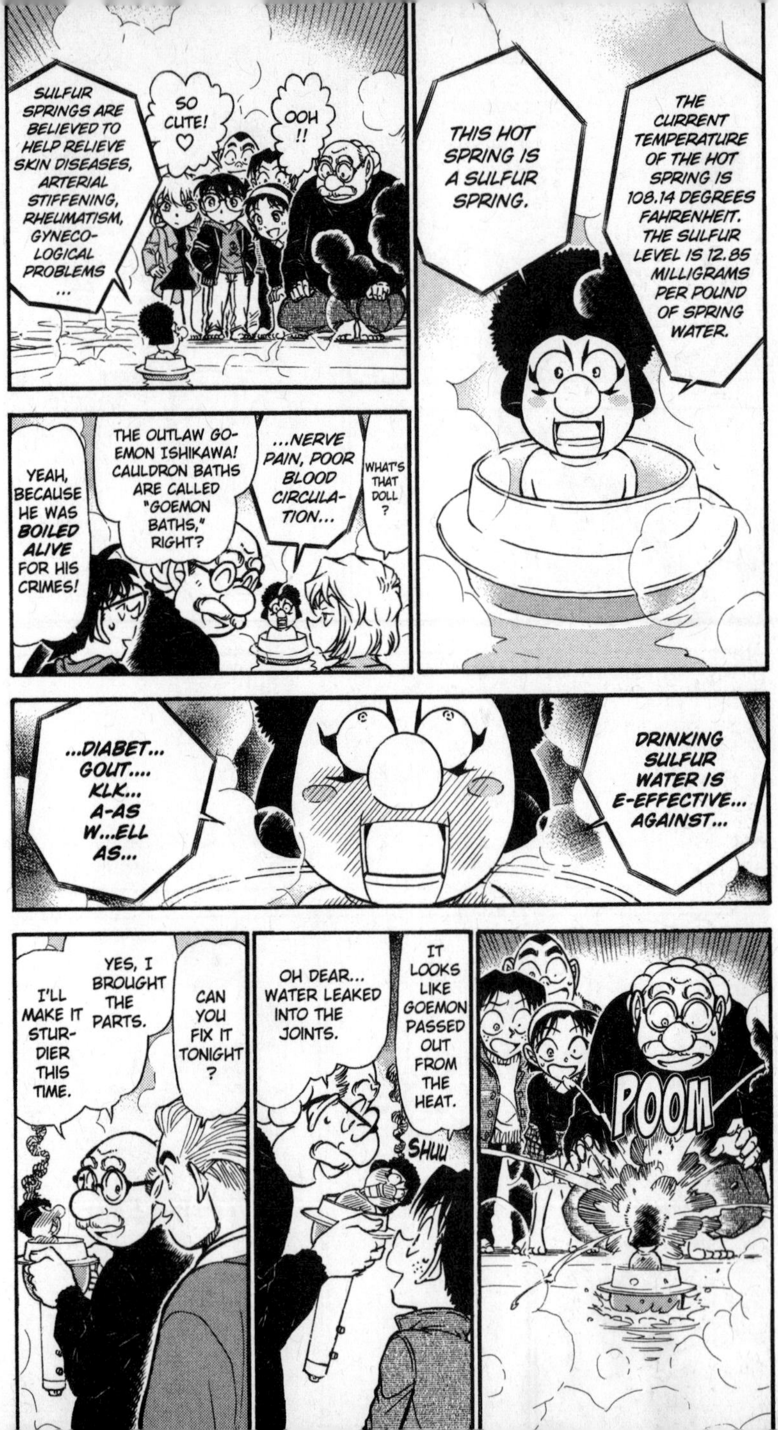
THE CURRENT TEMPERATURE OF THE HOT SPRING IS 108.14 DEGREES FAHRENHEIT. THE SULFUR LEVEL IS 12.85 MILLIGRAMS PER POUND OF SPRING WATER.
THIS HOT SPRING IS A SULFUR SPRING.
OOH !!
SO CUTE! ♡
SULFUR SPRINGS ARE BELIEVED TO HELP RELIEVE SKIN DISEASES, ARTERIAL STIFFENING, RHEUMATISM, GYNECO-LOGICAL PROBLEMS ...
WHAT'S THAT DOLL ?
...NERVE PAIN, POOR BLOOD CIRCULA-TION...
THE OUTLAW GO-EMON ISHIKAWA! CAULDRON BATHS ARE CALLED "GOEMON BATHS," RIGHT?
YEAH, BECAUSE HE WAS BOILED ALIVE FOR HIS CRIMES!
DRINKING SULFUR WATER IS E-EFFECTIVE... AGAINST...
...DIABET... GOUT.... KLK... A-AS W...ELL AS...
POOM
IT LOOKS LIKE GOEMON PASSED OUT FROM THE HEAT.
SHUU
OH DEAR... WATER LEAKED INTO THE JOINTS.
CAN YOU FIX IT TONIGHT ?
YES, I BROUGHT THE PARTS.
I'LL MAKE IT STUR-DIER THIS TIME.

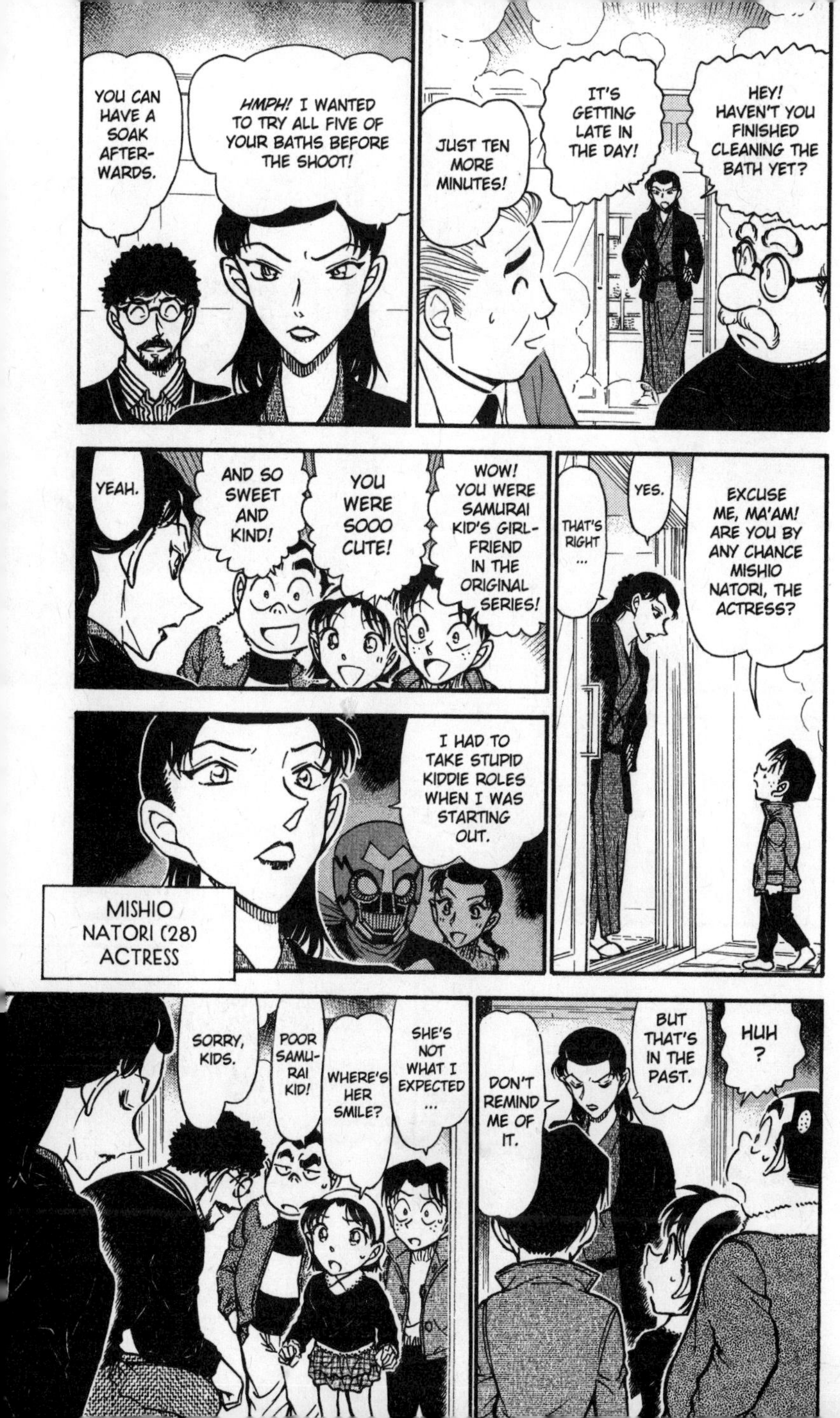
HEY! HAVEN'T YOU FINISHED CLEANING THE BATH YET?
IT'S GETTING LATE IN THE DAY!
JUST TEN MORE MINUTES!
HMPH! I WANTED TO TRY ALL FIVE OF YOUR BATHS BEFORE THE SHOOT!
YOU CAN HAVE A SOAK AFTER-WARDS.
EXCUSE ME, MA'AM! ARE YOU BY ANY CHANCE MISHIO NATORI, THE ACTRESS?
YES.
THAT'S RIGHT ...
WOW! YOU WERE SAMURAI KID'S GIRL-FRIEND IN THE ORIGINAL SERIES!
YOU WERE SOOO CUTE!
AND SO SWEET AND KIND!
YEAH.
I HAD TO TAKE STUPID KIDDIE ROLES WHEN I WAS STARTING OUT.
MISHIO NATORI (28) ACTRESS
HUH ?
BUT THAT'S IN THE PAST.
DON'T REMIND ME OF IT.
SHE'S NOT WHAT I EXPECTED ...
WHERE'S HER SMILE?
POOR SAMU-RAI KID!
SORRY, KIDS.

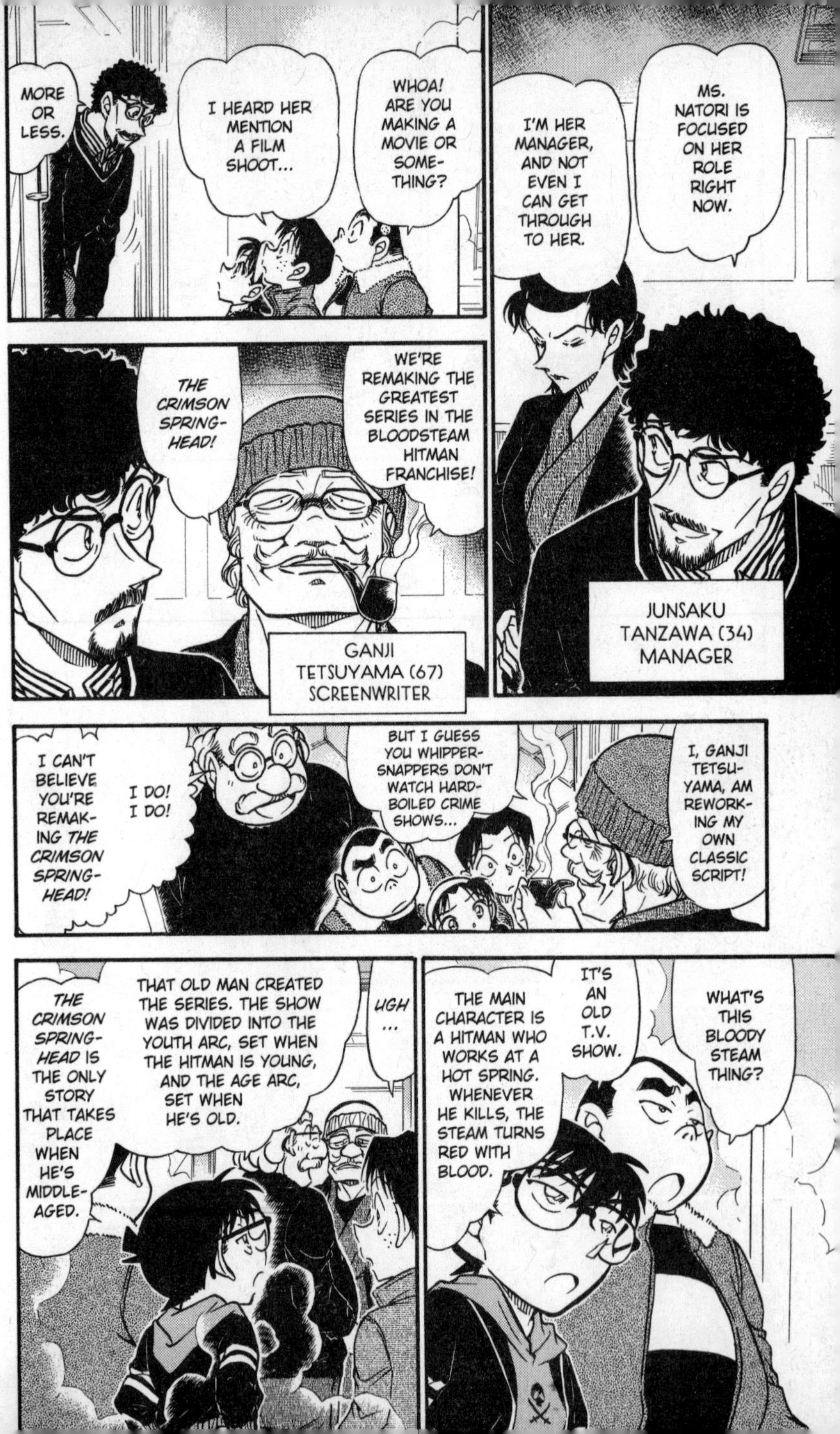
MS. NATORI IS FOCUSED ON HER ROLE RIGHT NOW.
I'M HER MANAGER, AND NOT EVEN I CAN GET THROUGH TO HER.
JUNSAKU TANZAWA (34) MANAGER
WHOA! ARE YOU MAKING A MOVIE OR SOMETHING?
I HEARD HER MENTION A FILM SHOOT...
MORE OR LESS.
WE'RE REMAKING THE GREATEST SERIES IN THE BLOODSTEAM HITMAN FRANCHISE!
THE CRIMSON SPRINGHEAD!
GANJI TETSUYAMA (67) SCREENWRITER
I, GANJI TETSUYAMA, AM REWORKING MY OWN CLASSIC SCRIPT!
BUT I GUESS YOU WHIPPERSNAPPERS DON'T WATCH HARD-BOILED CRIME SHOWS...
I DO! I DO!
I CAN'T BELIEVE YOU'RE REMAKING *THE CRIMSON SPRINGHEAD!*
WHAT'S THIS BLOODY STEAM THING?
IT'S AN OLD T.V. SHOW.
THE MAIN CHARACTER IS A HITMAN WHO WORKS AT A HOT SPRING. WHENEVER HE KILLS, THE STEAM TURNS RED WITH BLOOD.
UGH...
THAT OLD MAN CREATED THE SERIES. THE SHOW WAS DIVIDED INTO THE YOUTH ARC, SET WHEN THE HITMAN IS YOUNG, AND THE AGE ARC, SET WHEN HE'S OLD.
THE CRIMSON SPRINGHEAD IS THE ONLY STORY THAT TAKES PLACE WHEN HE'S MIDDLE-AGED.

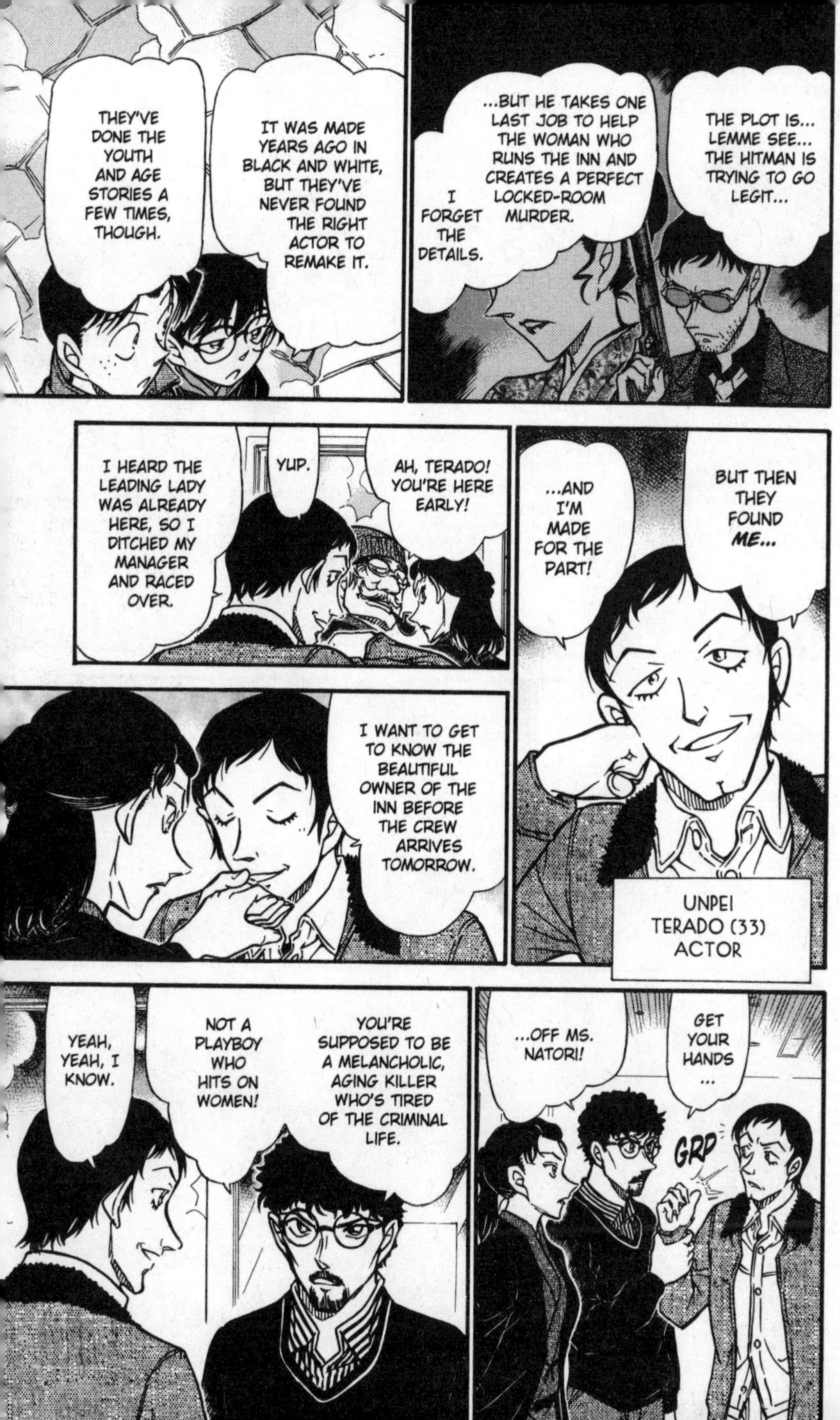
THE PLOT IS... LEMME SEE... THE HITMAN IS TRYING TO GO LEGIT...
...BUT HE TAKES ONE LAST JOB TO HELP THE WOMAN WHO RUNS THE INN AND CREATES A PERFECT LOCKED-ROOM MURDER.
I FORGET THE DETAILS.
IT WAS MADE YEARS AGO IN BLACK AND WHITE, BUT THEY'VE NEVER FOUND THE RIGHT ACTOR TO REMAKE IT.
THEY'VE DONE THE YOUTH AND AGE STORIES A FEW TIMES, THOUGH.
BUT THEN THEY FOUND *ME*...
...AND I'M MADE FOR THE PART!
UNPEI TERADO (33) ACTOR
AH, TERADO! YOU'RE HERE EARLY!
YUP.
I HEARD THE LEADING LADY WAS ALREADY HERE, SO I DITCHED MY MANAGER AND RACED OVER.
I WANT TO GET TO KNOW THE BEAUTIFUL OWNER OF THE INN BEFORE THE CREW ARRIVES TOMORROW.
GET YOUR HANDS ...
...OFF MS. NATORI!
GRP
YOU'RE SUPPOSED TO BE A MELANCHOLIC, AGING KILLER WHO'S TIRED OF THE CRIMINAL LIFE.
NOT A PLAYBOY WHO HITS ON WOMEN!
YEAH, YEAH, I KNOW.

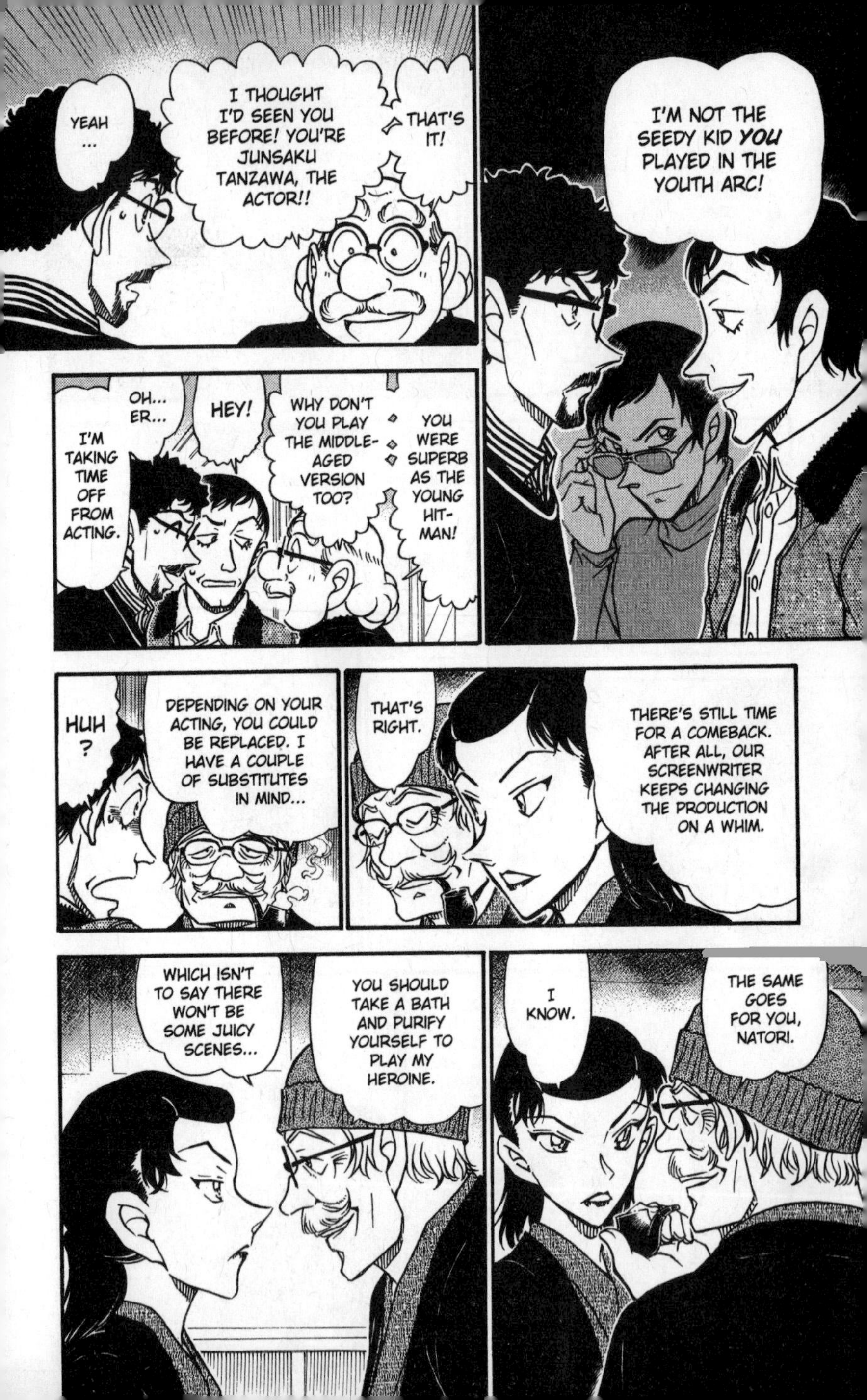
I'M NOT THE SEEDY KID YOU PLAYED IN THE YOUTH ARC!
THAT'S IT!
I THOUGHT I'D SEEN YOU BEFORE! YOU'RE JUNSAKU TANZAWA, THE ACTOR!!
YEAH ...
YOU WERE SUPERB AS THE YOUNG HIT-MAN!
WHY DON'T YOU PLAY THE MIDDLE-AGED VERSION TOO?
HEY!
OH... ER...
I'M TAKING TIME OFF FROM ACTING.
THERE'S STILL TIME FOR A COMEBACK. AFTER ALL, OUR SCREENWRITER KEEPS CHANGING THE PRODUCTION ON A WHIM.
THAT'S RIGHT.
DEPENDING ON YOUR ACTING, YOU COULD BE REPLACED. I HAVE A COUPLE OF SUBSTITUTES IN MIND...
HUH ?
THE SAME GOES FOR YOU, NATORI.
I KNOW.
YOU SHOULD TAKE A BATH AND PURIFY YOURSELF TO PLAY MY HEROINE.
WHICH ISN'T TO SAY THERE WON'T BE SOME JUICY SCENES...

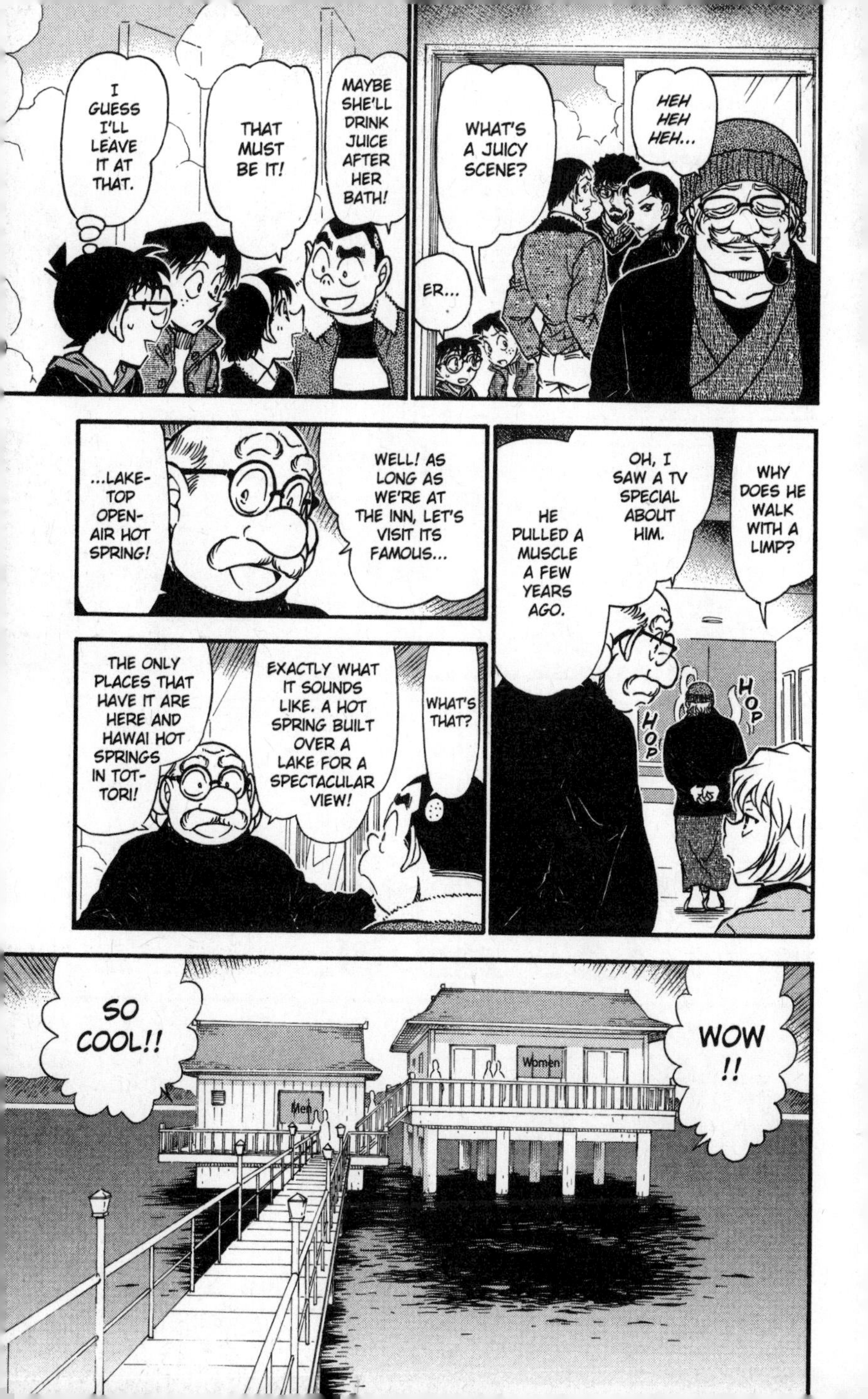
HEH HEH HEH...
WHAT'S A JUICY SCENE?
ER...
MAYBE SHE'LL DRINK JUICE AFTER HER BATH!
THAT MUST BE IT!
I GUESS I'LL LEAVE IT AT THAT.
WHY DOES HE WALK WITH A LIMP?
OH, I SAW A TV SPECIAL ABOUT HIM.
HE PULLED A MUSCLE A FEW YEARS AGO.
HOP
HOP
WELL! AS LONG AS WE'RE AT THE INN, LET'S VISIT ITS FAMOUS...
...LAKE-TOP OPEN-AIR HOT SPRING!
WHAT'S THAT?
EXACTLY WHAT IT SOUNDS LIKE. A HOT SPRING BUILT OVER A LAKE FOR A SPECTACULAR VIEW!
THE ONLY PLACES THAT HAVE IT ARE HERE AND HAWAI HOT SPRINGS IN TOT-TORI!
WOW!!
SO COOL!!
Women
Men

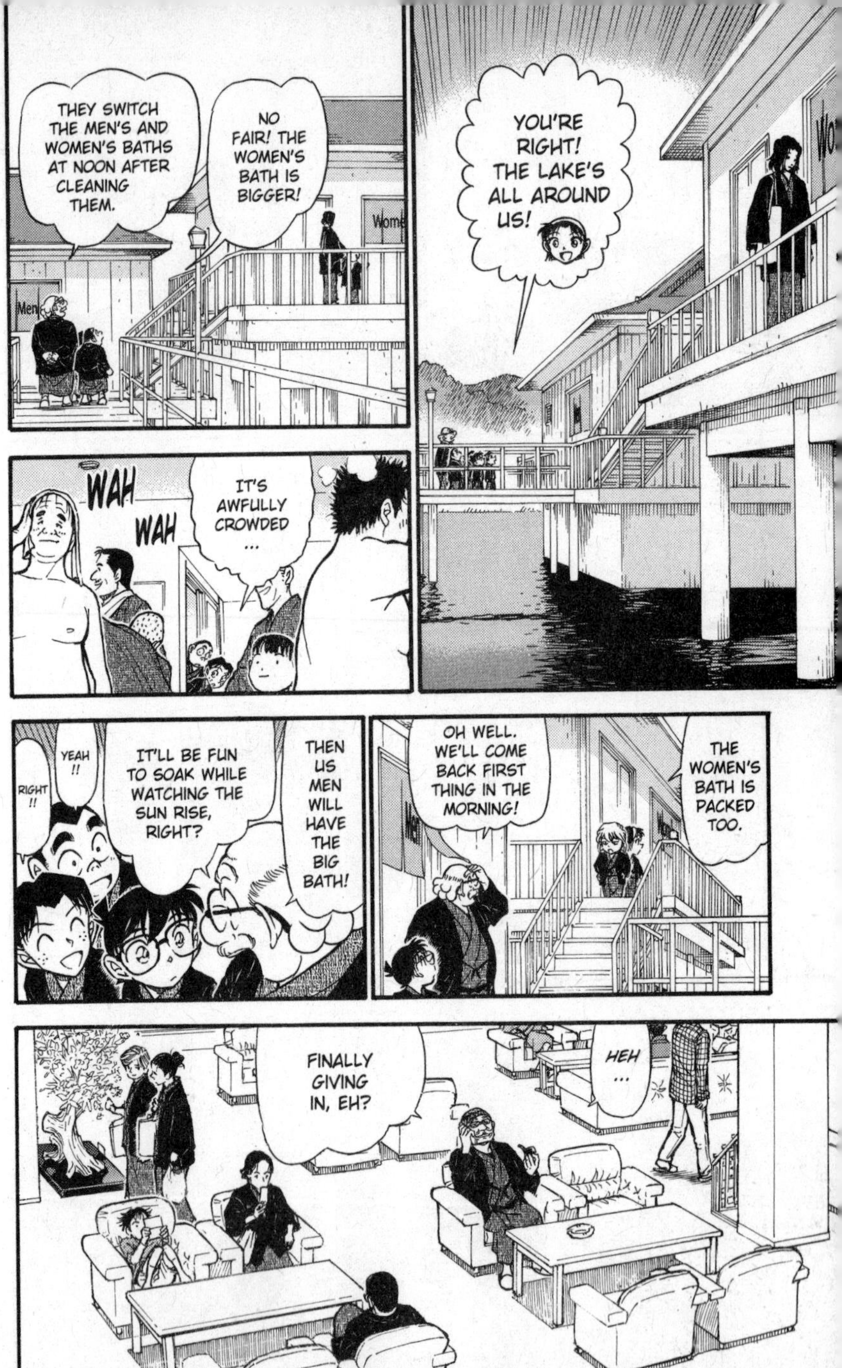
YOU'RE RIGHT! THE LAKE'S ALL AROUND US!
NO FAIR! THE WOMEN'S BATH IS BIGGER!
THEY SWITCH THE MEN'S AND WOMEN'S BATHS AT NOON AFTER CLEANING THEM.
IT'S AWFULLY CROWDED ...
WAH
WAH
THE WOMEN'S BATH IS PACKED TOO.
OH WELL. WE'LL COME BACK FIRST THING IN THE MORNING!
THEN US MEN WILL HAVE THE BIG BATH!
IT'LL BE FUN TO SOAK WHILE WATCHING THE SUN RISE, RIGHT?
YEAH !!
RIGHT !!
HEH ...
FINALLY GIVING IN, EH?

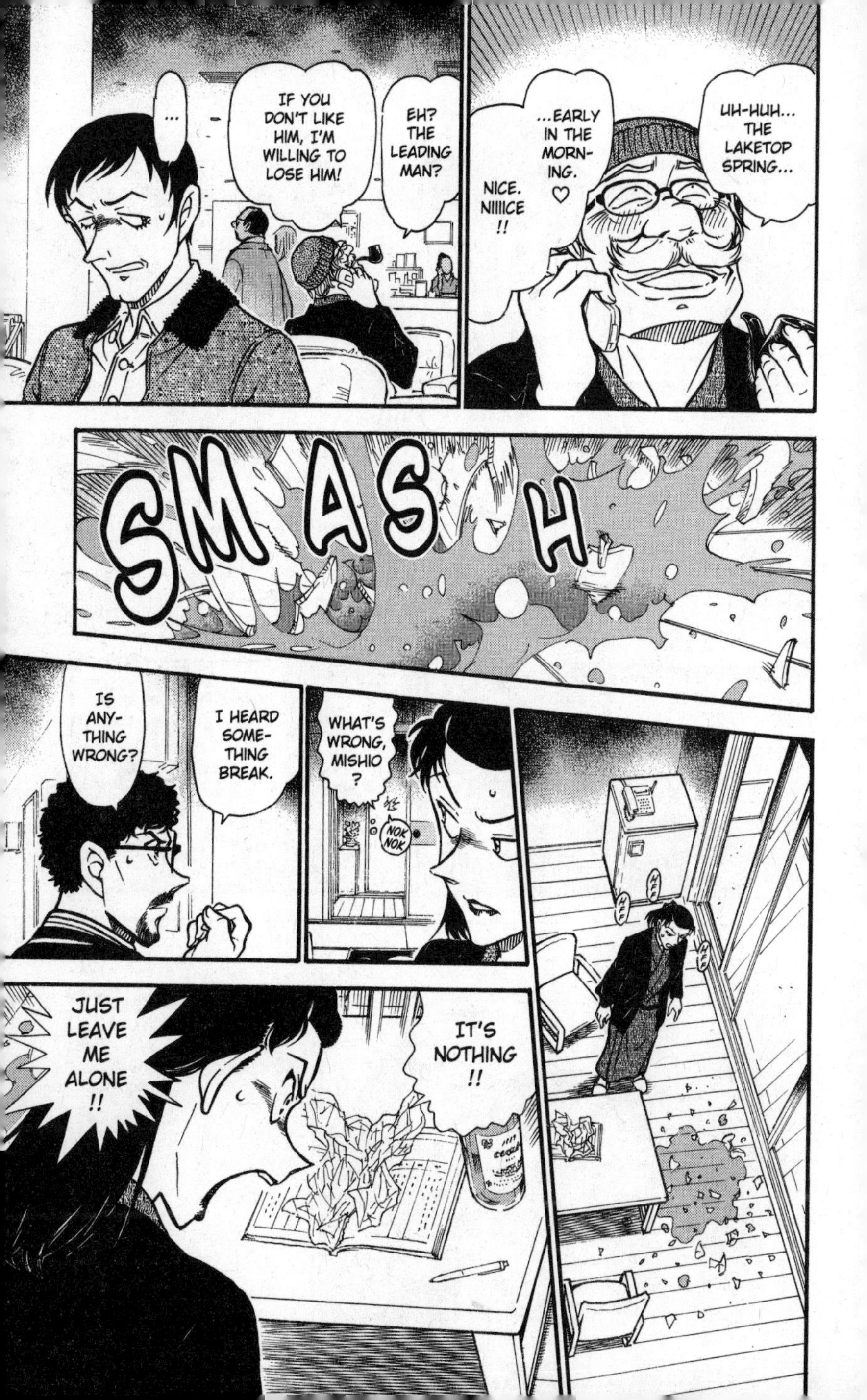
UH-HUH... THE LAKETOP SPRING...
...EARLY IN THE MORNING. ♡
NICE. NIIIICE !!
EH? THE LEADING MAN?
IF YOU DON'T LIKE HIM, I'M WILLING TO LOSE HIM!
...
SMASH
HEF
HEF
HEF
WHAT'S WRONG, MISHIO?
NOK NOK
I HEARD SOMETHING BREAK.
IS ANYTHING WRONG?
IT'S NOTHING !!
JUST LEAVE ME ALONE !!

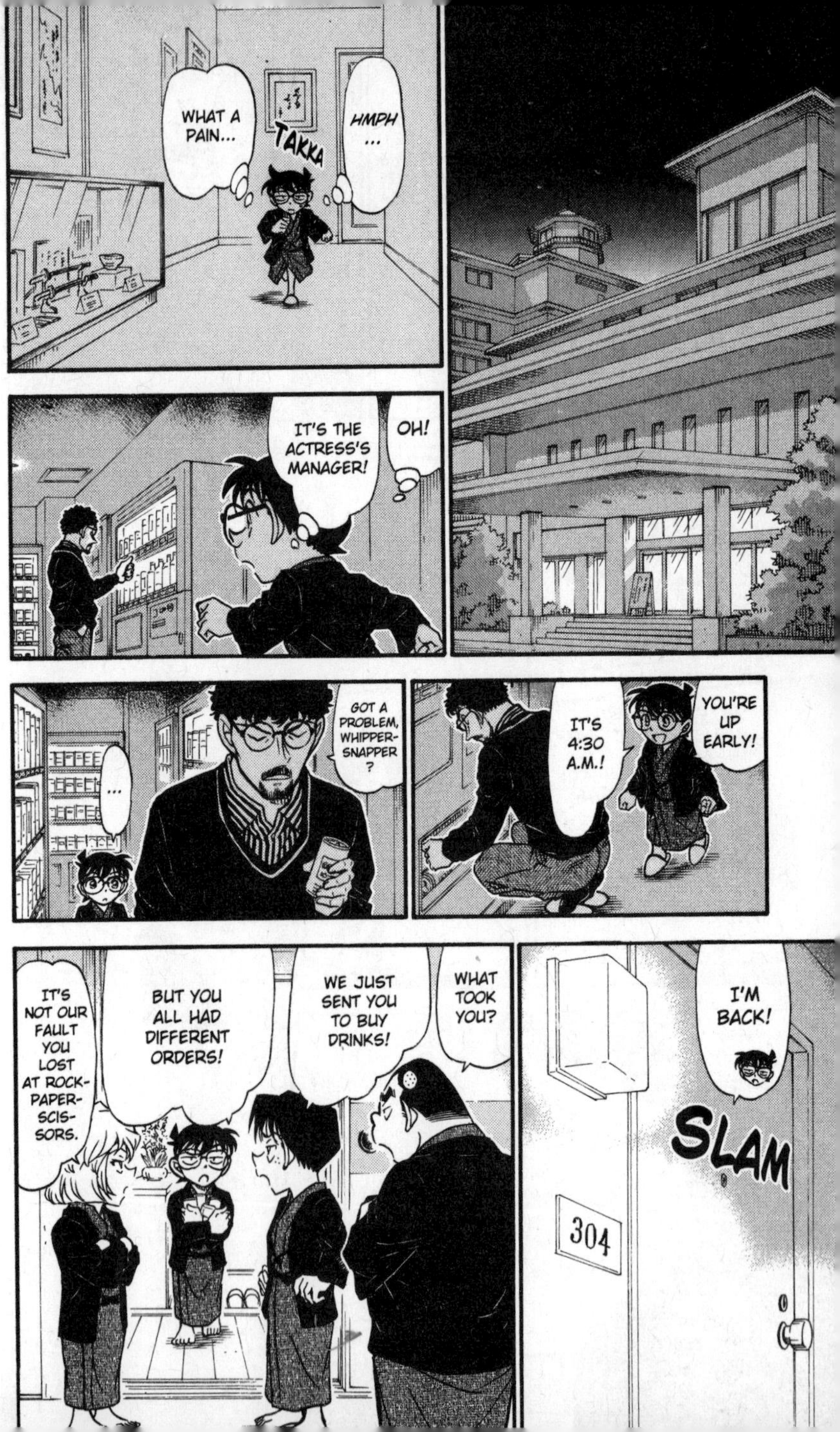
HMPH ...
TAKKA
WHAT A PAIN...
OH!
IT'S THE ACTRESS'S MANAGER!
YOU'RE UP EARLY!
IT'S 4:30 A.M.!
GOT A PROBLEM, WHIPPER-SNAPPER?
...
I'M BACK!
SLAM
304
WHAT TOOK YOU?
WE JUST SENT YOU TO BUY DRINKS!
BUT YOU ALL HAD DIFFERENT ORDERS!
IT'S NOT OUR FAULT YOU LOST AT ROCK-PAPER-SCISSORS.

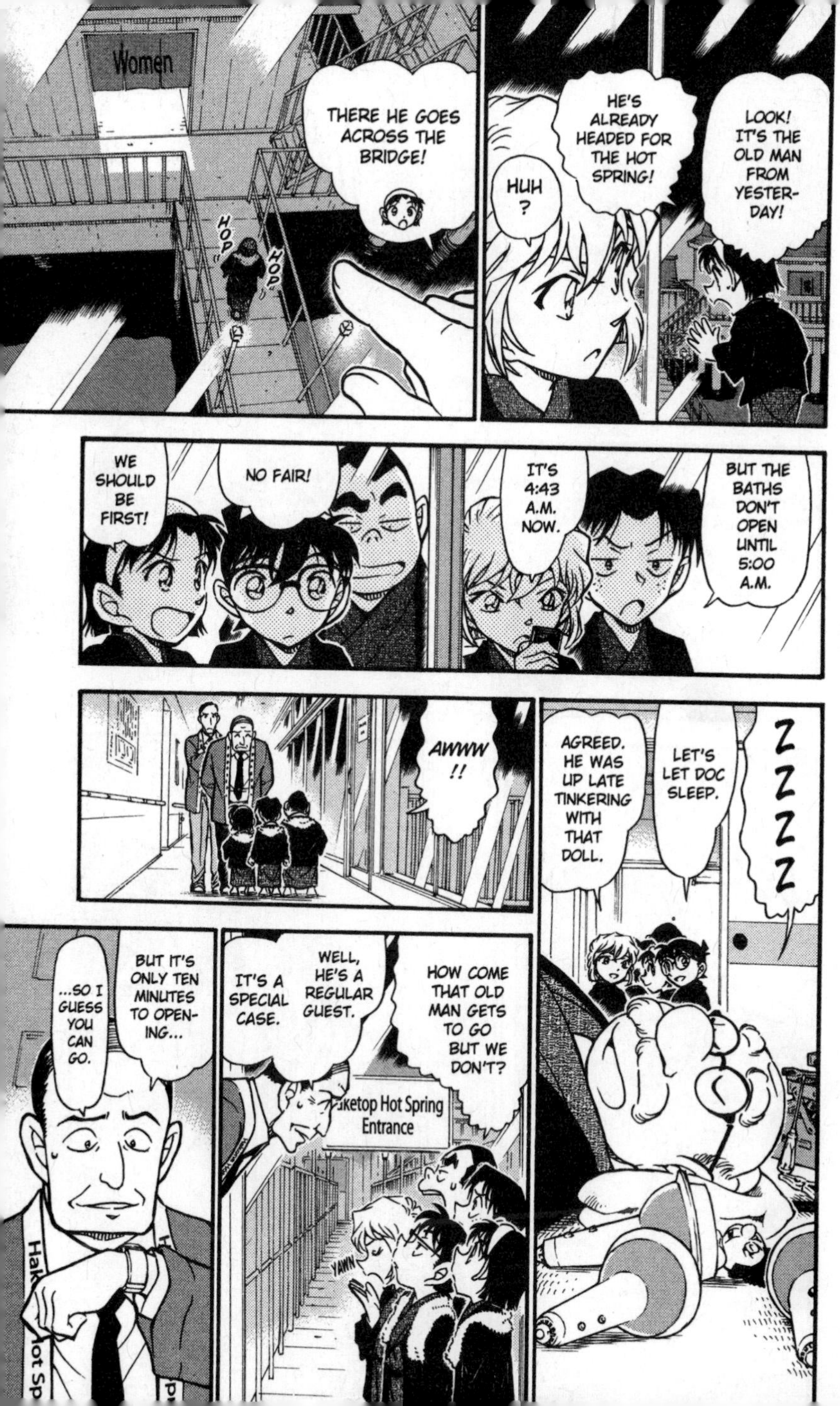
LOOK! IT'S THE OLD MAN FROM YESTER-DAY!
HE'S ALREADY HEADED FOR THE HOT SPRING!
HUH?
Women
THERE HE GOES ACROSS THE BRIDGE!
HOP
HOP
BUT THE BATHS DON'T OPEN UNTIL 5:00 A.M.
IT'S 4:43 A.M. NOW.
NO FAIR!
WE SHOULD BE FIRST!
ZZZZ
LET'S LET DOC SLEEP.
AGREED. HE WAS UP LATE TINKERING WITH THAT DOLL.
AWWW!!
HOW COME THAT OLD MAN GETS TO GO BUT WE DON'T?
WELL, HE'S A REGULAR GUEST.
IT'S A SPECIAL CASE.
YAWN
BUT IT'S ONLY TEN MINUTES TO OPEN-ING...
...SO I GUESS YOU CAN GO.

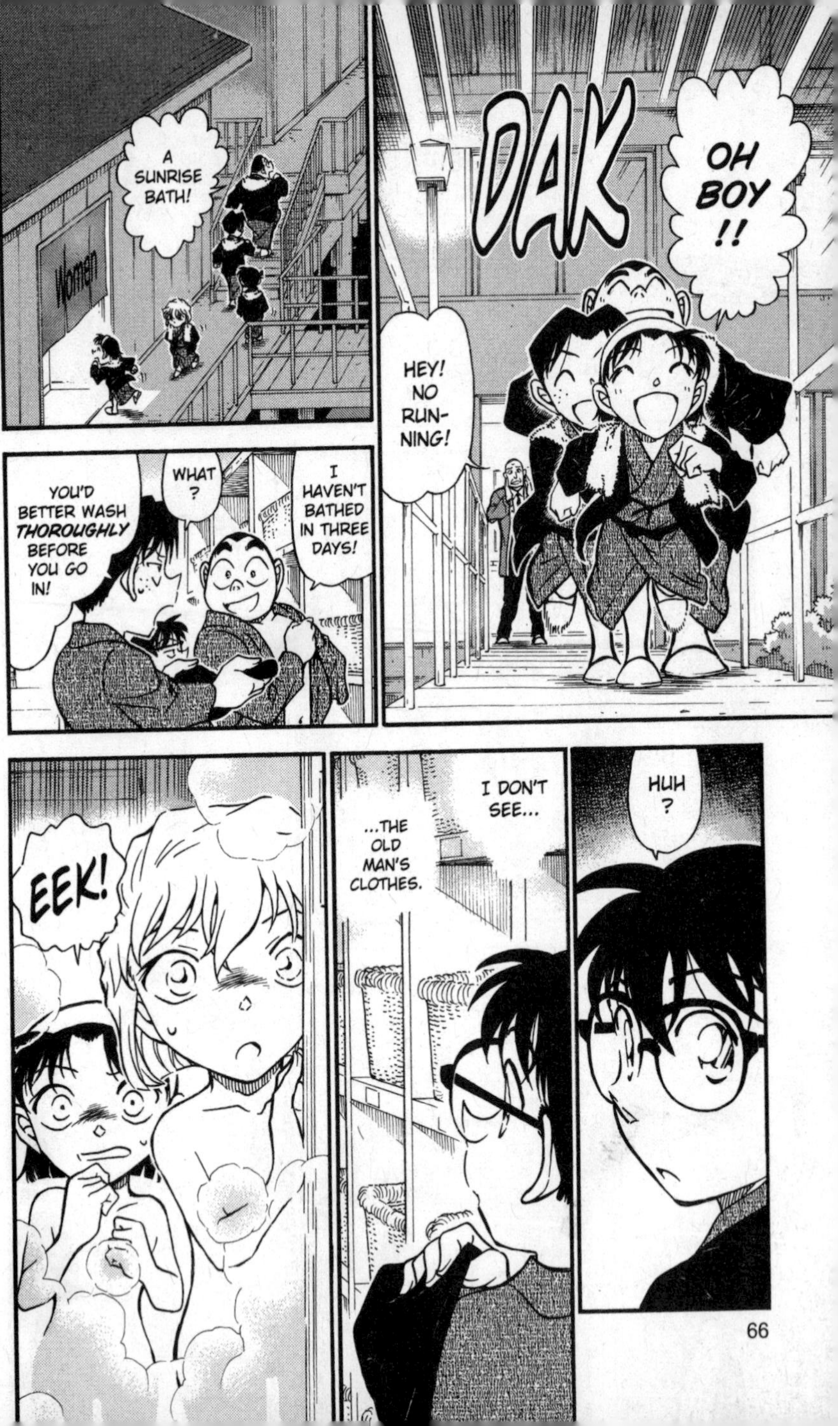
DAK
OH BOY!!
HEY! NO RUN-NING!
A SUNRISE BATH!
Women
I HAVEN'T BATHED IN THREE DAYS!
WHAT?
YOU'D BETTER WASH *THOROUGHLY* BEFORE YOU GO IN!
HUH?
I DON'T SEE...
...THE OLD MAN'S CLOTHES.
EEK!

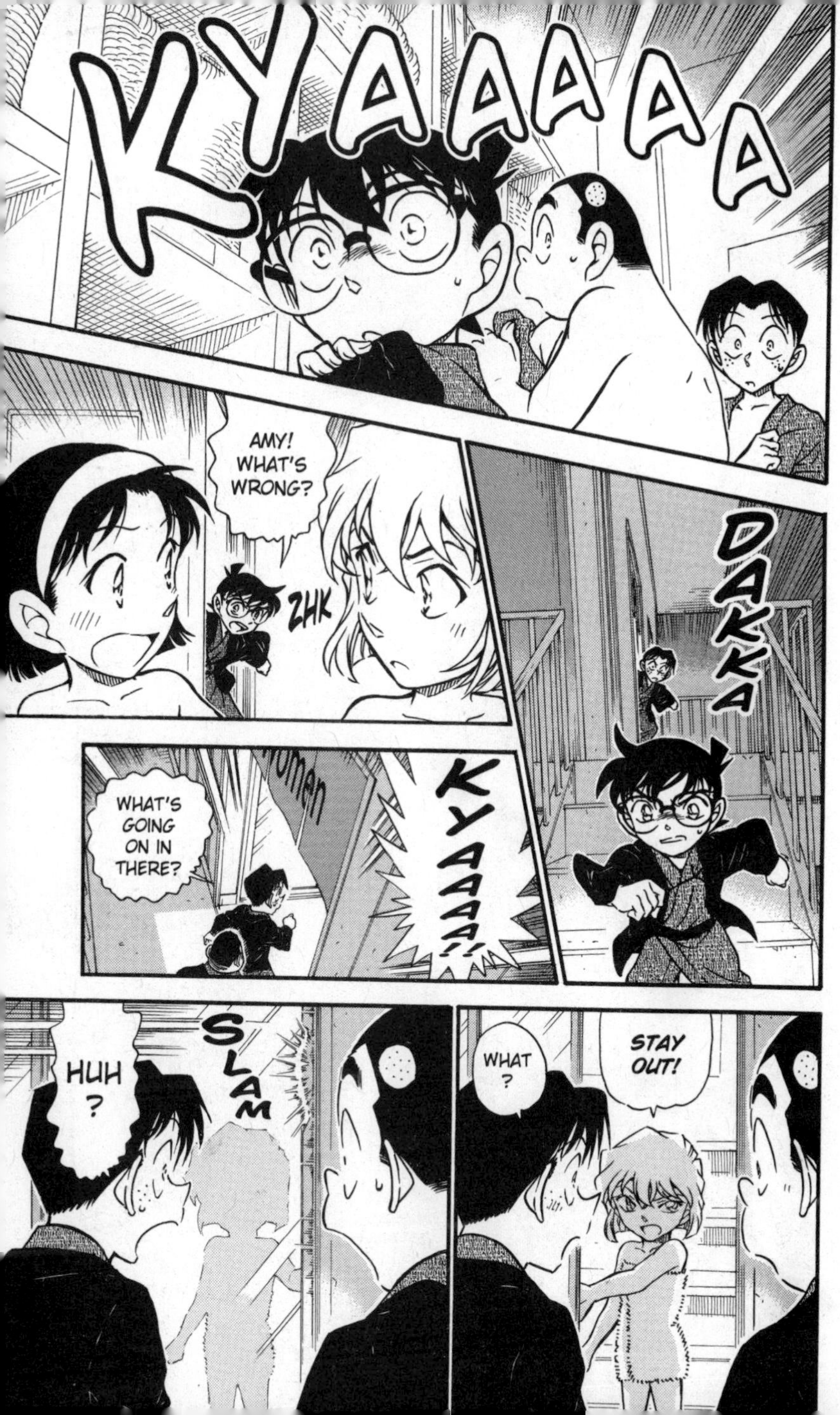
KYAAAAAA
DAKKA
AMY! WHAT'S WRONG?
ZHK
KYAAAAA!!
WHAT'S GOING ON IN THERE?
STAY OUT!
WHAT?
SLAM
HUH?

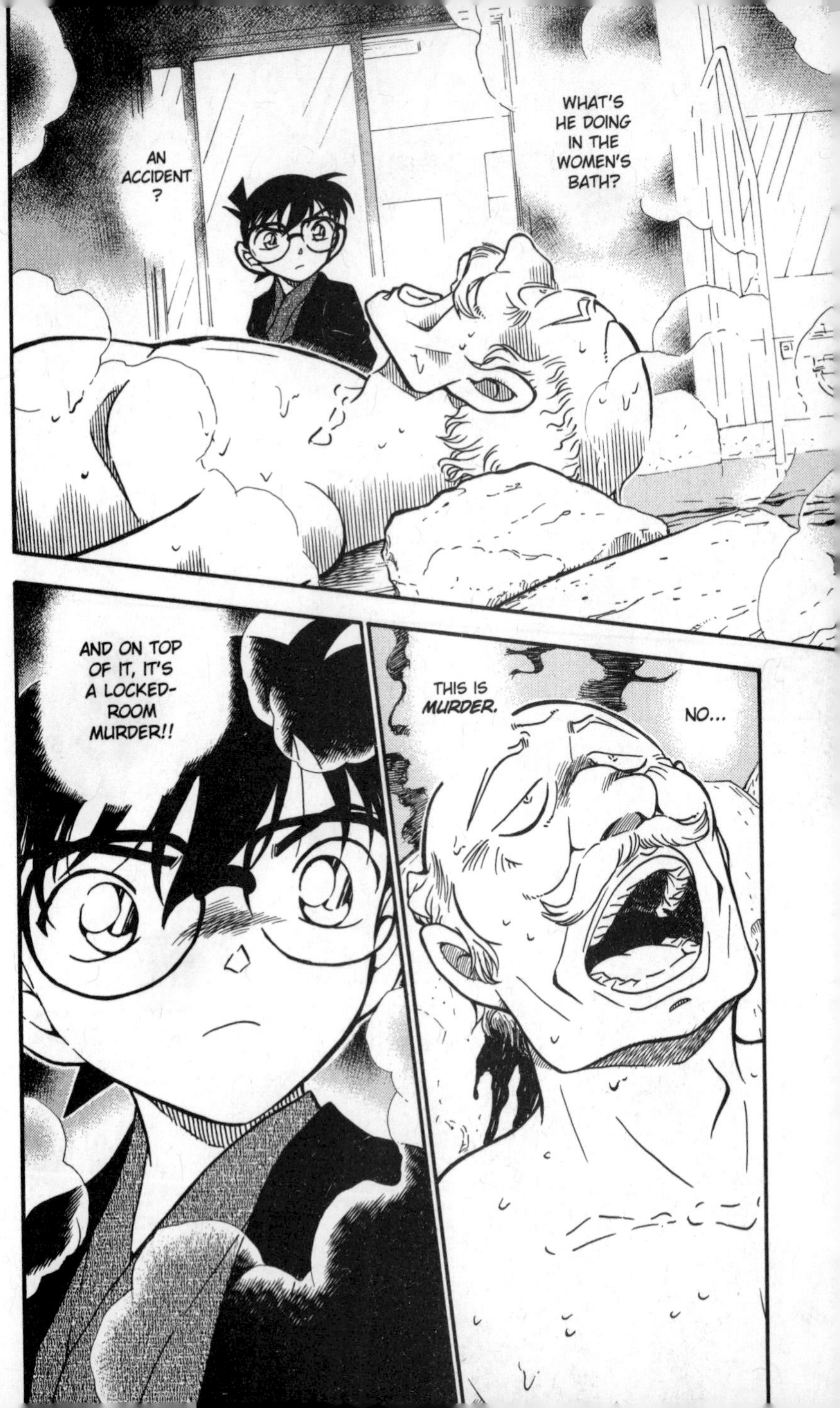
WHAT'S HE DOING IN THE WOMEN'S BATH?
AN ACCIDENT?
NO...
THIS IS *MURDER.*
AND ON TOP OF IT, IT'S A LOCKED-ROOM MURDER!!

FILE 5:
A LOCKED ROOM ON A LAKE

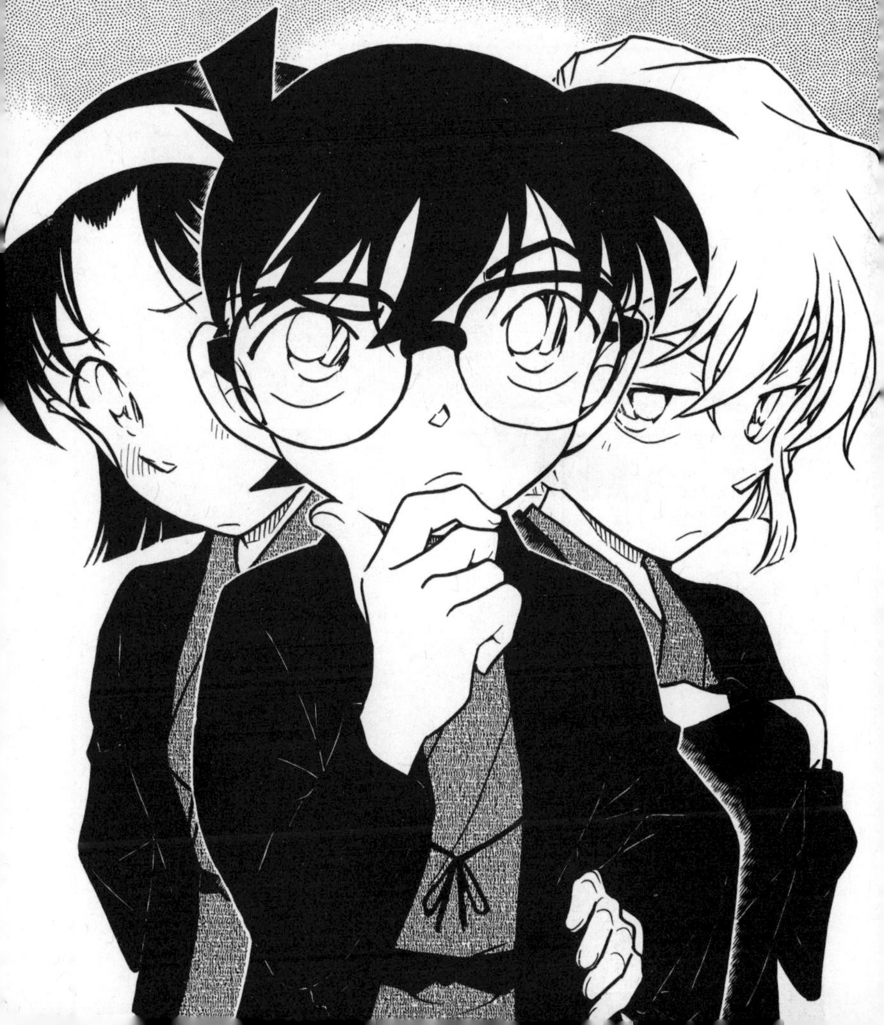

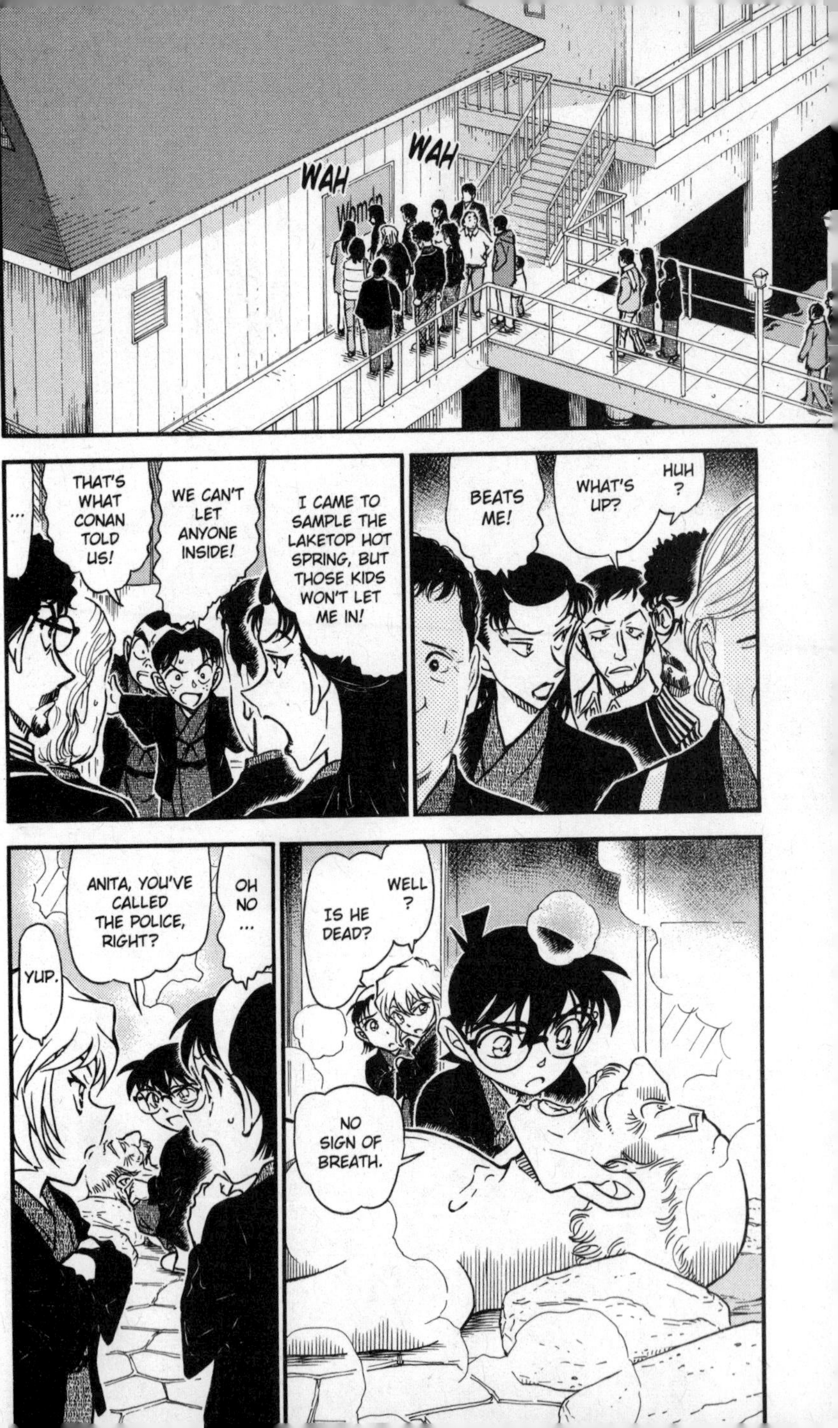
WAH
WAH
HUH?
WHAT'S UP?
BEATS ME!
I CAME TO SAMPLE THE LAKETOP HOT SPRING, BUT THOSE KIDS WON'T LET ME IN!
WE CAN'T LET ANYONE INSIDE!
THAT'S WHAT CONAN TOLD US!
...
WELL?
IS HE DEAD?
NO SIGN OF BREATH.
OH NO...
ANITA, YOU'VE CALLED THE POLICE, RIGHT?
YUP.

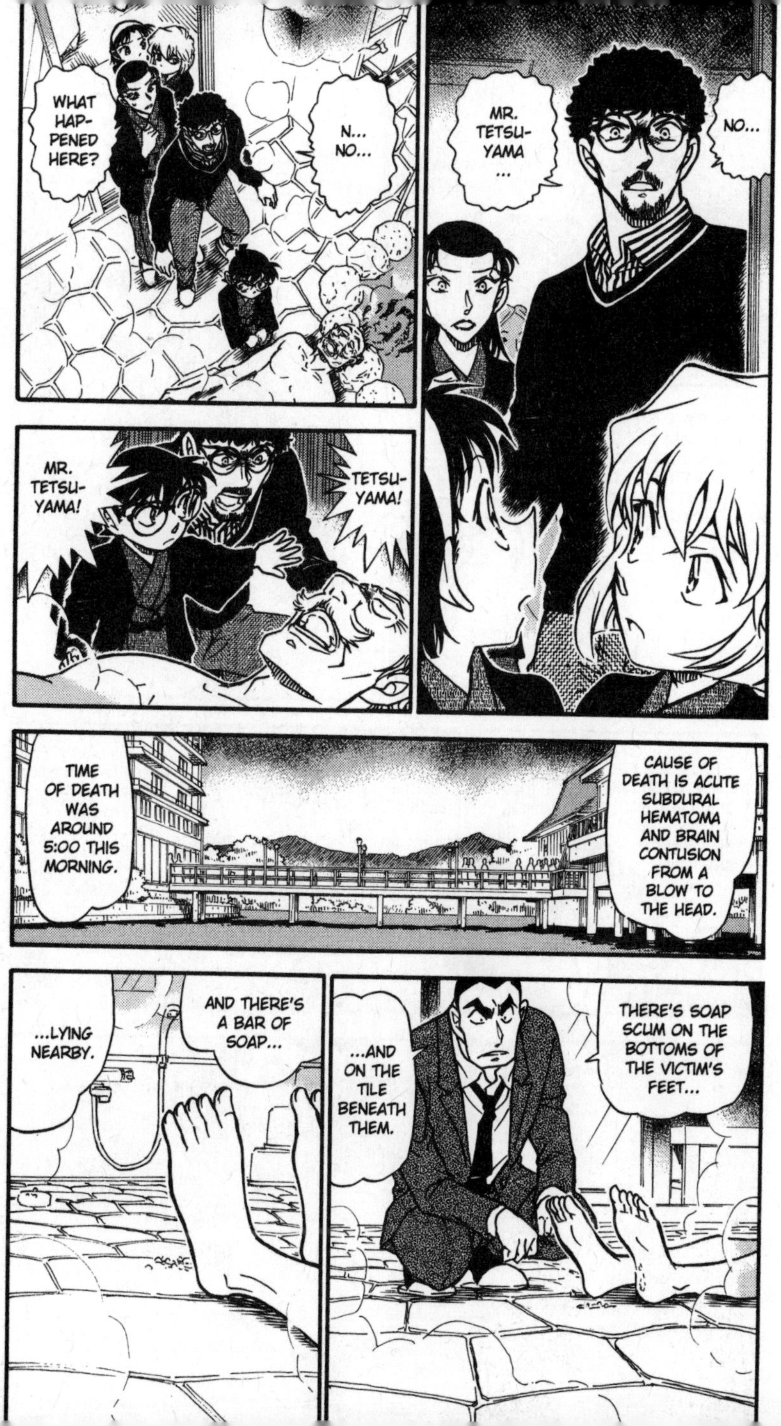
NO...
MR. TETSUYAMA...
N... NO...
WHAT HAPPENED HERE?
TETSUYAMA!
MR. TETSUYAMA!
CAUSE OF DEATH IS ACUTE SUBDURAL HEMATOMA AND BRAIN CONTUSION FROM A BLOW TO THE HEAD.
TIME OF DEATH WAS AROUND 5:00 THIS MORNING.
THERE'S SOAP SCUM ON THE BOTTOMS OF THE VICTIM'S FEET...
...AND ON THE TILE BENEATH THEM.
AND THERE'S A BAR OF SOAP...
...LYING NEARBY.

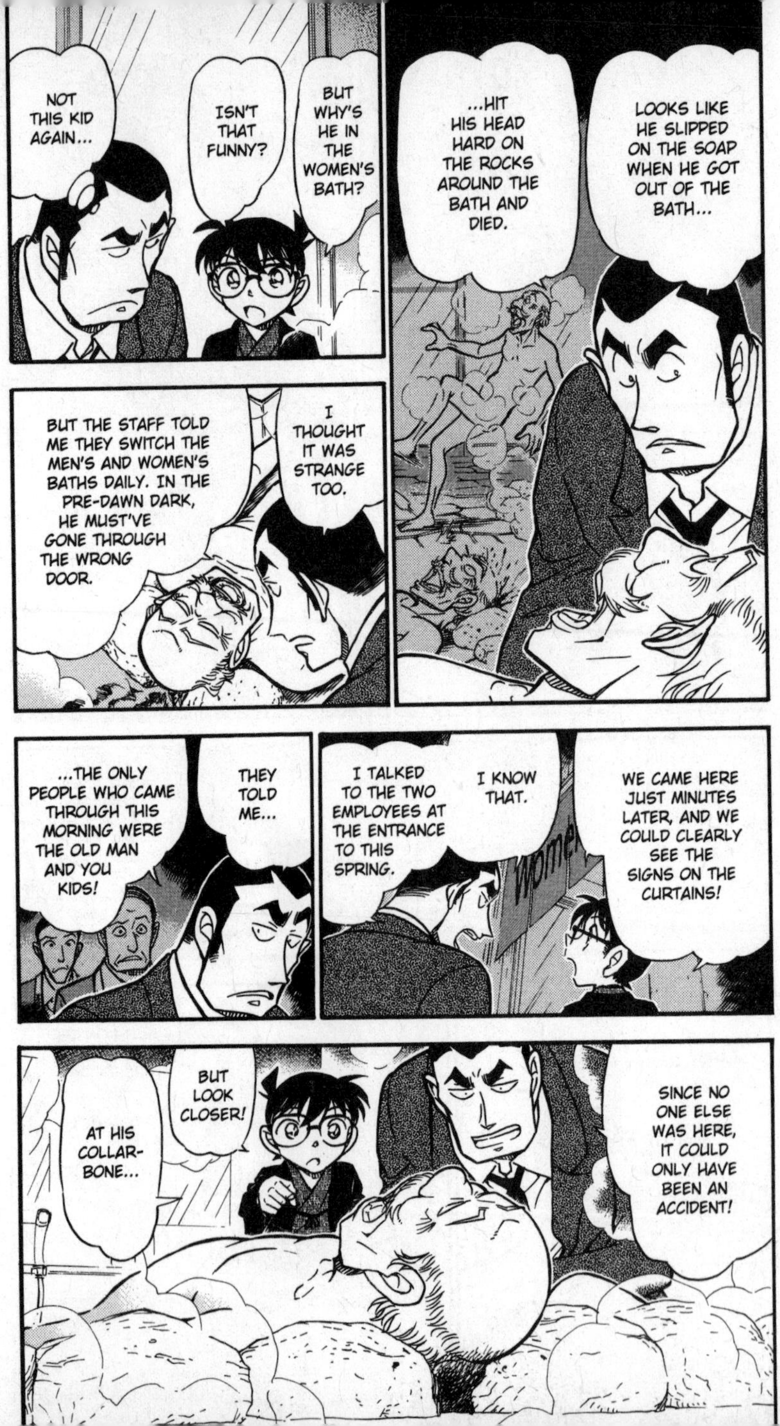
LOOKS LIKE HE SLIPPED ON THE SOAP WHEN HE GOT OUT OF THE BATH...
...HIT HIS HEAD HARD ON THE ROCKS AROUND THE BATH AND DIED.
BUT WHY'S HE IN THE WOMEN'S BATH?
ISN'T THAT FUNNY?
NOT THIS KID AGAIN...
I THOUGHT IT WAS STRANGE TOO.
BUT THE STAFF TOLD ME THEY SWITCH THE MEN'S AND WOMEN'S BATHS DAILY. IN THE PRE-DAWN DARK, HE MUST'VE GONE THROUGH THE WRONG DOOR.
WE CAME HERE JUST MINUTES LATER, AND WE COULD CLEARLY SEE THE SIGNS ON THE CURTAINS!
I KNOW THAT.
I TALKED TO THE TWO EMPLOYEES AT THE ENTRANCE TO THIS SPRING.
THEY TOLD ME...
...THE ONLY PEOPLE WHO CAME THROUGH THIS MORNING WERE THE OLD MAN AND YOU KIDS!
SINCE NO ONE ELSE WAS HERE, IT COULD ONLY HAVE BEEN AN ACCIDENT!
BUT LOOK CLOSER!
AT HIS COLLAR-BONE...

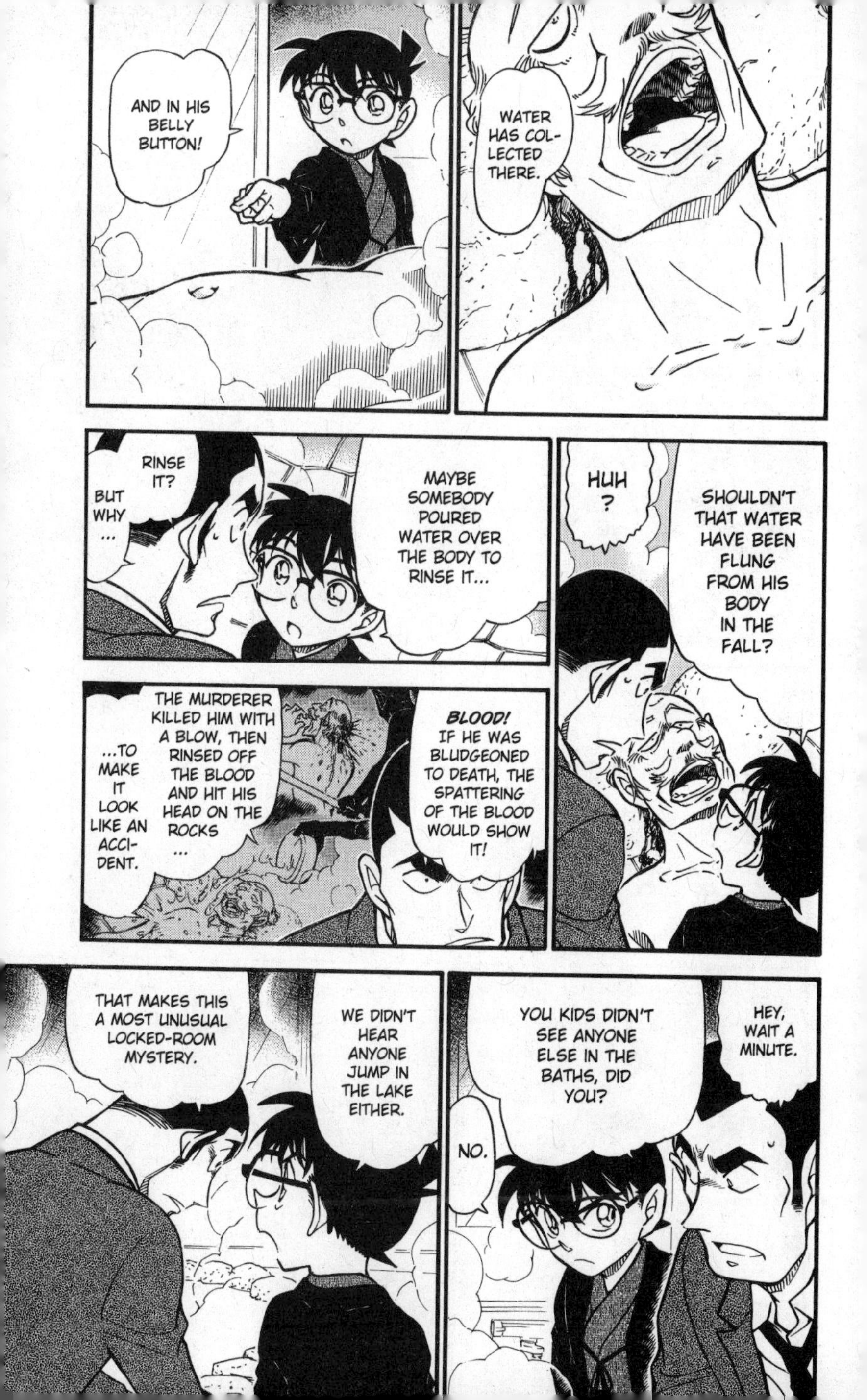
WATER HAS COLLECTED THERE.
AND IN HIS BELLY BUTTON!
SHOULDN'T THAT WATER HAVE BEEN FLUNG FROM HIS BODY IN THE FALL?
HUH?
MAYBE SOMEBODY POURED WATER OVER THE BODY TO RINSE IT...
RINSE IT?
BUT WHY...
BLOOD! IF HE WAS BLUDGEONED TO DEATH, THE SPATTERING OF THE BLOOD WOULD SHOW IT!
THE MURDERER KILLED HIM WITH A BLOW, THEN RINSED OFF THE BLOOD AND HIT HIS HEAD ON THE ROCKS...
...TO MAKE IT LOOK LIKE AN ACCIDENT.
HEY, WAIT A MINUTE.
YOU KIDS DIDN'T SEE ANYONE ELSE IN THE BATHS, DID YOU?
NO.
WE DIDN'T HEAR ANYONE JUMP IN THE LAKE EITHER.
THAT MAKES THIS A MOST UNUSUAL LOCKED-ROOM MYSTERY.

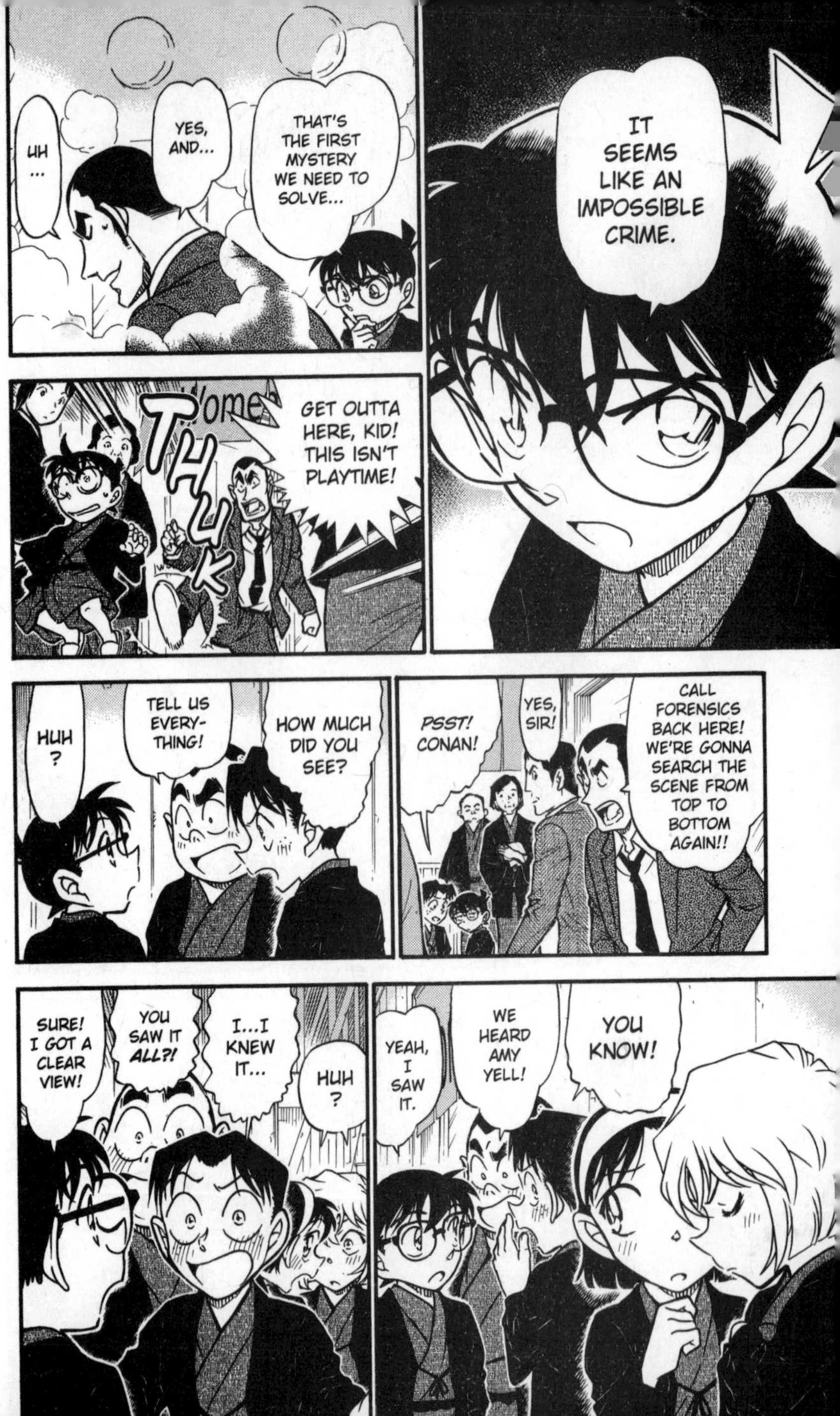
IT SEEMS LIKE AN IMPOSSIBLE CRIME.
THAT'S THE FIRST MYSTERY WE NEED TO SOLVE...
YES, AND...
UH ...
GET OUTTA HERE, KID! THIS ISN'T PLAYTIME!
THUK
CALL FORENSICS BACK HERE! WE'RE GONNA SEARCH THE SCENE FROM TOP TO BOTTOM AGAIN!!
YES, SIR!
PSST! CONAN!
HOW MUCH DID YOU SEE?
TELL US EVERY-THING!
HUH ?
YOU KNOW!
WE HEARD AMY YELL!
YEAH, I SAW IT.
HUH ?
I...I KNEW IT...
YOU SAW IT ALL?!
SURE! I GOT A CLEAR VIEW!

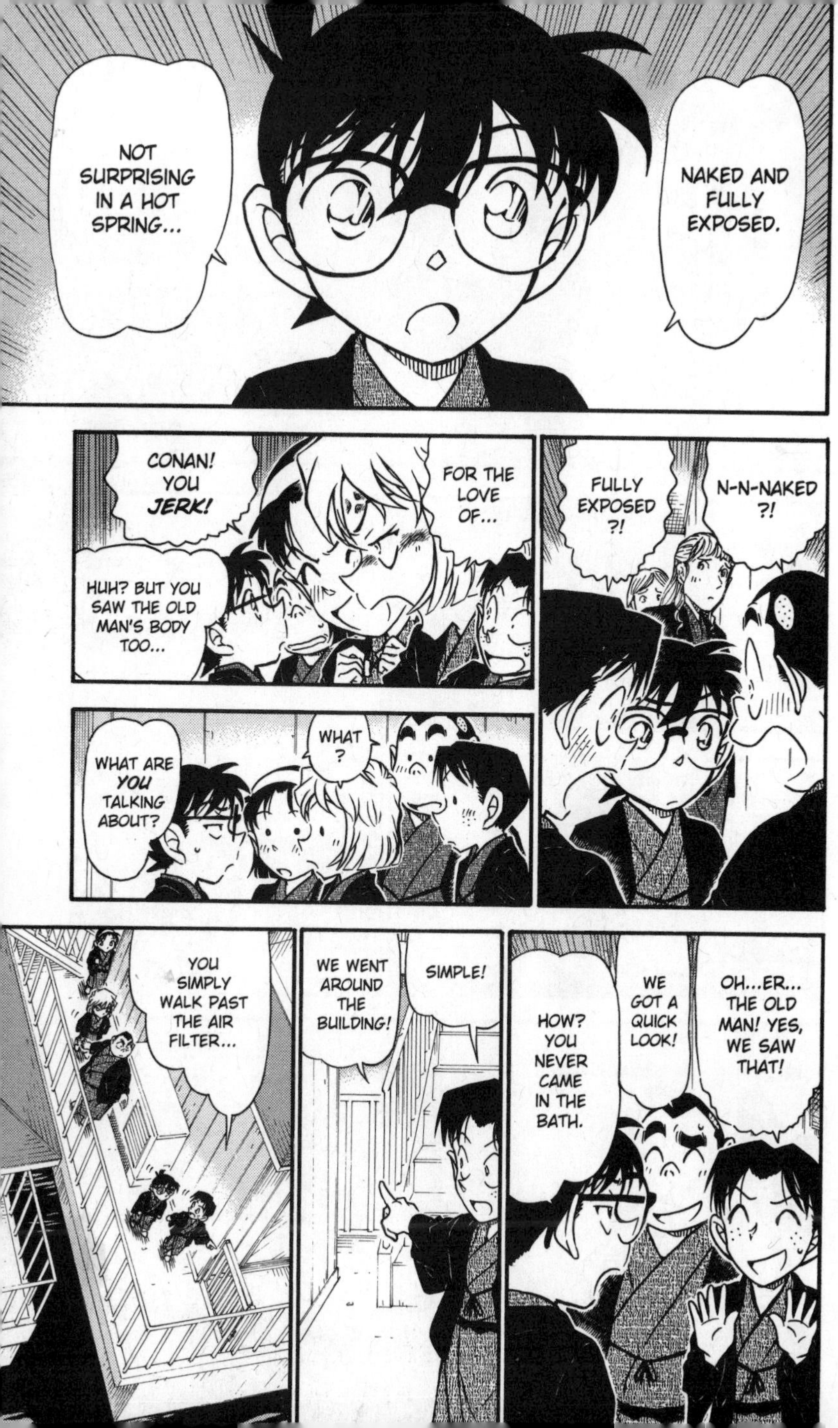
NAKED AND FULLY EXPOSED.
NOT SURPRISING IN A HOT SPRING...
N-N-NAKED ?!
FULLY EXPOSED ?!
FOR THE LOVE OF...
CONAN! YOU **JERK!**
HUH? BUT YOU SAW THE OLD MAN'S BODY TOO...
WHAT ?
WHAT ARE ***YOU*** TALKING ABOUT?
OH...ER... THE OLD MAN! YES, WE SAW THAT!
WE GOT A QUICK LOOK!
HOW? YOU NEVER CAME IN THE BATH.
SIMPLE!
WE WENT AROUND THE BUILDING!
YOU SIMPLY WALK PAST THE AIR FILTER...

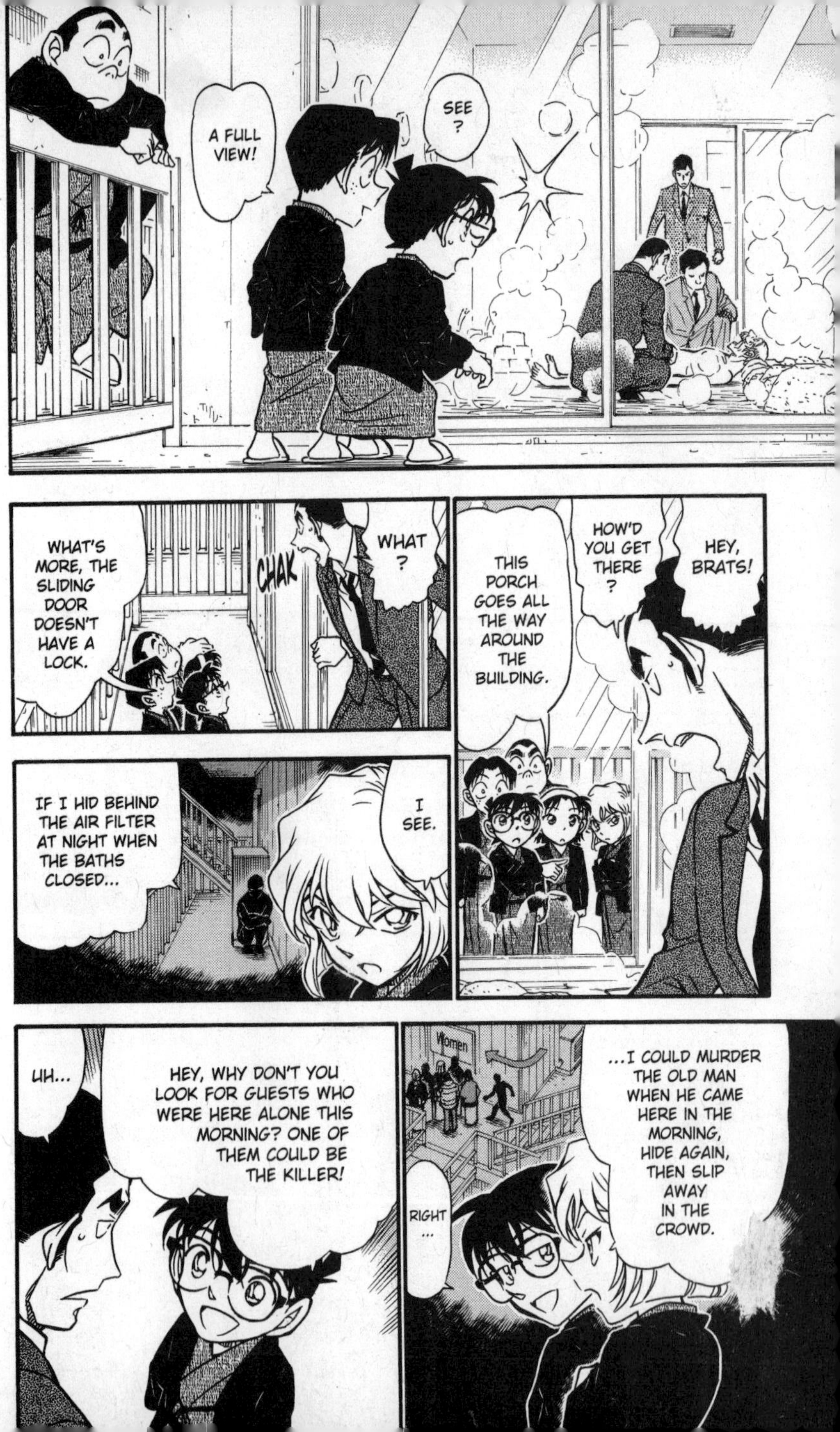
SEE?
A FULL VIEW!
HEY, BRATS!
HOW'D YOU GET THERE?
THIS PORCH GOES ALL THE WAY AROUND THE BUILDING.
WHAT?
CHAK
WHAT'S MORE, THE SLIDING DOOR DOESN'T HAVE A LOCK.
I SEE.
IF I HID BEHIND THE AIR FILTER AT NIGHT WHEN THE BATHS CLOSED...
Women
...I COULD MURDER THE OLD MAN WHEN HE CAME HERE IN THE MORNING, HIDE AGAIN, THEN SLIP AWAY IN THE CROWD.
RIGHT...
HEY, WHY DON'T YOU LOOK FOR GUESTS WHO WERE HERE ALONE THIS MORNING? ONE OF THEM COULD BE THE KILLER!
UH...

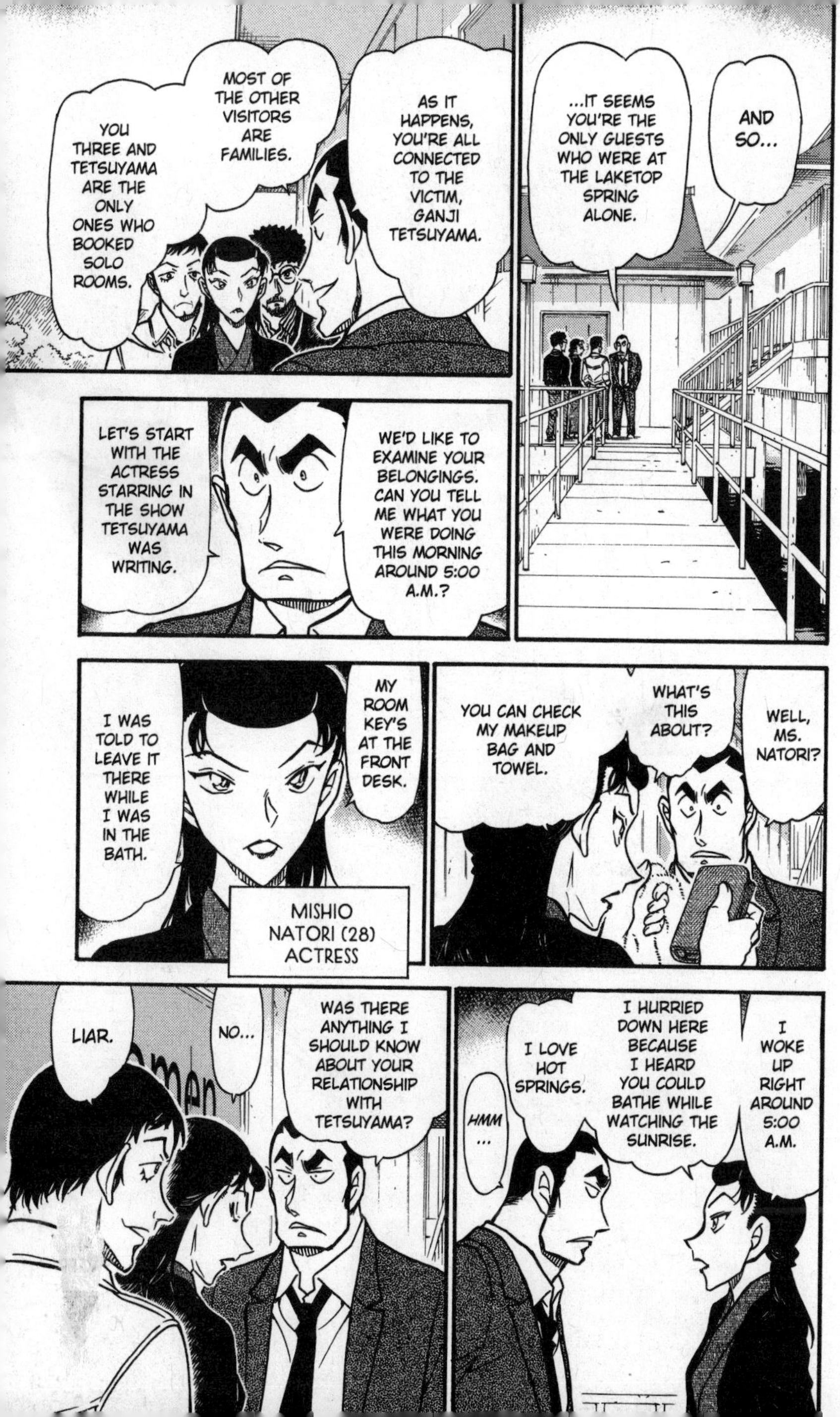
AND SO...
...IT SEEMS YOU'RE THE ONLY GUESTS WHO WERE AT THE LAKETOP SPRING ALONE.
AS IT HAPPENS, YOU'RE ALL CONNECTED TO THE VICTIM, GANJI TETSUYAMA.
MOST OF THE OTHER VISITORS ARE FAMILIES.
YOU THREE AND TETSUYAMA ARE THE ONLY ONES WHO BOOKED SOLO ROOMS.
WE'D LIKE TO EXAMINE YOUR BELONGINGS. CAN YOU TELL ME WHAT YOU WERE DOING THIS MORNING AROUND 5:00 A.M.?
LET'S START WITH THE ACTRESS STARRING IN THE SHOW TETSUYAMA WAS WRITING.
WELL, MS. NATORI?
WHAT'S THIS ABOUT?
YOU CAN CHECK MY MAKEUP BAG AND TOWEL.
MY ROOM KEY'S AT THE FRONT DESK.
I WAS TOLD TO LEAVE IT THERE WHILE I WAS IN THE BATH.
MISHIO NATORI (28) ACTRESS
I WOKE UP RIGHT AROUND 5:00 A.M.
I HURRIED DOWN HERE BECAUSE I HEARD YOU COULD BATHE WHILE WATCHING THE SUNRISE.
I LOVE HOT SPRINGS.
HMM...
WAS THERE ANYTHING I SHOULD KNOW ABOUT YOUR RELATIONSHIP WITH TETSUYAMA?
NO...
LIAR.

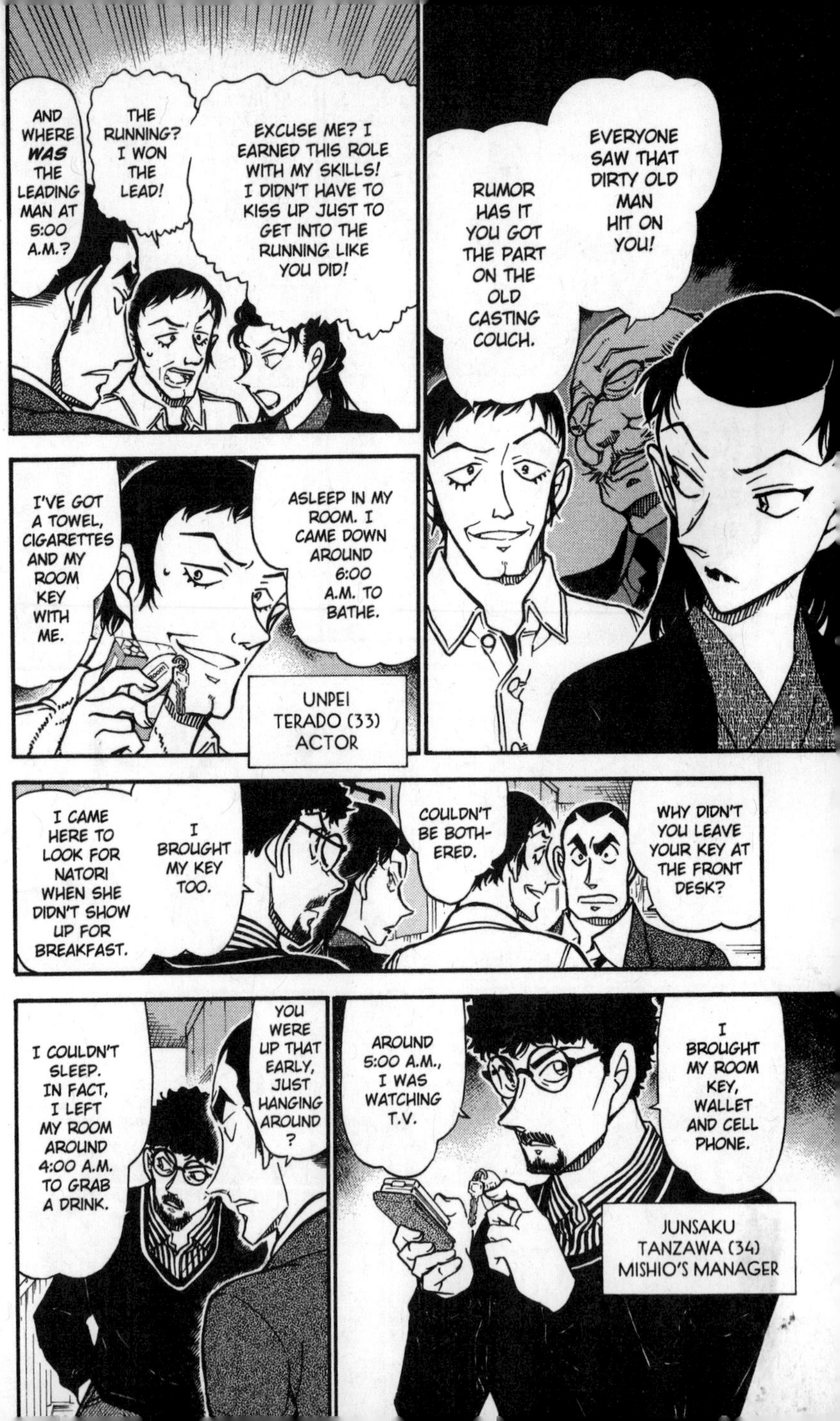
EVERYONE SAW THAT DIRTY OLD MAN HIT ON YOU!
RUMOR HAS IT YOU GOT THE PART ON THE OLD CASTING COUCH.
EXCUSE ME? I EARNED THIS ROLE WITH MY SKILLS! I DIDN'T HAVE TO KISS UP JUST TO GET INTO THE RUNNING LIKE YOU DID!
THE RUNNING? I WON THE LEAD!
AND WHERE *WAS* THE LEADING MAN AT 5:00 A.M.?
ASLEEP IN MY ROOM. I CAME DOWN AROUND 6:00 A.M. TO BATHE.
UNPEI TERADO (33) ACTOR
I'VE GOT A TOWEL, CIGARETTES AND MY ROOM KEY WITH ME.
WHY DIDN'T YOU LEAVE YOUR KEY AT THE FRONT DESK?
COULDN'T BE BOTHERED.
I BROUGHT MY KEY TOO.
I CAME HERE TO LOOK FOR NATORI WHEN SHE DIDN'T SHOW UP FOR BREAKFAST.
I BROUGHT MY ROOM KEY, WALLET AND CELL PHONE.
JUNSAKU TANZAWA (34) MISHIO'S MANAGER
AROUND 5:00 A.M., I WAS WATCHING T.V.
YOU WERE UP THAT EARLY, JUST HANGING AROUND?
I COULDN'T SLEEP. IN FACT, I LEFT MY ROOM AROUND 4:00 A.M. TO GRAB A DRINK.

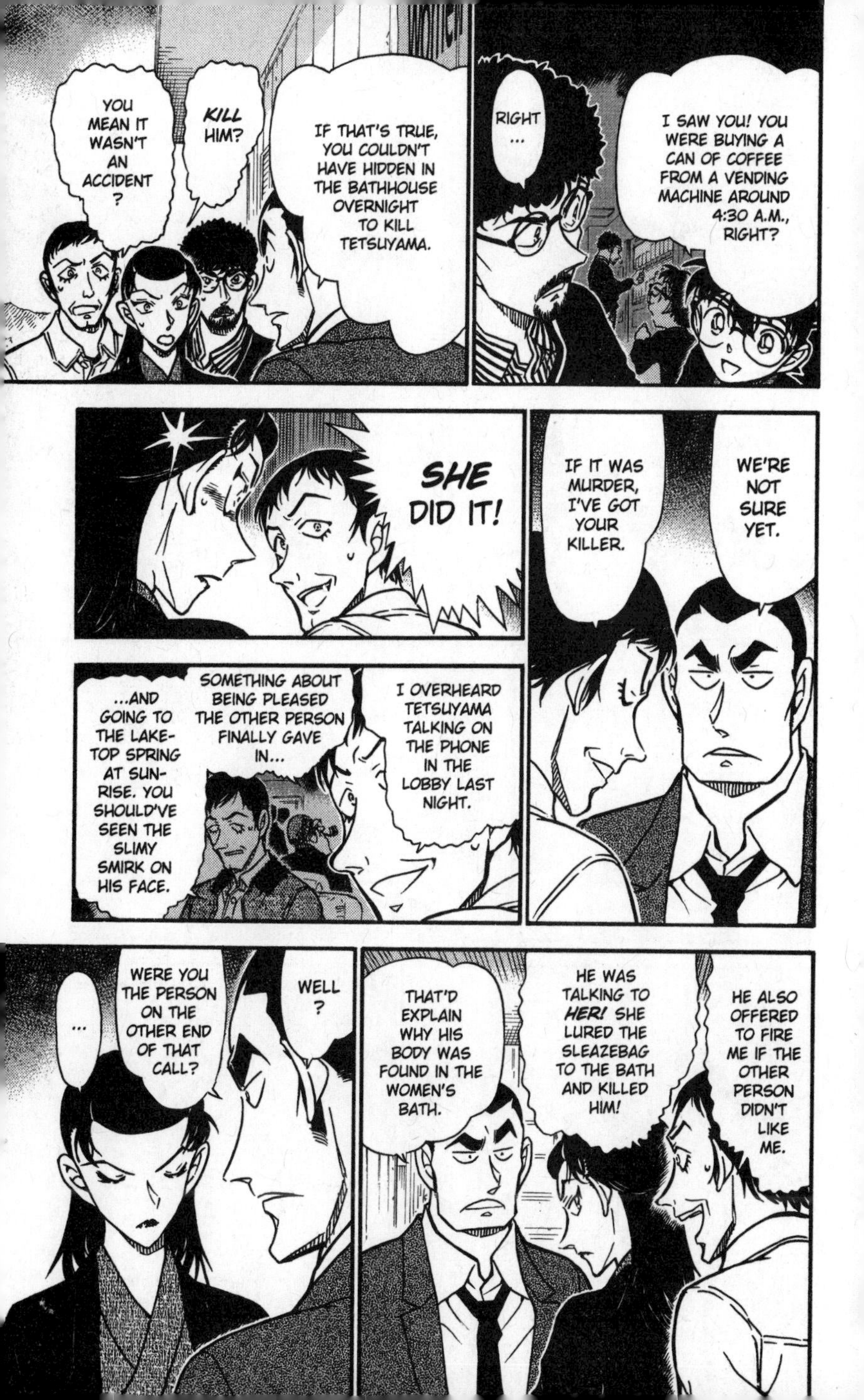
I SAW YOU! YOU WERE BUYING A CAN OF COFFEE FROM A VENDING MACHINE AROUND 4:30 A.M., RIGHT?
RIGHT...
IF THAT'S TRUE, YOU COULDN'T HAVE HIDDEN IN THE BATHHOUSE OVERNIGHT TO KILL TETSUYAMA.
KILL HIM?
YOU MEAN IT WASN'T AN ACCIDENT?
WE'RE NOT SURE YET.
IF IT WAS MURDER, I'VE GOT YOUR KILLER.
SHE DID IT!
I OVERHEARD TETSUYAMA TALKING ON THE PHONE IN THE LOBBY LAST NIGHT.
SOMETHING ABOUT BEING PLEASED THE OTHER PERSON FINALLY GAVE IN...
...AND GOING TO THE LAKE-TOP SPRING AT SUN-RISE. YOU SHOULD'VE SEEN THE SLIMY SMIRK ON HIS FACE.
HE ALSO OFFERED TO FIRE ME IF THE OTHER PERSON DIDN'T LIKE ME.
HE WAS TALKING TO *HER!* SHE LURED THE SLEAZEBAG TO THE BATH AND KILLED HIM!
THAT'D EXPLAIN WHY HIS BODY WAS FOUND IN THE WOMEN'S BATH.
WELL?
WERE YOU THE PERSON ON THE OTHER END OF THAT CALL?
...

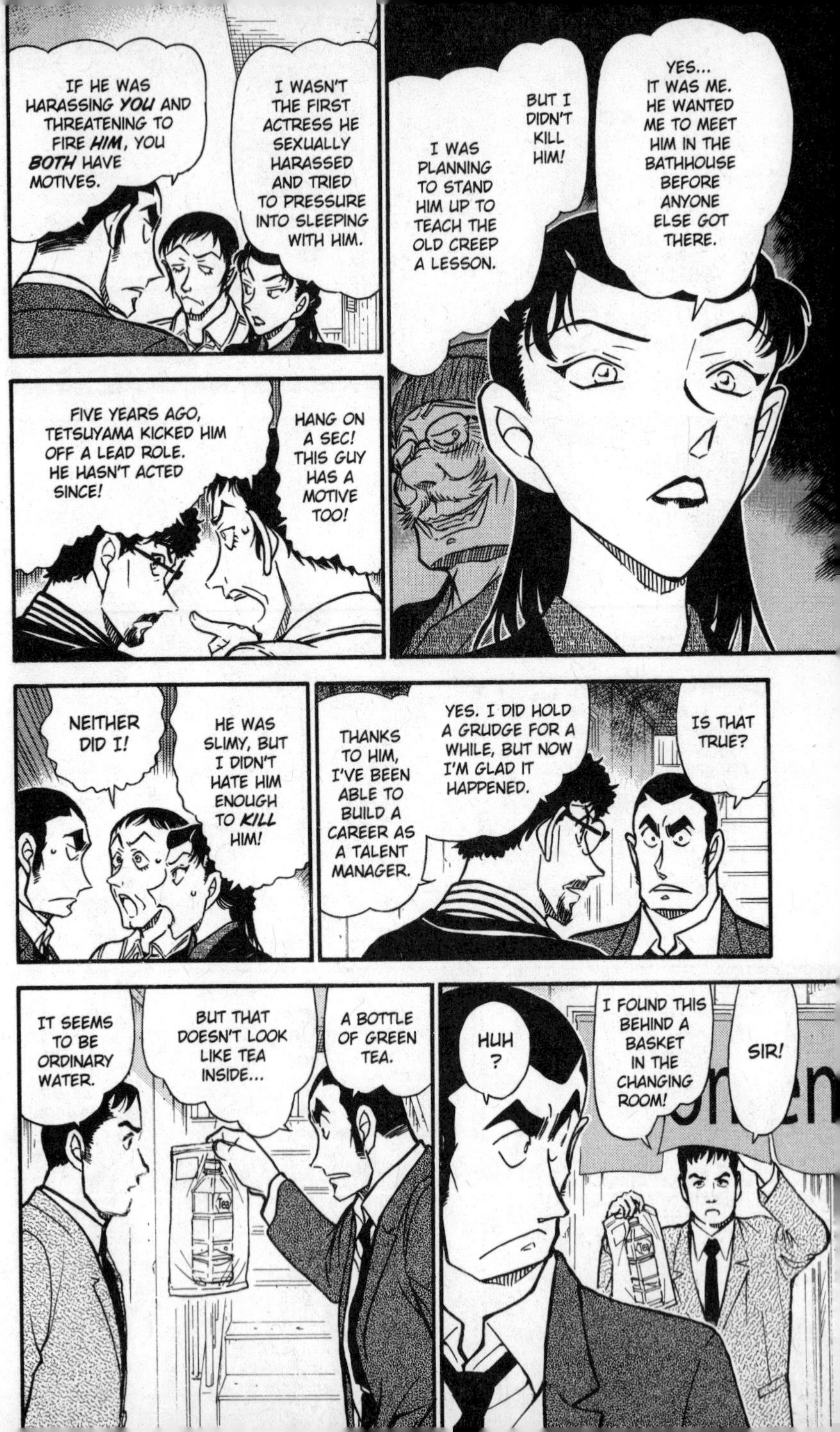
YES... IT WAS ME. HE WANTED ME TO MEET HIM IN THE BATHHOUSE BEFORE ANYONE ELSE GOT THERE.
BUT I DIDN'T KILL HIM!
I WAS PLANNING TO STAND HIM UP TO TEACH THE OLD CREEP A LESSON.
I WASN'T THE FIRST ACTRESS HE SEXUALLY HARASSED AND TRIED TO PRESSURE INTO SLEEPING WITH HIM.
IF HE WAS HARASSING YOU AND THREATENING TO FIRE HIM, YOU BOTH HAVE MOTIVES.
HANG ON A SEC! THIS GUY HAS A MOTIVE TOO!
FIVE YEARS AGO, TETSUYAMA KICKED HIM OFF A LEAD ROLE. HE HASN'T ACTED SINCE!
IS THAT TRUE?
YES. I DID HOLD A GRUDGE FOR A WHILE, BUT NOW I'M GLAD IT HAPPENED.
THANKS TO HIM, I'VE BEEN ABLE TO BUILD A CAREER AS A TALENT MANAGER.
HE WAS SLIMY, BUT I DIDN'T HATE HIM ENOUGH TO KILL HIM!
NEITHER DID I!
SIR!
I FOUND THIS BEHIND A BASKET IN THE CHANGING ROOM!
HUH?
A BOTTLE OF GREEN TEA.
BUT THAT DOESN'T LOOK LIKE TEA INSIDE...
IT SEEMS TO BE ORDINARY WATER.

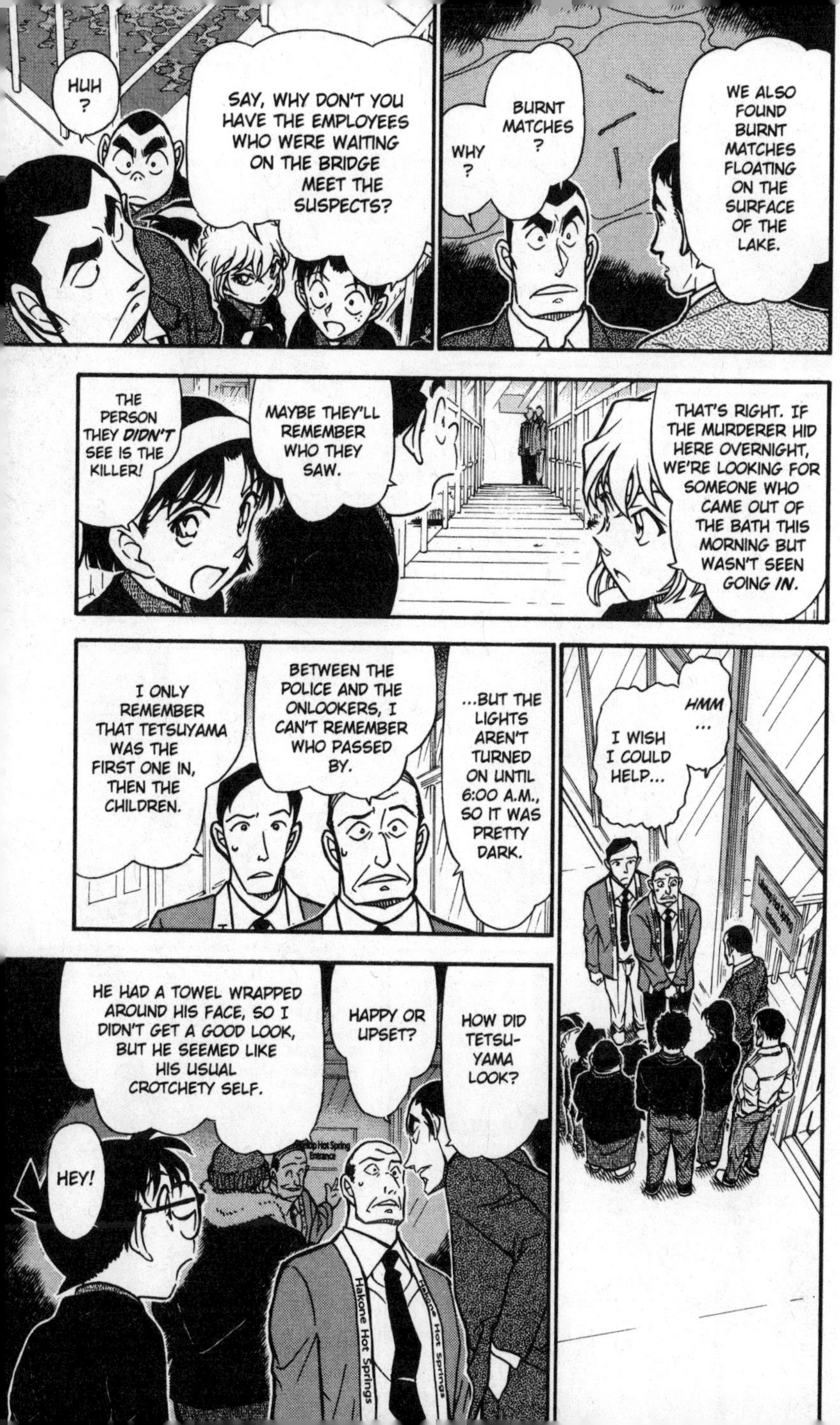
WE ALSO FOUND BURNT MATCHES FLOATING ON THE SURFACE OF THE LAKE.
BURNT MATCHES?
WHY?
SAY, WHY DON'T YOU HAVE THE EMPLOYEES WHO WERE WAITING ON THE BRIDGE MEET THE SUSPECTS?
HUH?
THAT'S RIGHT. IF THE MURDERER HID HERE OVERNIGHT, WE'RE LOOKING FOR SOMEONE WHO CAME OUT OF THE BATH THIS MORNING BUT WASN'T SEEN GOING *IN*.
MAYBE THEY'LL REMEMBER WHO THEY SAW.
THE PERSON THEY *DIDN'T* SEE IS THE KILLER!
HMM...
I WISH I COULD HELP...
...BUT THE LIGHTS AREN'T TURNED ON UNTIL 6:00 A.M., SO IT WAS PRETTY DARK.
BETWEEN THE POLICE AND THE ONLOOKERS, I CAN'T REMEMBER WHO PASSED BY.
I ONLY REMEMBER THAT TETSUYAMA WAS THE FIRST ONE IN, THEN THE CHILDREN.
HOW DID TETSUYAMA LOOK?
HAPPY OR UPSET?
HE HAD A TOWEL WRAPPED AROUND HIS FACE, SO I DIDN'T GET A GOOD LOOK, BUT HE SEEMED LIKE HIS USUAL CROTCHETY SELF.
Hakone Hot Spring Entrance
HEY!
Hakone Hot Springs
Hakone Hot Springs

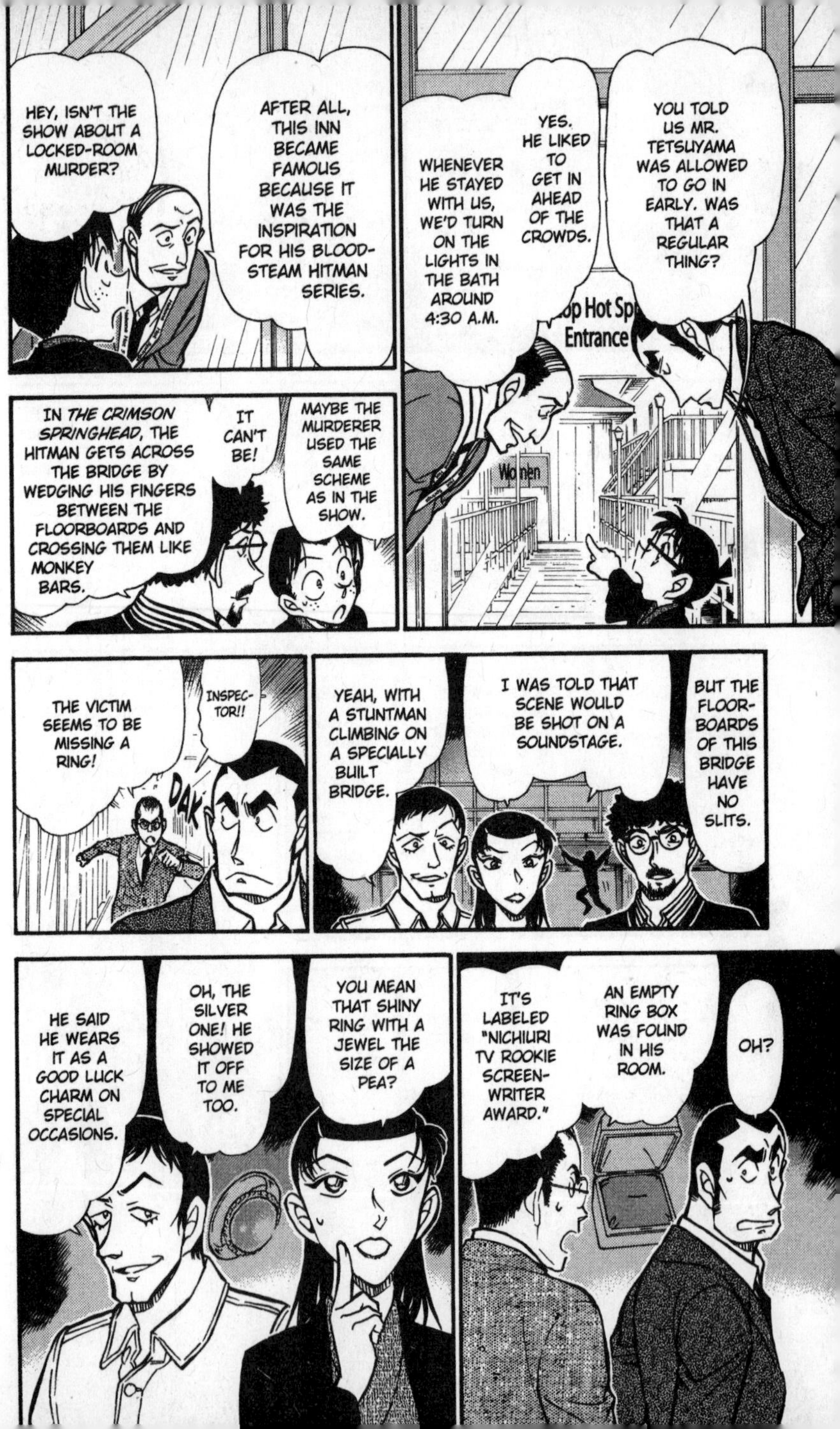
YOU TOLD US MR. TETSUYAMA WAS ALLOWED TO GO IN EARLY. WAS THAT A REGULAR THING?
YES. HE LIKED TO GET IN AHEAD OF THE CROWDS.
WHENEVER HE STAYED WITH US, WE'D TURN ON THE LIGHTS IN THE BATH AROUND 4:30 A.M.
Entrance
Women
AFTER ALL, THIS INN BECAME FAMOUS BECAUSE IT WAS THE INSPIRATION FOR HIS BLOOD-STEAM HITMAN SERIES.
HEY, ISN'T THE SHOW ABOUT A LOCKED-ROOM MURDER?
MAYBE THE MURDERER USED THE SAME SCHEME AS IN THE SHOW.
IT CAN'T BE!
IN *THE CRIMSON SPRINGHEAD*, THE HITMAN GETS ACROSS THE BRIDGE BY WEDGING HIS FINGERS BETWEEN THE FLOORBOARDS AND CROSSING THEM LIKE MONKEY BARS.
BUT THE FLOORBOARDS OF THIS BRIDGE HAVE NO SLITS.
I WAS TOLD THAT SCENE WOULD BE SHOT ON A SOUNDSTAGE.
YEAH, WITH A STUNTMAN CLIMBING ON A SPECIALLY BUILT BRIDGE.
INSPECTOR!!
DAK
THE VICTIM SEEMS TO BE MISSING A RING!
OH?
AN EMPTY RING BOX WAS FOUND IN HIS ROOM.
IT'S LABELED "NICHIURI TV ROOKIE SCREENWRITER AWARD."
YOU MEAN THAT SHINY RING WITH A JEWEL THE SIZE OF A PEA?
OH, THE SILVER ONE! HE SHOWED IT OFF TO ME TOO.
HE SAID HE WEARS IT AS A GOOD LUCK CHARM ON SPECIAL OCCASIONS.

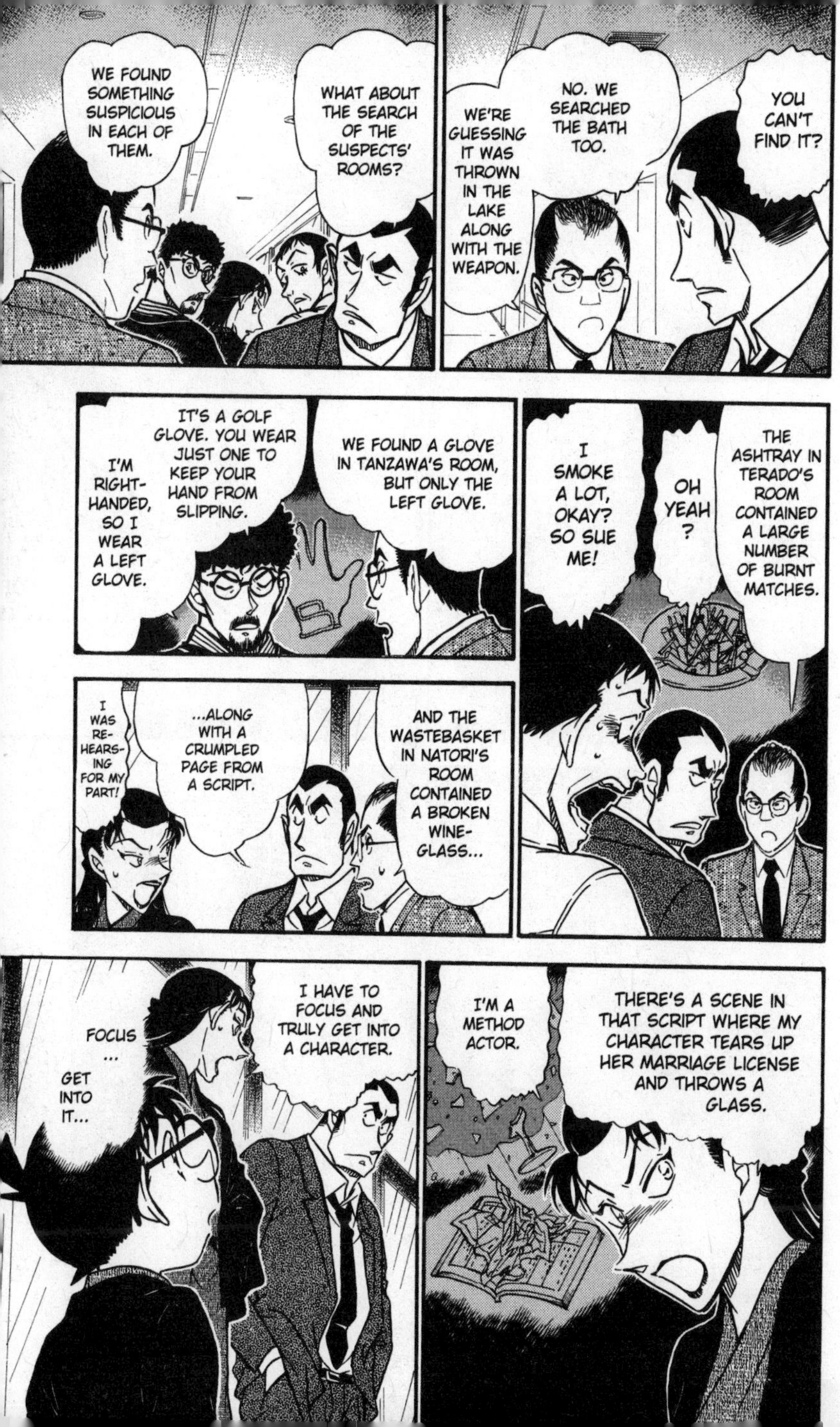
YOU CAN'T FIND IT?
NO. WE SEARCHED THE BATH TOO.
WE'RE GUESSING IT WAS THROWN IN THE LAKE ALONG WITH THE WEAPON.
WHAT ABOUT THE SEARCH OF THE SUSPECTS' ROOMS?
WE FOUND SOMETHING SUSPICIOUS IN EACH OF THEM.
THE ASHTRAY IN TERADO'S ROOM CONTAINED A LARGE NUMBER OF BURNT MATCHES.
OH YEAH?
I SMOKE A LOT, OKAY? SO SUE ME!
WE FOUND A GLOVE IN TANZAWA'S ROOM, BUT ONLY THE LEFT GLOVE.
IT'S A GOLF GLOVE. YOU WEAR JUST ONE TO KEEP YOUR HAND FROM SLIPPING.
I'M RIGHT-HANDED, SO I WEAR A LEFT GLOVE.
AND THE WASTEBASKET IN NATORI'S ROOM CONTAINED A BROKEN WINE-GLASS...
...ALONG WITH A CRUMPLED PAGE FROM A SCRIPT.
I WAS RE-HEARSING FOR MY PART!
THERE'S A SCENE IN THAT SCRIPT WHERE MY CHARACTER TEARS UP HER MARRIAGE LICENSE AND THROWS A GLASS.
I'M A METHOD ACTOR.
I HAVE TO FOCUS AND TRULY GET INTO A CHARACTER.
FOCUS... GET INTO IT...

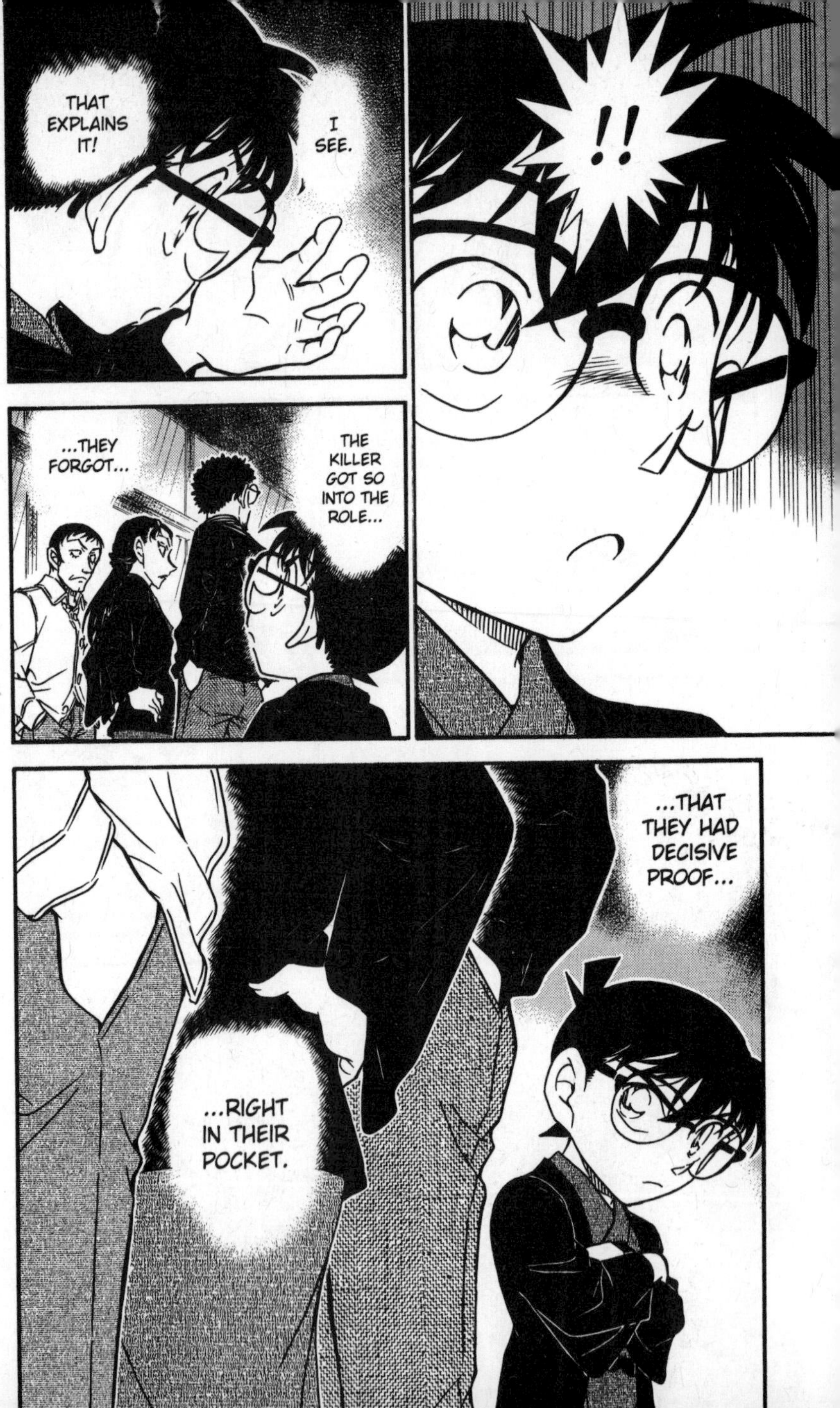
!!
I SEE.
THAT EXPLAINS IT!
THE KILLER GOT SO INTO THE ROLE...
...THEY FORGOT...
...THAT THEY HAD DECISIVE PROOF...
...RIGHT IN THEIR POCKET.

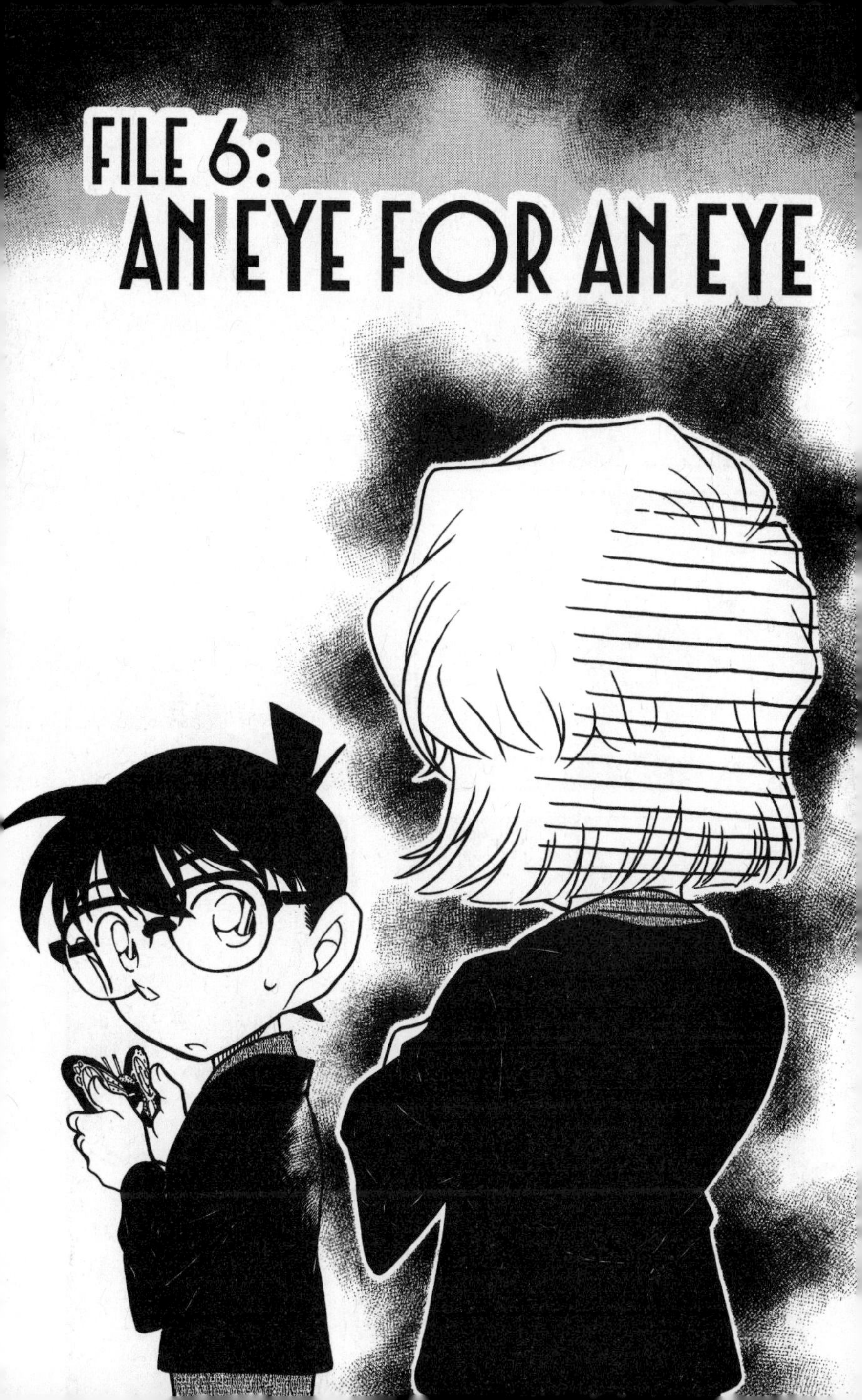
FILE 6:
AN EYE FOR AN EYE

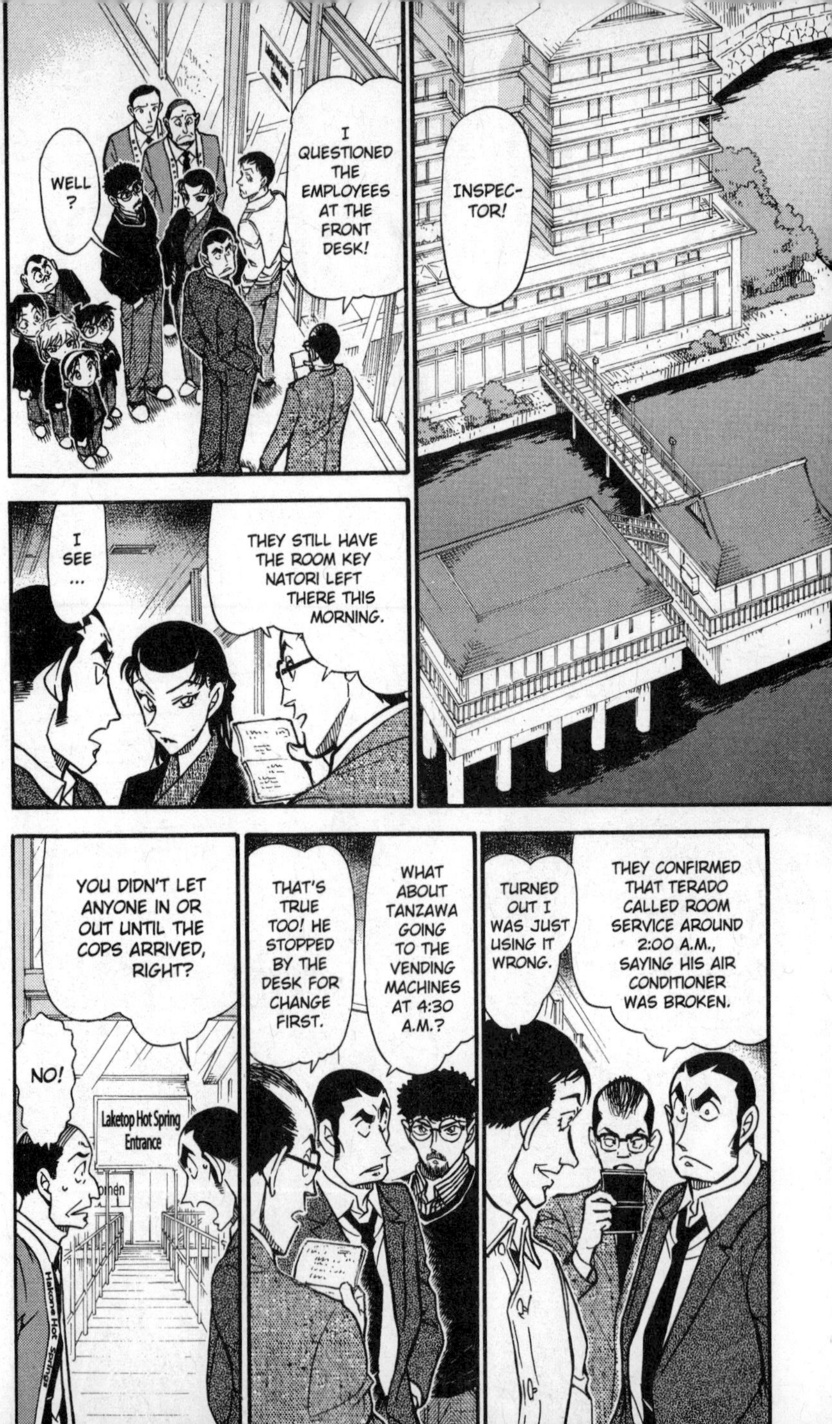
INSPECTOR!
I QUESTIONED THE EMPLOYEES AT THE FRONT DESK!
WELL?
THEY STILL HAVE THE ROOM KEY NATORI LEFT THERE THIS MORNING.
I SEE...
THEY CONFIRMED THAT TERADO CALLED ROOM SERVICE AROUND 2:00 A.M., SAYING HIS AIR CONDITIONER WAS BROKEN.
TURNED OUT I WAS JUST USING IT WRONG.
WHAT ABOUT TANZAWA GOING TO THE VENDING MACHINES AT 4:30 A.M.?
THAT'S TRUE TOO! HE STOPPED BY THE DESK FOR CHANGE FIRST.
YOU DIDN'T LET ANYONE IN OR OUT UNTIL THE COPS ARRIVED, RIGHT?
NO!
Laketop Hot Spring Entrance
Hakone Hot Springs

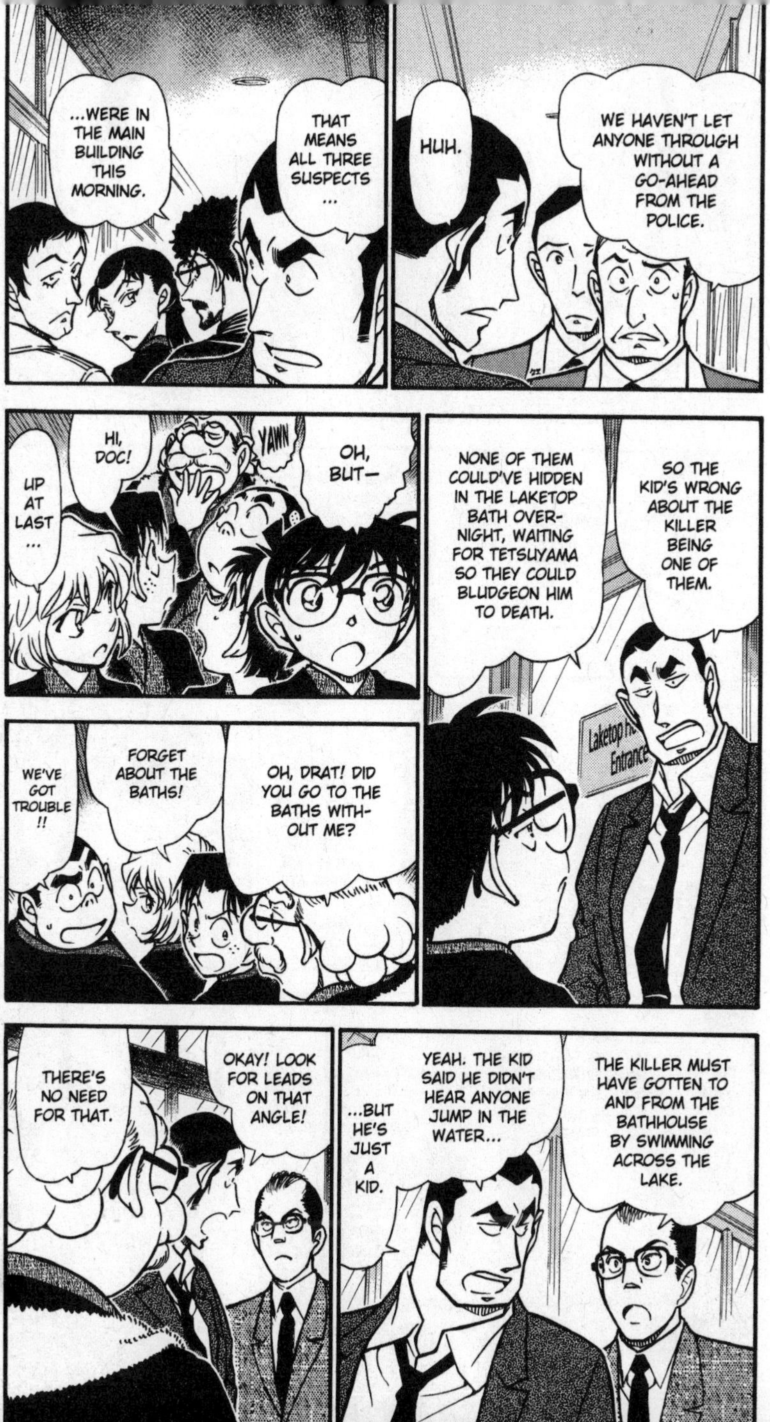
WE HAVEN'T LET ANYONE THROUGH WITHOUT A GO-AHEAD FROM THE POLICE.
HUH.
THAT MEANS ALL THREE SUSPECTS ...
...WERE IN THE MAIN BUILDING THIS MORNING.
SO THE KID'S WRONG ABOUT THE KILLER BEING ONE OF THEM.
NONE OF THEM COULD'VE HIDDEN IN THE LAKETOP BATH OVER-NIGHT, WAITING FOR TETSUYAMA SO THEY COULD BLUDGEON HIM TO DEATH.
Laketop H
Entrance
OH, BUT—
YAWN
HI, DOC!
UP AT LAST ...
OH, DRAT! DID YOU GO TO THE BATHS WITH-OUT ME?
FORGET ABOUT THE BATHS!
WE'VE GOT TROUBLE !!
THE KILLER MUST HAVE GOTTEN TO AND FROM THE BATHHOUSE BY SWIMMING ACROSS THE LAKE.
YEAH. THE KID SAID HE DIDN'T HEAR ANYONE JUMP IN THE WATER...
...BUT HE'S JUST A KID.
OKAY! LOOK FOR LEADS ON THAT ANGLE!
THERE'S NO NEED FOR THAT.

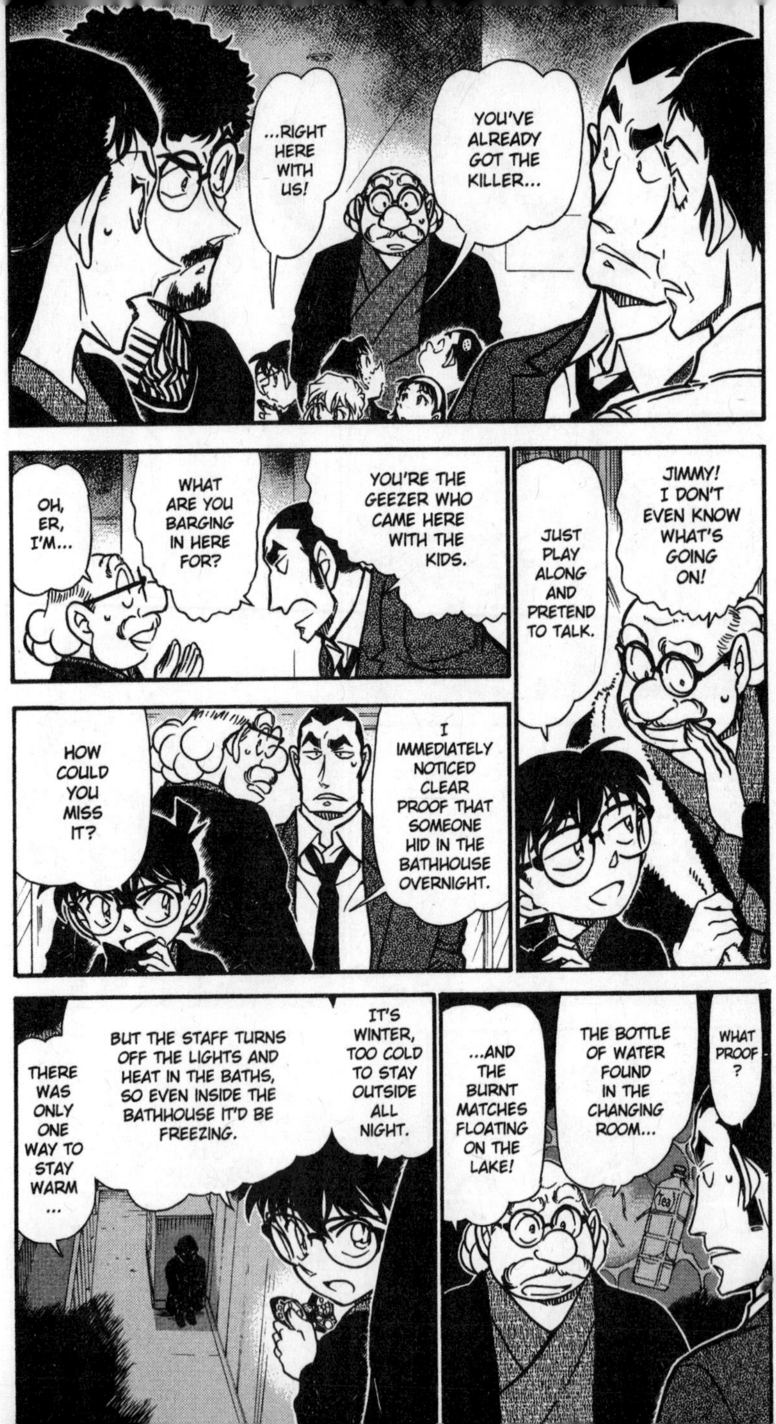
YOU'VE ALREADY GOT THE KILLER...
...RIGHT HERE WITH US!
JIMMY! I DON'T EVEN KNOW WHAT'S GOING ON!
JUST PLAY ALONG AND PRETEND TO TALK.
YOU'RE THE GEEZER WHO CAME HERE WITH THE KIDS.
WHAT ARE YOU BARGING IN HERE FOR?
OH, ER, I'M...
I IMMEDIATELY NOTICED CLEAR PROOF THAT SOMEONE HID IN THE BATHHOUSE OVERNIGHT.
HOW COULD YOU MISS IT?
WHAT PROOF?
THE BOTTLE OF WATER FOUND IN THE CHANGING ROOM...
...AND THE BURNT MATCHES FLOATING ON THE LAKE!
IT'S WINTER, TOO COLD TO STAY OUTSIDE ALL NIGHT.
BUT THE STAFF TURNS OFF THE LIGHTS AND HEAT IN THE BATHS, SO EVEN INSIDE THE BATHHOUSE IT'D BE FREEZING.
THERE WAS ONLY ONE WAY TO STAY WARM...

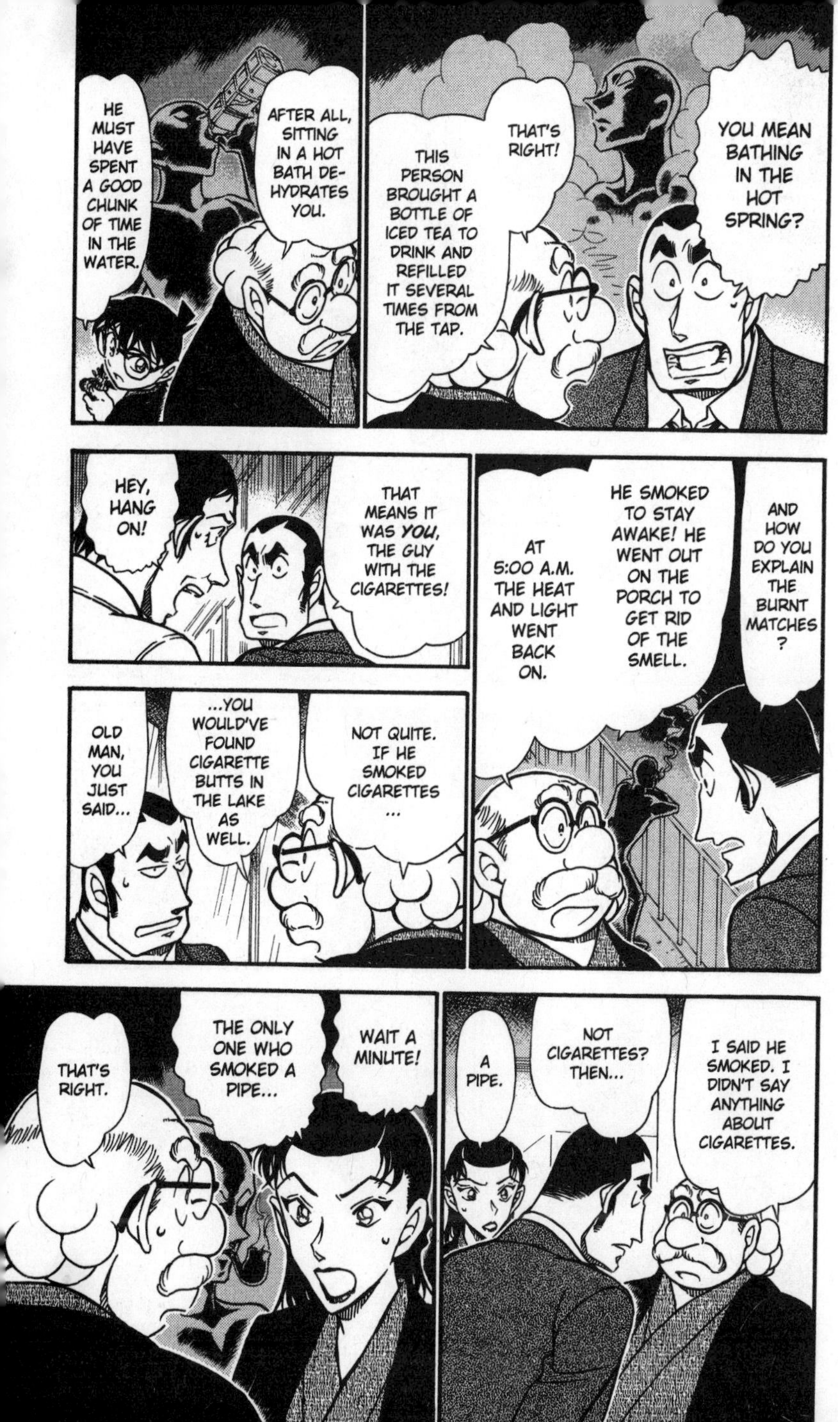
YOU MEAN BATHING IN THE HOT SPRING?
THAT'S RIGHT!
THIS PERSON BROUGHT A BOTTLE OF ICED TEA TO DRINK AND REFILLED IT SEVERAL TIMES FROM THE TAP.
AFTER ALL, SITTING IN A HOT BATH DE-HYDRATES YOU.
HE MUST HAVE SPENT A GOOD CHUNK OF TIME IN THE WATER.
AND HOW DO YOU EXPLAIN THE BURNT MATCHES?
HE SMOKED TO STAY AWAKE! HE WENT OUT ON THE PORCH TO GET RID OF THE SMELL.
AT 5:00 A.M. THE HEAT AND LIGHT WENT BACK ON.
THAT MEANS IT WAS *YOU*, THE GUY WITH THE CIGARETTES!
HEY, HANG ON!
NOT QUITE. IF HE SMOKED CIGARETTES ...
...YOU WOULD'VE FOUND CIGARETTE BUTTS IN THE LAKE AS WELL.
OLD MAN, YOU JUST SAID...
I SAID HE SMOKED. I DIDN'T SAY ANYTHING ABOUT CIGARETTES.
NOT CIGARETTES? THEN...
A PIPE.
WAIT A MINUTE!
THE ONLY ONE WHO SMOKED A PIPE...
THAT'S RIGHT.

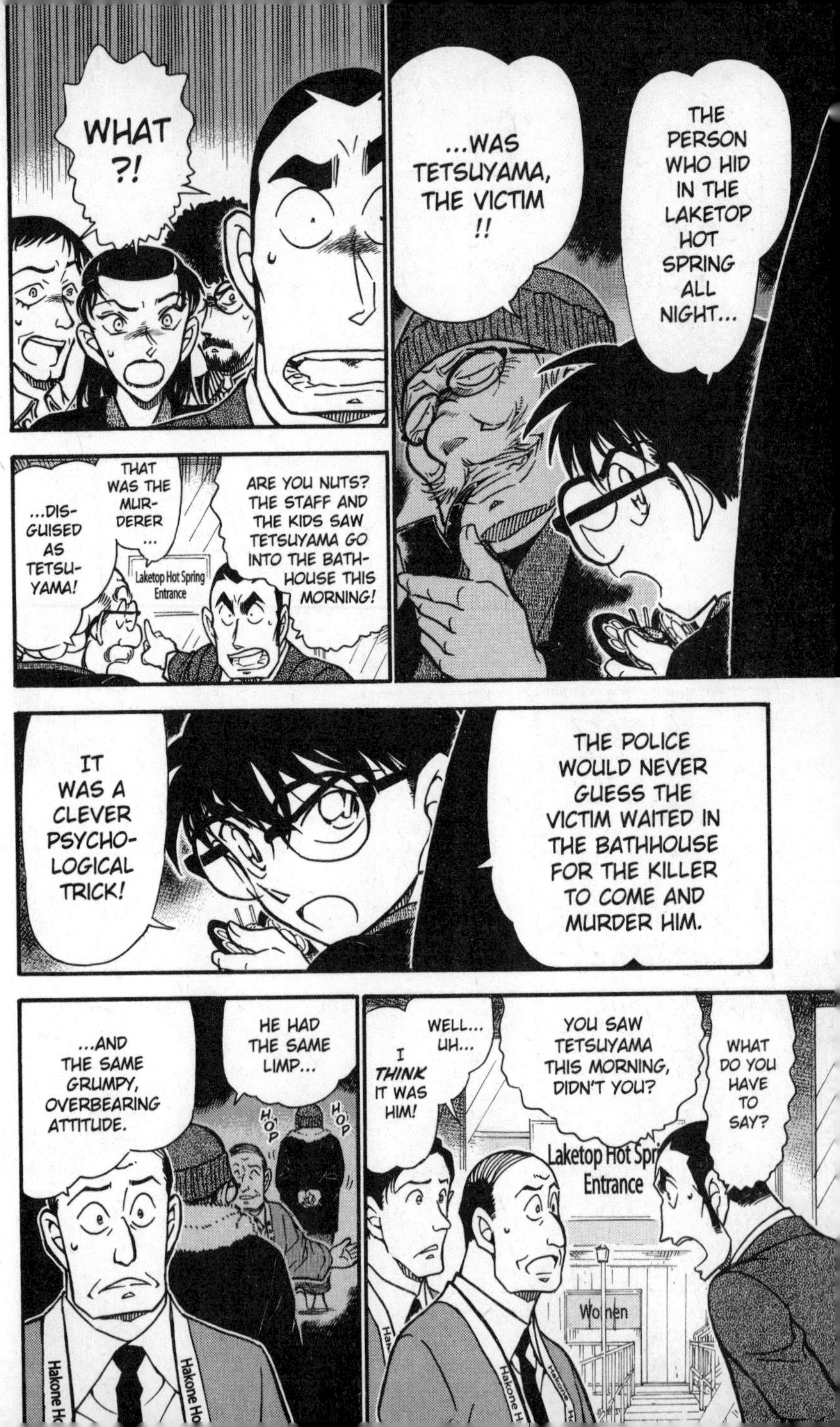
THE PERSON WHO HID IN THE LAKETOP HOT SPRING ALL NIGHT...
...WAS TETSUYAMA, THE VICTIM!!
WHAT?!
ARE YOU NUTS? THE STAFF AND THE KIDS SAW TETSUYAMA GO INTO THE BATHHOUSE THIS MORNING!
Laketop Hot Spring Entrance
THAT WAS THE MURDERER...
...DISGUISED AS TETSUYAMA!
THE POLICE WOULD NEVER GUESS THE VICTIM WAITED IN THE BATHHOUSE FOR THE KILLER TO COME AND MURDER HIM.
IT WAS A CLEVER PSYCHOLOGICAL TRICK!
WHAT DO YOU HAVE TO SAY?
YOU SAW TETSUYAMA THIS MORNING, DIDN'T YOU?
WELL... UH...
I *THINK* IT WAS HIM!
Laketop Hot Spri
Entrance
HE HAD THE SAME LIMP...
HOP
HOP
...AND THE SAME GRUMPY, OVERBEARING ATTITUDE.

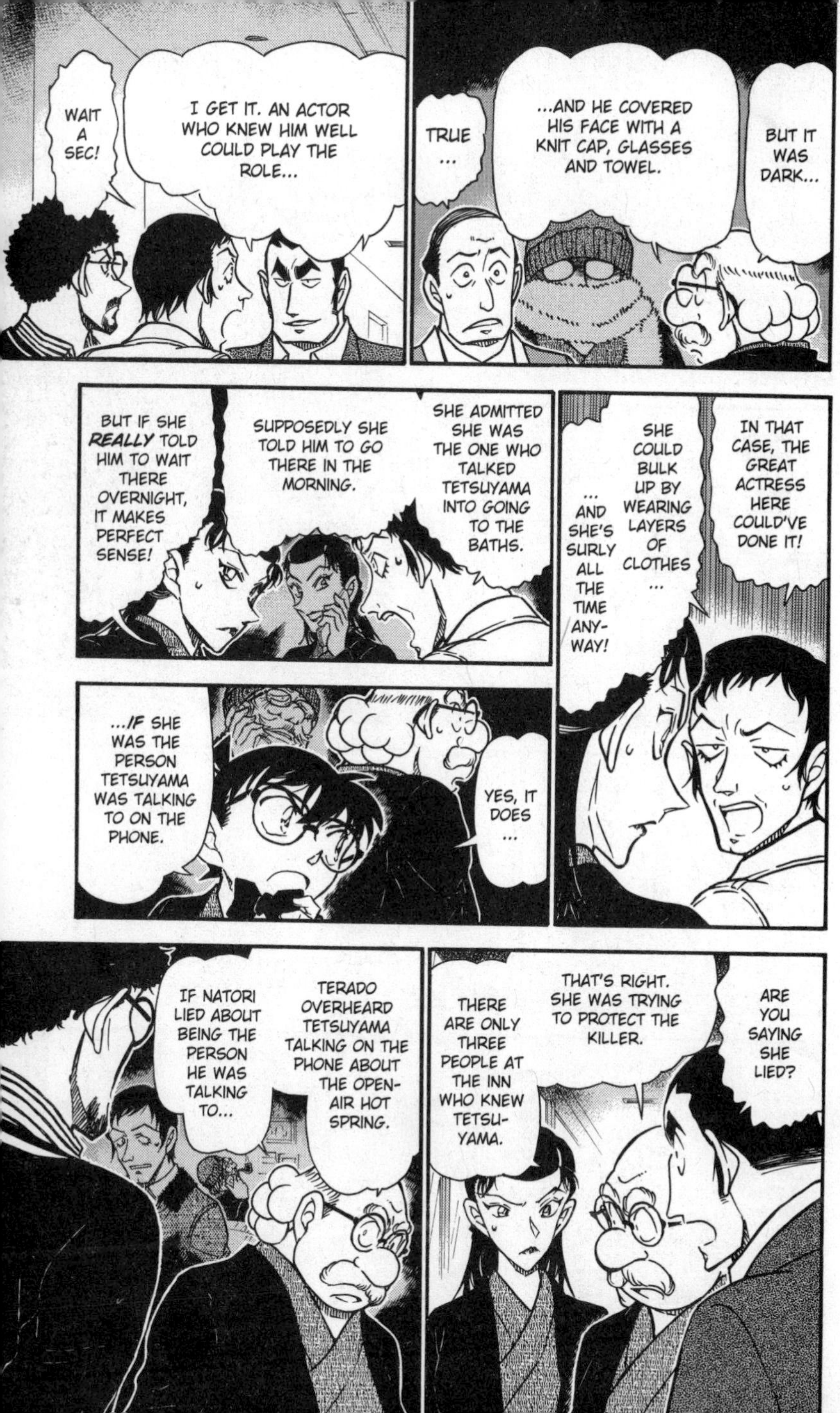
BUT IT WAS DARK...
...AND HE COVERED HIS FACE WITH A KNIT CAP, GLASSES AND TOWEL.
TRUE ...
I GET IT. AN ACTOR WHO KNEW HIM WELL COULD PLAY THE ROLE...
WAIT A SEC!
IN THAT CASE, THE GREAT ACTRESS HERE COULD'VE DONE IT!
SHE COULD BULK UP BY WEARING LAYERS OF CLOTHES ...
... AND SHE'S SURLY ALL THE TIME ANY-WAY!
SHE ADMITTED SHE WAS THE ONE WHO TALKED TETSUYAMA INTO GOING TO THE BATHS.
SUPPOSEDLY SHE TOLD HIM TO GO THERE IN THE MORNING.
BUT IF SHE ***REALLY*** TOLD HIM TO WAIT THERE OVERNIGHT, IT MAKES PERFECT SENSE!
YES, IT DOES ...
...***IF*** SHE WAS THE PERSON TETSUYAMA WAS TALKING TO ON THE PHONE.
ARE YOU SAYING SHE LIED?
THAT'S RIGHT. SHE WAS TRYING TO PROTECT THE KILLER.
THERE ARE ONLY THREE PEOPLE AT THE INN WHO KNEW TETSU-YAMA.
TERADO OVERHEARD TETSUYAMA TALKING ON THE PHONE ABOUT THE OPEN-AIR HOT SPRING.
IF NATORI LIED ABOUT BEING THE PERSON HE WAS TALKING TO...

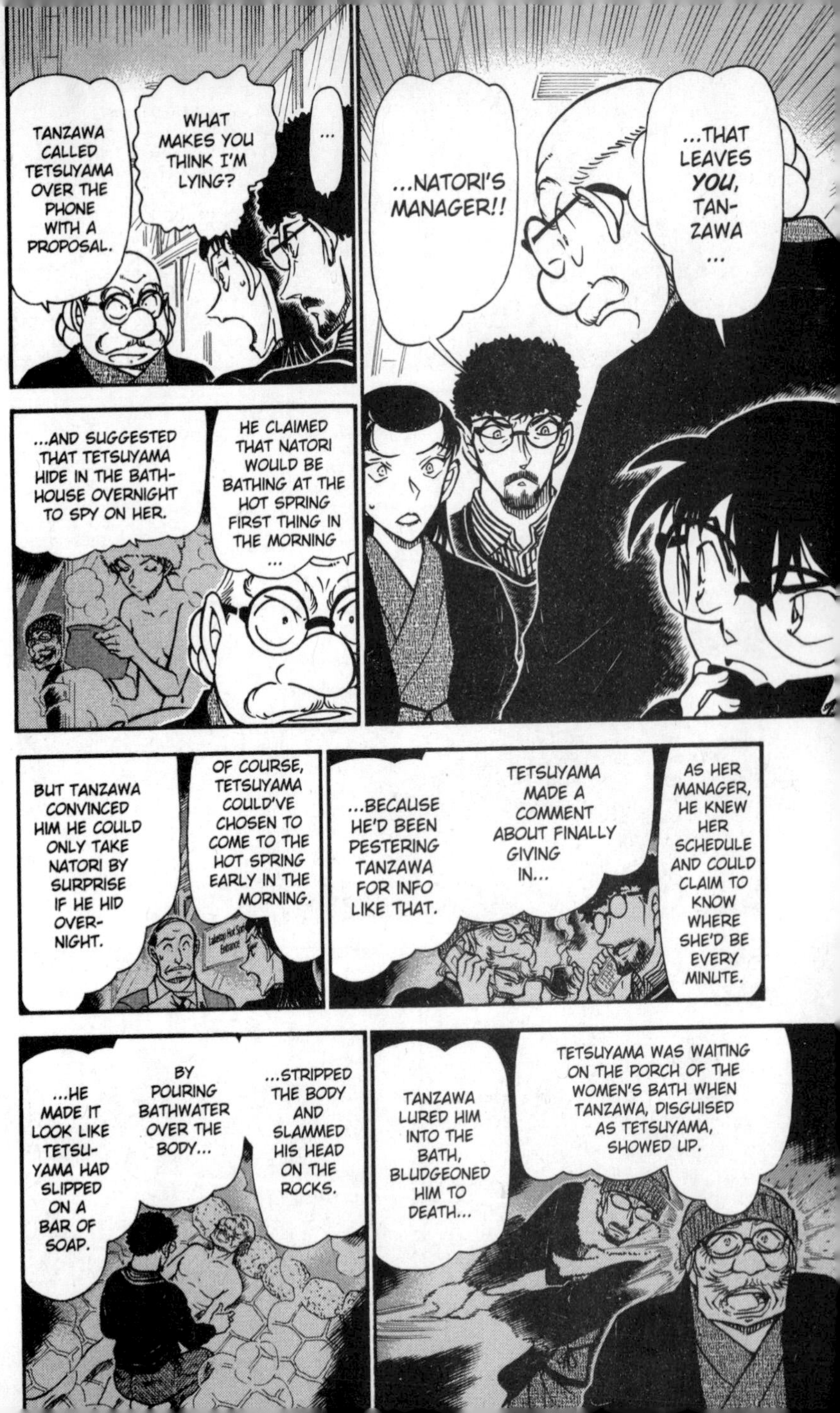
...THAT LEAVES YOU, TANZAWA...
...NATORI'S MANAGER!!
...
WHAT MAKES YOU THINK I'M LYING?
TANZAWA CALLED TETSUYAMA OVER THE PHONE WITH A PROPOSAL.
HE CLAIMED THAT NATORI WOULD BE BATHING AT THE HOT SPRING FIRST THING IN THE MORNING...
...AND SUGGESTED THAT TETSUYAMA HIDE IN THE BATHHOUSE OVERNIGHT TO SPY ON HER.
AS HER MANAGER, HE KNEW HER SCHEDULE AND COULD CLAIM TO KNOW WHERE SHE'D BE EVERY MINUTE.
TETSUYAMA MADE A COMMENT ABOUT FINALLY GIVING IN...
...BECAUSE HE'D BEEN PESTERING TANZAWA FOR INFO LIKE THAT.
OF COURSE, TETSUYAMA COULD'VE CHOSEN TO COME TO THE HOT SPRING EARLY IN THE MORNING.
BUT TANZAWA CONVINCED HIM HE COULD ONLY TAKE NATORI BY SURPRISE IF HE HID OVERNIGHT.
TETSUYAMA WAS WAITING ON THE PORCH OF THE WOMEN'S BATH WHEN TANZAWA, DISGUISED AS TETSUYAMA, SHOWED UP.
TANZAWA LURED HIM INTO THE BATH, BLUDGEONED HIM TO DEATH...
...STRIPPED THE BODY AND SLAMMED HIS HEAD ON THE ROCKS.
BY POURING BATHWATER OVER THE BODY...
...HE MADE IT LOOK LIKE TETSUYAMA HAD SLIPPED ON A BAR OF SOAP.

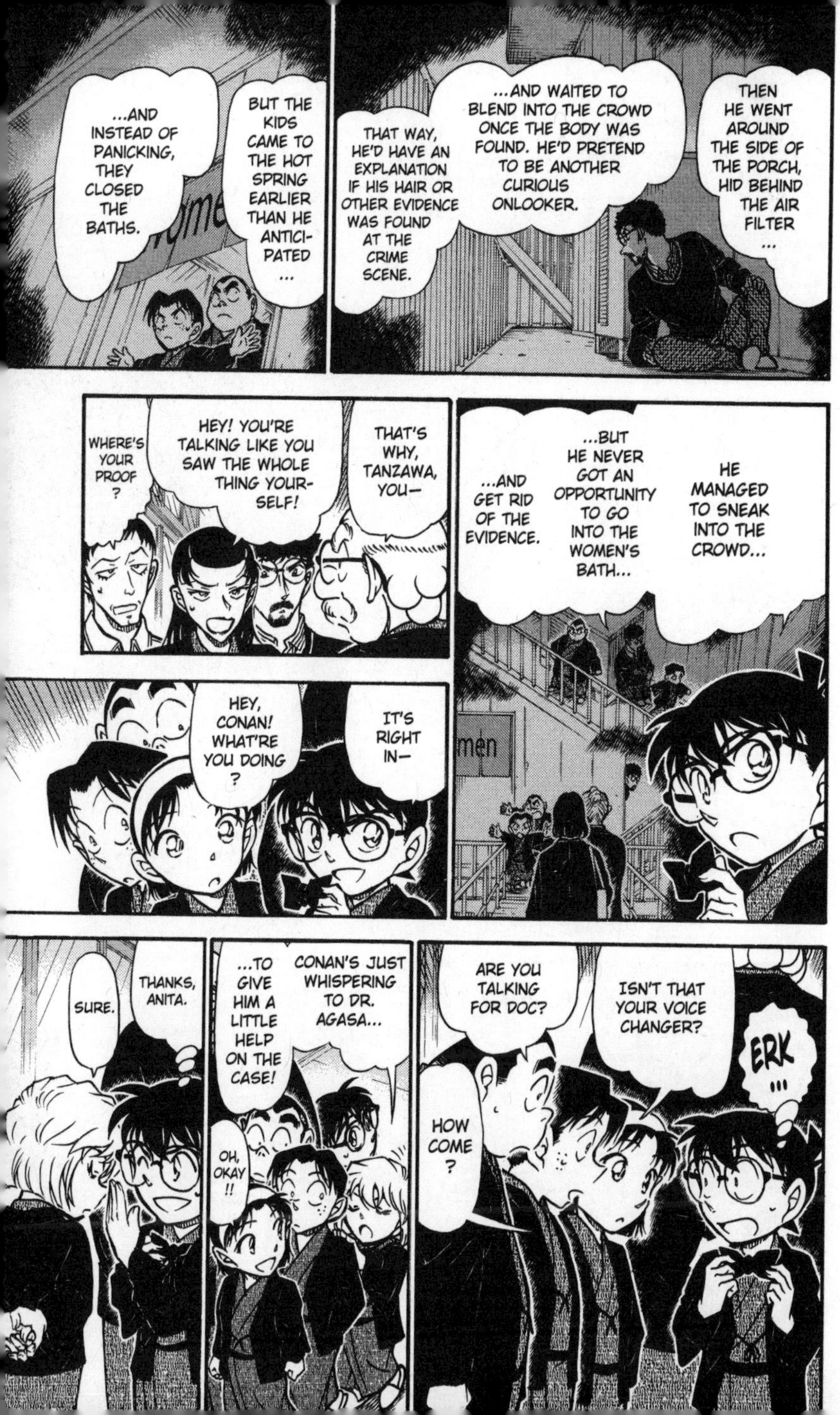
THEN HE WENT AROUND THE SIDE OF THE PORCH, HID BEHIND THE AIR FILTER ...
...AND WAITED TO BLEND INTO THE CROWD ONCE THE BODY WAS FOUND. HE'D PRETEND TO BE ANOTHER CURIOUS ONLOOKER.
THAT WAY, HE'D HAVE AN EXPLANATION IF HIS HAIR OR OTHER EVIDENCE WAS FOUND AT THE CRIME SCENE.
BUT THE KIDS CAME TO THE HOT SPRING EARLIER THAN HE ANTICI-PATED ...
...AND INSTEAD OF PANICKING, THEY CLOSED THE BATHS.
HE MANAGED TO SNEAK INTO THE CROWD...
...BUT HE NEVER GOT AN OPPORTUNITY TO GO INTO THE WOMEN'S BATH...
...AND GET RID OF THE EVIDENCE.
THAT'S WHY, TANZAWA, YOU—
HEY! YOU'RE TALKING LIKE YOU SAW THE WHOLE THING YOUR-SELF!
WHERE'S YOUR PROOF?
IT'S RIGHT IN—
HEY, CONAN! WHAT'RE YOU DOING?
ERK ...
ISN'T THAT YOUR VOICE CHANGER?
ARE YOU TALKING FOR DOC?
HOW COME?
CONAN'S JUST WHISPERING TO DR. AGASA...
...TO GIVE HIM A LITTLE HELP ON THE CASE!
OH, OKAY!!
THANKS, ANITA.
SURE.

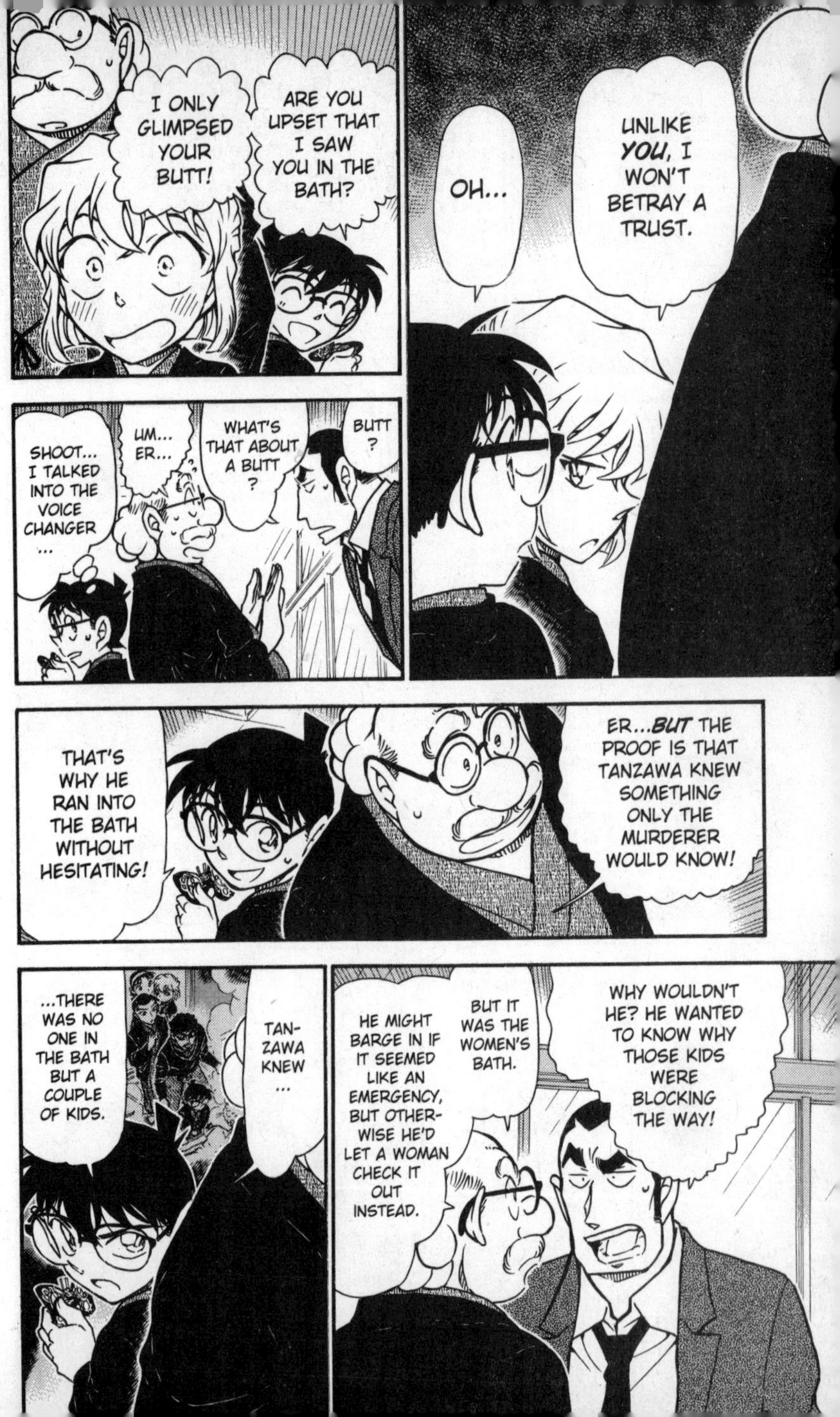
UNLIKE *YOU*, I WON'T BETRAY A TRUST.
OH...
ARE YOU UPSET THAT I SAW YOU IN THE BATH?
I ONLY GLIMPSED YOUR BUTT!
BUTT?
WHAT'S THAT ABOUT A BUTT?
UM... ER...
SHOOT... I TALKED INTO THE VOICE CHANGER...
ER...*BUT* THE PROOF IS THAT TANZAWA KNEW SOMETHING ONLY THE MURDERER WOULD KNOW!
THAT'S WHY HE RAN INTO THE BATH WITHOUT HESITATING!
WHY WOULDN'T HE? HE WANTED TO KNOW WHY THOSE KIDS WERE BLOCKING THE WAY!
BUT IT WAS THE WOMEN'S BATH.
HE MIGHT BARGE IN IF IT SEEMED LIKE AN EMERGENCY, BUT OTHERWISE HE'D LET A WOMAN CHECK IT OUT INSTEAD.
TANZAWA KNEW...
...THERE WAS NO ONE IN THE BATH BUT A COUPLE OF KIDS.

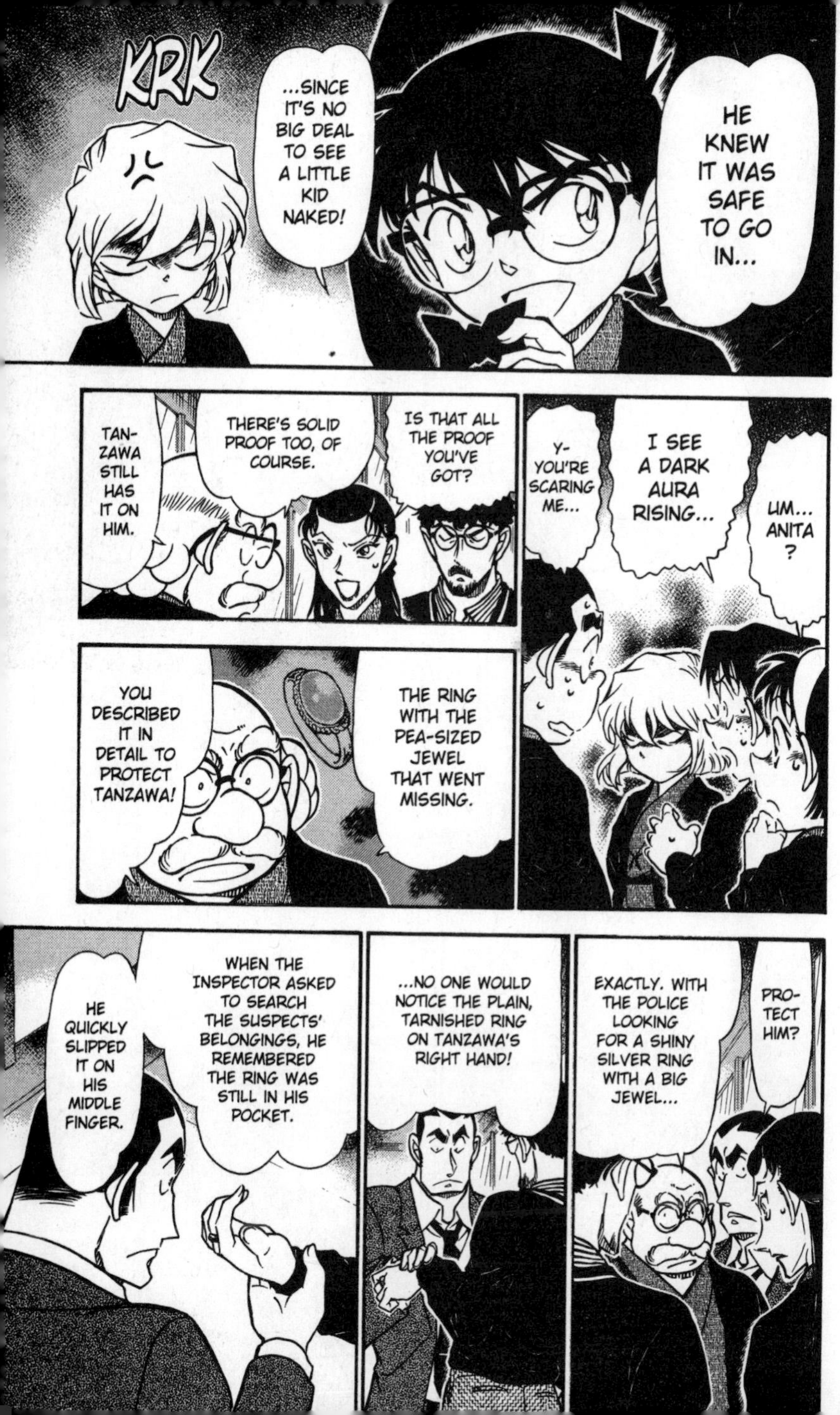
HE KNEW IT WAS SAFE TO GO IN...
...SINCE IT'S NO BIG DEAL TO SEE A LITTLE KID NAKED!
KRK
UM... ANITA?
I SEE A DARK AURA RISING...
Y-YOU'RE SCARING ME...
IS THAT ALL THE PROOF YOU'VE GOT?
THERE'S SOLID PROOF TOO, OF COURSE.
TANZAWA STILL HAS IT ON HIM.
THE RING WITH THE PEA-SIZED JEWEL THAT WENT MISSING.
YOU DESCRIBED IT IN DETAIL TO PROTECT TANZAWA!
PROTECT HIM?
EXACTLY. WITH THE POLICE LOOKING FOR A SHINY SILVER RING WITH A BIG JEWEL...
...NO ONE WOULD NOTICE THE PLAIN, TARNISHED RING ON TANZAWA'S RIGHT HAND!
WHEN THE INSPECTOR ASKED TO SEARCH THE SUSPECTS' BELONGINGS, HE REMEMBERED THE RING WAS STILL IN HIS POCKET.
HE QUICKLY SLIPPED IT ON HIS MIDDLE FINGER.

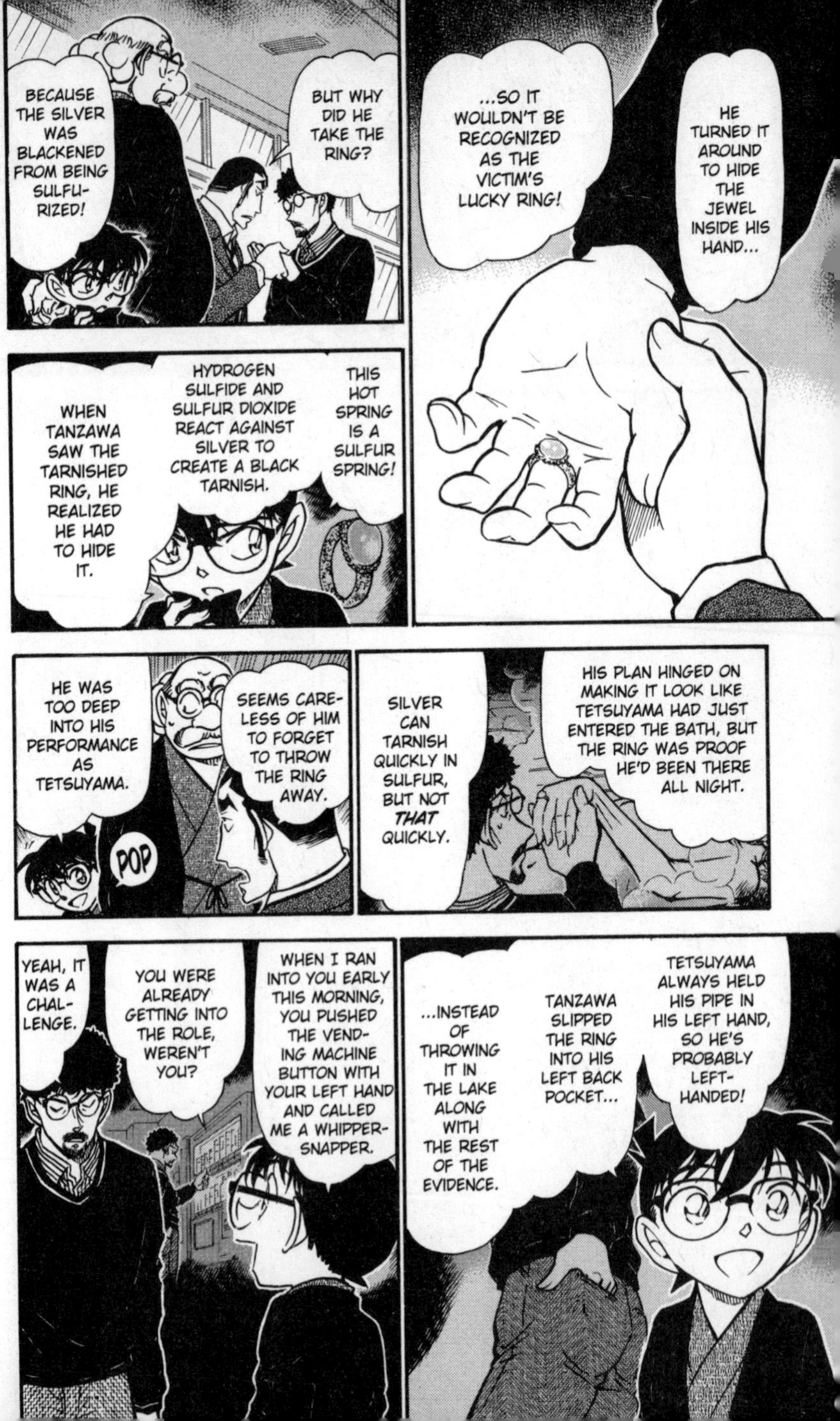
BUT WHY DID HE TAKE THE RING?
BECAUSE THE SILVER WAS BLACKENED FROM BEING SULFU-RIZED!
THIS HOT SPRING IS A SULFUR SPRING!
HYDROGEN SULFIDE AND SULFUR DIOXIDE REACT AGAINST SILVER TO CREATE A BLACK TARNISH.
WHEN TANZAWA SAW THE TARNISHED RING, HE REALIZED HE HAD TO HIDE IT.
HE TURNED IT AROUND TO HIDE THE JEWEL INSIDE HIS HAND...
...SO IT WOULDN'T BE RECOGNIZED AS THE VICTIM'S LUCKY RING!
HIS PLAN HINGED ON MAKING IT LOOK LIKE TETSUYAMA HAD JUST ENTERED THE BATH, BUT THE RING WAS PROOF HE'D BEEN THERE ALL NIGHT.
SILVER CAN TARNISH QUICKLY IN SULFUR, BUT NOT *THAT* QUICKLY.
SEEMS CARE-LESS OF HIM TO FORGET TO THROW THE RING AWAY.
HE WAS TOO DEEP INTO HIS PERFORMANCE AS TETSUYAMA.
POP
TETSUYAMA ALWAYS HELD HIS PIPE IN HIS LEFT HAND, SO HE'S PROBABLY LEFT-HANDED!
TANZAWA SLIPPED THE RING INTO HIS LEFT BACK POCKET...
...INSTEAD OF THROWING IT IN THE LAKE ALONG WITH THE REST OF THE EVIDENCE.
WHEN I RAN INTO YOU EARLY THIS MORNING, YOU PUSHED THE VEND-ING MACHINE BUTTON WITH YOUR LEFT HAND AND CALLED ME A WHIPPER-SNAPPER.
YOU WERE ALREADY GETTING INTO THE ROLE, WEREN'T YOU?
YEAH, IT WAS A CHAL-LENGE.

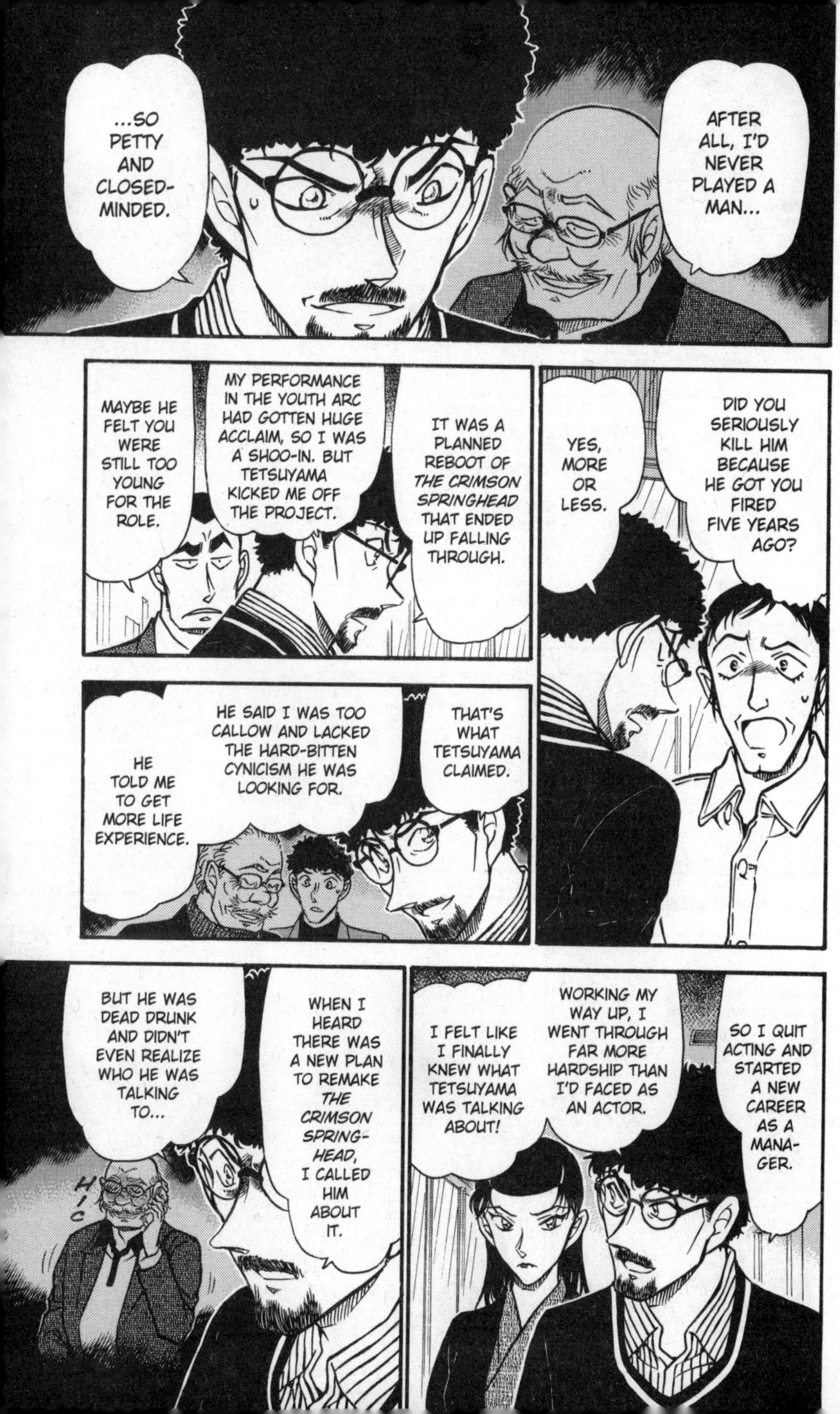
AFTER ALL, I'D NEVER PLAYED A MAN...
...SO PETTY AND CLOSED-MINDED.
DID YOU SERIOUSLY KILL HIM BECAUSE HE GOT YOU FIRED FIVE YEARS AGO?
YES, MORE OR LESS.
IT WAS A PLANNED REBOOT OF *THE CRIMSON SPRINGHEAD* THAT ENDED UP FALLING THROUGH.
MY PERFORMANCE IN THE YOUTH ARC HAD GOTTEN HUGE ACCLAIM, SO I WAS A SHOO-IN. BUT TETSUYAMA KICKED ME OFF THE PROJECT.
MAYBE HE FELT YOU WERE STILL TOO YOUNG FOR THE ROLE.
THAT'S WHAT TETSUYAMA CLAIMED.
HE SAID I WAS TOO CALLOW AND LACKED THE HARD-BITTEN CYNICISM HE WAS LOOKING FOR.
HE TOLD ME TO GET MORE LIFE EXPERIENCE.
SO I QUIT ACTING AND STARTED A NEW CAREER AS A MANA-GER.
WORKING MY WAY UP, I WENT THROUGH FAR MORE HARDSHIP THAN I'D FACED AS AN ACTOR.
I FELT LIKE I FINALLY KNEW WHAT TETSUYAMA WAS TALKING ABOUT!
WHEN I HEARD THERE WAS A NEW PLAN TO REMAKE *THE CRIMSON SPRING-HEAD*, I CALLED HIM ABOUT IT.
BUT HE WAS DEAD DRUNK AND DIDN'T EVEN REALIZE WHO HE WAS TALKING TO...
HIC

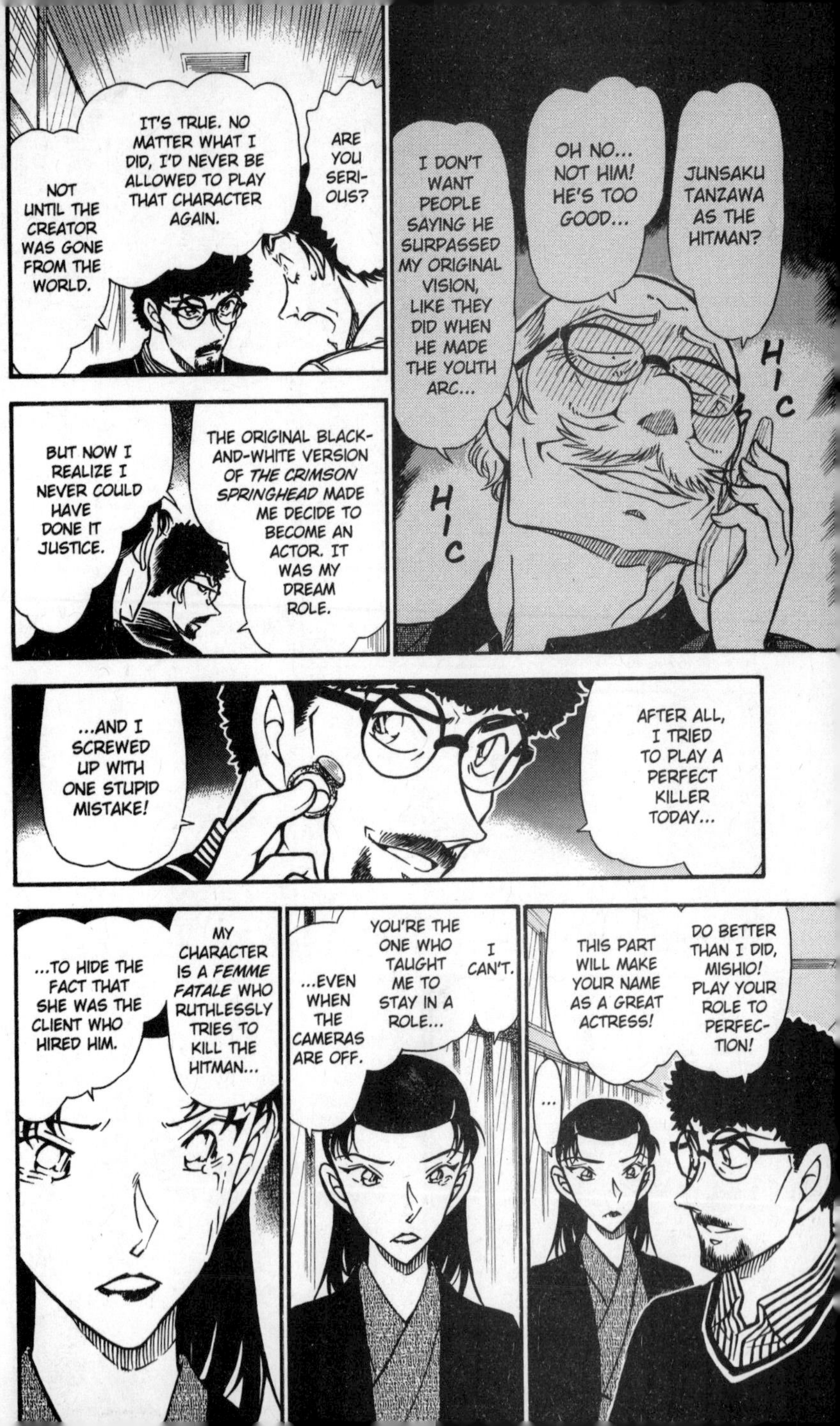
JUNSAKU TANZAWA AS THE HITMAN?
OH NO... NOT HIM! HE'S TOO GOOD...
I DON'T WANT PEOPLE SAYING HE SURPASSED MY ORIGINAL VISION, LIKE THEY DID WHEN HE MADE THE YOUTH ARC...
HIC
HIC
ARE YOU SERIOUS?
IT'S TRUE. NO MATTER WHAT I DID, I'D NEVER BE ALLOWED TO PLAY THAT CHARACTER AGAIN.
NOT UNTIL THE CREATOR WAS GONE FROM THE WORLD.
THE ORIGINAL BLACK-AND-WHITE VERSION OF *THE CRIMSON SPRINGHEAD* MADE ME DECIDE TO BECOME AN ACTOR. IT WAS MY DREAM ROLE.
BUT NOW I REALIZE I NEVER COULD HAVE DONE IT JUSTICE.
AFTER ALL, I TRIED TO PLAY A PERFECT KILLER TODAY...
...AND I SCREWED UP WITH ONE STUPID MISTAKE!
DO BETTER THAN I DID, MISHIO! PLAY YOUR ROLE TO PERFECTION!
THIS PART WILL MAKE YOUR NAME AS A GREAT ACTRESS!
...
I CAN'T.
YOU'RE THE ONE WHO TAUGHT ME TO STAY IN A ROLE...
...EVEN WHEN THE CAMERAS ARE OFF.
MY CHARACTER IS A *FEMME FATALE* WHO RUTHLESSLY TRIES TO KILL THE HITMAN...
...TO HIDE THE FACT THAT SHE WAS THE CLIENT WHO HIRED HIM.

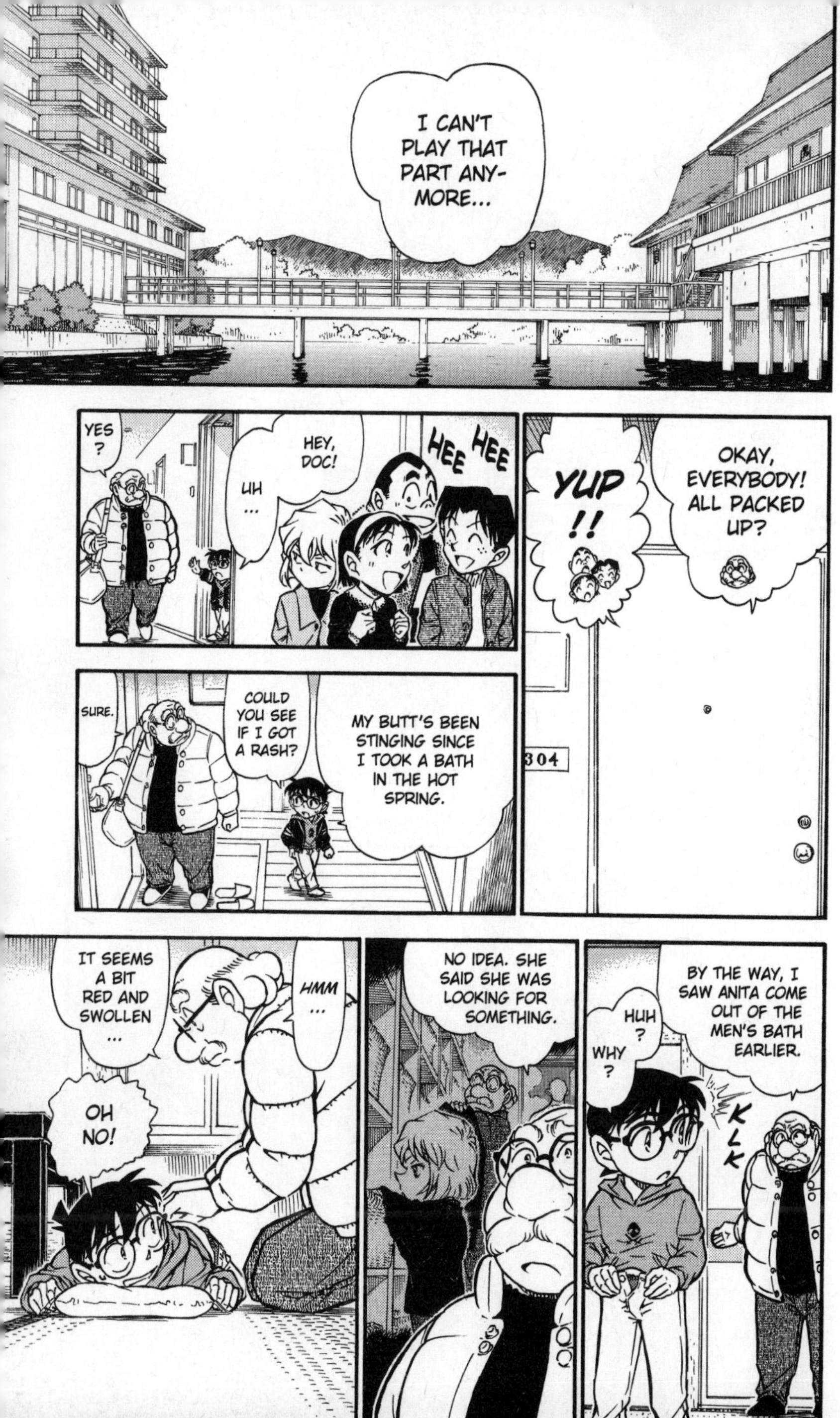
I CAN'T PLAY THAT PART ANY-MORE...
OKAY, EVERYBODY! ALL PACKED UP?
YUP !!
304
HEE HEE
HEY, DOC!
UH ...
YES ?
MY BUTT'S BEEN STINGING SINCE I TOOK A BATH IN THE HOT SPRING.
COULD YOU SEE IF I GOT A RASH?
SURE.
BY THE WAY, I SAW ANITA COME OUT OF THE MEN'S BATH EARLIER.
KLK
HUH ?
WHY ?
NO IDEA. SHE SAID SHE WAS LOOKING FOR SOMETHING.
HMM ...
IT SEEMS A BIT RED AND SWOLLEN ...
OH NO!

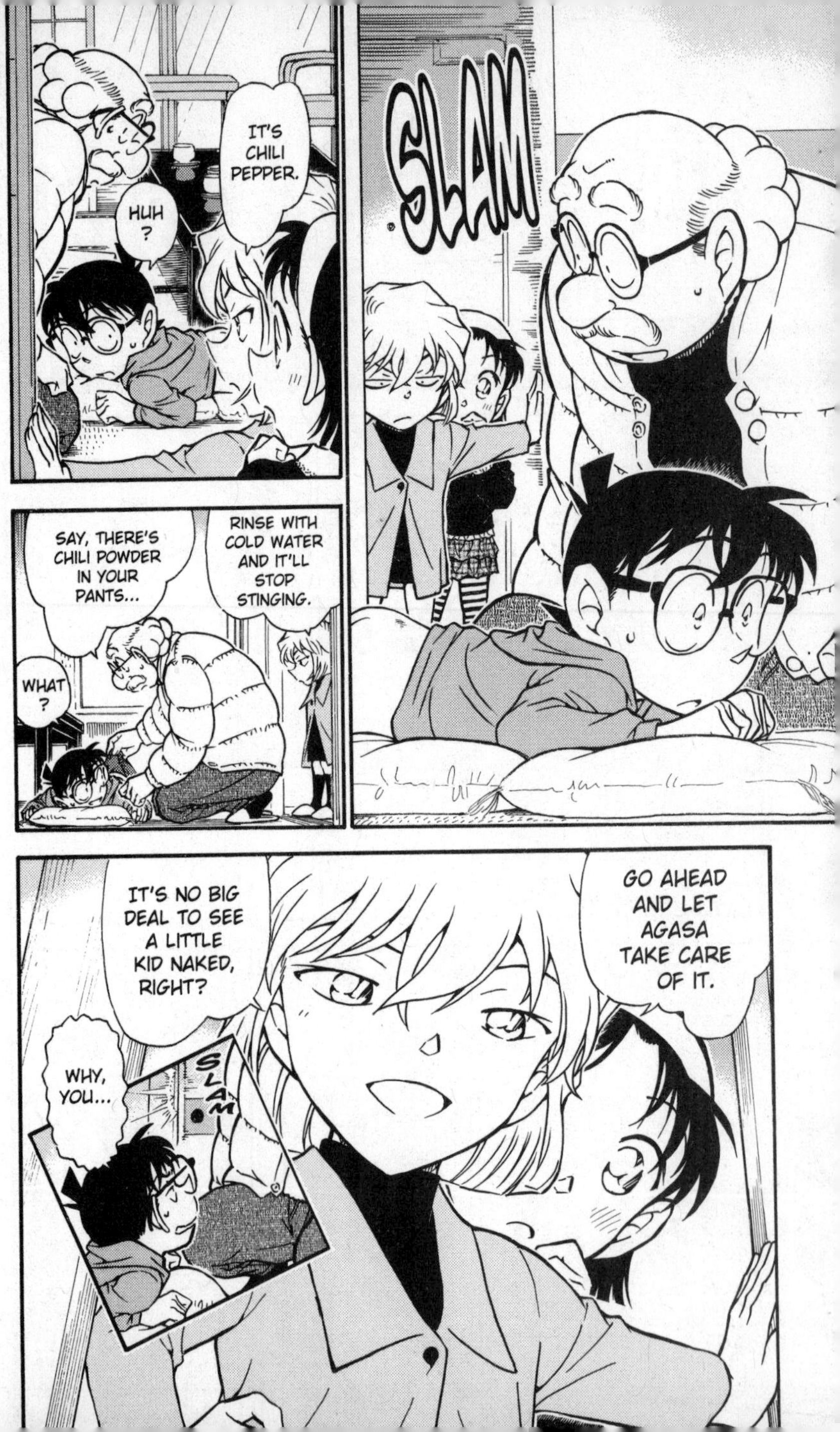
SLAM
IT'S CHILI PEPPER.
HUH?
RINSE WITH COLD WATER AND IT'LL STOP STINGING.
SAY, THERE'S CHILI POWDER IN YOUR PANTS...
WHAT?
GO AHEAD AND LET AGASA TAKE CARE OF IT.
IT'S NO BIG DEAL TO SEE A LITTLE KID NAKED, RIGHT?
SLAM
WHY, YOU...

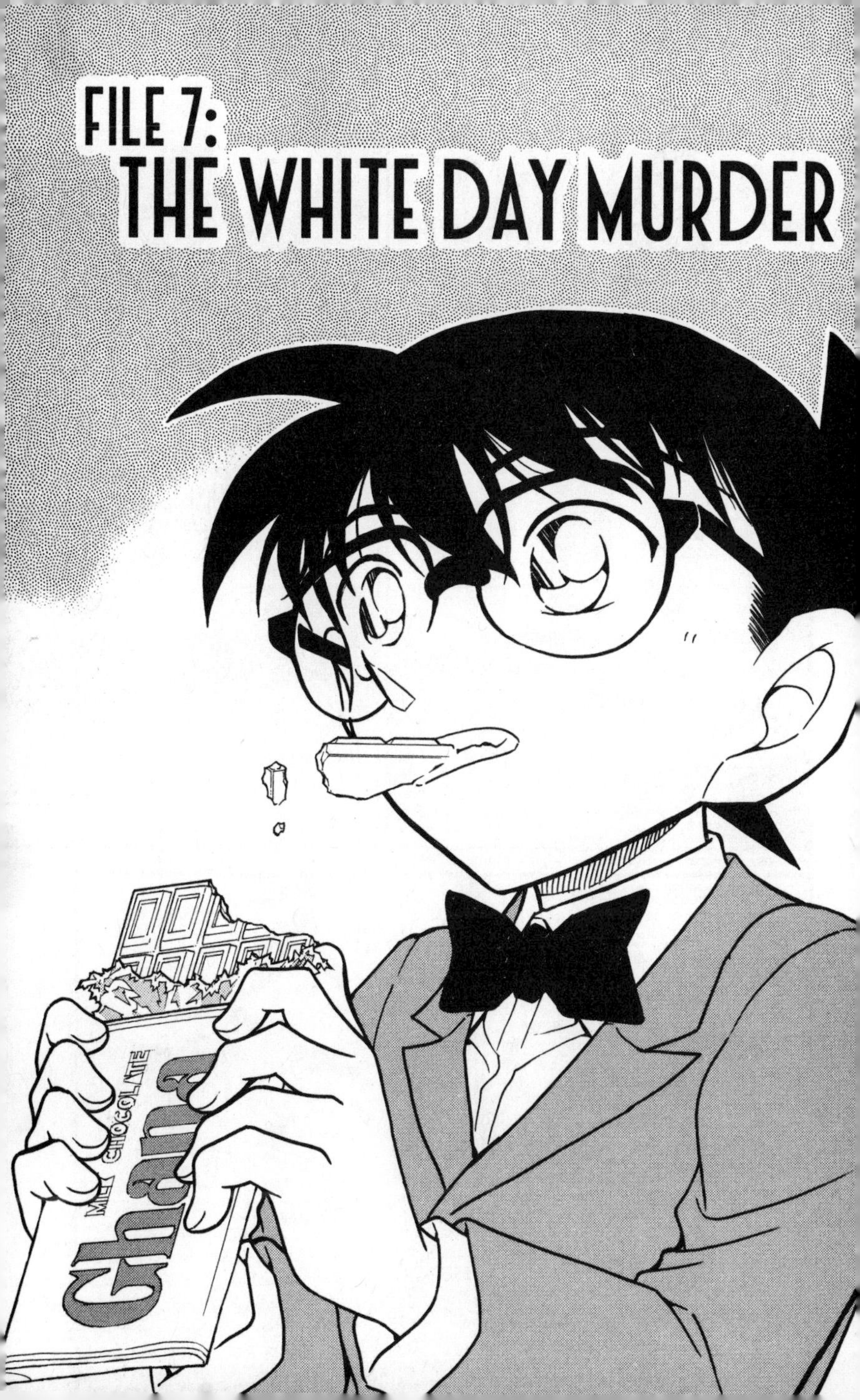
FILE 7:
THE WHITE DAY MURDER

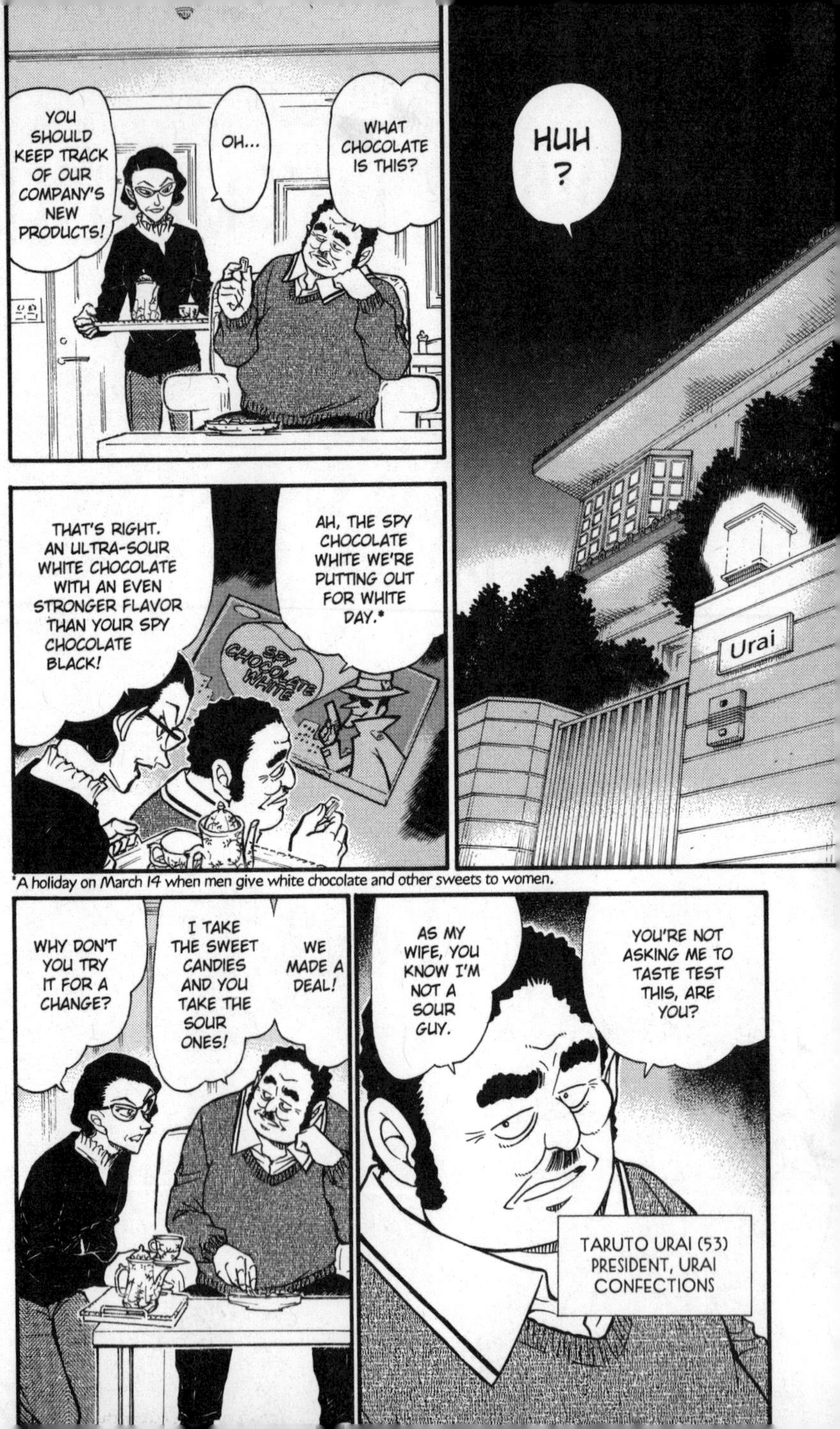
HUH ?
WHAT CHOCOLATE IS THIS?
OH...
YOU SHOULD KEEP TRACK OF OUR COMPANY'S NEW PRODUCTS!
AH, THE SPY CHOCOLATE WHITE WE'RE PUTTING OUT FOR WHITE DAY.*
THAT'S RIGHT. AN ULTRA-SOUR WHITE CHOCOLATE WITH AN EVEN STRONGER FLAVOR THAN YOUR SPY CHOCOLATE BLACK!
SPY CHOCOLATE WHITE
Urai
YOU'RE NOT ASKING ME TO TASTE TEST THIS, ARE YOU?
AS MY WIFE, YOU KNOW I'M NOT A SOUR GUY.
TARUTO URAI (53) PRESIDENT, URAI CONFECTIONS
WE MADE A DEAL!
I TAKE THE SWEET CANDIES AND YOU TAKE THE SOUR ONES!
WHY DON'T YOU TRY IT FOR A CHANGE?

*A holiday on March 14 when men give white chocolate and other sweets to women.

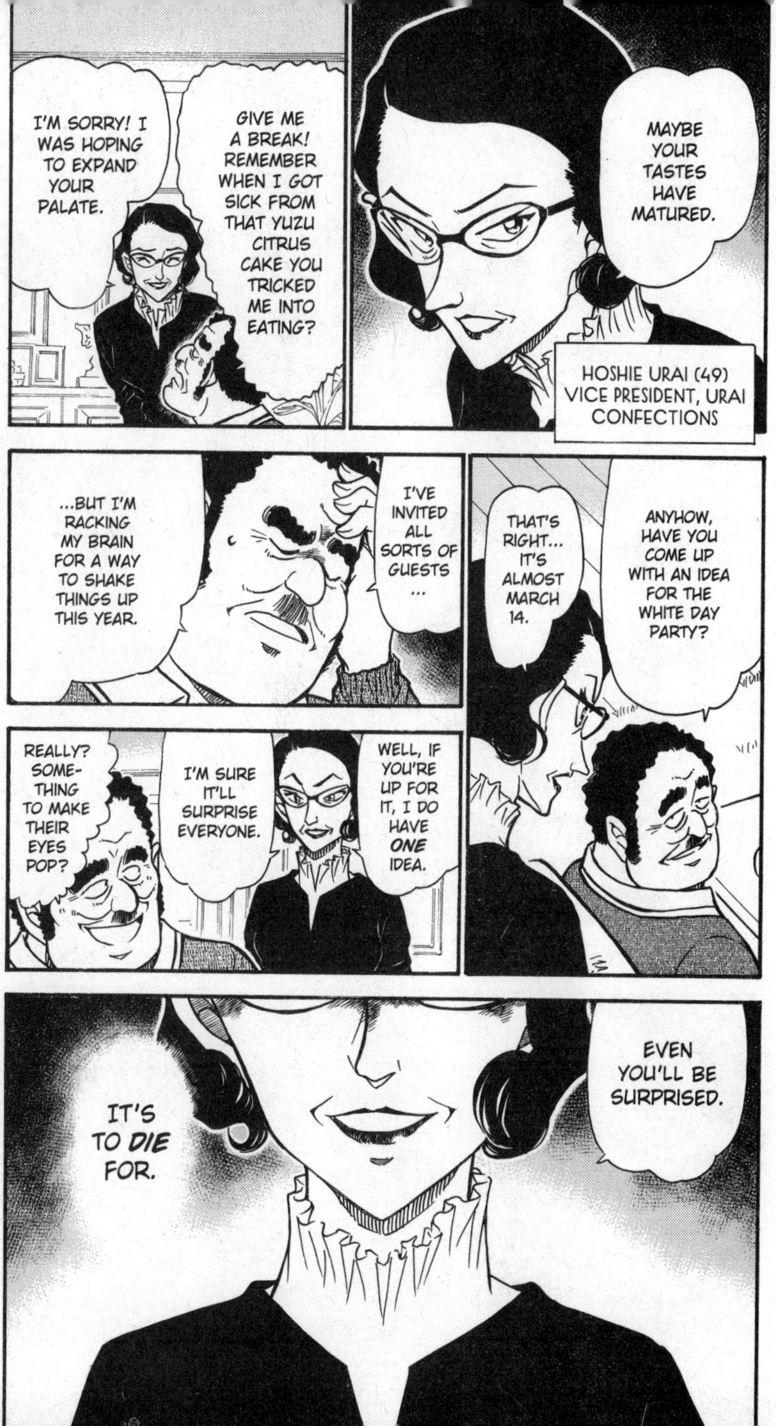
MAYBE YOUR TASTES HAVE MATURED.
HOSHIE URAI (49) VICE PRESIDENT, URAI CONFECTIONS
GIVE ME A BREAK! REMEMBER WHEN I GOT SICK FROM THAT YUZU CITRUS CAKE YOU TRICKED ME INTO EATING?
I'M SORRY! I WAS HOPING TO EXPAND YOUR PALATE.
ANYHOW, HAVE YOU COME UP WITH AN IDEA FOR THE WHITE DAY PARTY?
THAT'S RIGHT... IT'S ALMOST MARCH 14.
I'VE INVITED ALL SORTS OF GUESTS ...
...BUT I'M RACKING MY BRAIN FOR A WAY TO SHAKE THINGS UP THIS YEAR.
WELL, IF YOU'RE UP FOR IT, I DO HAVE *ONE* IDEA.
I'M SURE IT'LL SURPRISE EVERYONE.
REALLY? SOME-THING TO MAKE THEIR EYES POP?
EVEN YOU'LL BE SURPRISED.
IT'S TO *DIE* FOR.

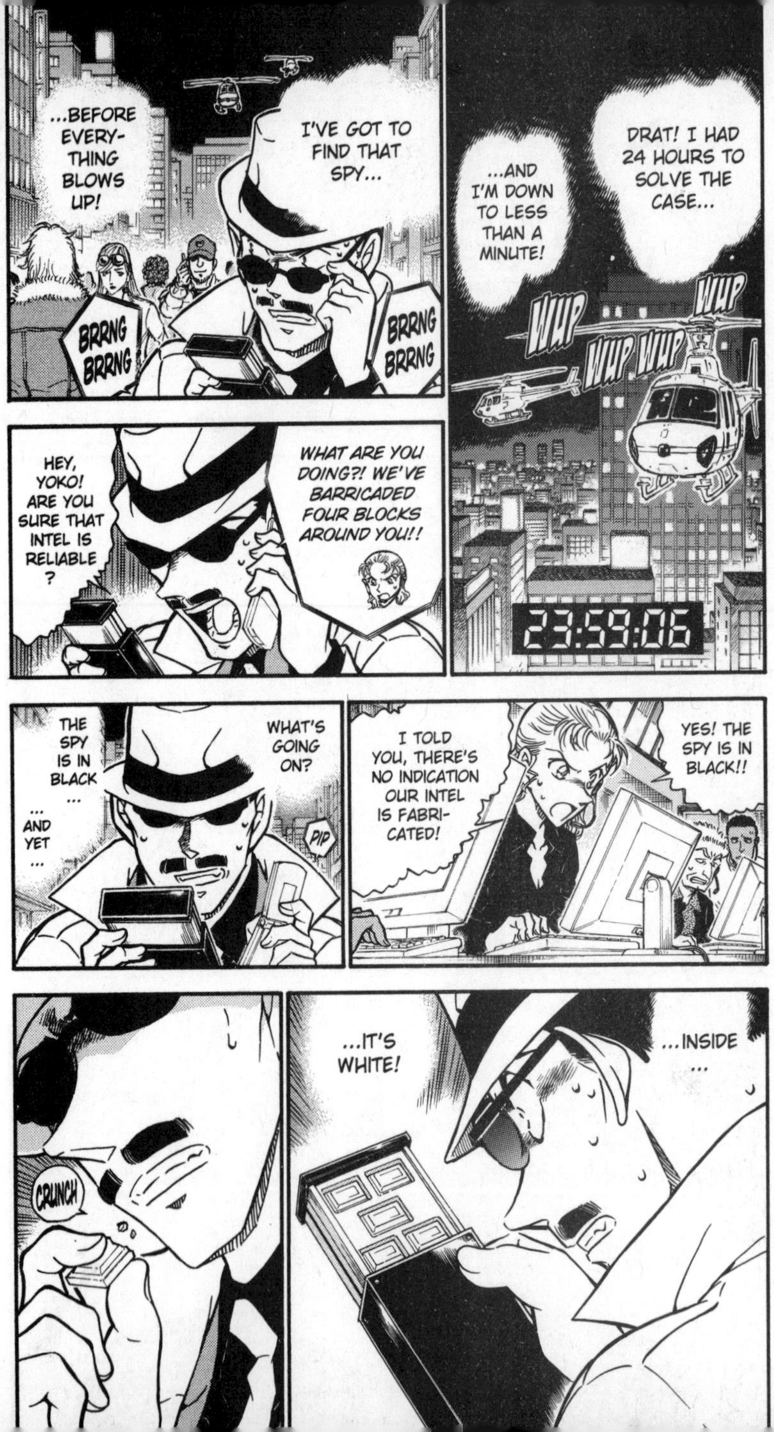
DRAT! I HAD 24 HOURS TO SOLVE THE CASE...
...AND I'M DOWN TO LESS THAN A MINUTE!
WUP
WUP
WUP WUP
23:59:06
I'VE GOT TO FIND THAT SPY...
...BEFORE EVERYTHING BLOWS UP!
BRRNG BRRNG
BRRNG BRRNG
WHAT ARE YOU DOING?! WE'VE BARRICADED FOUR BLOCKS AROUND YOU!!
HEY, YOKO! ARE YOU SURE THAT INTEL IS RELIABLE?
YES! THE SPY IS IN BLACK!!
I TOLD YOU, THERE'S NO INDICATION OUR INTEL IS FABRICATED!
WHAT'S GOING ON?
PIP
THE SPY IS IN BLACK...
...AND YET...
...INSIDE...
...IT'S WHITE!
CRUNCH

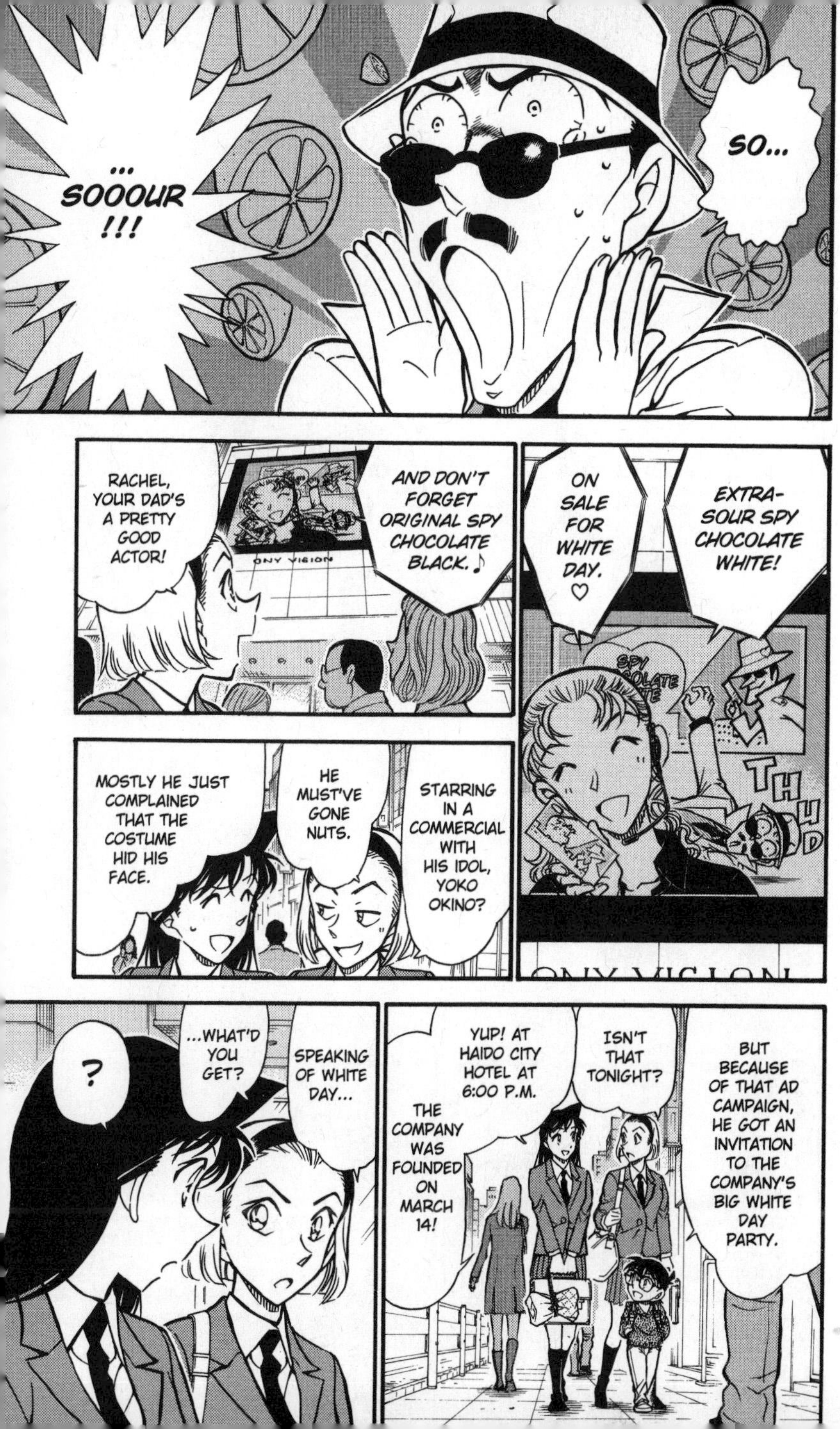
SO...
... SOOOUR !!!
EXTRA-SOUR SPY CHOCOLATE WHITE!
ON SALE FOR WHITE DAY. ♡
THUD
ONY VISION
AND DON'T FORGET ORIGINAL SPY CHOCOLATE BLACK. ♪
RACHEL, YOUR DAD'S A PRETTY GOOD ACTOR!
ONY VISION
STARRING IN A COMMERCIAL WITH HIS IDOL, YOKO OKINO?
HE MUST'VE GONE NUTS.
MOSTLY HE JUST COMPLAINED THAT THE COSTUME HID HIS FACE.
BUT BECAUSE OF THAT AD CAMPAIGN, HE GOT AN INVITATION TO THE COMPANY'S BIG WHITE DAY PARTY.
ISN'T THAT TONIGHT?
YUP! AT HAIDO CITY HOTEL AT 6:00 P.M.
THE COMPANY WAS FOUNDED ON MARCH 14!
SPEAKING OF WHITE DAY...
...WHAT'D YOU GET?
?

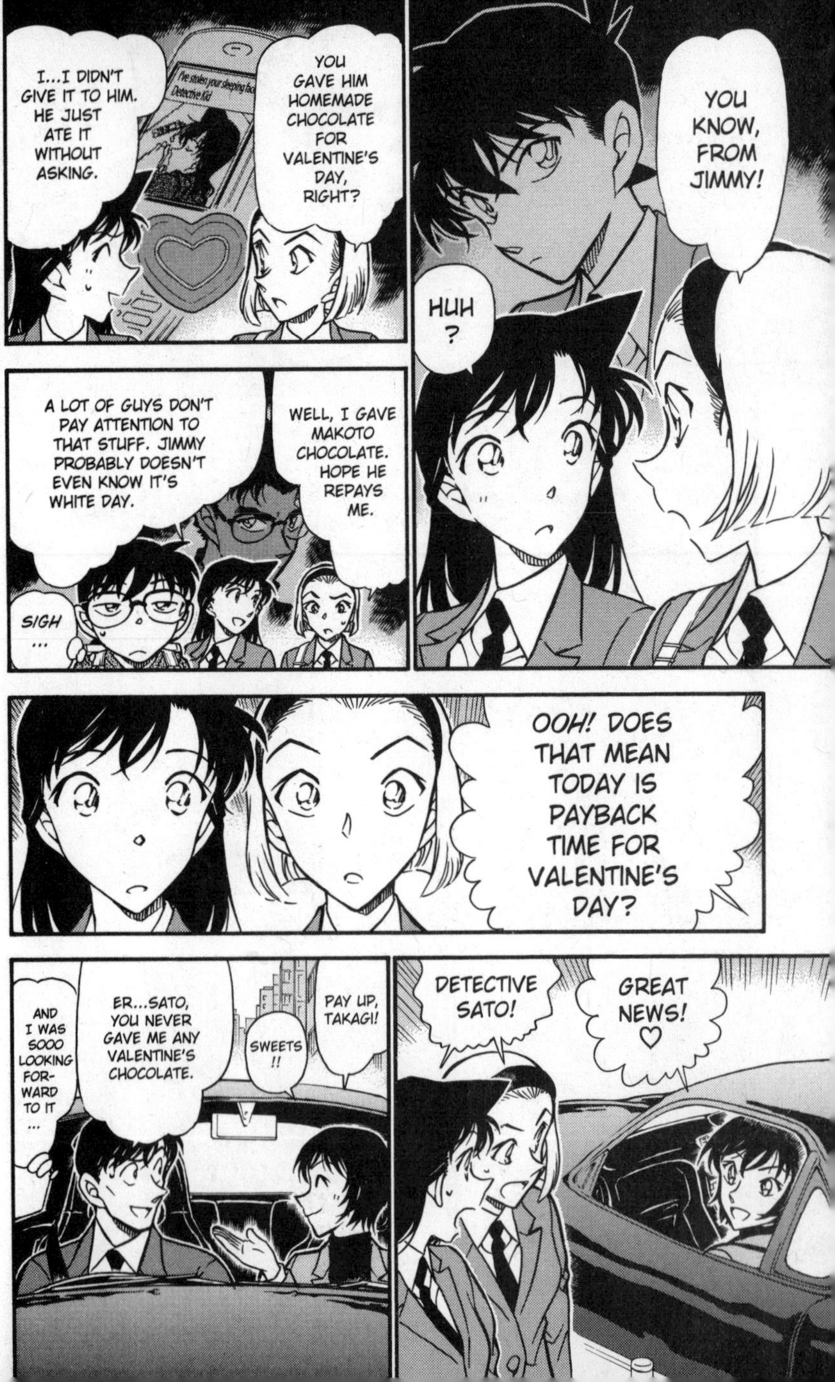
YOU KNOW, FROM JIMMY!
HUH ?
YOU GAVE HIM HOMEMADE CHOCOLATE FOR VALENTINE'S DAY, RIGHT?
I...I DIDN'T GIVE IT TO HIM. HE JUST ATE IT WITHOUT ASKING.
WELL, I GAVE MAKOTO CHOCOLATE. HOPE HE REPAYS ME.
A LOT OF GUYS DON'T PAY ATTENTION TO THAT STUFF. JIMMY PROBABLY DOESN'T EVEN KNOW IT'S WHITE DAY.
SIGH ...
OOH! DOES THAT MEAN TODAY IS PAYBACK TIME FOR VALENTINE'S DAY?
GREAT NEWS! ♡
DETECTIVE SATO!
PAY UP, TAKAGI!
SWEETS !!
ER...SATO, YOU NEVER GAVE ME ANY VALENTINE'S CHOCOLATE.
AND I WAS SOOO LOOKING FOR-WARD TO IT ...

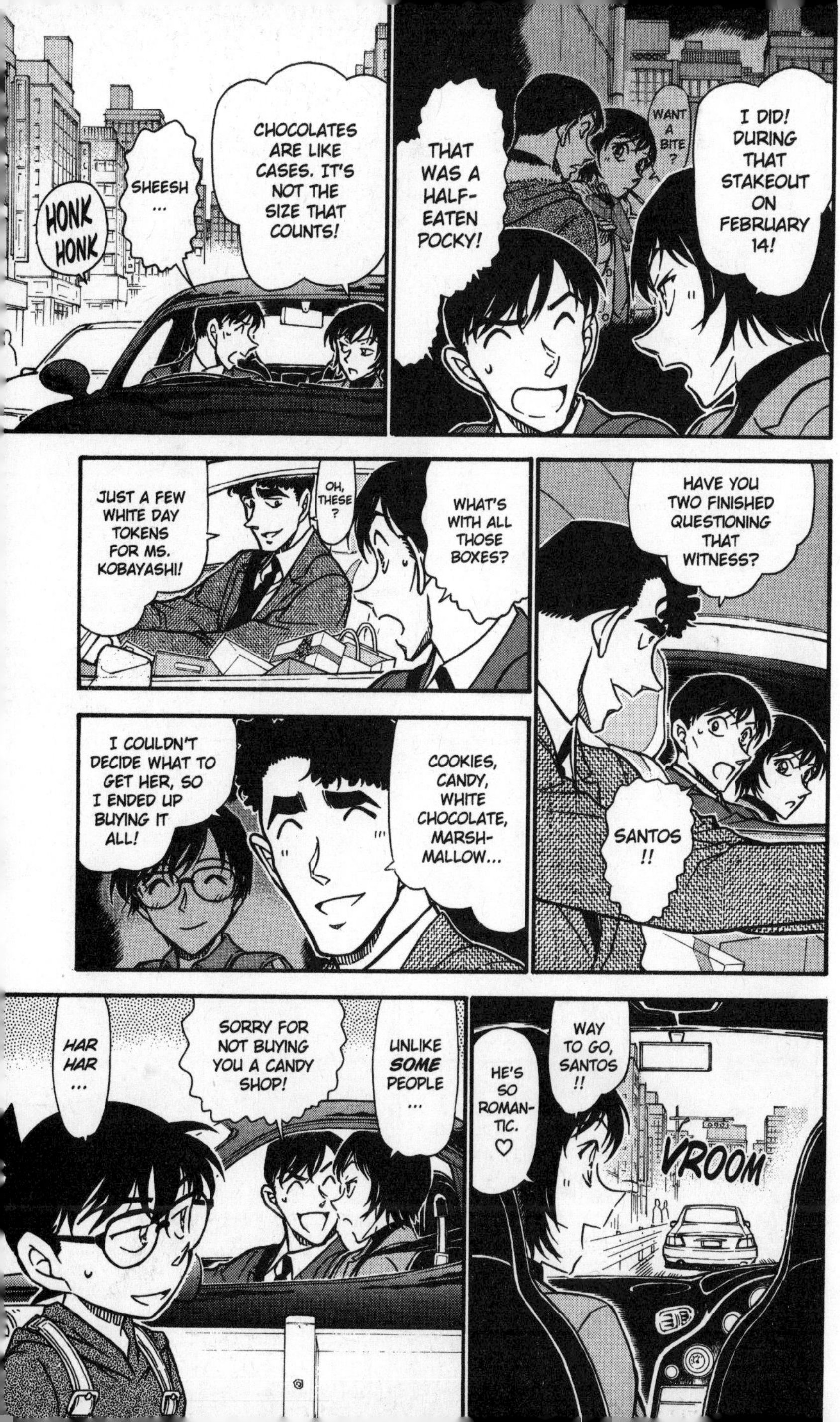
I DID! DURING THAT STAKEOUT ON FEBRUARY 14!
WANT A BITE?
THAT WAS A HALF-EATEN POCKY!
CHOCOLATES ARE LIKE CASES. IT'S NOT THE SIZE THAT COUNTS!
SHEESH...
HONK HONK
HAVE YOU TWO FINISHED QUESTIONING THAT WITNESS?
SANTOS!!
WHAT'S WITH ALL THOSE BOXES?
OH, THESE?
JUST A FEW WHITE DAY TOKENS FOR MS. KOBAYASHI!
COOKIES, CANDY, WHITE CHOCOLATE, MARSH-MALLOW...
I COULDN'T DECIDE WHAT TO GET HER, SO I ENDED UP BUYING IT ALL!
WAY TO GO, SANTOS!!
HE'S SO ROMAN-TIC. ♡
VROOM
UNLIKE *SOME* PEOPLE...
SORRY FOR NOT BUYING YOU A CANDY SHOP!
HAR HAR...

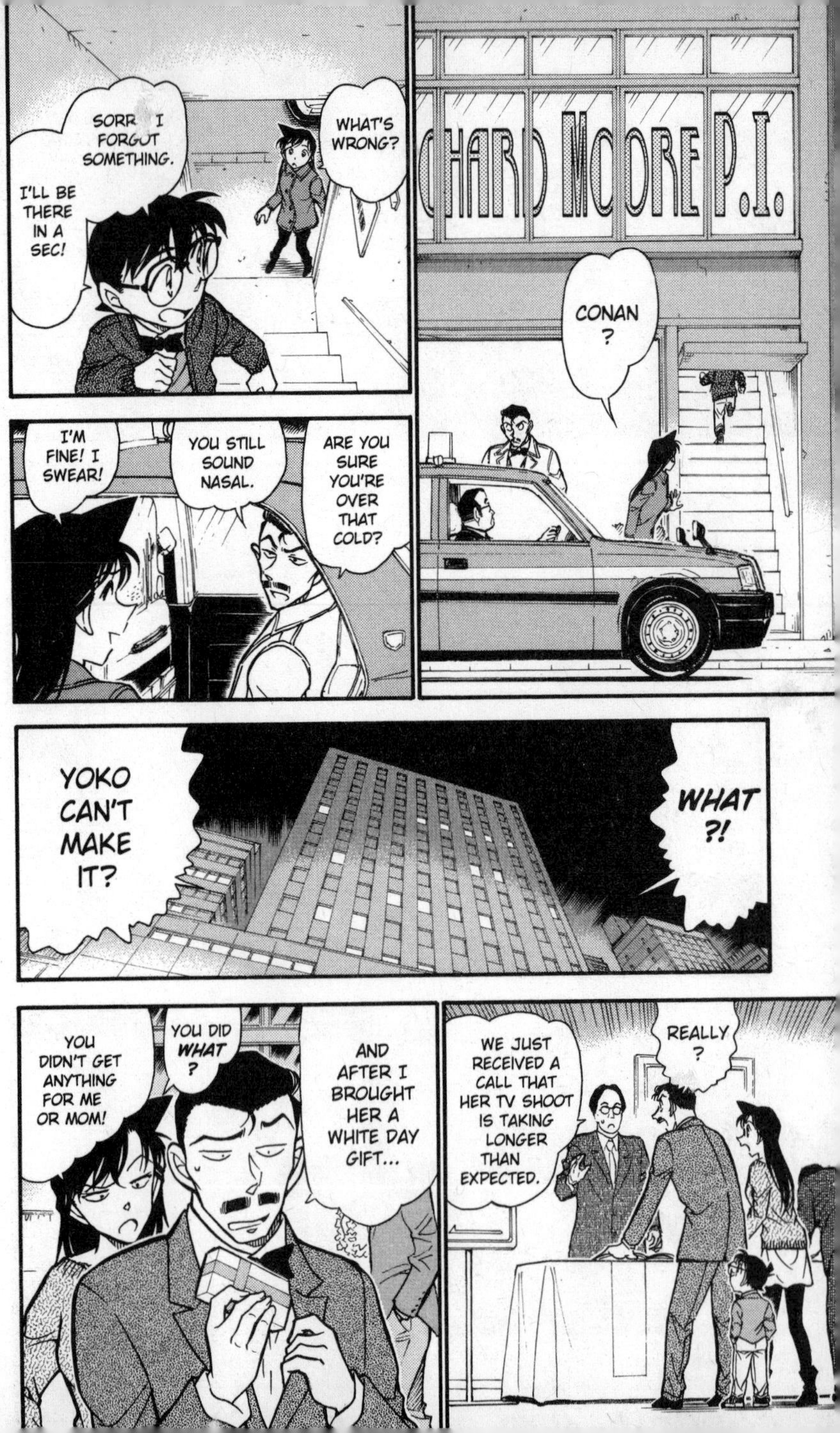
CHARD MOORE P.I.
CONAN?
WHAT'S WRONG?
SORRY I FORGOT SOMETHING.
I'LL BE THERE IN A SEC!
ARE YOU SURE YOU'RE OVER THAT COLD?
YOU STILL SOUND NASAL.
I'M FINE! I SWEAR!
WHAT?!
YOKO CAN'T MAKE IT?
REALLY?
WE JUST RECEIVED A CALL THAT HER TV SHOOT IS TAKING LONGER THAN EXPECTED.
AND AFTER I BROUGHT HER A WHITE DAY GIFT...
YOU DID WHAT?
YOU DIDN'T GET ANYTHING FOR ME OR MOM!

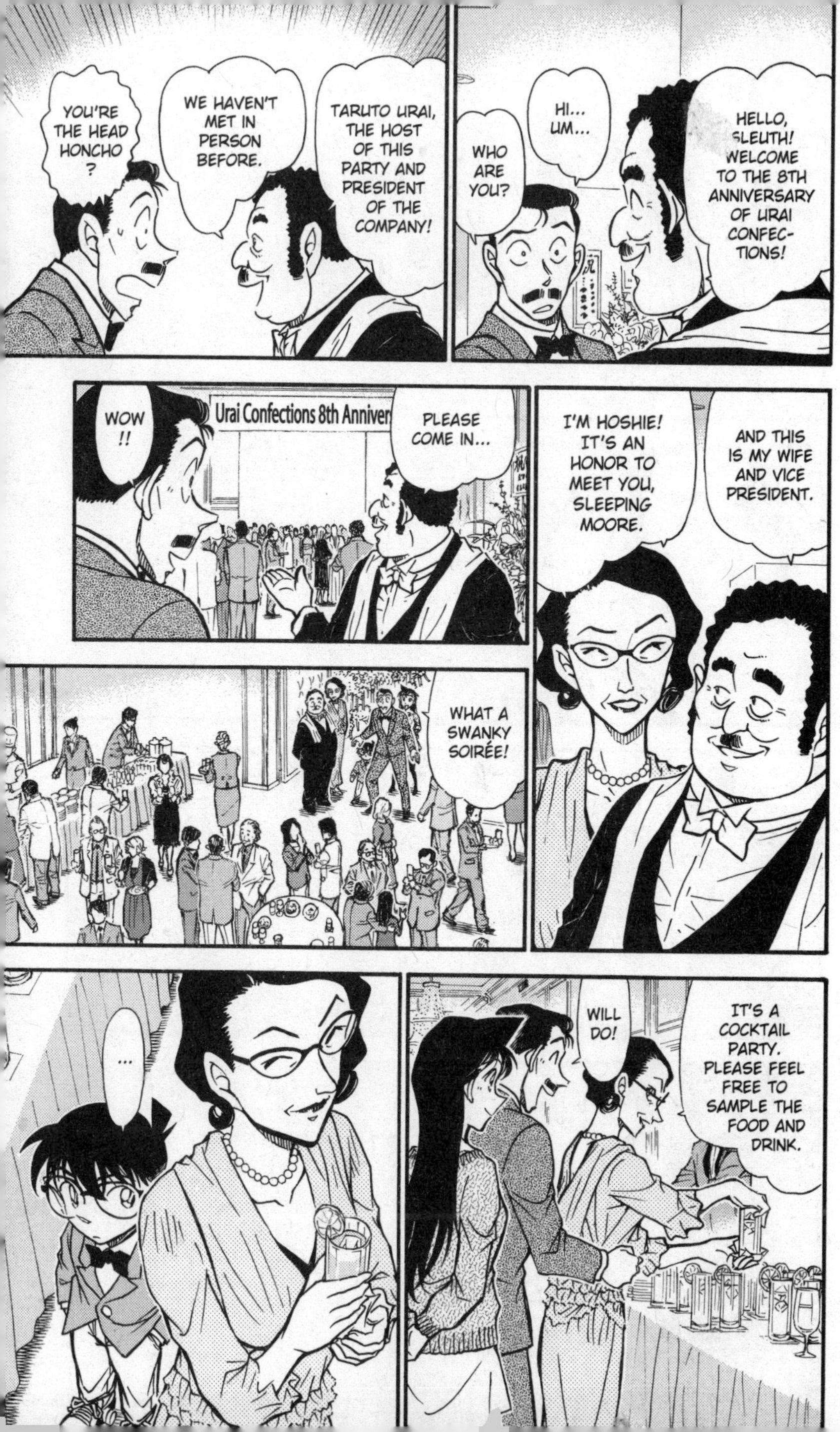
HELLO, SLEUTH! WELCOME TO THE 8TH ANNIVERSARY OF URAI CONFECTIONS!
HI... UM...
WHO ARE YOU?
TARUTO URAI, THE HOST OF THIS PARTY AND PRESIDENT OF THE COMPANY!
WE HAVEN'T MET IN PERSON BEFORE.
YOU'RE THE HEAD HONCHO?
AND THIS IS MY WIFE AND VICE PRESIDENT.
I'M HOSHIE! IT'S AN HONOR TO MEET YOU, SLEEPING MOORE.
Urai Confections 8th Annivers
PLEASE COME IN...
WOW!!
WHAT A SWANKY SOIRÉE!
IT'S A COCKTAIL PARTY. PLEASE FEEL FREE TO SAMPLE THE FOOD AND DRINK.
WILL DO!
...

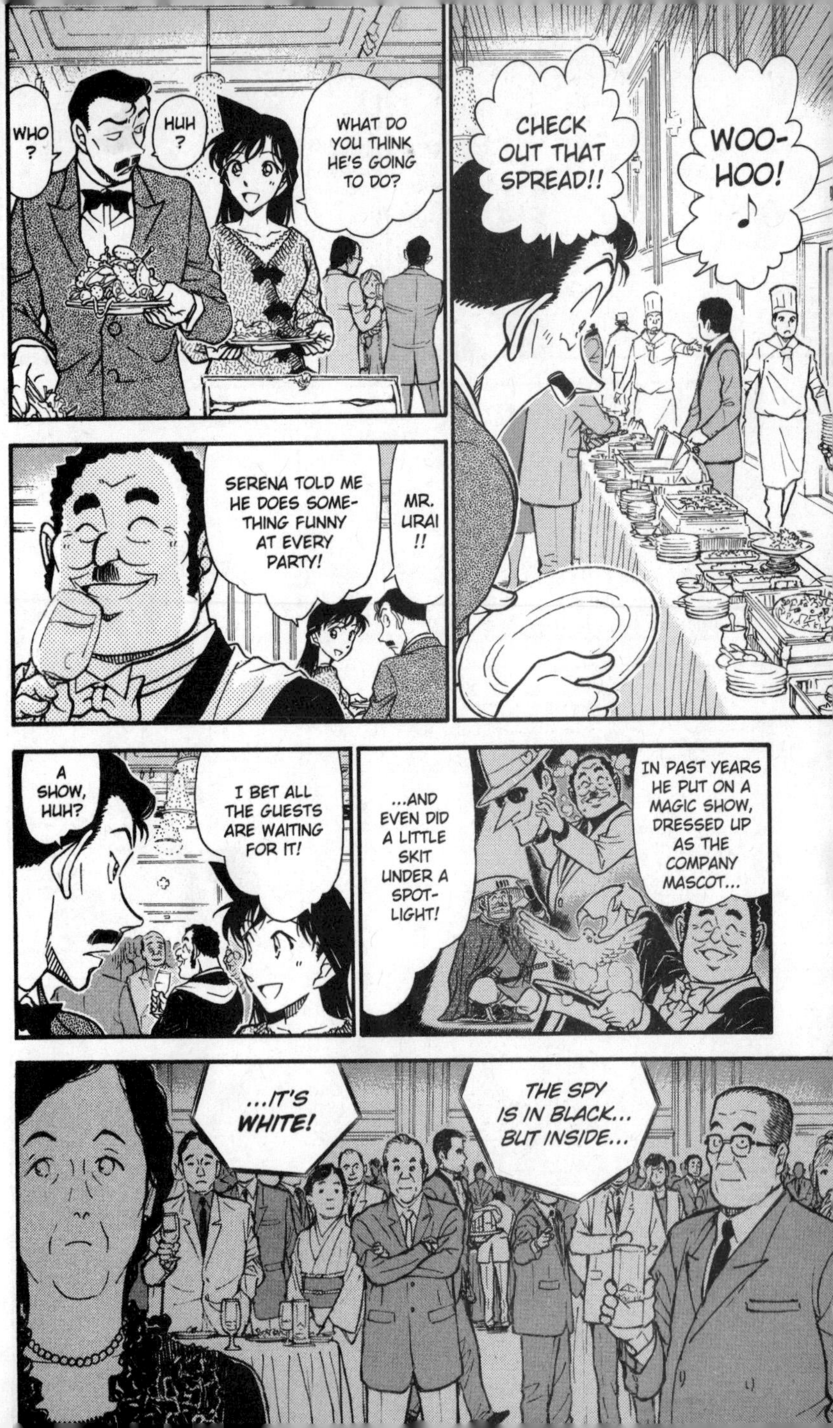
WOO-HOO! ♪
CHECK OUT THAT SPREAD!!
WHAT DO YOU THINK HE'S GOING TO DO?
HUH?
WHO?
MR. URAI!!
SERENA TOLD ME HE DOES SOME-THING FUNNY AT EVERY PARTY!
IN PAST YEARS HE PUT ON A MAGIC SHOW, DRESSED UP AS THE COMPANY MASCOT...
...AND EVEN DID A LITTLE SKIT UNDER A SPOT-LIGHT!
I BET ALL THE GUESTS ARE WAITING FOR IT!
A SHOW, HUH?
THE SPY IS IN BLACK... BUT INSIDE...
...IT'S WHITE!

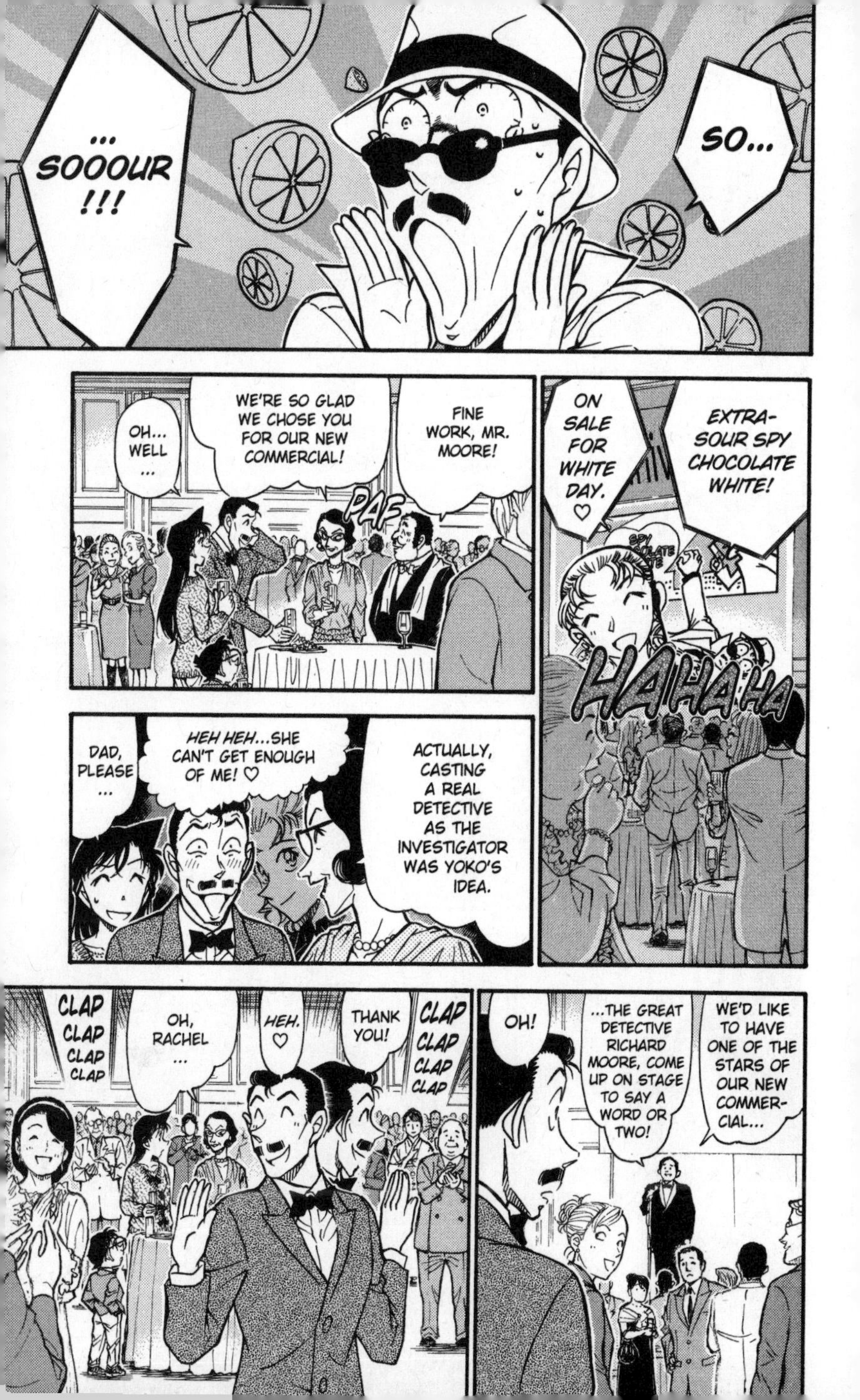
SO...
... SOOOUR !!!
EXTRA-SOUR SPY CHOCOLATE WHITE!
ON SALE FOR WHITE DAY. ♡
HAHAHA
FINE WORK, MR. MOORE!
WE'RE SO GLAD WE CHOSE YOU FOR OUR NEW COMMERCIAL!
PAF
OH... WELL ...
ACTUALLY, CASTING A REAL DETECTIVE AS THE INVESTIGATOR WAS YOKO'S IDEA.
HEH HEH...SHE CAN'T GET ENOUGH OF ME! ♡
DAD, PLEASE ...
WE'D LIKE TO HAVE ONE OF THE STARS OF OUR NEW COMMER-CIAL...
...THE GREAT DETECTIVE RICHARD MOORE, COME UP ON STAGE TO SAY A WORD OR TWO!
OH!
CLAP CLAP CLAP CLAP
THANK YOU!
HEH. ♡
OH, RACHEL ...
CLAP CLAP CLAP CLAP

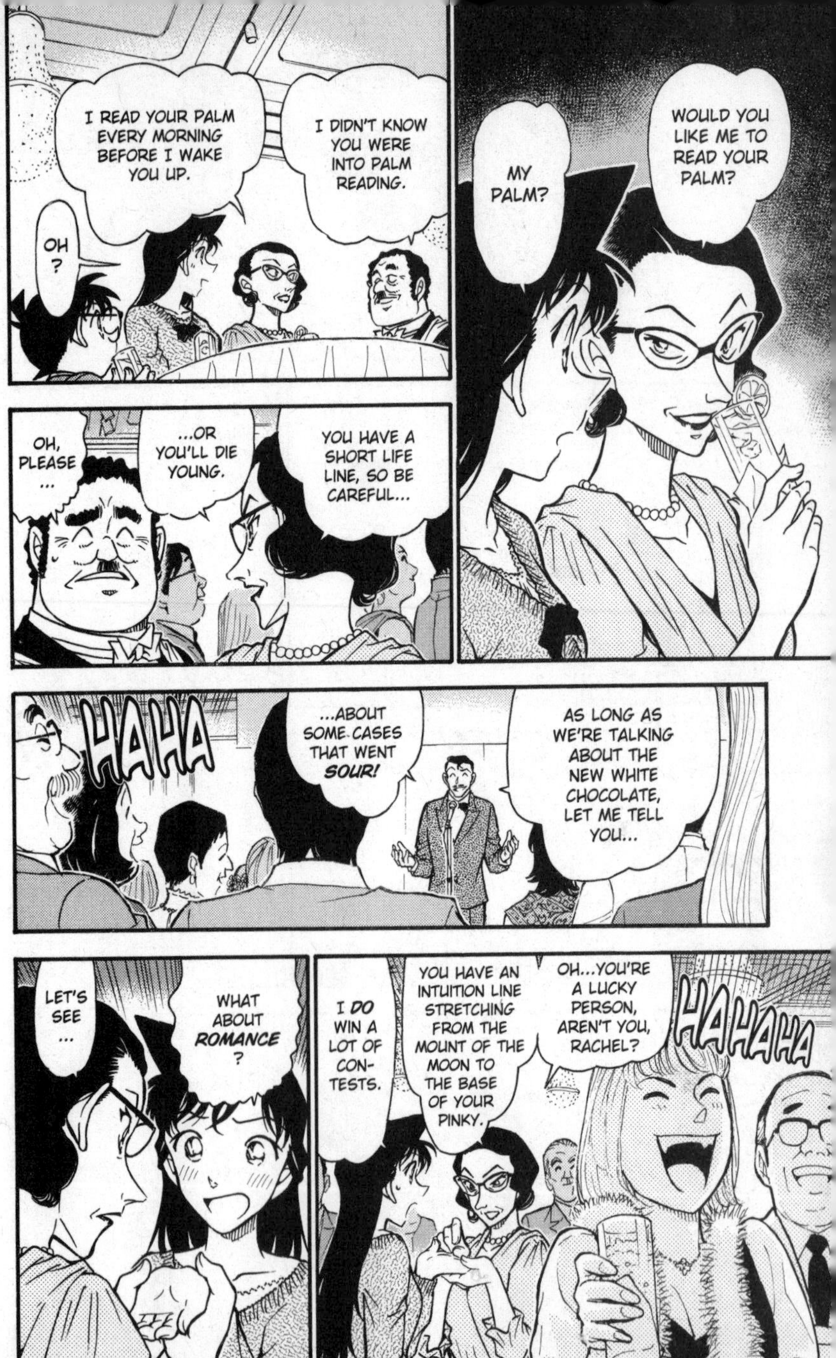
WOULD YOU LIKE ME TO READ YOUR PALM?
MY PALM?
I DIDN'T KNOW YOU WERE INTO PALM READING.
I READ YOUR PALM EVERY MORNING BEFORE I WAKE YOU UP.
OH?
YOU HAVE A SHORT LIFE LINE, SO BE CAREFUL...
...OR YOU'LL DIE YOUNG.
OH, PLEASE...
AS LONG AS WE'RE TALKING ABOUT THE NEW WHITE CHOCOLATE, LET ME TELL YOU...
...ABOUT SOME CASES THAT WENT *SOUR!*
HAHA
HAHAHA
OH...YOU'RE A LUCKY PERSON, AREN'T YOU, RACHEL?
YOU HAVE AN INTUITION LINE STRETCHING FROM THE MOUNT OF THE MOON TO THE BASE OF YOUR PINKY.
I *DO* WIN A LOT OF CON-TESTS.
WHAT ABOUT *ROMANCE*?
LET'S SEE...

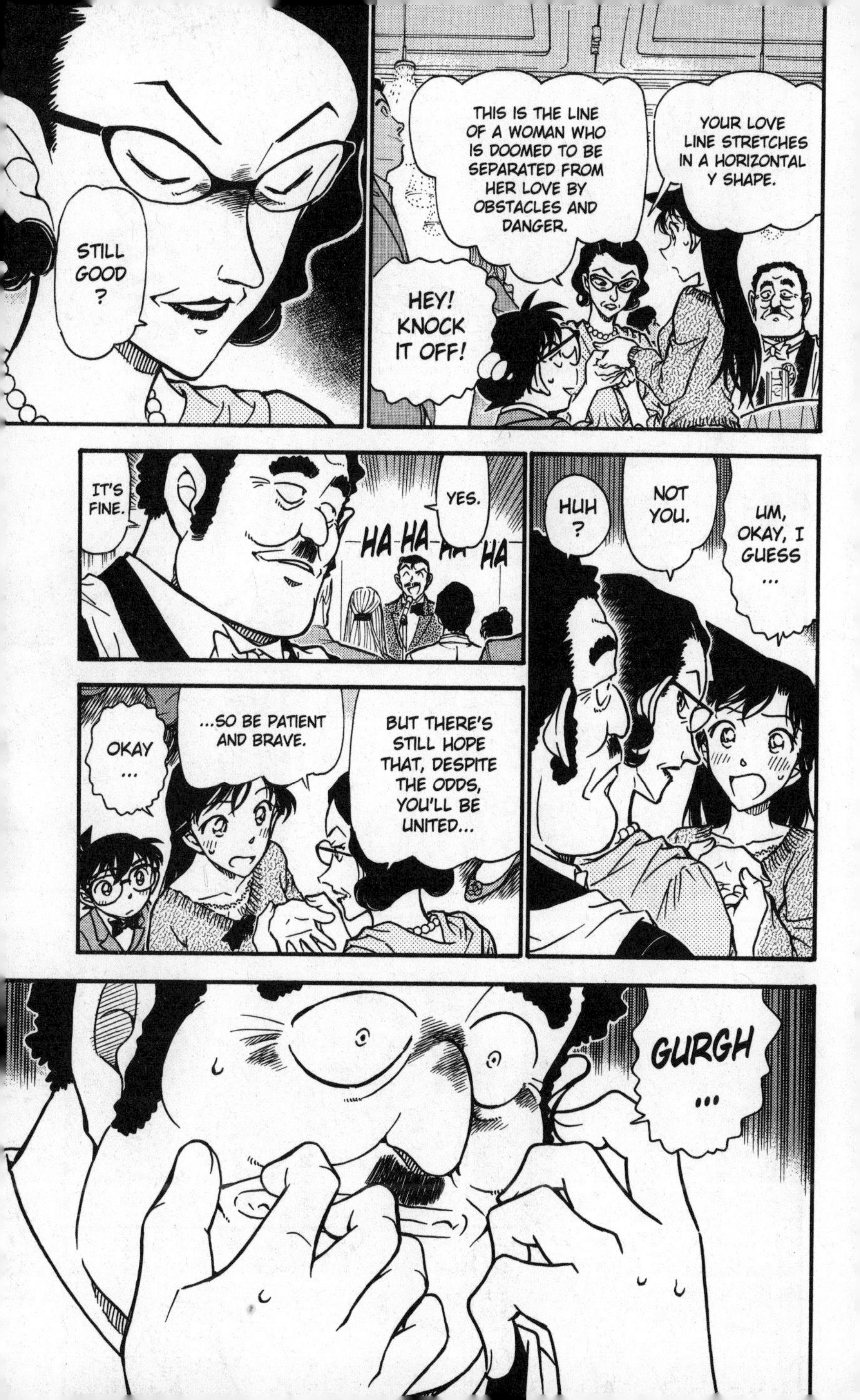
YOUR LOVE LINE STRETCHES IN A HORIZONTAL Y SHAPE.
THIS IS THE LINE OF A WOMAN WHO IS DOOMED TO BE SEPARATED FROM HER LOVE BY OBSTACLES AND DANGER.
HEY! KNOCK IT OFF!
STILL GOOD?
UM, OKAY, I GUESS...
NOT YOU.
HUH?
YES.
HA HA HA HA
IT'S FINE.
BUT THERE'S STILL HOPE THAT, DESPITE THE ODDS, YOU'LL BE UNITED...
...SO BE PATIENT AND BRAVE.
OKAY...
GURGH...

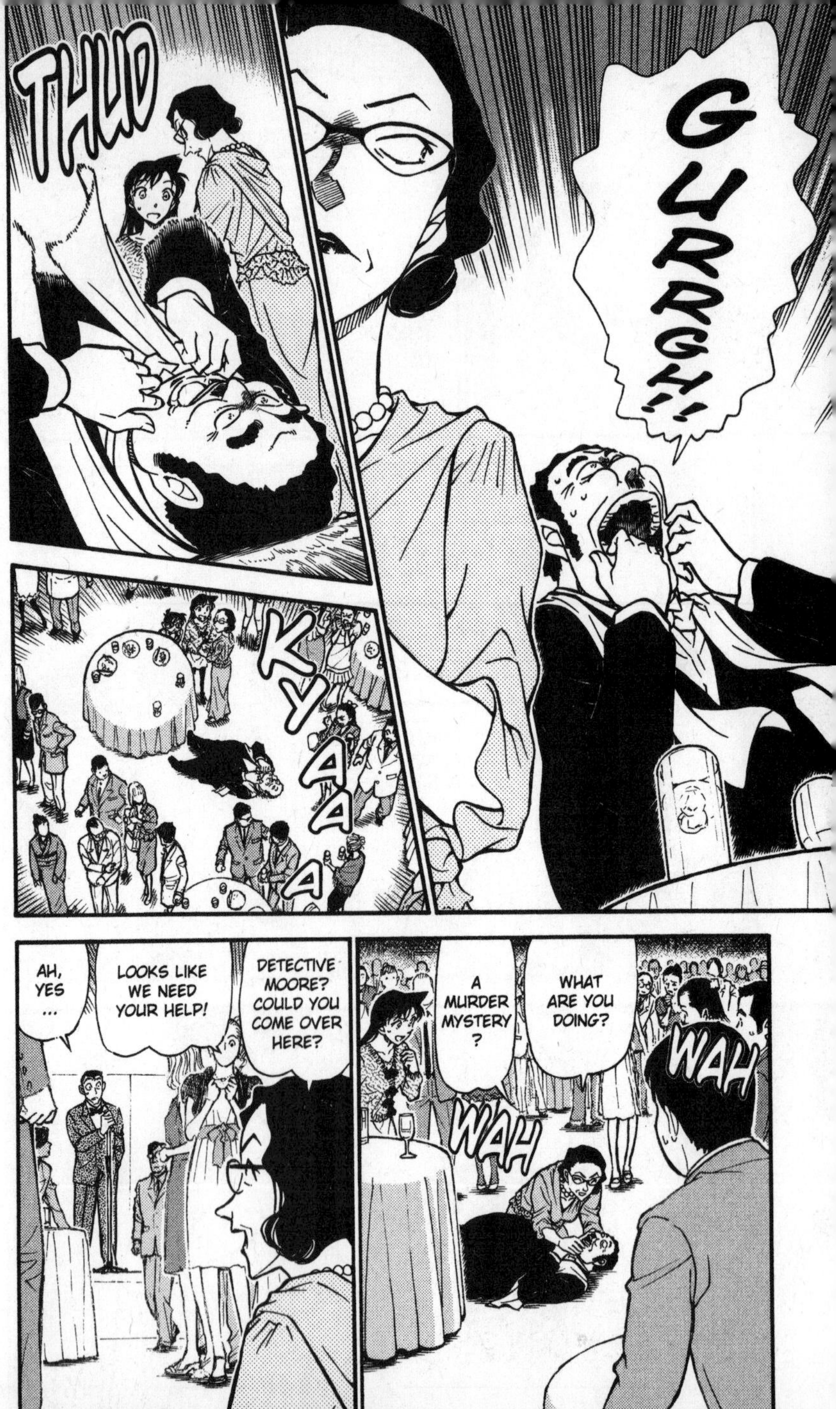
GURRGH!!
THUD
KYAAA
WHAT ARE YOU DOING?
A MURDER MYSTERY?
WAH
WAH
DETECTIVE MOORE? COULD YOU COME OVER HERE?
LOOKS LIKE WE NEED YOUR HELP!
AH, YES ...

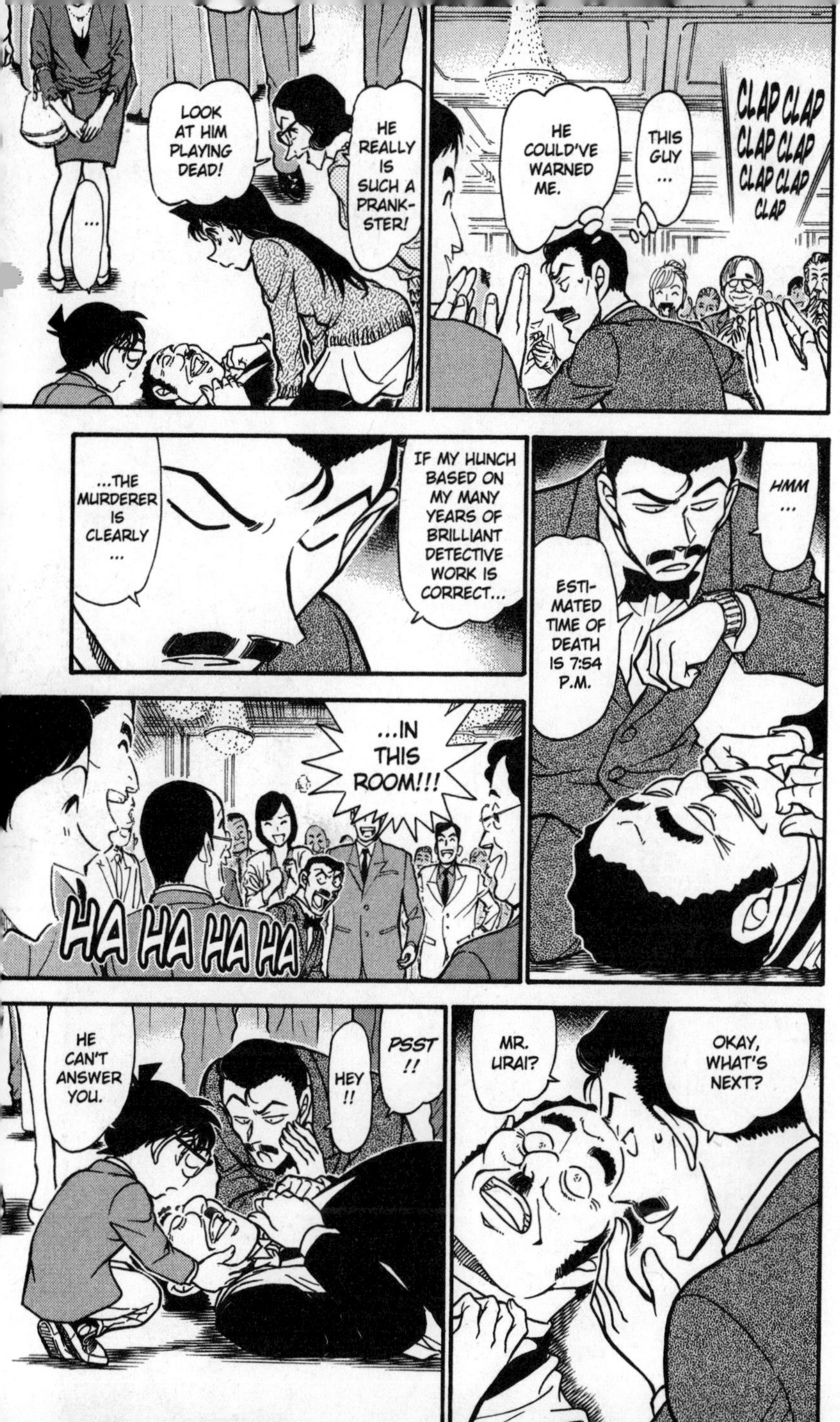
CLAP CLAP CLAP CLAP CLAP CLAP CLAP
THIS GUY ...
HE COULD'VE WARNED ME.
HE REALLY IS SUCH A PRANKSTER!
LOOK AT HIM PLAYING DEAD!
...
HMM ...
ESTIMATED TIME OF DEATH IS 7:54 P.M.
IF MY HUNCH BASED ON MY MANY YEARS OF BRILLIANT DETECTIVE WORK IS CORRECT...
...THE MURDERER IS CLEARLY ...
...IN THIS ROOM!!!
HA HA HA HA
OKAY, WHAT'S NEXT?
MR. URAI?
PSST !!
HEY !!
HE CAN'T ANSWER YOU.

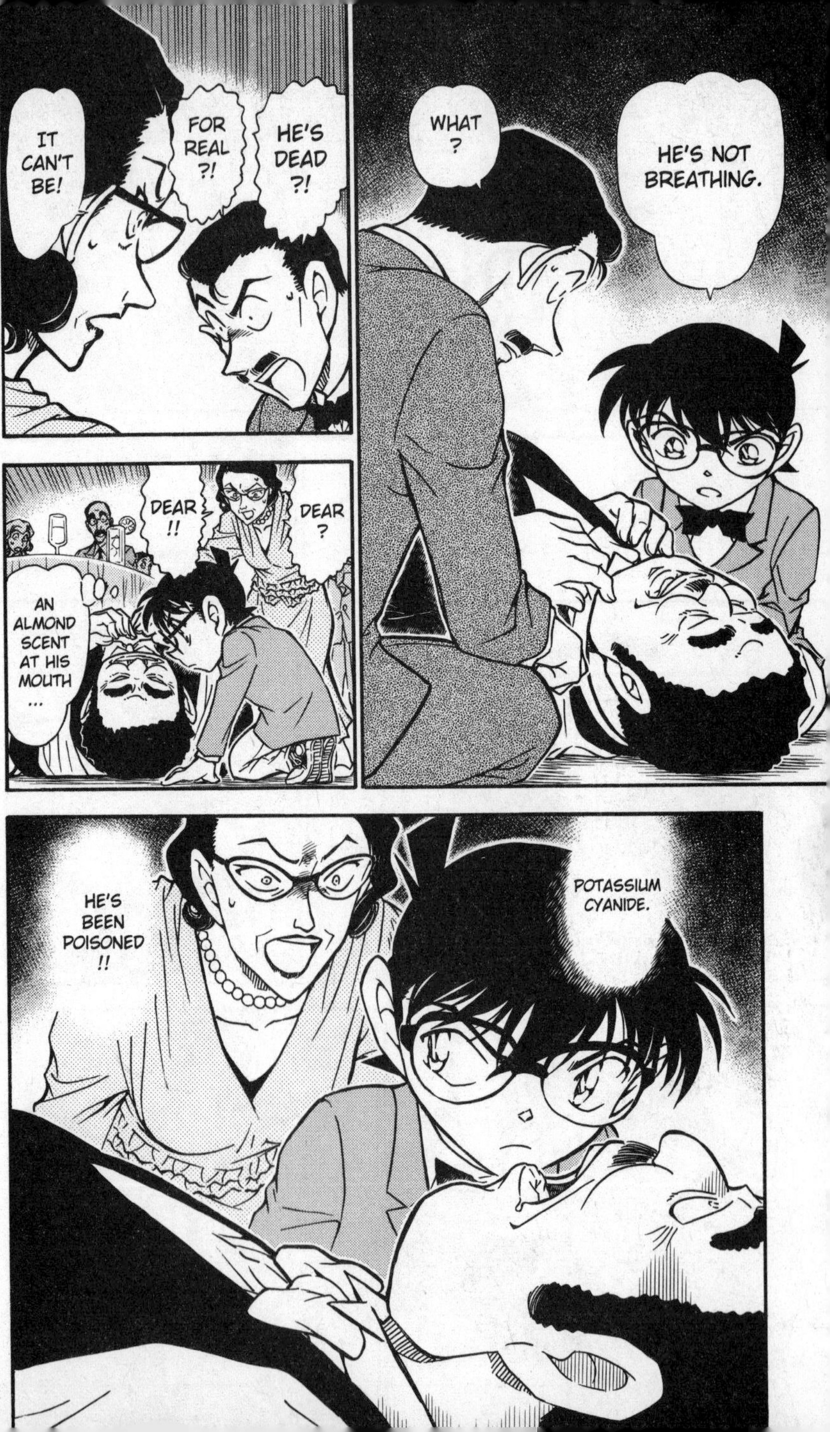
HE'S NOT BREATHING.
WHAT?
HE'S DEAD?!
FOR REAL?!
IT CAN'T BE!
DEAR?
DEAR!!
AN ALMOND SCENT AT HIS MOUTH...
POTASSIUM CYANIDE.
HE'S BEEN POISONED!!

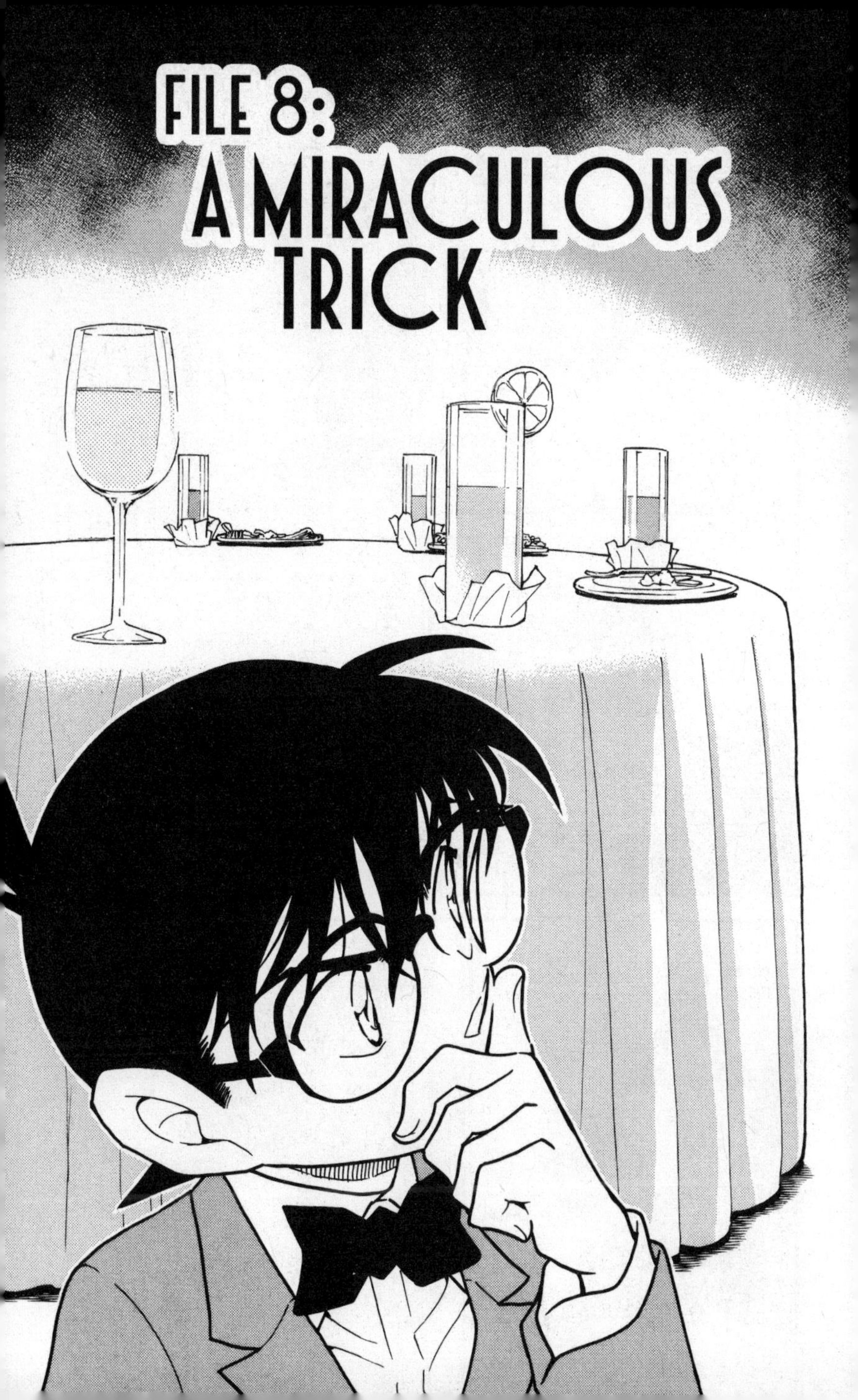
FILE 8:
A MIRACULOUS TRICK

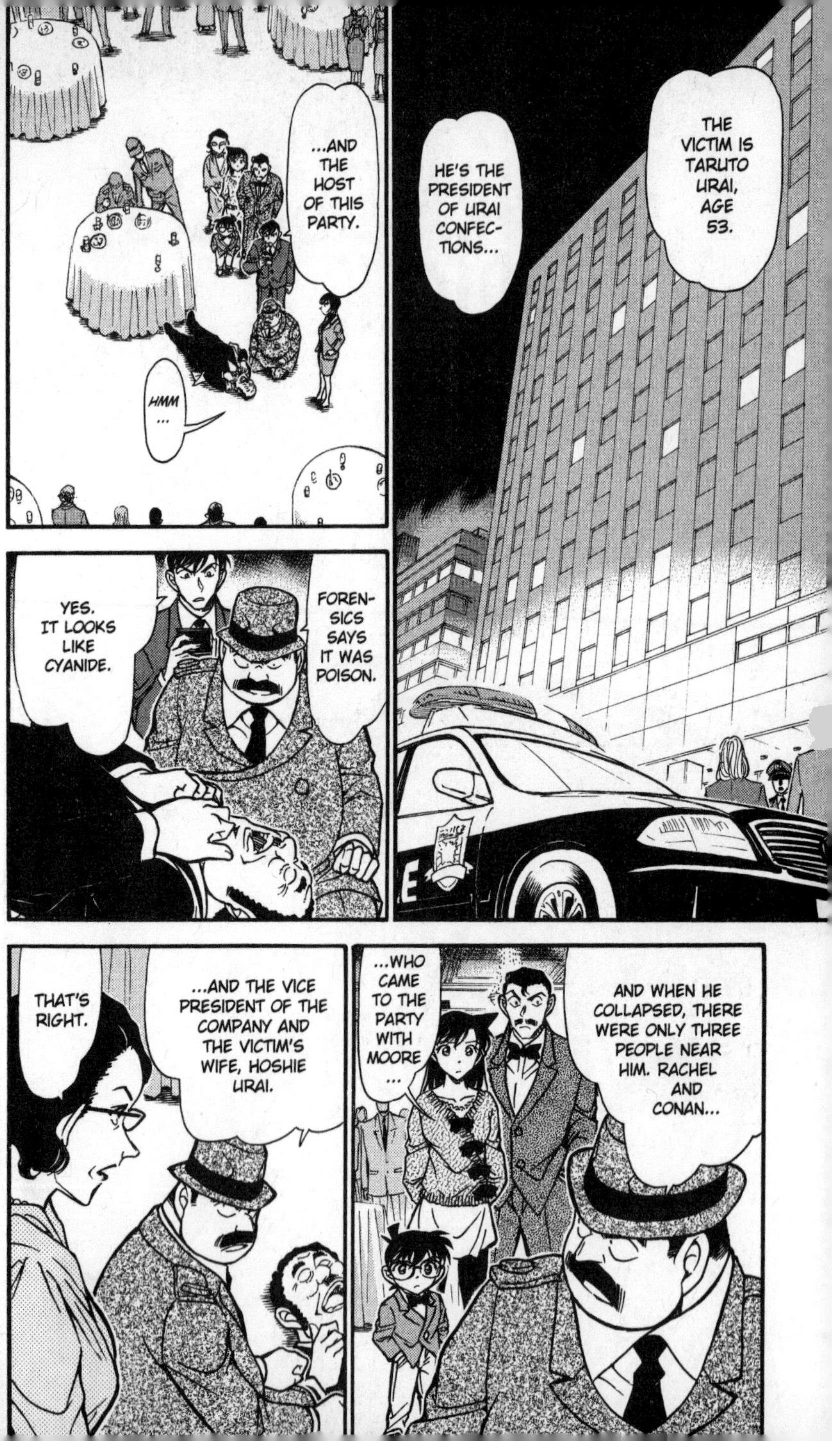
THE VICTIM IS TARUTO URAI, AGE 53.
HE'S THE PRESIDENT OF URAI CONFEC-TIONS...
...AND THE HOST OF THIS PARTY.
HMM ...
FOREN-SICS SAYS IT WAS POISON.
YES. IT LOOKS LIKE CYANIDE.
AND WHEN HE COLLAPSED, THERE WERE ONLY THREE PEOPLE NEAR HIM. RACHEL AND CONAN...
...WHO CAME TO THE PARTY WITH MOORE ...
...AND THE VICE PRESIDENT OF THE COMPANY AND THE VICTIM'S WIFE, HOSHIE URAI.
THAT'S RIGHT.

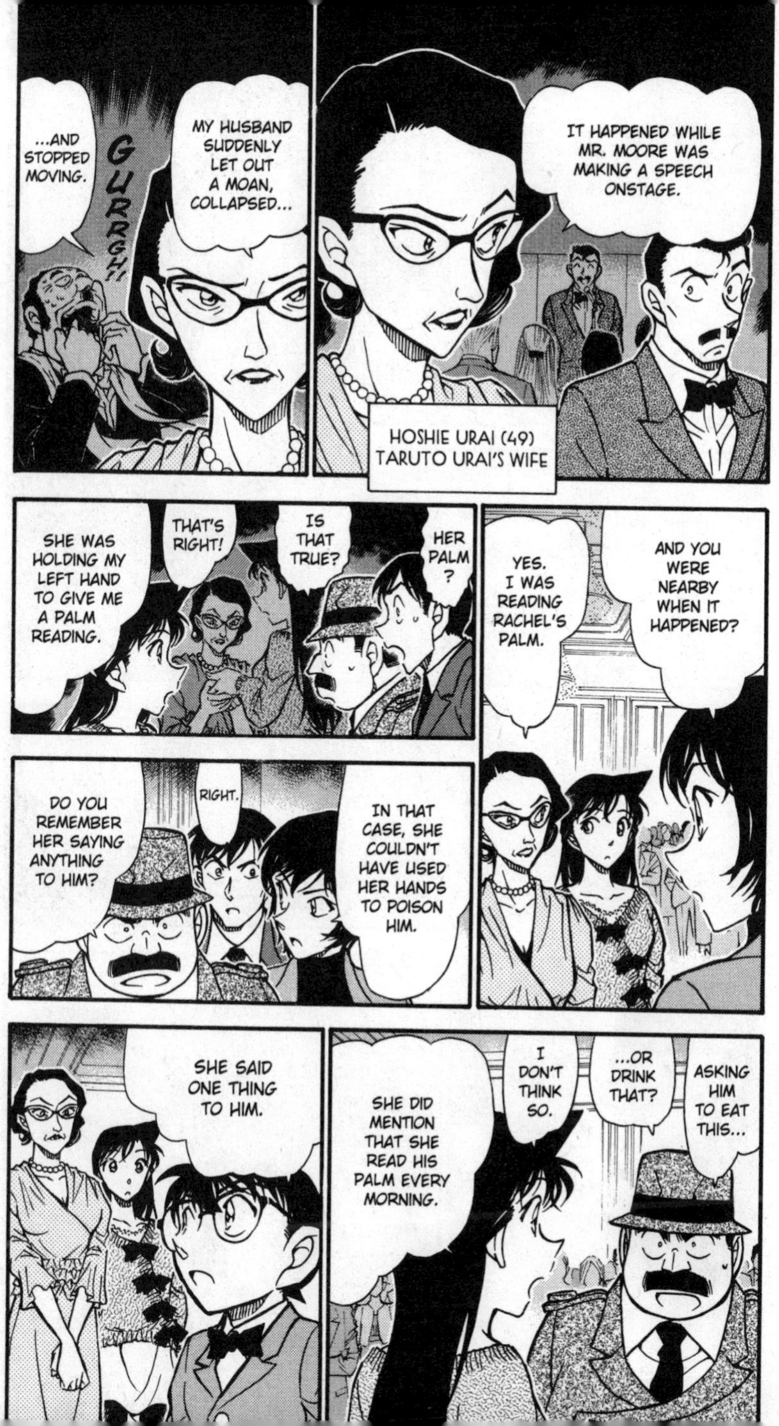
IT HAPPENED WHILE MR. MOORE WAS MAKING A SPEECH ONSTAGE.
HOSHIE URAI (49) TARUTO URAI'S WIFE
MY HUSBAND SUDDENLY LET OUT A MOAN, COLLAPSED...
GURRGH!!
...AND STOPPED MOVING.
AND YOU WERE NEARBY WHEN IT HAPPENED?
YES. I WAS READING RACHEL'S PALM.
HER PALM?
IS THAT TRUE?
THAT'S RIGHT!
SHE WAS HOLDING MY LEFT HAND TO GIVE ME A PALM READING.
IN THAT CASE, SHE COULDN'T HAVE USED HER HANDS TO POISON HIM.
RIGHT.
DO YOU REMEMBER HER SAYING ANYTHING TO HIM?
ASKING HIM TO EAT THIS...
...OR DRINK THAT?
I DON'T THINK SO.
SHE DID MENTION THAT SHE READ HIS PALM EVERY MORNING.
SHE SAID ONE THING TO HIM.

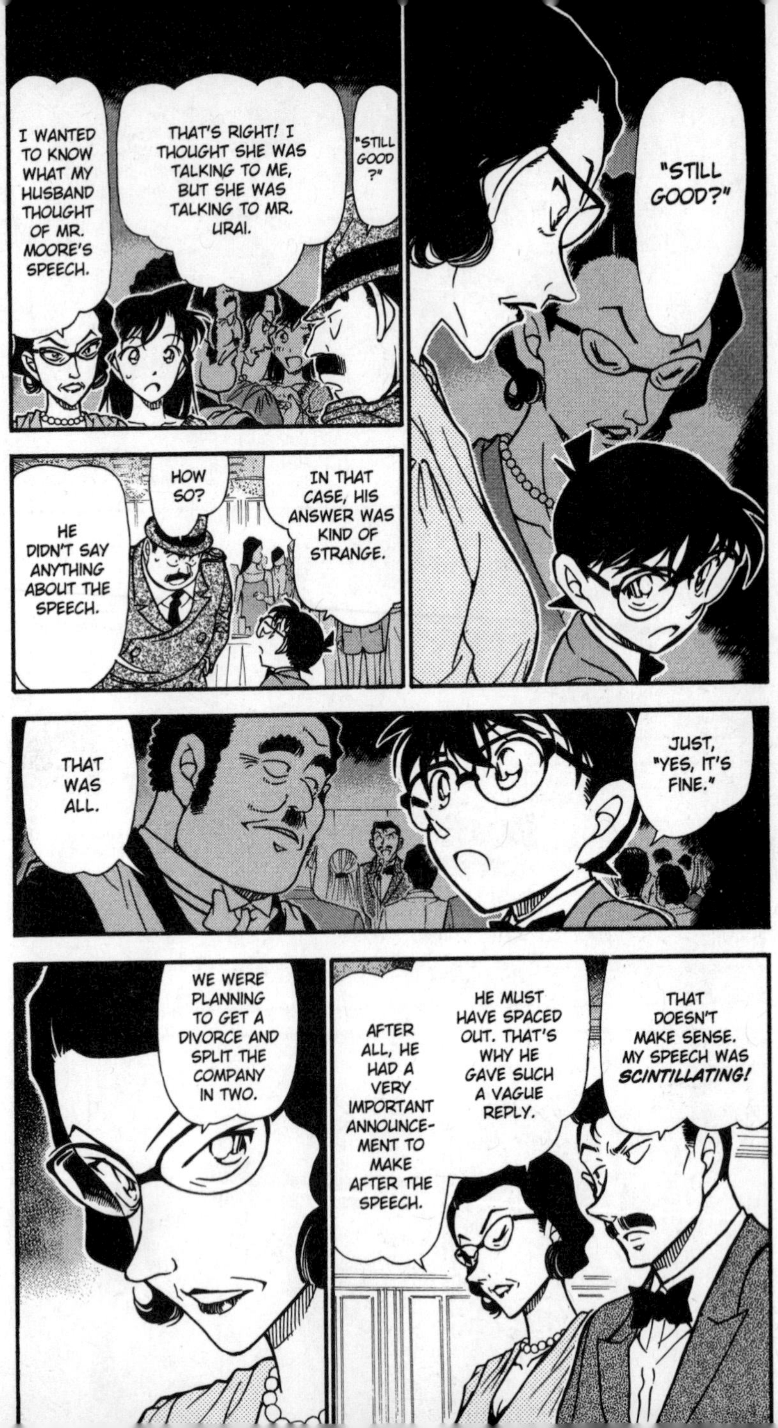
"STILL GOOD?"
"STILL GOOD?"
THAT'S RIGHT! I THOUGHT SHE WAS TALKING TO ME, BUT SHE WAS TALKING TO MR. URAI.
I WANTED TO KNOW WHAT MY HUSBAND THOUGHT OF MR. MOORE'S SPEECH.
IN THAT CASE, HIS ANSWER WAS KIND OF STRANGE.
HOW SO?
HE DIDN'T SAY ANYTHING ABOUT THE SPEECH.
JUST, "YES, IT'S FINE."
THAT WAS ALL.
THAT DOESN'T MAKE SENSE. MY SPEECH WAS *SCINTILLATING!*
HE MUST HAVE SPACED OUT. THAT'S WHY HE GAVE SUCH A VAGUE REPLY.
AFTER ALL, HE HAD A VERY IMPORTANT ANNOUNCEMENT TO MAKE AFTER THE SPEECH.
WE WERE PLANNING TO GET A DIVORCE AND SPLIT THE COMPANY IN TWO.

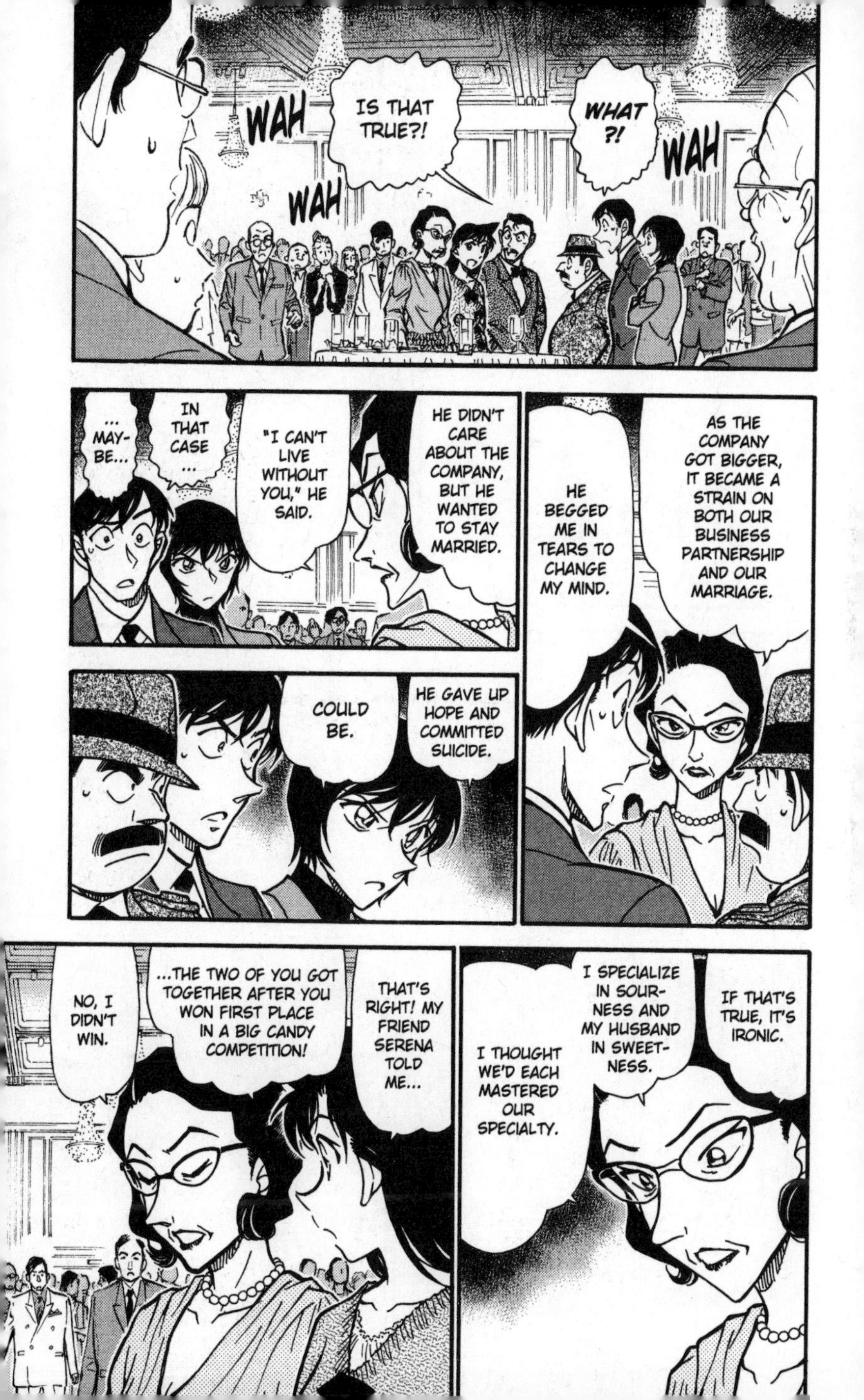
WHAT ?!
WAH
IS THAT TRUE?!
WAH
WAH
AS THE COMPANY GOT BIGGER, IT BECAME A STRAIN ON BOTH OUR BUSINESS PARTNERSHIP AND OUR MARRIAGE.
HE BEGGED ME IN TEARS TO CHANGE MY MIND.
HE DIDN'T CARE ABOUT THE COMPANY, BUT HE WANTED TO STAY MARRIED.
"I CAN'T LIVE WITHOUT YOU," HE SAID.
IN THAT CASE...
...MAYBE...
HE GAVE UP HOPE AND COMMITTED SUICIDE.
COULD BE.
IF THAT'S TRUE, IT'S IRONIC.
I SPECIALIZE IN SOURNESS AND MY HUSBAND IN SWEETNESS.
I THOUGHT WE'D EACH MASTERED OUR SPECIALTY.
THAT'S RIGHT! MY FRIEND SERENA TOLD ME...
...THE TWO OF YOU GOT TOGETHER AFTER YOU WON FIRST PLACE IN A BIG CANDY COMPETITION!
NO, I DIDN'T WIN.

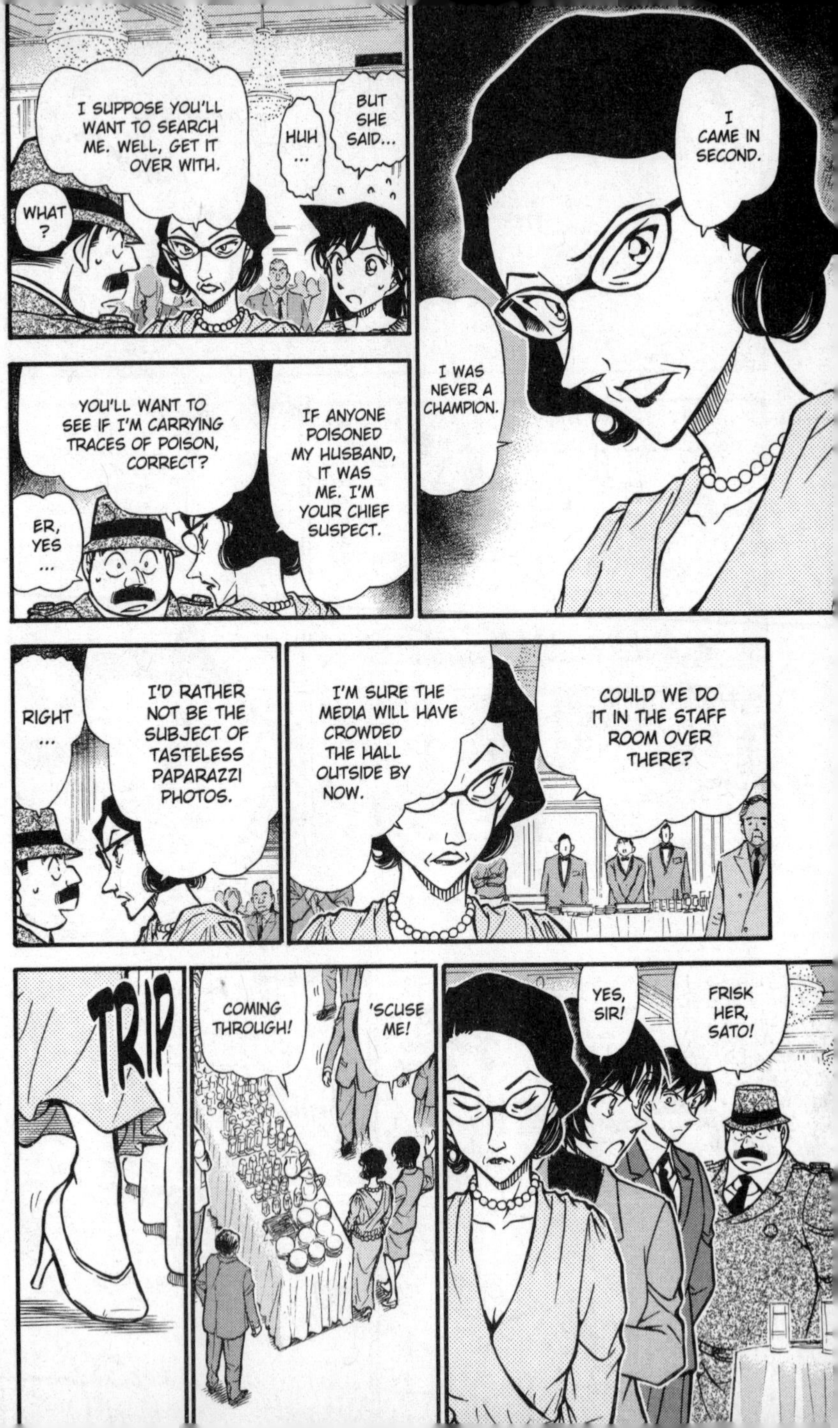
I CAME IN SECOND.
I WAS NEVER A CHAMPION.
BUT SHE SAID...
HUH...
I SUPPOSE YOU'LL WANT TO SEARCH ME. WELL, GET IT OVER WITH.
WHAT?
IF ANYONE POISONED MY HUSBAND, IT WAS ME. I'M YOUR CHIEF SUSPECT.
YOU'LL WANT TO SEE IF I'M CARRYING TRACES OF POISON, CORRECT?
ER, YES...
COULD WE DO IT IN THE STAFF ROOM OVER THERE?
I'M SURE THE MEDIA WILL HAVE CROWDED THE HALL OUTSIDE BY NOW.
I'D RATHER NOT BE THE SUBJECT OF TASTELESS PAPARAZZI PHOTOS.
RIGHT...
FRISK HER, SATO!
YES, SIR!
'SCUSE ME!
COMING THROUGH!
TRIP

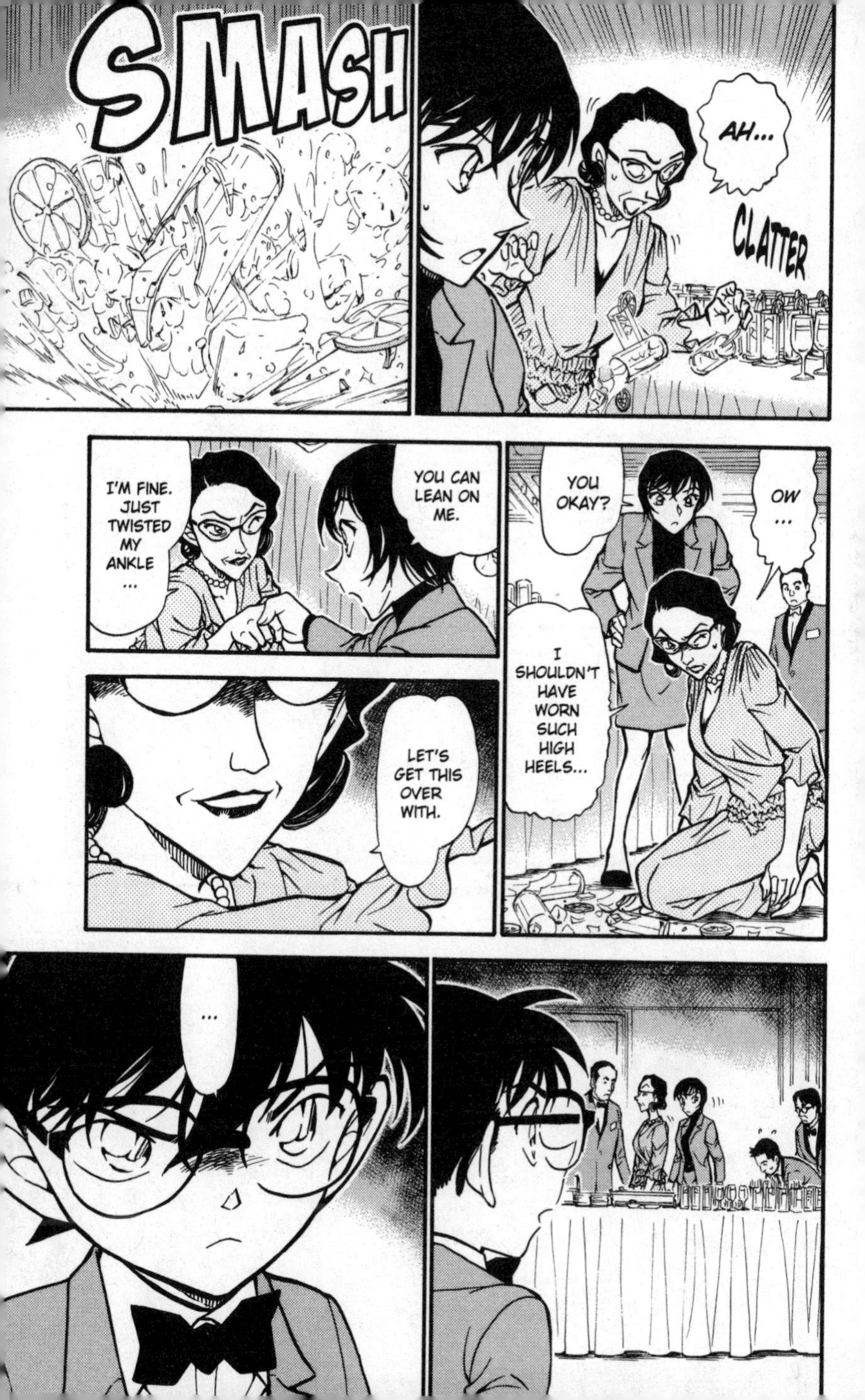
AH...
CLATTER
SMASH
OW ...
YOU OKAY?
I SHOULDN'T HAVE WORN SUCH HIGH HEELS...
YOU CAN LEAN ON ME.
I'M FINE. JUST TWISTED MY ANKLE ...
LET'S GET THIS OVER WITH.
...

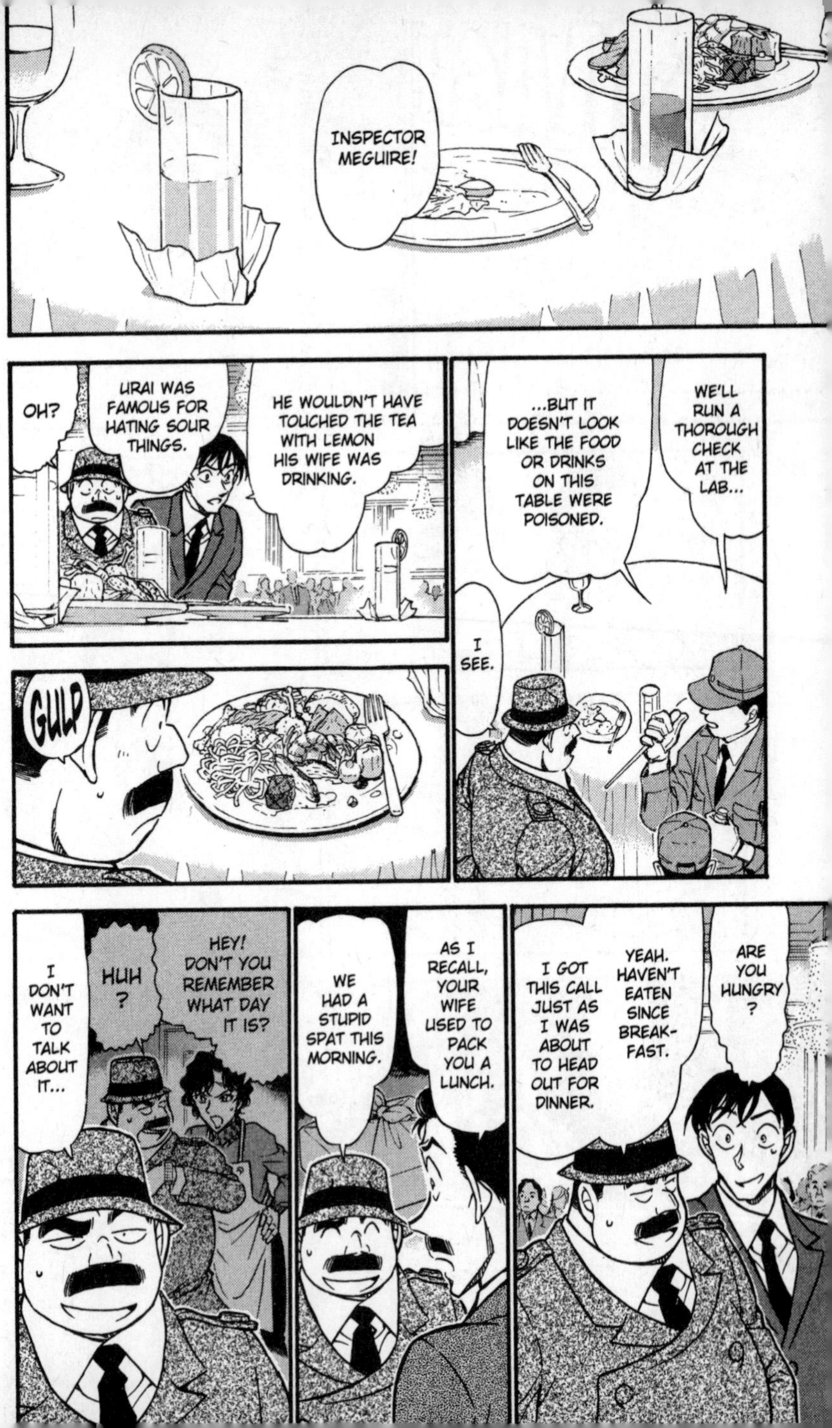
INSPECTOR MEGUIRE!
WE'LL RUN A THOROUGH CHECK AT THE LAB...
...BUT IT DOESN'T LOOK LIKE THE FOOD OR DRINKS ON THIS TABLE WERE POISONED.
I SEE.
HE WOULDN'T HAVE TOUCHED THE TEA WITH LEMON HIS WIFE WAS DRINKING.
URAI WAS FAMOUS FOR HATING SOUR THINGS.
OH?
GULP
ARE YOU HUNGRY?
YEAH. HAVEN'T EATEN SINCE BREAK-FAST.
I GOT THIS CALL JUST AS I WAS ABOUT TO HEAD OUT FOR DINNER.
AS I RECALL, YOUR WIFE USED TO PACK YOU A LUNCH.
WE HAD A STUPID SPAT THIS MORNING.
HEY! DON'T YOU REMEMBER WHAT DAY IT IS?
HUH?
I DON'T WANT TO TALK ABOUT IT...

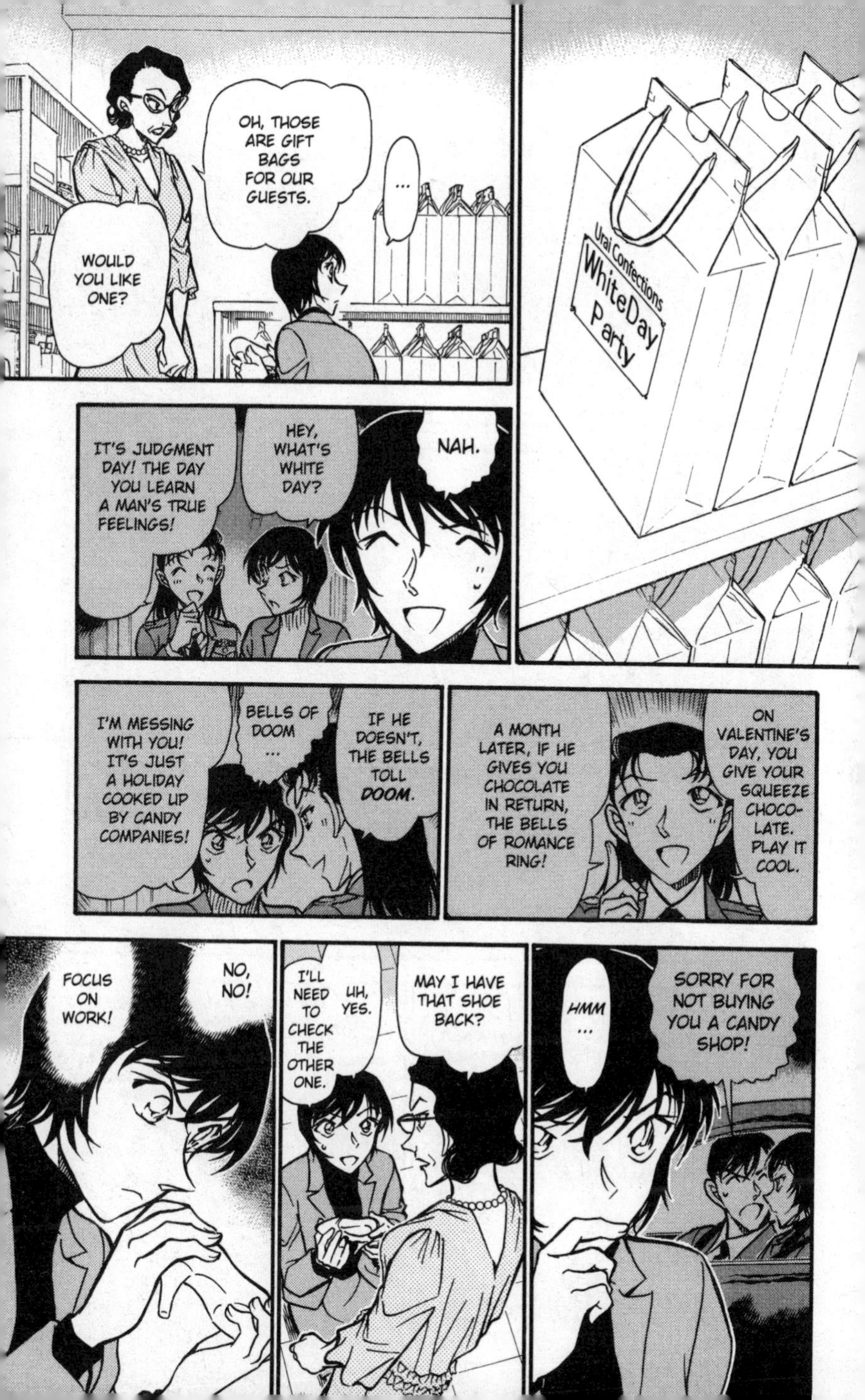
Urai Confections
WhiteDay Party
OH, THOSE ARE GIFT BAGS FOR OUR GUESTS.
...
WOULD YOU LIKE ONE?
NAH.
HEY, WHAT'S WHITE DAY?
IT'S JUDGMENT DAY! THE DAY YOU LEARN A MAN'S TRUE FEELINGS!
ON VALENTINE'S DAY, YOU GIVE YOUR SQUEEZE CHOCO-LATE. PLAY IT COOL.
A MONTH LATER, IF HE GIVES YOU CHOCOLATE IN RETURN, THE BELLS OF ROMANCE RING!
IF HE DOESN'T, THE BELLS TOLL DOOM.
BELLS OF DOOM ...
I'M MESSING WITH YOU! IT'S JUST A HOLIDAY COOKED UP BY CANDY COMPANIES!
SORRY FOR NOT BUYING YOU A CANDY SHOP!
HMM ...
MAY I HAVE THAT SHOE BACK?
UH, YES.
I'LL NEED TO CHECK THE OTHER ONE.
NO, NO!
FOCUS ON WORK!

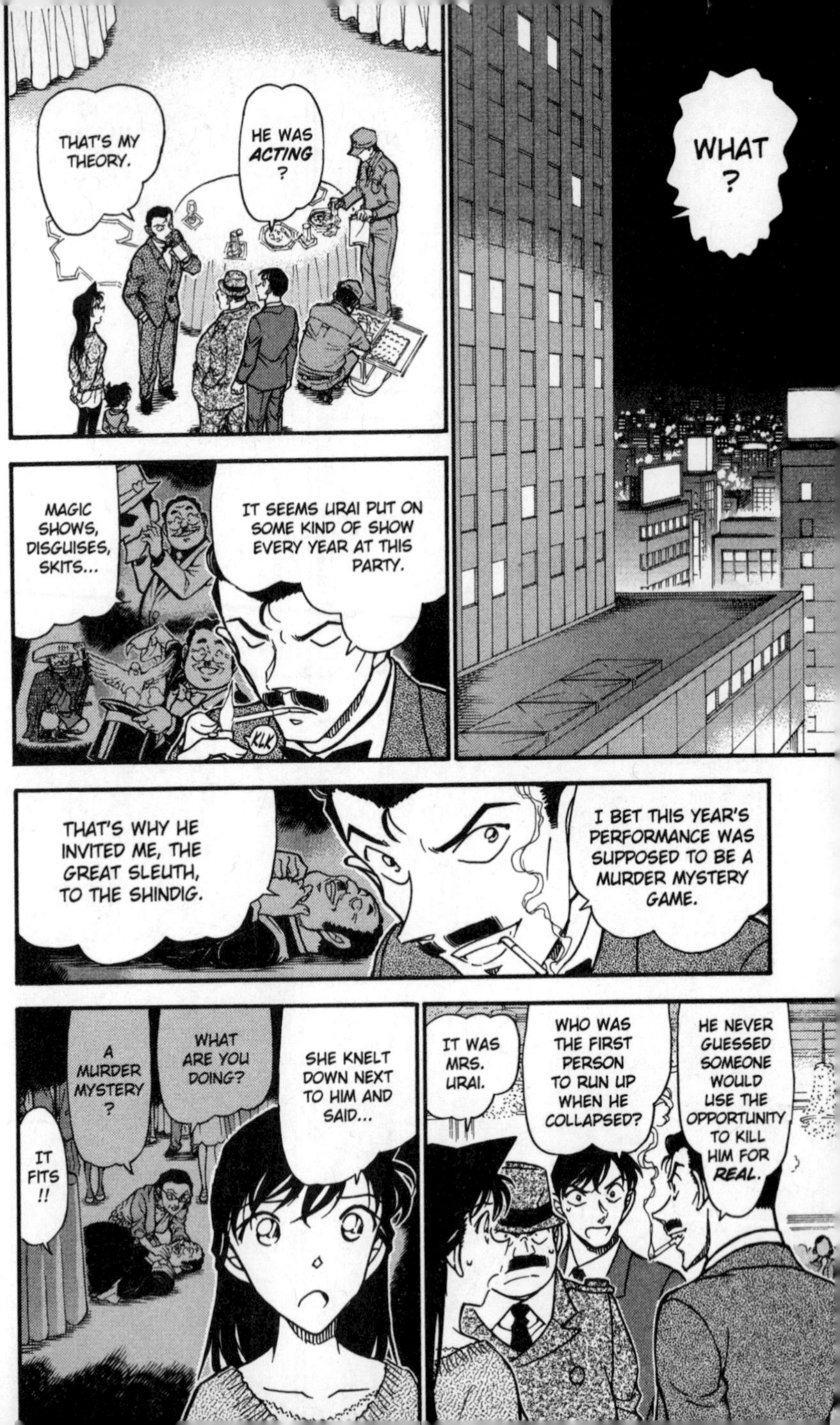
WHAT ?
HE WAS ACTING ?
THAT'S MY THEORY.
IT SEEMS URAI PUT ON SOME KIND OF SHOW EVERY YEAR AT THIS PARTY.
MAGIC SHOWS, DISGUISES, SKITS...
KLIK
I BET THIS YEAR'S PERFORMANCE WAS SUPPOSED TO BE A MURDER MYSTERY GAME.
THAT'S WHY HE INVITED ME, THE GREAT SLEUTH, TO THE SHINDIG.
HE NEVER GUESSED SOMEONE WOULD USE THE OPPORTUNITY TO KILL HIM FOR REAL.
WHO WAS THE FIRST PERSON TO RUN UP WHEN HE COLLAPSED?
IT WAS MRS. URAI.
SHE KNELT DOWN NEXT TO HIM AND SAID...
WHAT ARE YOU DOING?
A MURDER MYSTERY ?
IT FITS !!

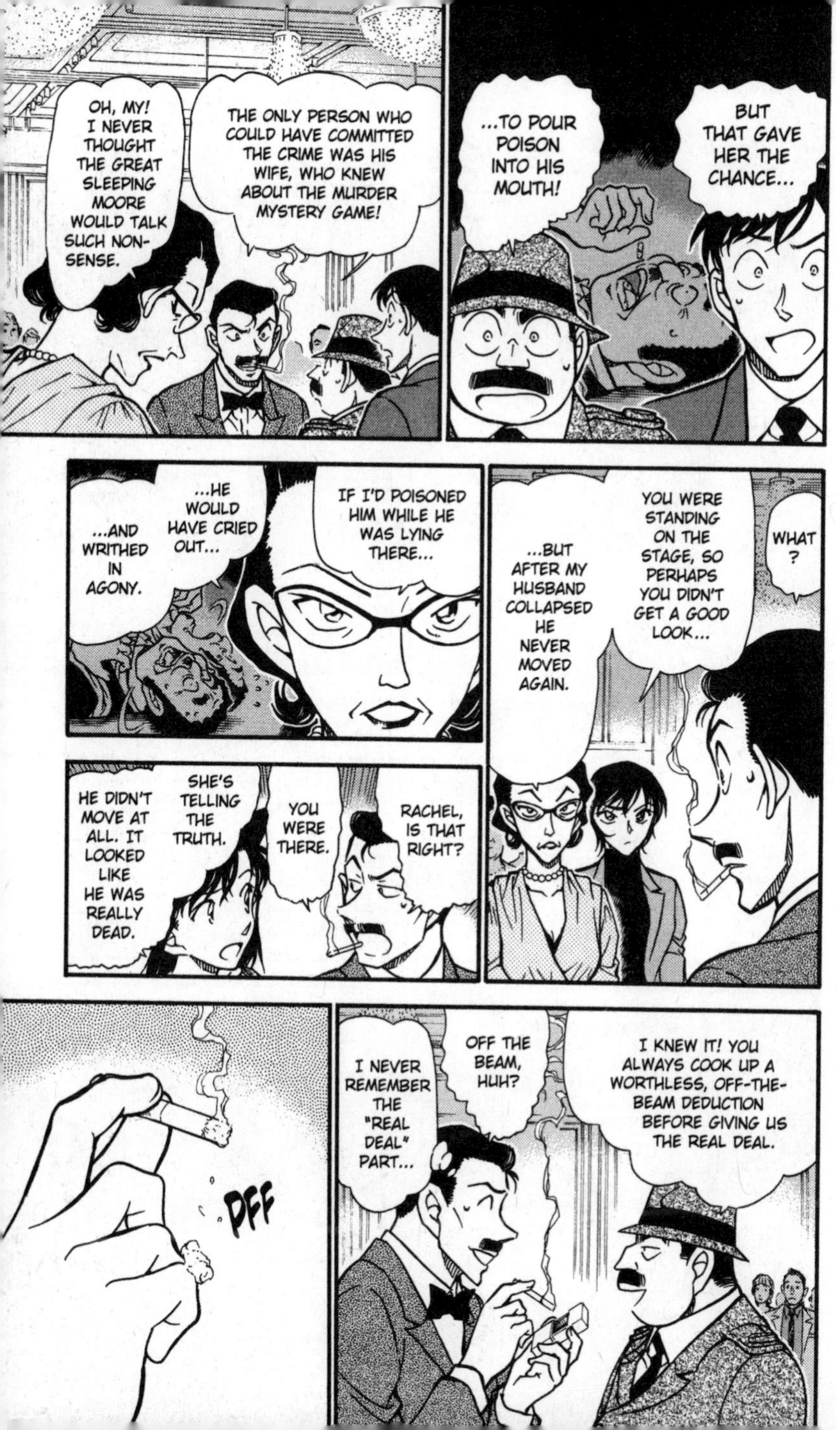
BUT THAT GAVE HER THE CHANCE...
...TO POUR POISON INTO HIS MOUTH!
THE ONLY PERSON WHO COULD HAVE COMMITTED THE CRIME WAS HIS WIFE, WHO KNEW ABOUT THE MURDER MYSTERY GAME!
OH, MY! I NEVER THOUGHT THE GREAT SLEEPING MOORE WOULD TALK SUCH NON-SENSE.
WHAT?
YOU WERE STANDING ON THE STAGE, SO PERHAPS YOU DIDN'T GET A GOOD LOOK...
...BUT AFTER MY HUSBAND COLLAPSED HE NEVER MOVED AGAIN.
IF I'D POISONED HIM WHILE HE WAS LYING THERE...
...HE WOULD HAVE CRIED OUT...
...AND WRITHED IN AGONY.
RACHEL, IS THAT RIGHT?
YOU WERE THERE.
SHE'S TELLING THE TRUTH.
HE DIDN'T MOVE AT ALL. IT LOOKED LIKE HE WAS REALLY DEAD.
I KNEW IT! YOU ALWAYS COOK UP A WORTHLESS, OFF-THE-BEAM DEDUCTION BEFORE GIVING US THE REAL DEAL.
OFF THE BEAM, HUH?
I NEVER REMEMBER THE "REAL DEAL" PART...
PFF

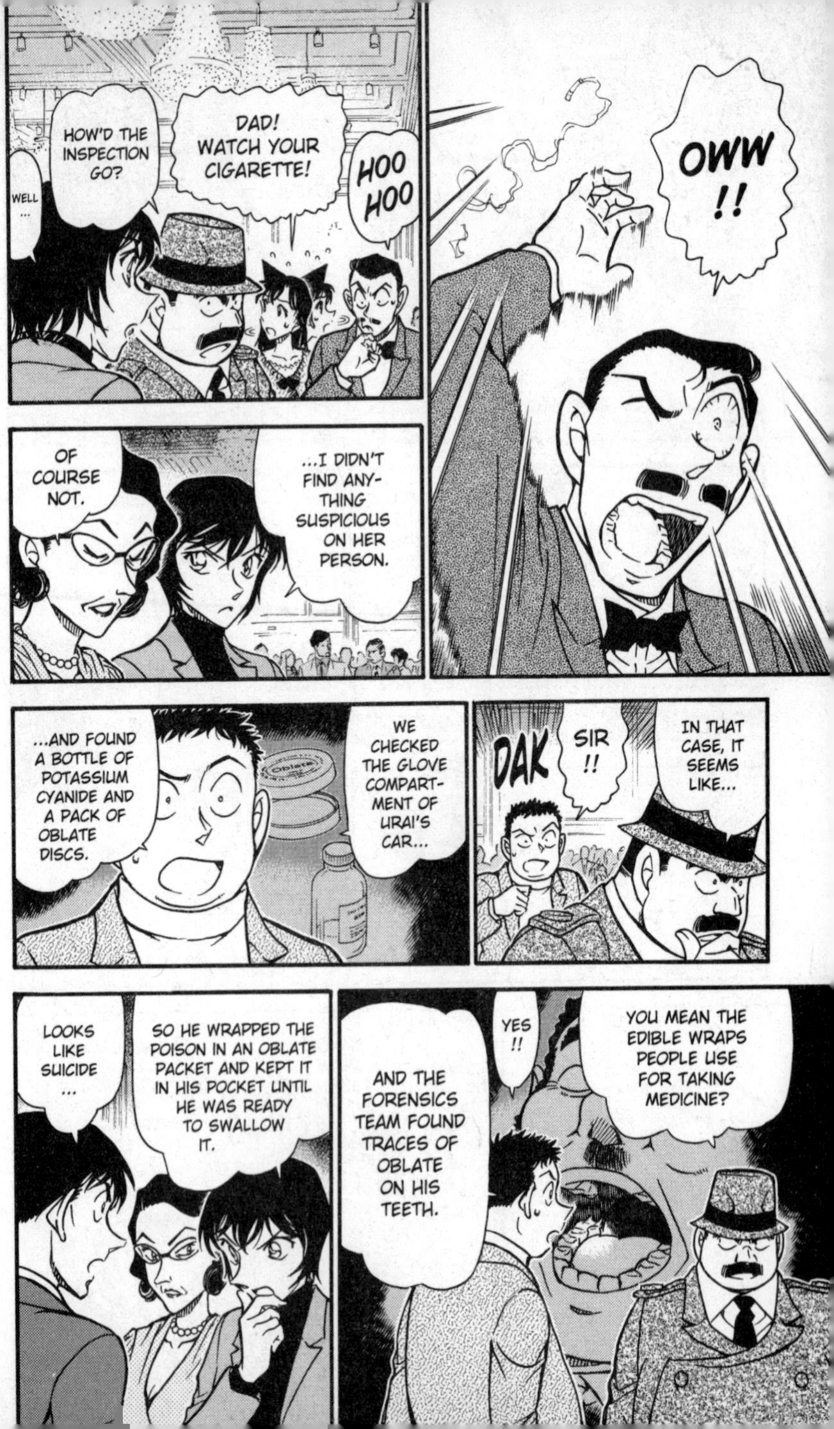
OWW !!
HOO HOO
DAD! WATCH YOUR CIGARETTE!
HOW'D THE INSPECTION GO?
WELL ...
...I DIDN'T FIND ANYTHING SUSPICIOUS ON HER PERSON.
OF COURSE NOT.
IN THAT CASE, IT SEEMS LIKE...
SIR !!
DAK
WE CHECKED THE GLOVE COMPARTMENT OF URAI'S CAR...
...AND FOUND A BOTTLE OF POTASSIUM CYANIDE AND A PACK OF OBLATE DISCS.
YOU MEAN THE EDIBLE WRAPS PEOPLE USE FOR TAKING MEDICINE?
YES !!
AND THE FORENSICS TEAM FOUND TRACES OF OBLATE ON HIS TEETH.
SO HE WRAPPED THE POISON IN AN OBLATE PACKET AND KEPT IT IN HIS POCKET UNTIL HE WAS READY TO SWALLOW IT.
LOOKS LIKE SUICIDE ...

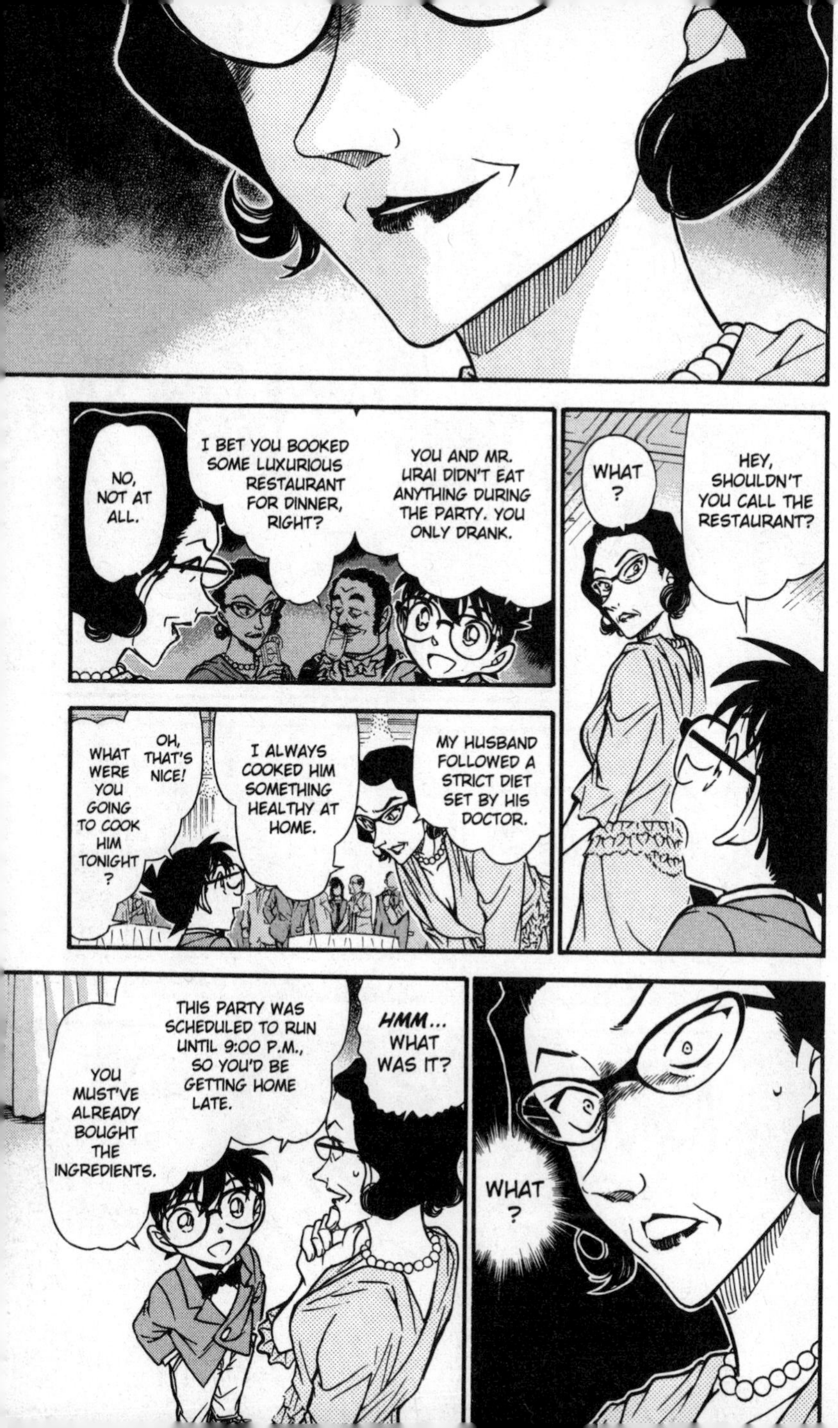
HEY, SHOULDN'T YOU CALL THE RESTAURANT?
WHAT?
YOU AND MR. URAI DIDN'T EAT ANYTHING DURING THE PARTY. YOU ONLY DRANK.
I BET YOU BOOKED SOME LUXURIOUS RESTAURANT FOR DINNER, RIGHT?
NO, NOT AT ALL.
MY HUSBAND FOLLOWED A STRICT DIET SET BY HIS DOCTOR.
I ALWAYS COOKED HIM SOMETHING HEALTHY AT HOME.
OH, THAT'S NICE!
WHAT WERE YOU GOING TO COOK HIM TONIGHT?
WHAT?
HMM... WHAT WAS IT?
THIS PARTY WAS SCHEDULED TO RUN UNTIL 9:00 P.M., SO YOU'D BE GETTING HOME LATE.
YOU MUST'VE ALREADY BOUGHT THE INGREDIENTS.

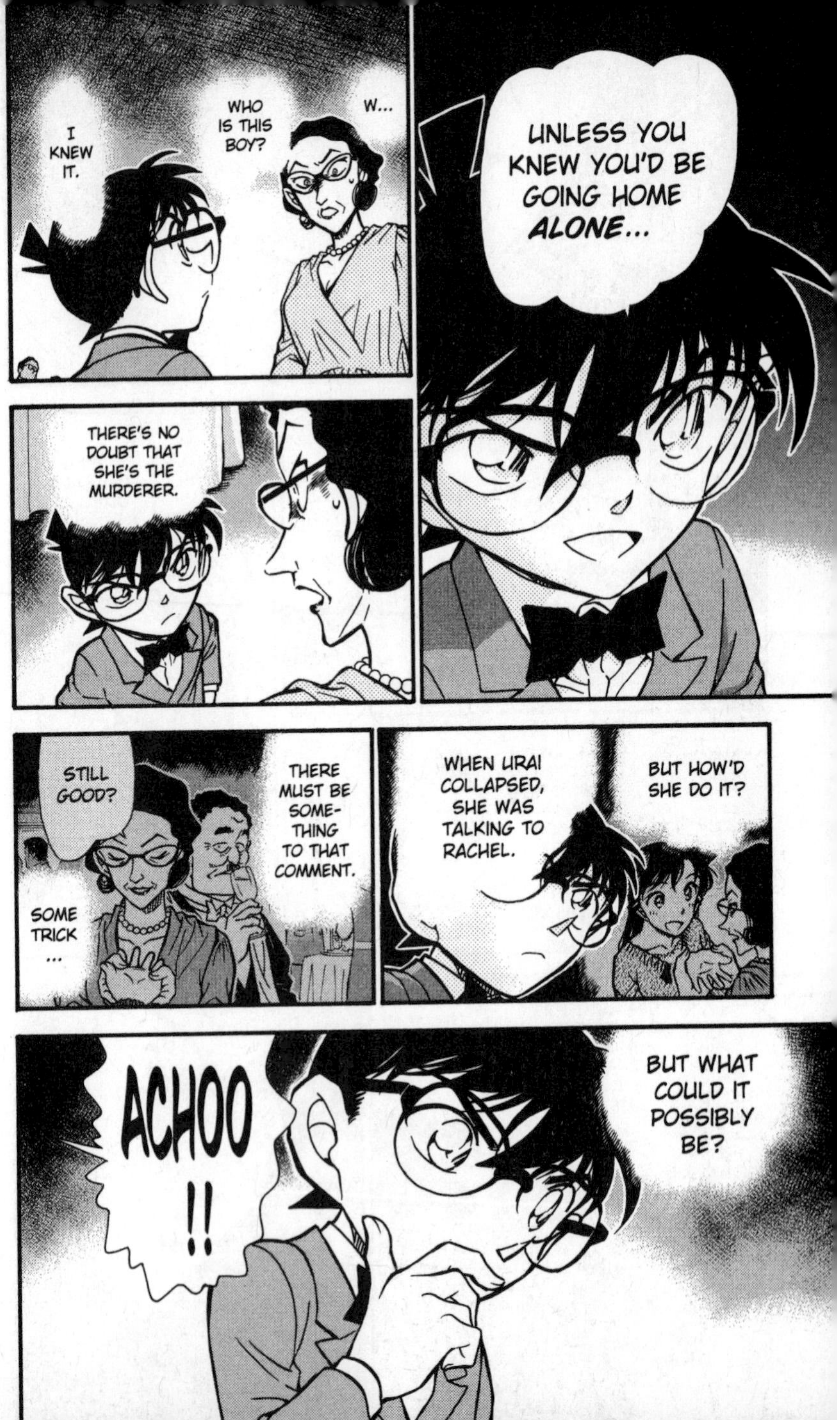
UNLESS YOU KNEW YOU'D BE GOING HOME *ALONE*...
W...
WHO IS THIS BOY?
I KNEW IT.
THERE'S NO DOUBT THAT SHE'S THE MURDERER.
BUT HOW'D SHE DO IT?
WHEN URAI COLLAPSED, SHE WAS TALKING TO RACHEL.
THERE MUST BE SOME-THING TO THAT COMMENT.
STILL GOOD?
SOME TRICK ...
BUT WHAT COULD IT POSSIBLY BE?
ACHOO !!

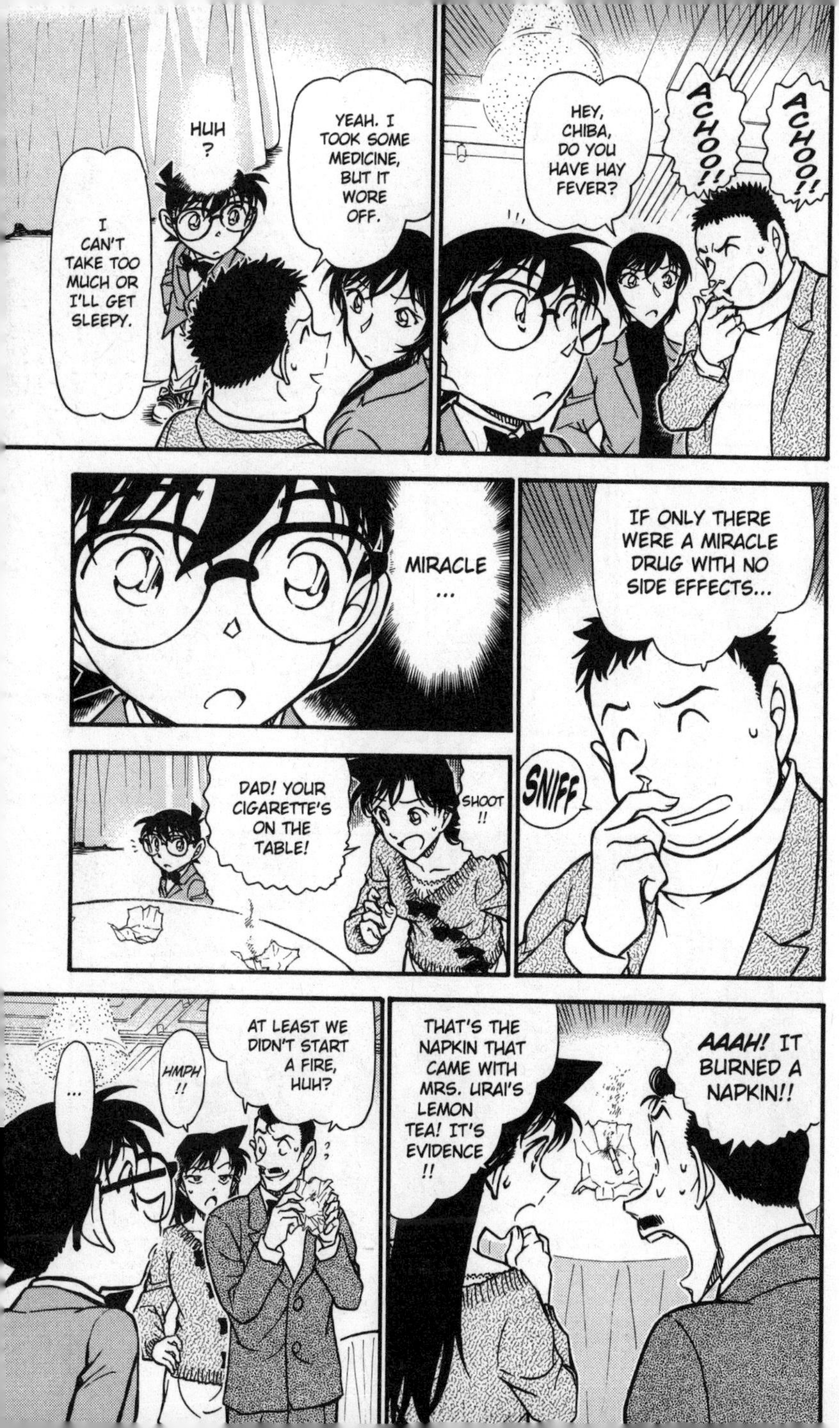
ACHOO!!
ACHOO!!
HEY, CHIBA, DO YOU HAVE HAY FEVER?
YEAH. I TOOK SOME MEDICINE, BUT IT WORE OFF.
HUH?
I CAN'T TAKE TOO MUCH OR I'LL GET SLEEPY.
IF ONLY THERE WERE A MIRACLE DRUG WITH NO SIDE EFFECTS...
SNIFF
MIRACLE...
SHOOT!!
DAD! YOUR CIGARETTE'S ON THE TABLE!
AAAH! IT BURNED A NAPKIN!!
THAT'S THE NAPKIN THAT CAME WITH MRS. URAI'S LEMON TEA! IT'S EVIDENCE!!
AT LEAST WE DIDN'T START A FIRE, HUH?
HMPH!!
...

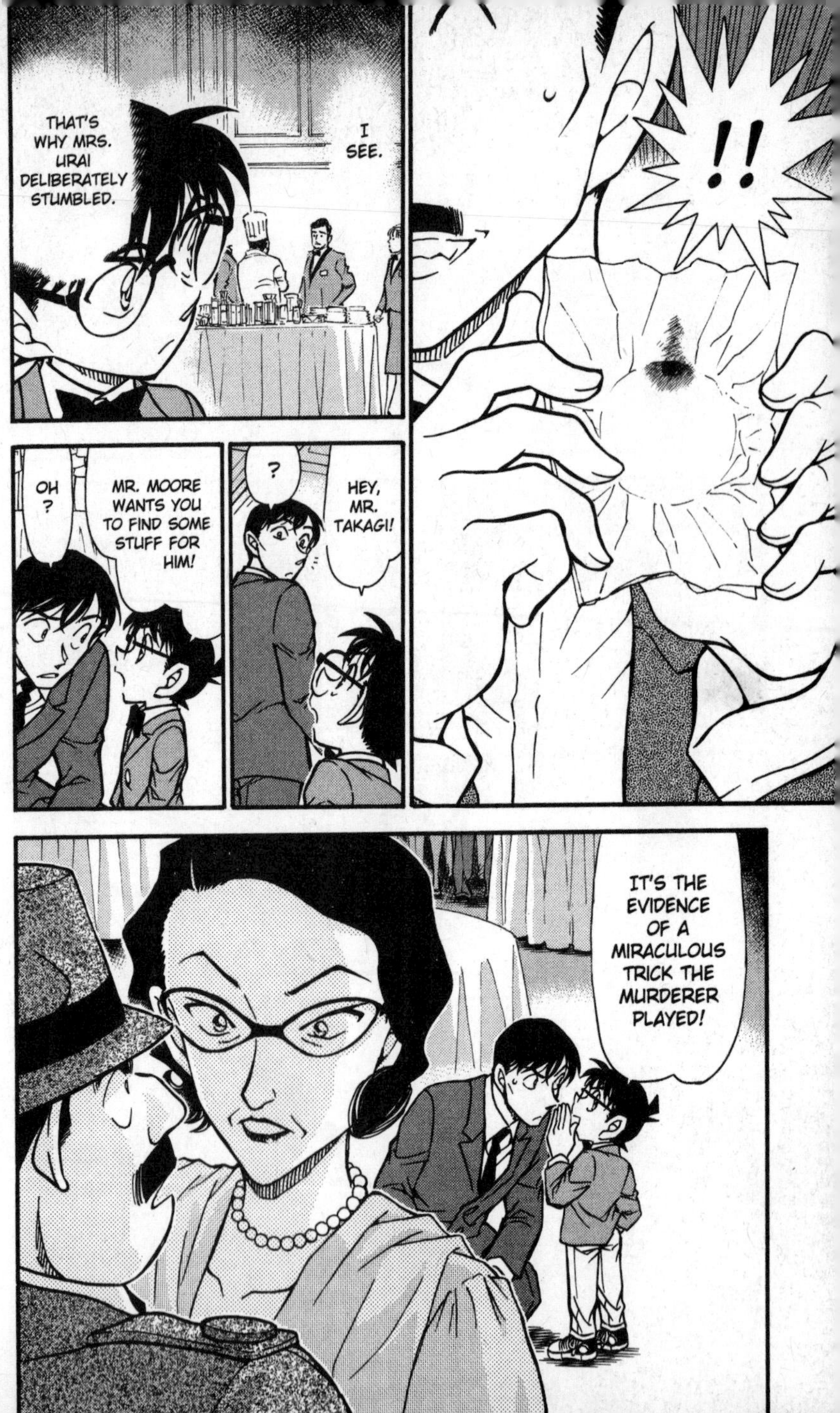
!!
I SEE.
THAT'S WHY MRS. URAI DELIBERATELY STUMBLED.
HEY, MR. TAKAGI!
?
MR. MOORE WANTS YOU TO FIND SOME STUFF FOR HIM!
OH?
IT'S THE EVIDENCE OF A MIRACULOUS TRICK THE MURDERER PLAYED!

FILE 9: HAPPY WHITE DAY

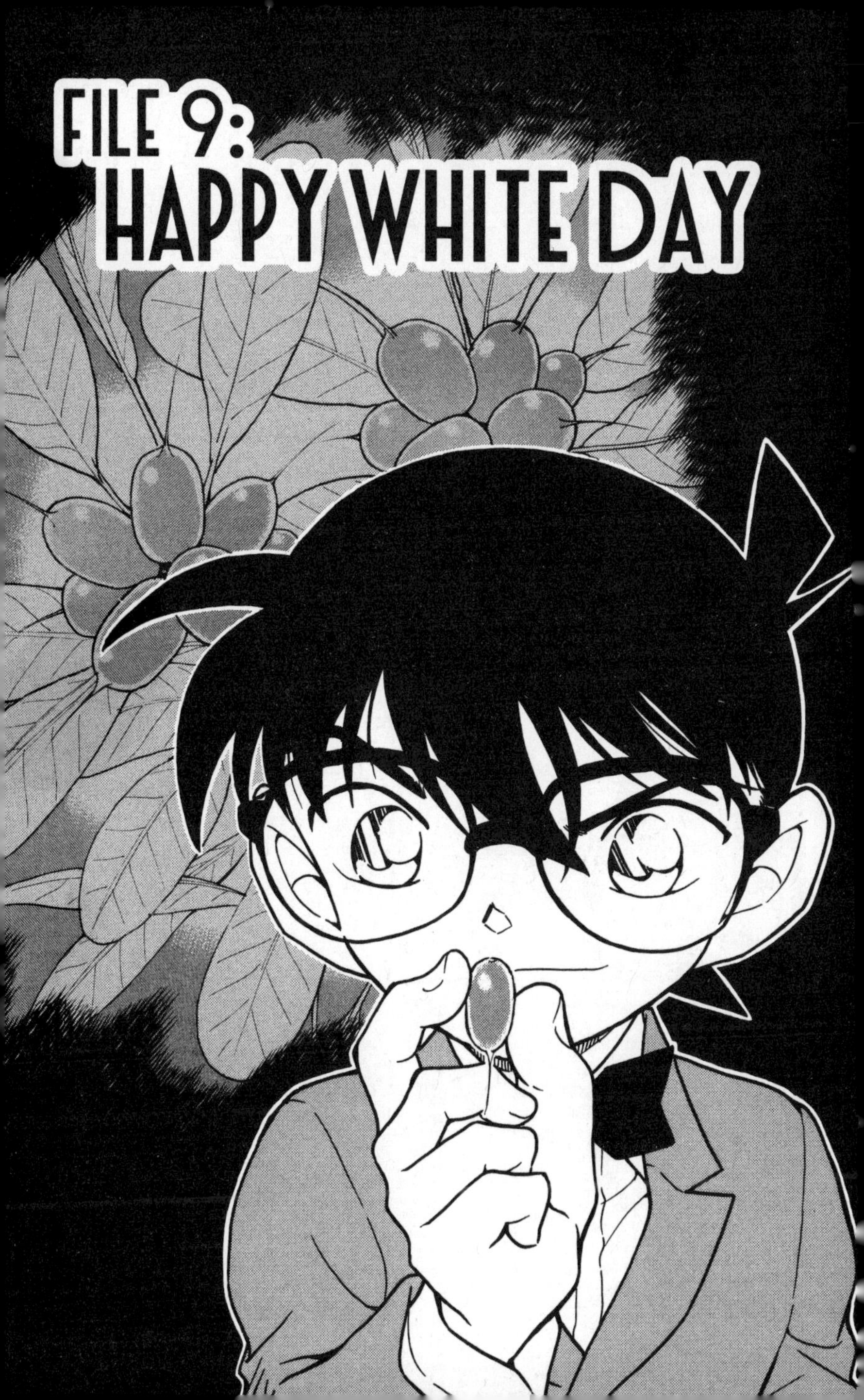

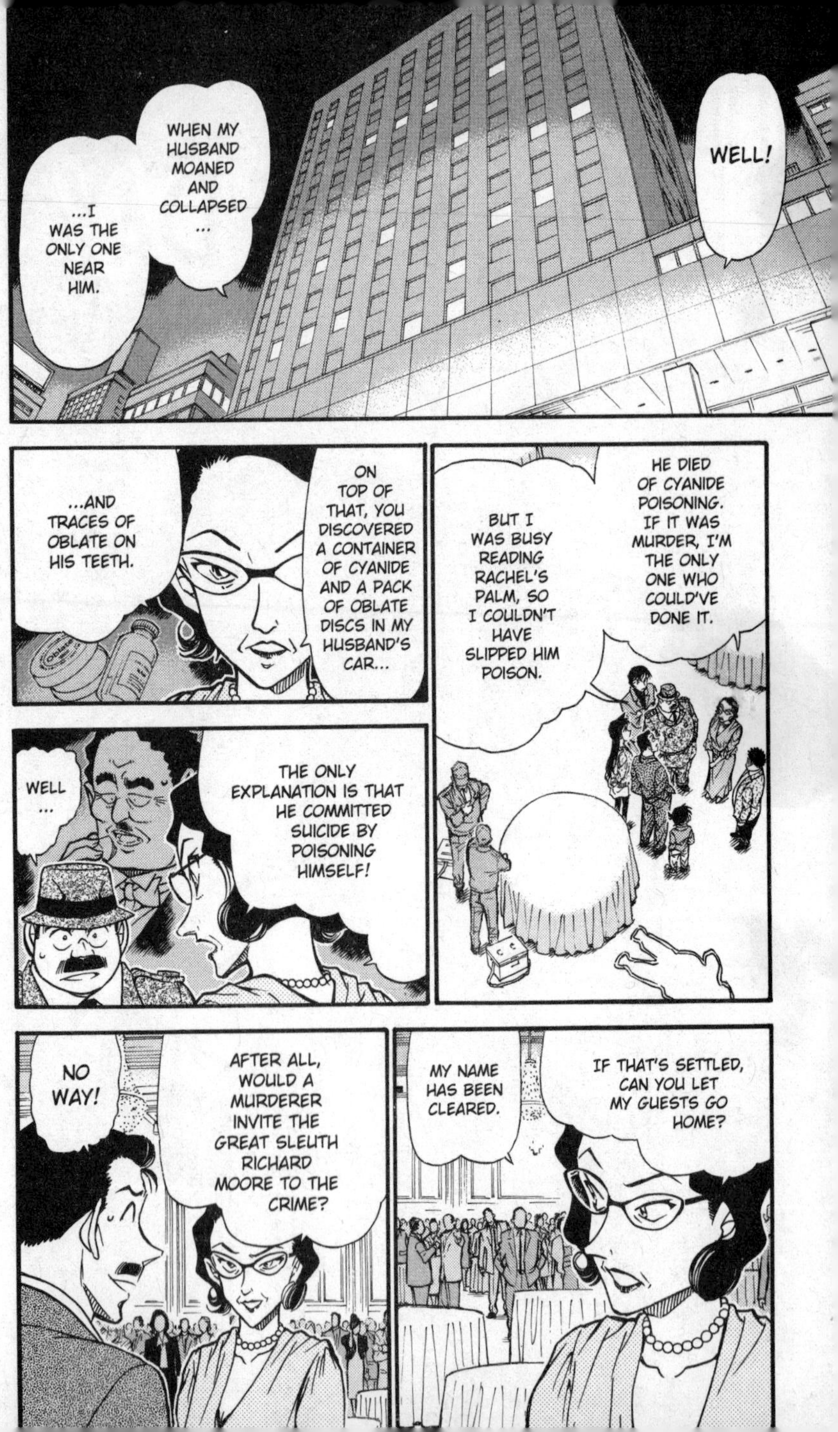
WELL!
WHEN MY HUSBAND MOANED AND COLLAPSED...
...I WAS THE ONLY ONE NEAR HIM.
HE DIED OF CYANIDE POISONING. IF IT WAS MURDER, I'M THE ONLY ONE WHO COULD'VE DONE IT.
BUT I WAS BUSY READING RACHEL'S PALM, SO I COULDN'T HAVE SLIPPED HIM POISON.
ON TOP OF THAT, YOU DISCOVERED A CONTAINER OF CYANIDE AND A PACK OF OBLATE DISCS IN MY HUSBAND'S CAR...
...AND TRACES OF OBLATE ON HIS TEETH.
THE ONLY EXPLANATION IS THAT HE COMMITTED SUICIDE BY POISONING HIMSELF!
WELL...
IF THAT'S SETTLED, CAN YOU LET MY GUESTS GO HOME?
MY NAME HAS BEEN CLEARED.
AFTER ALL, WOULD A MURDERER INVITE THE GREAT SLEUTH RICHARD MOORE TO THE CRIME?
NO WAY!

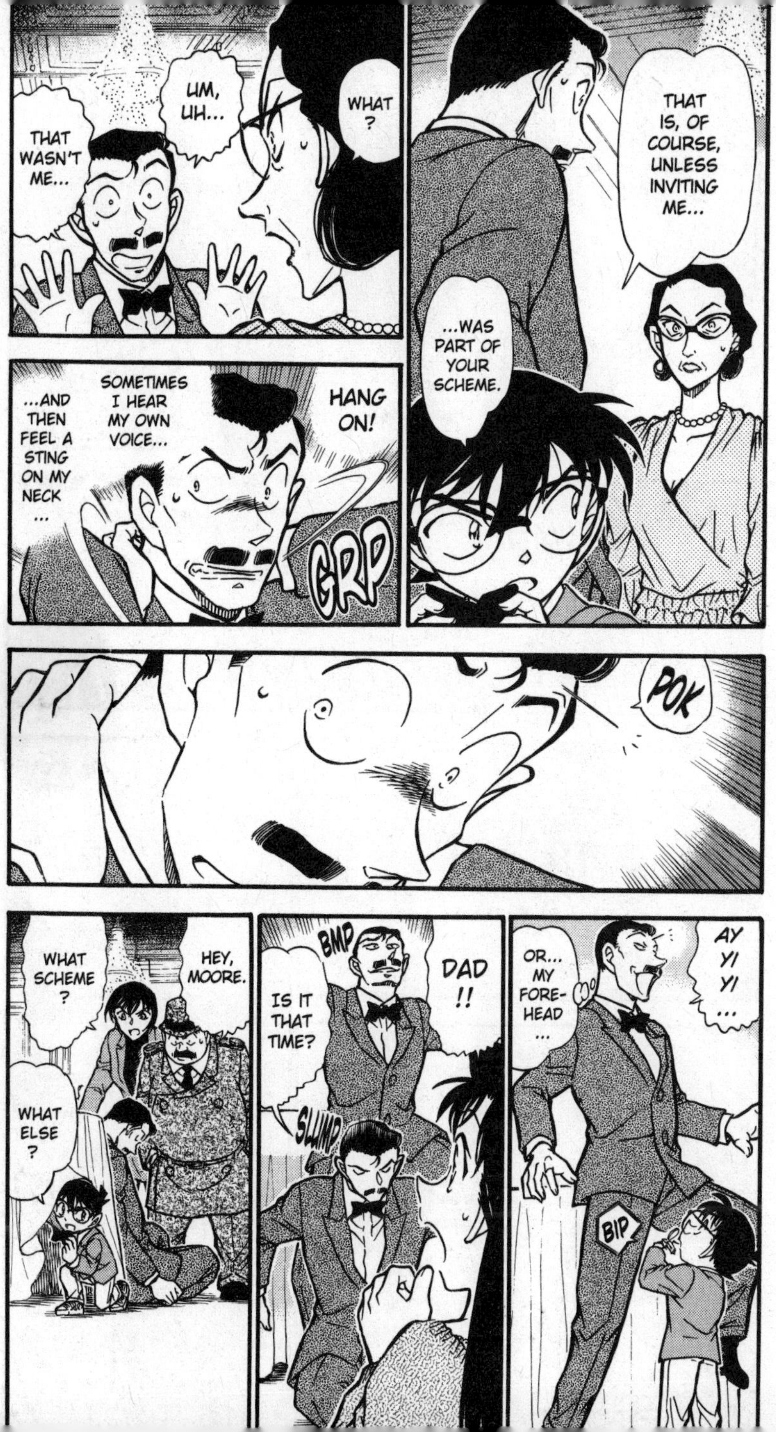
THAT IS, OF COURSE, UNLESS INVITING ME...
...WAS PART OF YOUR SCHEME.
WHAT ?
UM, UH...
THAT WASN'T ME...
HANG ON!
SOMETIMES I HEAR MY OWN VOICE...
...AND THEN FEEL A STING ON MY NECK ...
GRP
POK
AY YI YI ...
OR... MY FORE-HEAD ...
BIP
DAD !!
BMP
IS IT THAT TIME?
SLUMP
HEY, MOORE.
WHAT SCHEME ?
WHAT ELSE ?

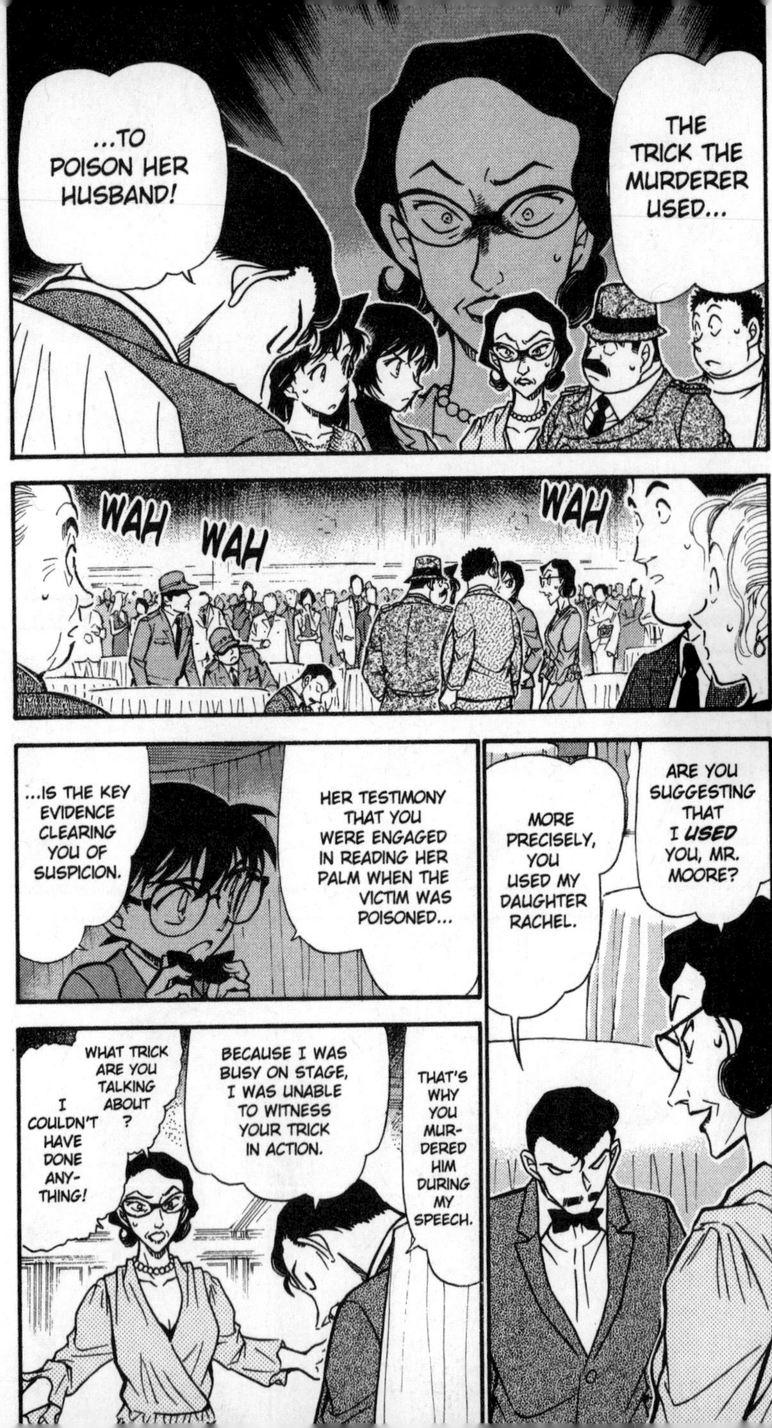
THE TRICK THE MURDERER USED...
...TO POISON HER HUSBAND!
WAH
WAH
WAH
ARE YOU SUGGESTING THAT I *USED* YOU, MR. MOORE?
MORE PRECISELY, YOU USED MY DAUGHTER RACHEL.
HER TESTIMONY THAT YOU WERE ENGAGED IN READING HER PALM WHEN THE VICTIM WAS POISONED...
...IS THE KEY EVIDENCE CLEARING YOU OF SUSPICION.
THAT'S WHY YOU MURDERED HIM DURING MY SPEECH.
BECAUSE I WAS BUSY ON STAGE, I WAS UNABLE TO WITNESS YOUR TRICK IN ACTION.
WHAT TRICK ARE YOU TALKING ABOUT?
I COULDN'T HAVE DONE ANYTHING!

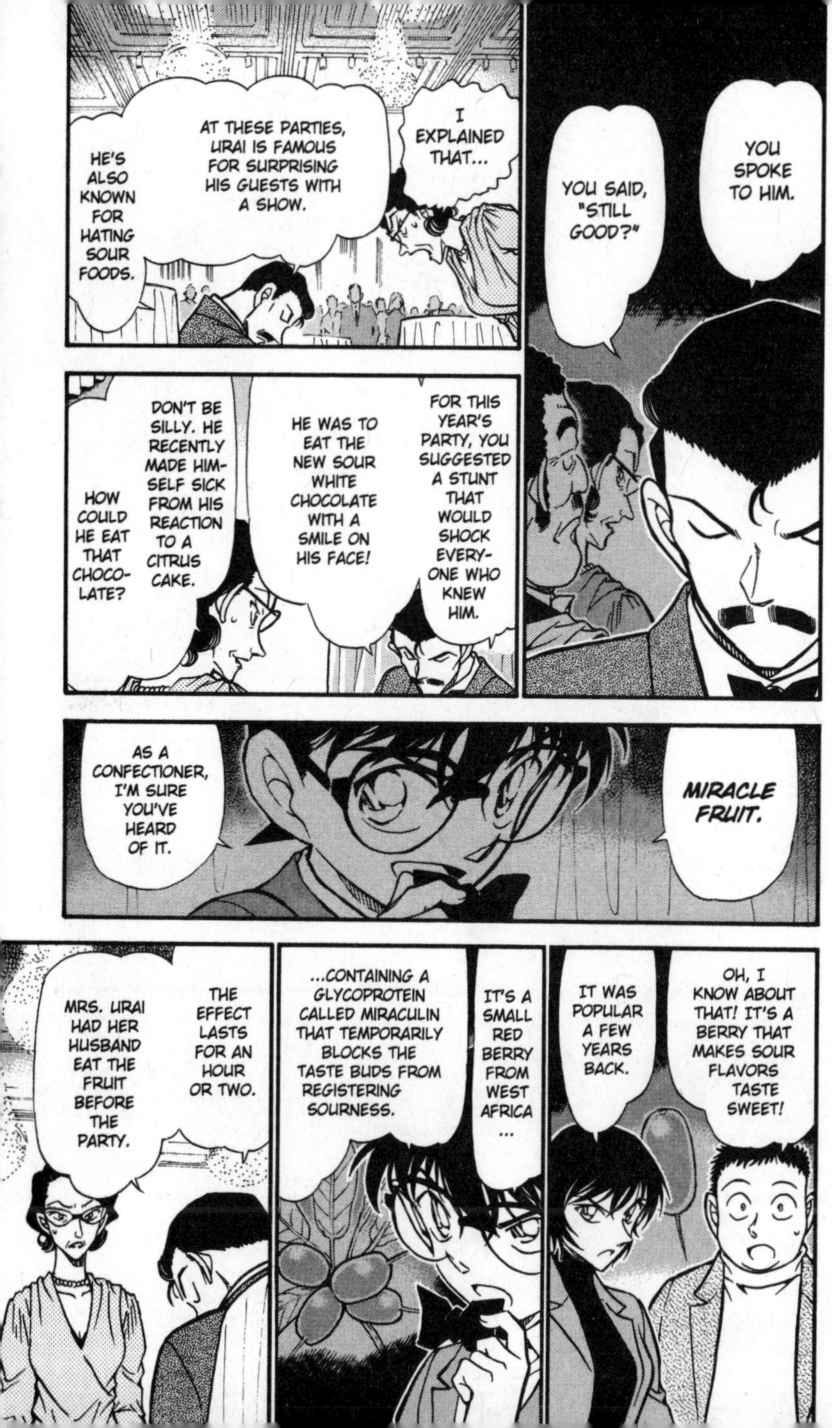
YOU SPOKE TO HIM.
YOU SAID, "STILL GOOD?"
I EXPLAINED THAT...
AT THESE PARTIES, URAI IS FAMOUS FOR SURPRISING HIS GUESTS WITH A SHOW.
HE'S ALSO KNOWN FOR HATING SOUR FOODS.
FOR THIS YEAR'S PARTY, YOU SUGGESTED A STUNT THAT WOULD SHOCK EVERY-ONE WHO KNEW HIM.
HE WAS TO EAT THE NEW SOUR WHITE CHOCOLATE WITH A SMILE ON HIS FACE!
DON'T BE SILLY. HE RECENTLY MADE HIM-SELF SICK FROM HIS REACTION TO A CITRUS CAKE.
HOW COULD HE EAT THAT CHOCO-LATE?
MIRACLE FRUIT.
AS A CONFECTIONER, I'M SURE YOU'VE HEARD OF IT.
OH, I KNOW ABOUT THAT! IT'S A BERRY THAT MAKES SOUR FLAVORS TASTE SWEET!
IT WAS POPULAR A FEW YEARS BACK.
IT'S A SMALL RED BERRY FROM WEST AFRICA ...
...CONTAINING A GLYCOPROTEIN CALLED MIRACULIN THAT TEMPORARILY BLOCKS THE TASTE BUDS FROM REGISTERING SOURNESS.
THE EFFECT LASTS FOR AN HOUR OR TWO.
MRS. URAI HAD HER HUSBAND EAT THE FRUIT BEFORE THE PARTY.

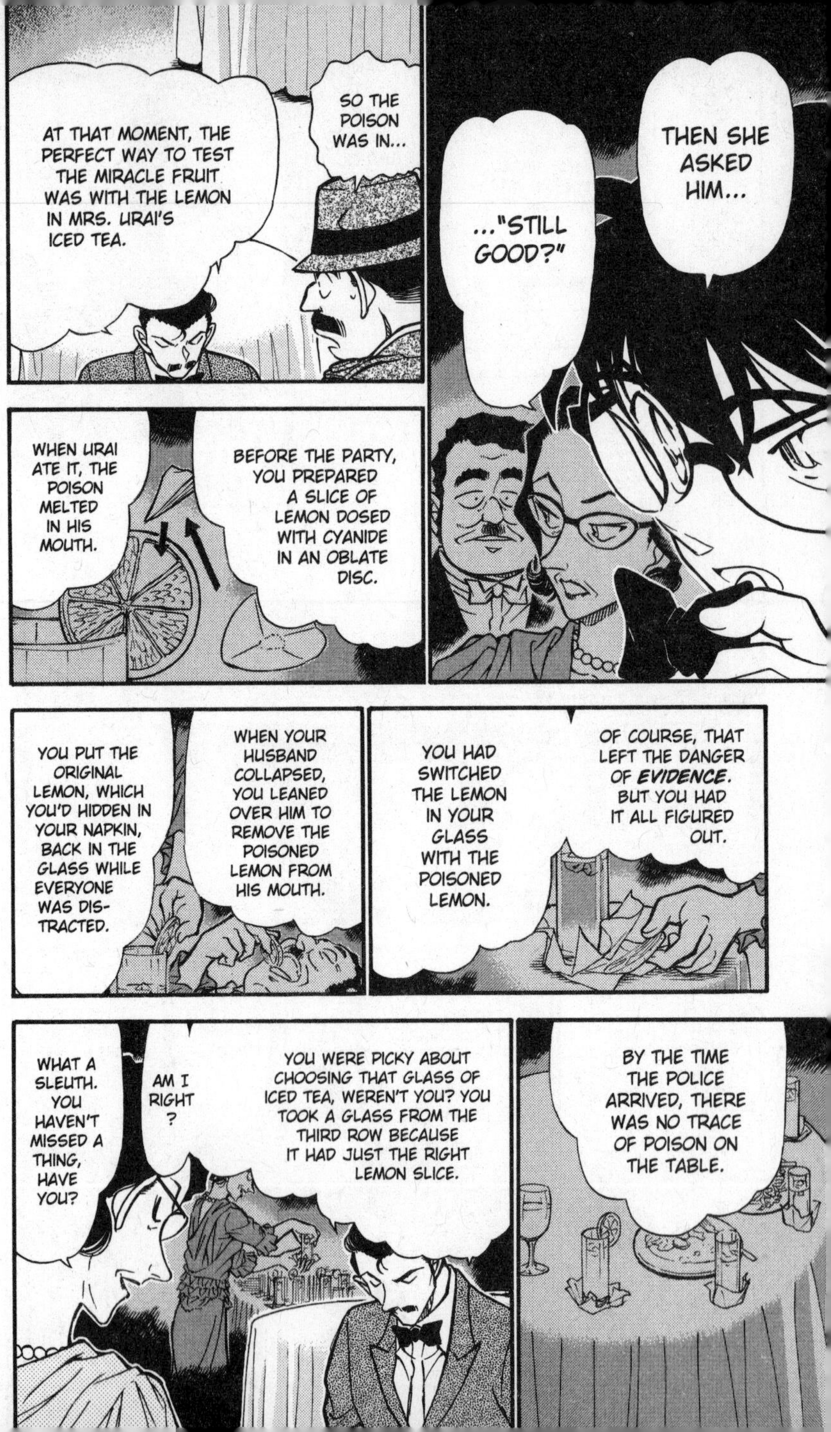
THEN SHE ASKED HIM...
..."STILL GOOD?"
SO THE POISON WAS IN...
AT THAT MOMENT, THE PERFECT WAY TO TEST THE MIRACLE FRUIT WAS WITH THE LEMON IN MRS. URAI'S ICED TEA.
BEFORE THE PARTY, YOU PREPARED A SLICE OF LEMON DOSED WITH CYANIDE IN AN OBLATE DISC.
WHEN URAI ATE IT, THE POISON MELTED IN HIS MOUTH.
OF COURSE, THAT LEFT THE DANGER OF *EVIDENCE*. BUT YOU HAD IT ALL FIGURED OUT.
YOU HAD SWITCHED THE LEMON IN YOUR GLASS WITH THE POISONED LEMON.
WHEN YOUR HUSBAND COLLAPSED, YOU LEANED OVER HIM TO REMOVE THE POISONED LEMON FROM HIS MOUTH.
YOU PUT THE ORIGINAL LEMON, WHICH YOU'D HIDDEN IN YOUR NAPKIN, BACK IN THE GLASS WHILE EVERYONE WAS DISTRACTED.
BY THE TIME THE POLICE ARRIVED, THERE WAS NO TRACE OF POISON ON THE TABLE.
YOU WERE PICKY ABOUT CHOOSING THAT GLASS OF ICED TEA, WEREN'T YOU? YOU TOOK A GLASS FROM THE THIRD ROW BECAUSE IT HAD JUST THE RIGHT LEMON SLICE.
AM I RIGHT?
WHAT A SLEUTH. YOU HAVEN'T MISSED A THING, HAVE YOU?

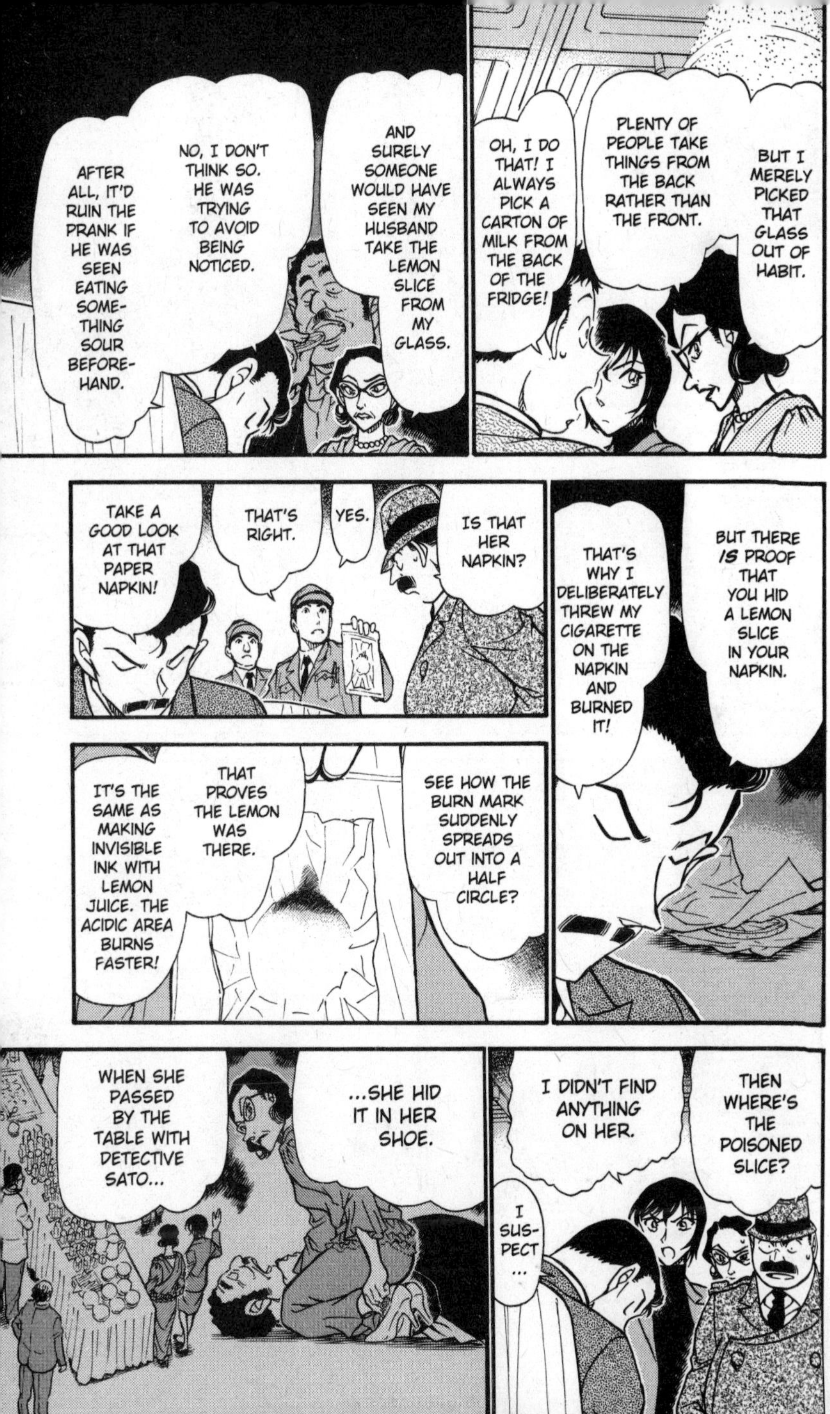
BUT I MERELY PICKED THAT GLASS OUT OF HABIT.
PLENTY OF PEOPLE TAKE THINGS FROM THE BACK RATHER THAN THE FRONT.
OH, I DO THAT! I ALWAYS PICK A CARTON OF MILK FROM THE BACK OF THE FRIDGE!
AND SURELY SOMEONE WOULD HAVE SEEN MY HUSBAND TAKE THE LEMON SLICE FROM MY GLASS.
NO, I DON'T THINK SO. HE WAS TRYING TO AVOID BEING NOTICED.
AFTER ALL, IT'D RUIN THE PRANK IF HE WAS SEEN EATING SOMETHING SOUR BEFOREHAND.
BUT THERE *IS* PROOF THAT YOU HID A LEMON SLICE IN YOUR NAPKIN.
THAT'S WHY I DELIBERATELY THREW MY CIGARETTE ON THE NAPKIN AND BURNED IT!
IS THAT HER NAPKIN?
YES.
THAT'S RIGHT.
TAKE A GOOD LOOK AT THAT PAPER NAPKIN!
SEE HOW THE BURN MARK SUDDENLY SPREADS OUT INTO A HALF CIRCLE?
THAT PROVES THE LEMON WAS THERE.
IT'S THE SAME AS MAKING INVISIBLE INK WITH LEMON JUICE. THE ACIDIC AREA BURNS FASTER!
THEN WHERE'S THE POISONED SLICE?
I DIDN'T FIND ANYTHING ON HER.
I SUSPECT...
WHEN SHE PASSED BY THE TABLE WITH DETECTIVE SATO...
...SHE HID IT IN HER SHOE.

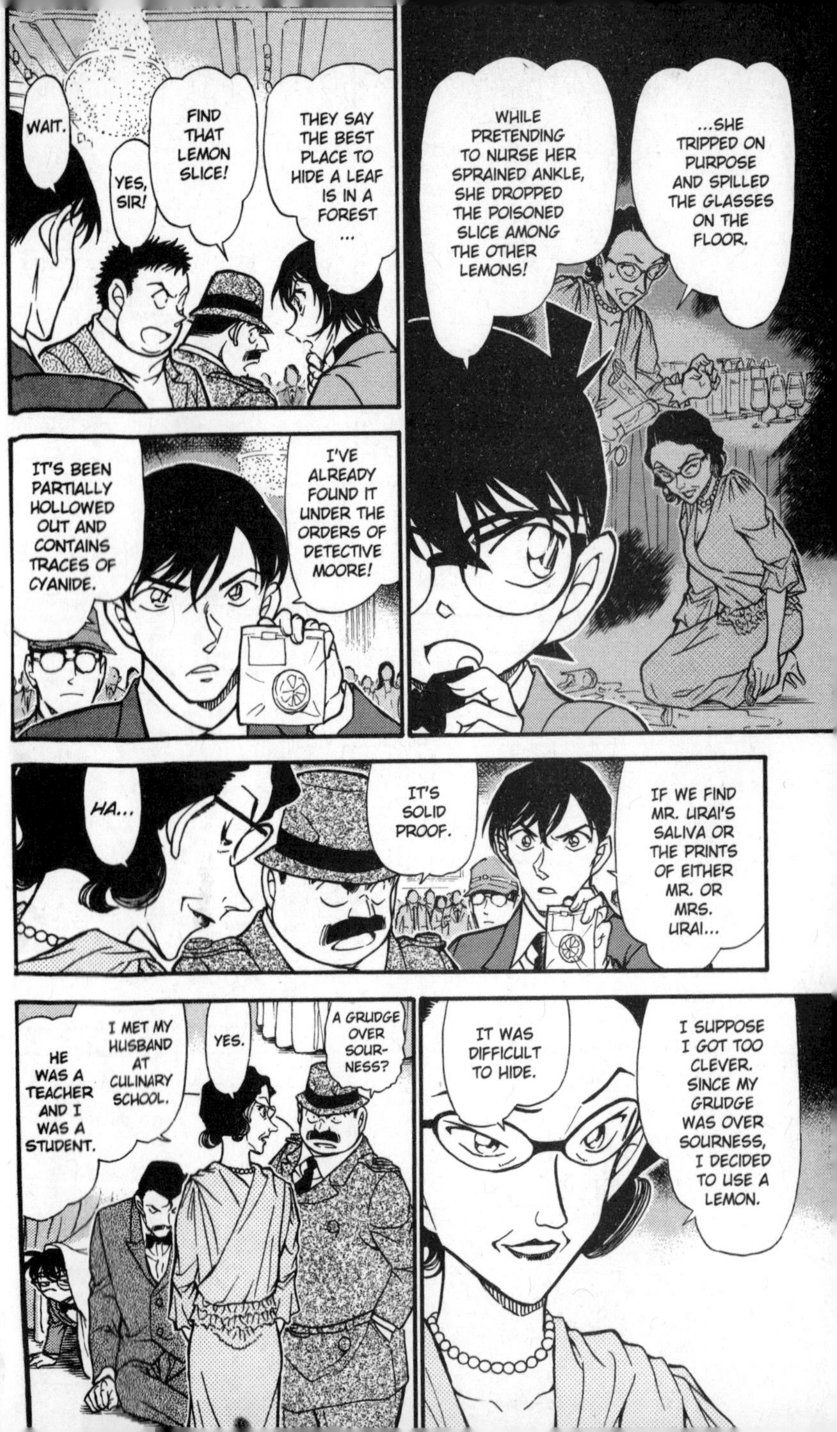
...SHE TRIPPED ON PURPOSE AND SPILLED THE GLASSES ON THE FLOOR.
WHILE PRETENDING TO NURSE HER SPRAINED ANKLE, SHE DROPPED THE POISONED SLICE AMONG THE OTHER LEMONS!
THEY SAY THE BEST PLACE TO HIDE A LEAF IS IN A FOREST ...
FIND THAT LEMON SLICE!
YES, SIR!
WAIT.
I'VE ALREADY FOUND IT UNDER THE ORDERS OF DETECTIVE MOORE!
IT'S BEEN PARTIALLY HOLLOWED OUT AND CONTAINS TRACES OF CYANIDE.
IF WE FIND MR. URAI'S SALIVA OR THE PRINTS OF EITHER MR. OR MRS. URAI...
IT'S SOLID PROOF.
HA...
I SUPPOSE I GOT TOO CLEVER. SINCE MY GRUDGE WAS OVER SOURNESS, I DECIDED TO USE A LEMON.
IT WAS DIFFICULT TO HIDE.
A GRUDGE OVER SOUR-NESS?
YES.
I MET MY HUSBAND AT CULINARY SCHOOL.
HE WAS A TEACHER AND I WAS A STUDENT.

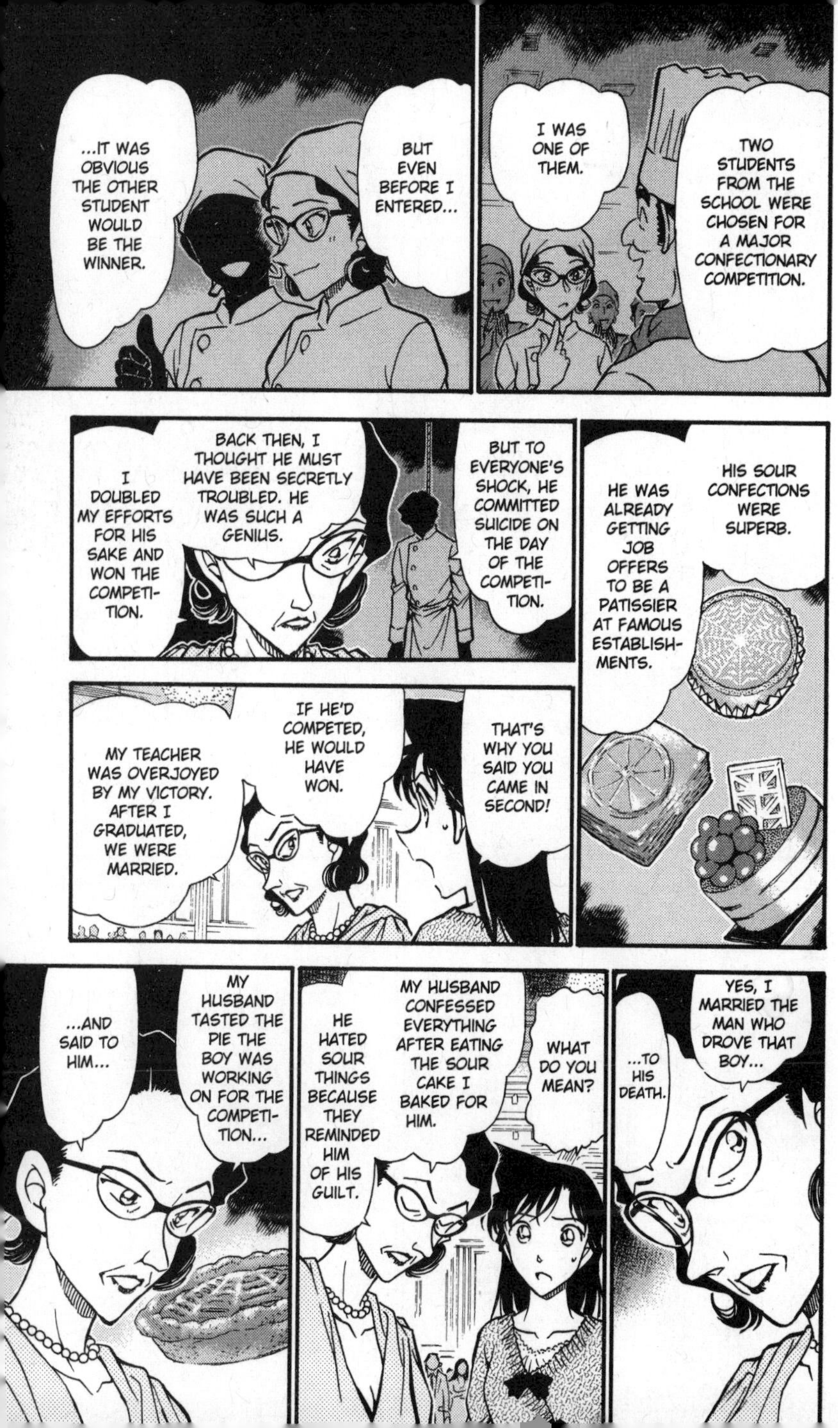
TWO STUDENTS FROM THE SCHOOL WERE CHOSEN FOR A MAJOR CONFECTIONARY COMPETITION.
I WAS ONE OF THEM.
BUT EVEN BEFORE I ENTERED...
...IT WAS OBVIOUS THE OTHER STUDENT WOULD BE THE WINNER.
HIS SOUR CONFECTIONS WERE SUPERB.
HE WAS ALREADY GETTING JOB OFFERS TO BE A PATISSIER AT FAMOUS ESTABLISHMENTS.
BUT TO EVERYONE'S SHOCK, HE COMMITTED SUICIDE ON THE DAY OF THE COMPETITION.
BACK THEN, I THOUGHT HE MUST HAVE BEEN SECRETLY TROUBLED. HE WAS SUCH A GENIUS.
I DOUBLED MY EFFORTS FOR HIS SAKE AND WON THE COMPETITION.
THAT'S WHY YOU SAID YOU CAME IN SECOND!
IF HE'D COMPETED, HE WOULD HAVE WON.
MY TEACHER WAS OVERJOYED BY MY VICTORY. AFTER I GRADUATED, WE WERE MARRIED.
YES, I MARRIED THE MAN WHO DROVE THAT BOY...
...TO HIS DEATH.
WHAT DO YOU MEAN?
MY HUSBAND CONFESSED EVERYTHING AFTER EATING THE SOUR CAKE I BAKED FOR HIM.
HE HATED SOUR THINGS BECAUSE THEY REMINDED HIM OF HIS GUILT.
MY HUSBAND TASTED THE PIE THE BOY WAS WORKING ON FOR THE COMPETITION...
...AND SAID TO HIM...

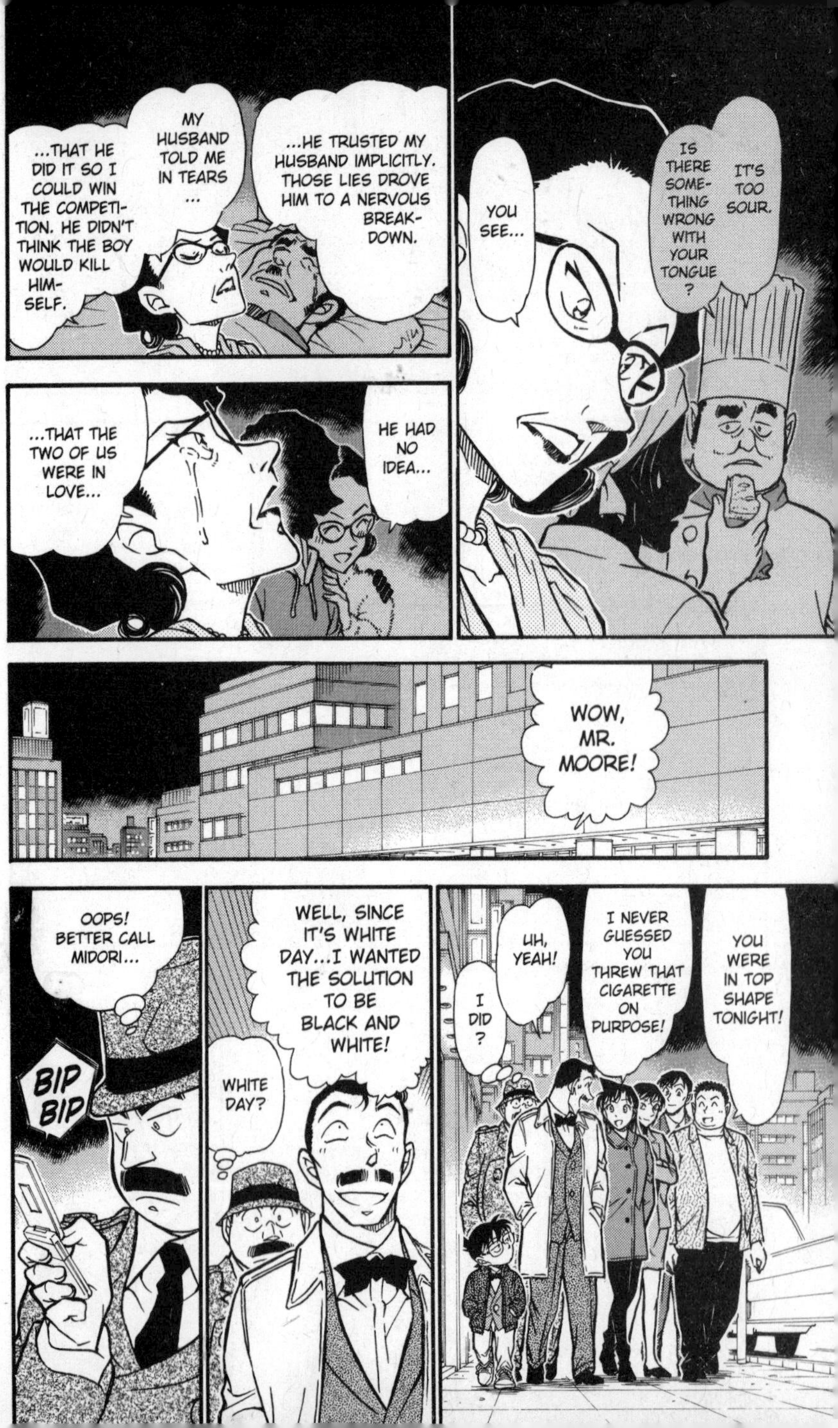

IT'S TOO SOUR.
IS THERE SOMETHING WRONG WITH YOUR TONGUE?
YOU SEE...
...HE TRUSTED MY HUSBAND IMPLICITLY. THOSE LIES DROVE HIM TO A NERVOUS BREAKDOWN.
MY HUSBAND TOLD ME IN TEARS...
...THAT HE DID IT SO I COULD WIN THE COMPETITION. HE DIDN'T THINK THE BOY WOULD KILL HIMSELF.
HE HAD NO IDEA...
...THAT THE TWO OF US WERE IN LOVE...
WOW, MR. MOORE!
YOU WERE IN TOP SHAPE TONIGHT!
I NEVER GUESSED YOU THREW THAT CIGARETTE ON PURPOSE!
UH, YEAH!
I DID?
WELL, SINCE IT'S WHITE DAY...I WANTED THE SOLUTION TO BE BLACK AND WHITE!
WHITE DAY?
OOPS! BETTER CALL MIDORI...
BIP BIP

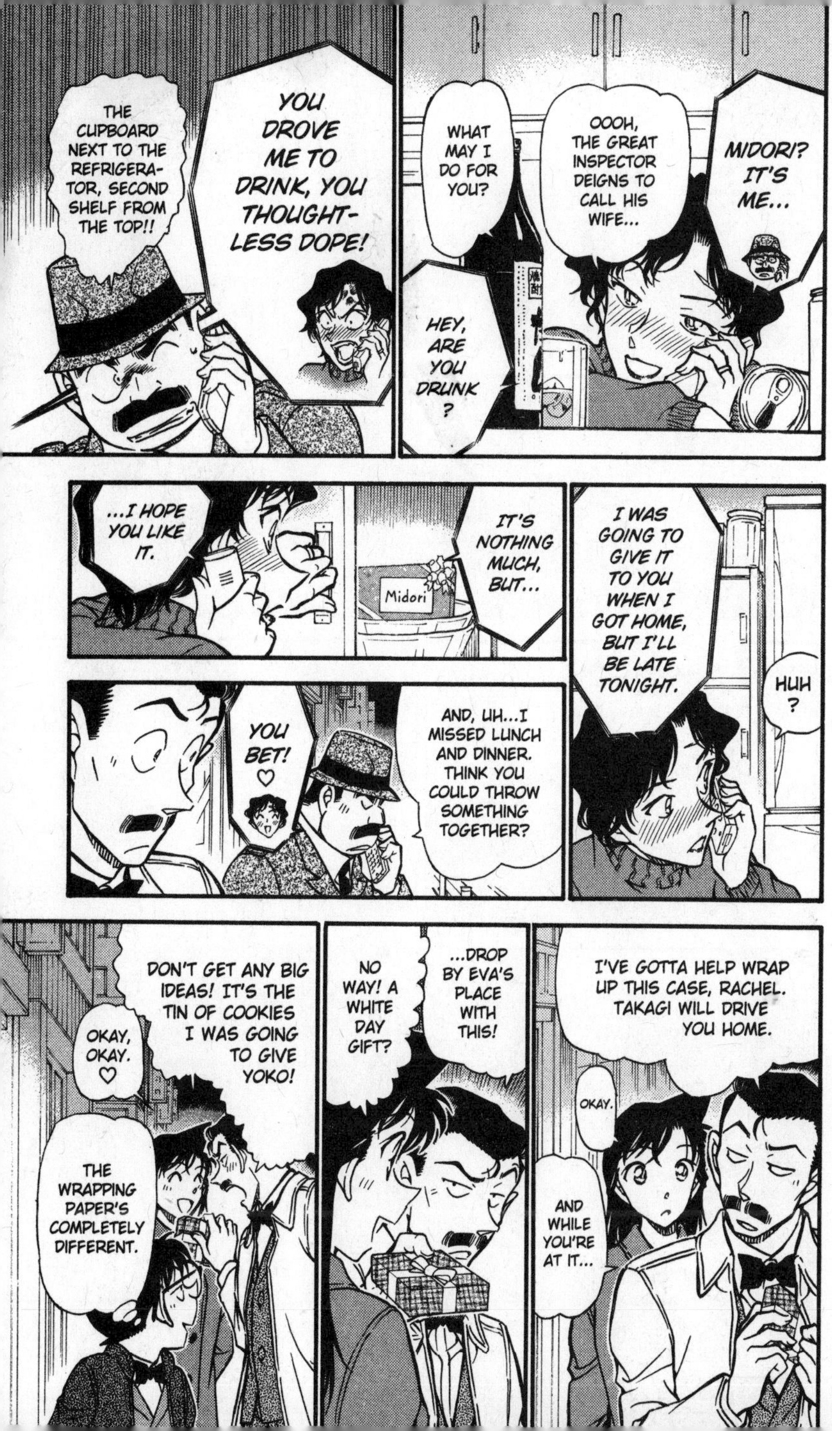
MIDORI? IT'S ME...
OOOH, THE GREAT INSPECTOR DEIGNS TO CALL HIS WIFE...
WHAT MAY I DO FOR YOU?
HEY, ARE YOU DRUNK?
YOU DROVE ME TO DRINK, YOU THOUGHT-LESS DOPE!
THE CUPBOARD NEXT TO THE REFRIGERA-TOR, SECOND SHELF FROM THE TOP!!
I WAS GOING TO GIVE IT TO YOU WHEN I GOT HOME, BUT I'LL BE LATE TONIGHT.
HUH?
IT'S NOTHING MUCH, BUT...
Midori
...I HOPE YOU LIKE IT.
AND, UH...I MISSED LUNCH AND DINNER. THINK YOU COULD THROW SOMETHING TOGETHER?
YOU BET! ♡
I'VE GOTTA HELP WRAP UP THIS CASE, RACHEL. TAKAGI WILL DRIVE YOU HOME.
OKAY.
AND WHILE YOU'RE AT IT...
...DROP BY EVA'S PLACE WITH THIS!
NO WAY! A WHITE DAY GIFT?
DON'T GET ANY BIG IDEAS! IT'S THE TIN OF COOKIES I WAS GOING TO GIVE YOKO!
OKAY, OKAY. ♡
THE WRAPPING PAPER'S COMPLETELY DIFFERENT.

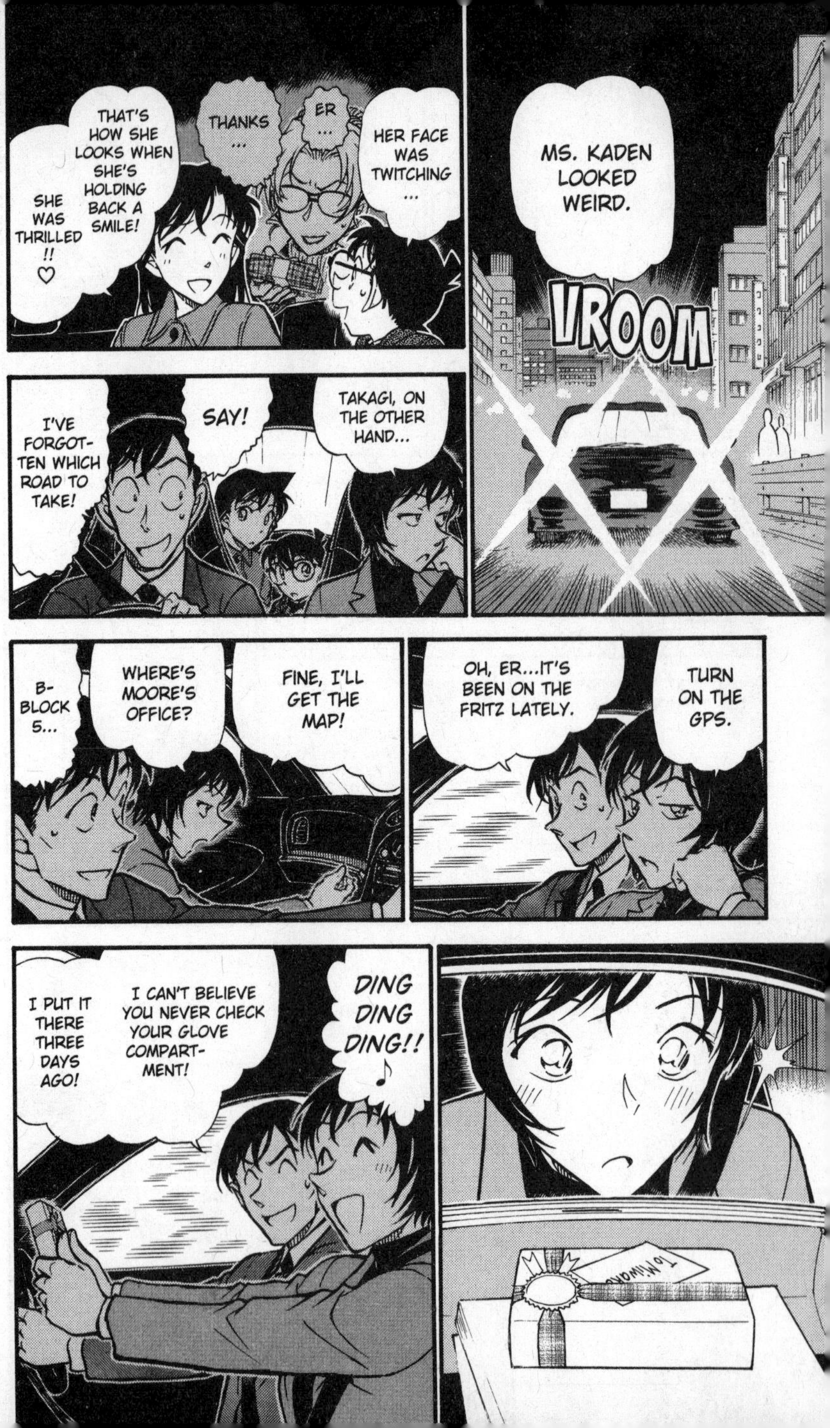
MS. KADEN LOOKED WEIRD.
VROOM
HER FACE WAS TWITCHING...
ER...
THANKS...
THAT'S HOW SHE LOOKS WHEN SHE'S HOLDING BACK A SMILE!
SHE WAS THRILLED!! ♡
TAKAGI, ON THE OTHER HAND...
SAY!
I'VE FORGOTTEN WHICH ROAD TO TAKE!
TURN ON THE GPS.
OH, ER...IT'S BEEN ON THE FRITZ LATELY.
FINE, I'LL GET THE MAP!
WHERE'S MOORE'S OFFICE?
B-BLOCK 5...
To Miwako
DING DING DING!! ♪
I CAN'T BELIEVE YOU NEVER CHECK YOUR GLOVE COMPARTMENT!
I PUT IT THERE THREE DAYS AGO!

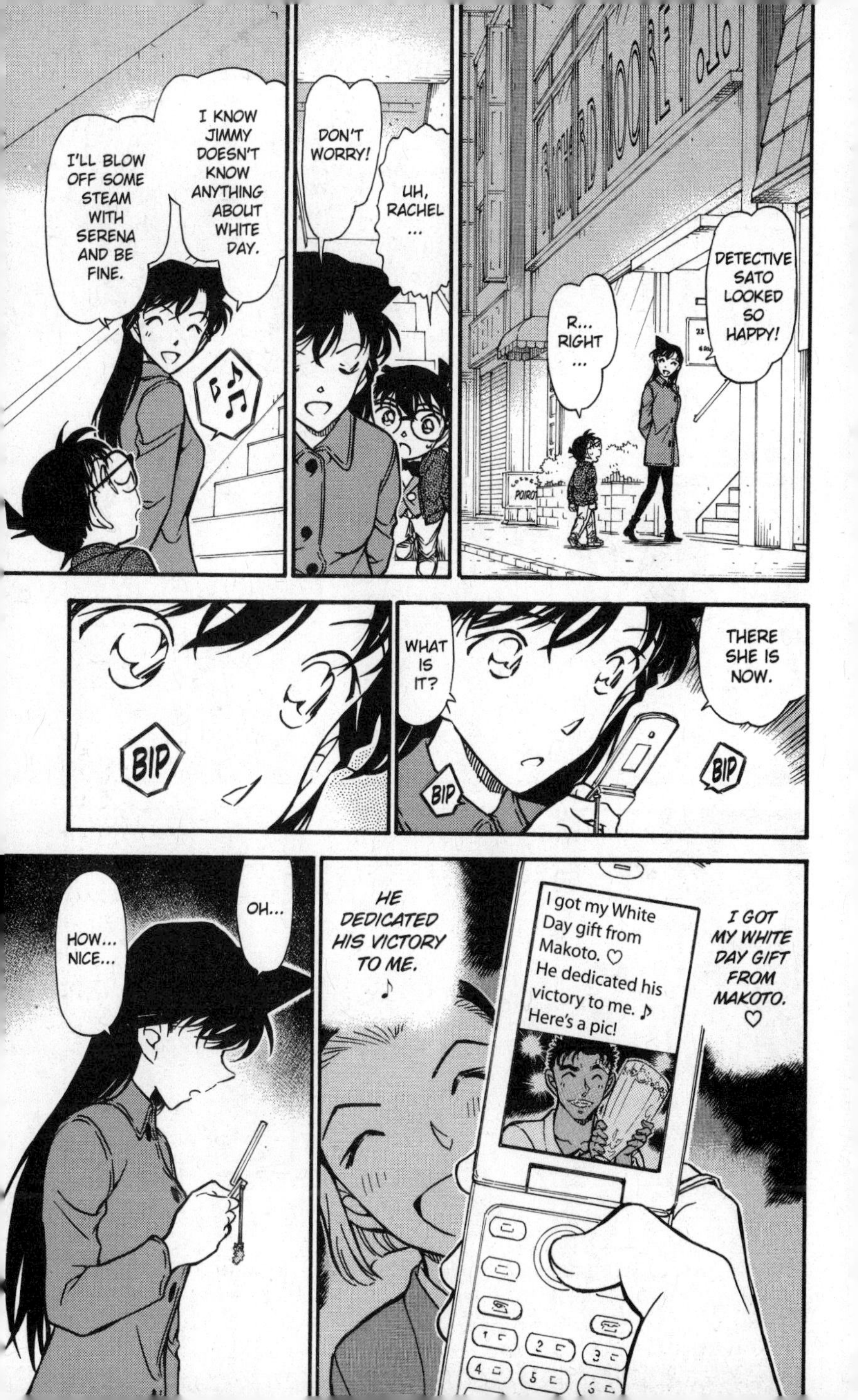
DETECTIVE SATO LOOKED SO HAPPY!
R... RIGHT ...
UH, RACHEL ...
DON'T WORRY!
I KNOW JIMMY DOESN'T KNOW ANYTHING ABOUT WHITE DAY.
I'LL BLOW OFF SOME STEAM WITH SERENA AND BE FINE.
THERE SHE IS NOW.
BIP
BIP
WHAT IS IT?
BIP
I GOT MY WHITE DAY GIFT FROM MAKOTO. ♡
I got my White Day gift from Makoto. ♡ He dedicated his victory to me. ♪ Here's a pic!
HE DEDICATED HIS VICTORY TO ME. ♪
OH...
HOW... NICE...

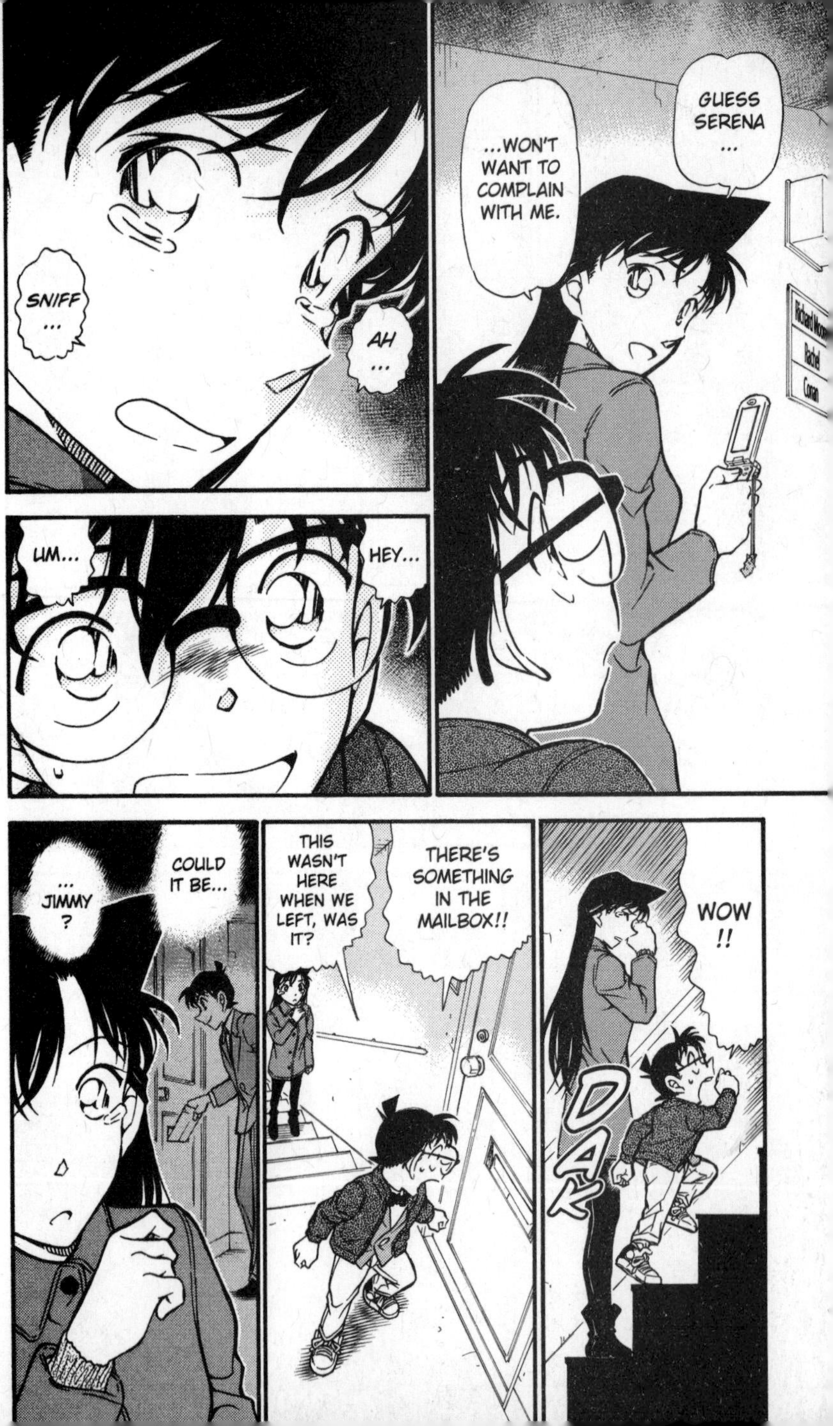
GUESS SERENA ...
...WON'T WANT TO COMPLAIN WITH ME.
Rachel
Conan
AH ...
SNIFF ...
HEY...
UM...
WOW !!
DAK
THERE'S SOMETHING IN THE MAILBOX!!
THIS WASN'T HERE WHEN WE LEFT, WAS IT?
COULD IT BE...
... JIMMY ?

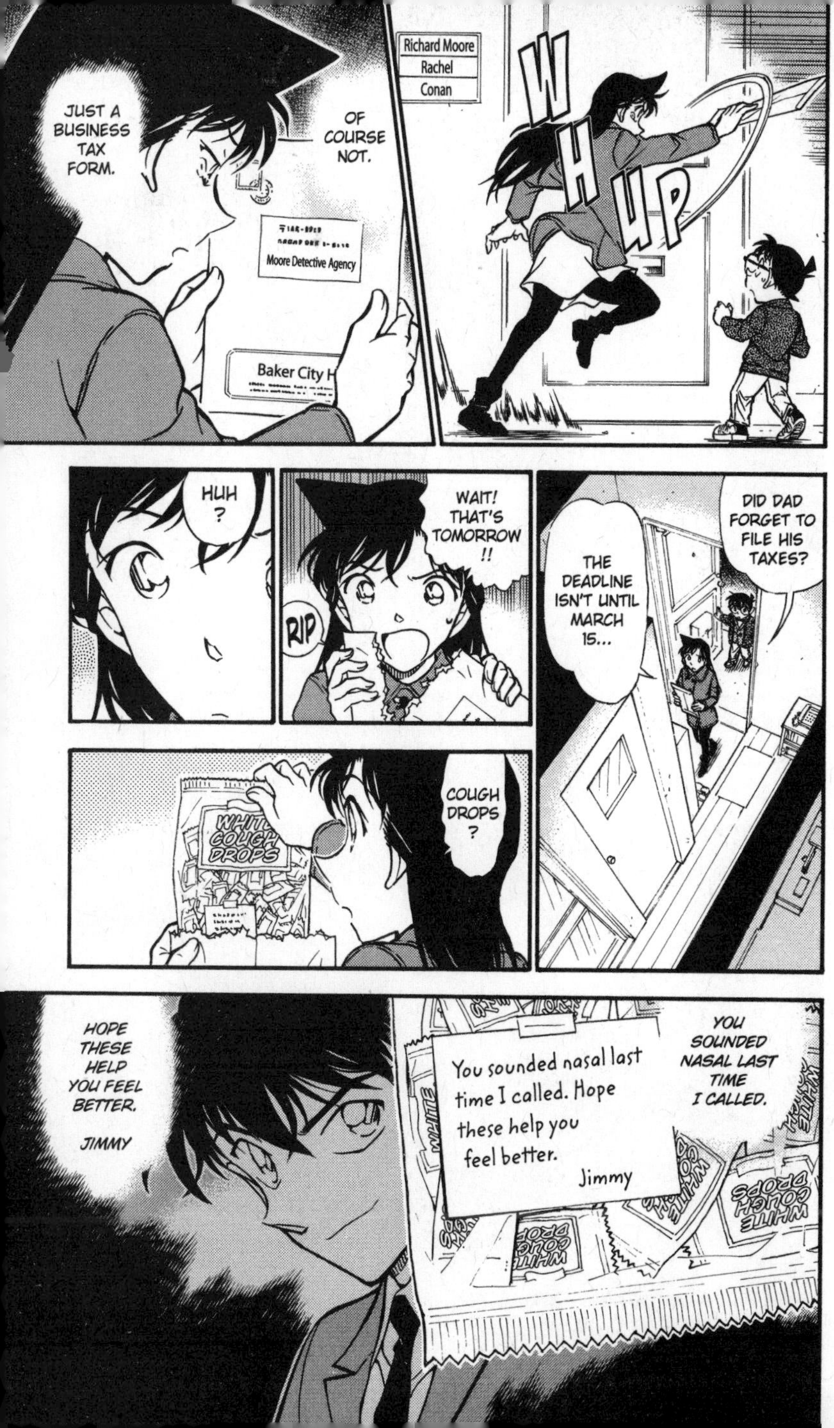

Richard Moore
Rachel
Conan
WHUP
OF COURSE NOT.
JUST A BUSINESS TAX FORM.
Moore Detective Agency
Baker City H
DID DAD FORGET TO FILE HIS TAXES?
THE DEADLINE ISN'T UNTIL MARCH 15...
WAIT! THAT'S TOMORROW!!
RIP
HUH?
COUGH DROPS?
WHITE COUGH DROPS
YOU SOUNDED NASAL LAST TIME I CALLED.
You sounded nasal last time I called. Hope these help you feel better.
Jimmy
HOPE THESE HELP YOU FEEL BETTER.
JIMMY

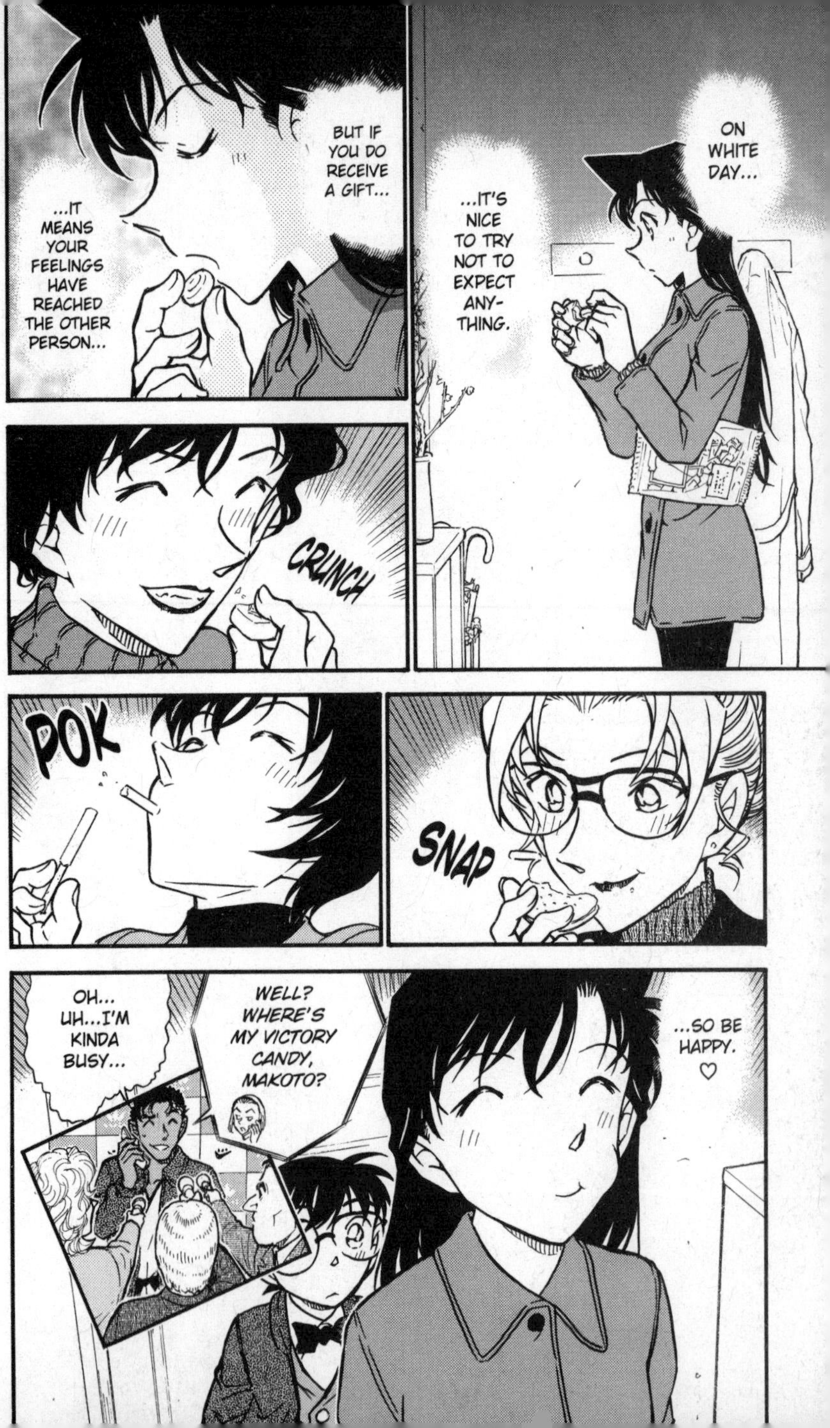
ON WHITE DAY...
...IT'S NICE TO TRY NOT TO EXPECT ANYTHING.
BUT IF YOU DO RECEIVE A GIFT...
...IT MEANS YOUR FEELINGS HAVE REACHED THE OTHER PERSON...
CRUNCH
SNAP
POK
...SO BE HAPPY. ♡
WELL? WHERE'S MY VICTORY CANDY, MAKOTO?
OH... UH...I'M KINDA BUSY...

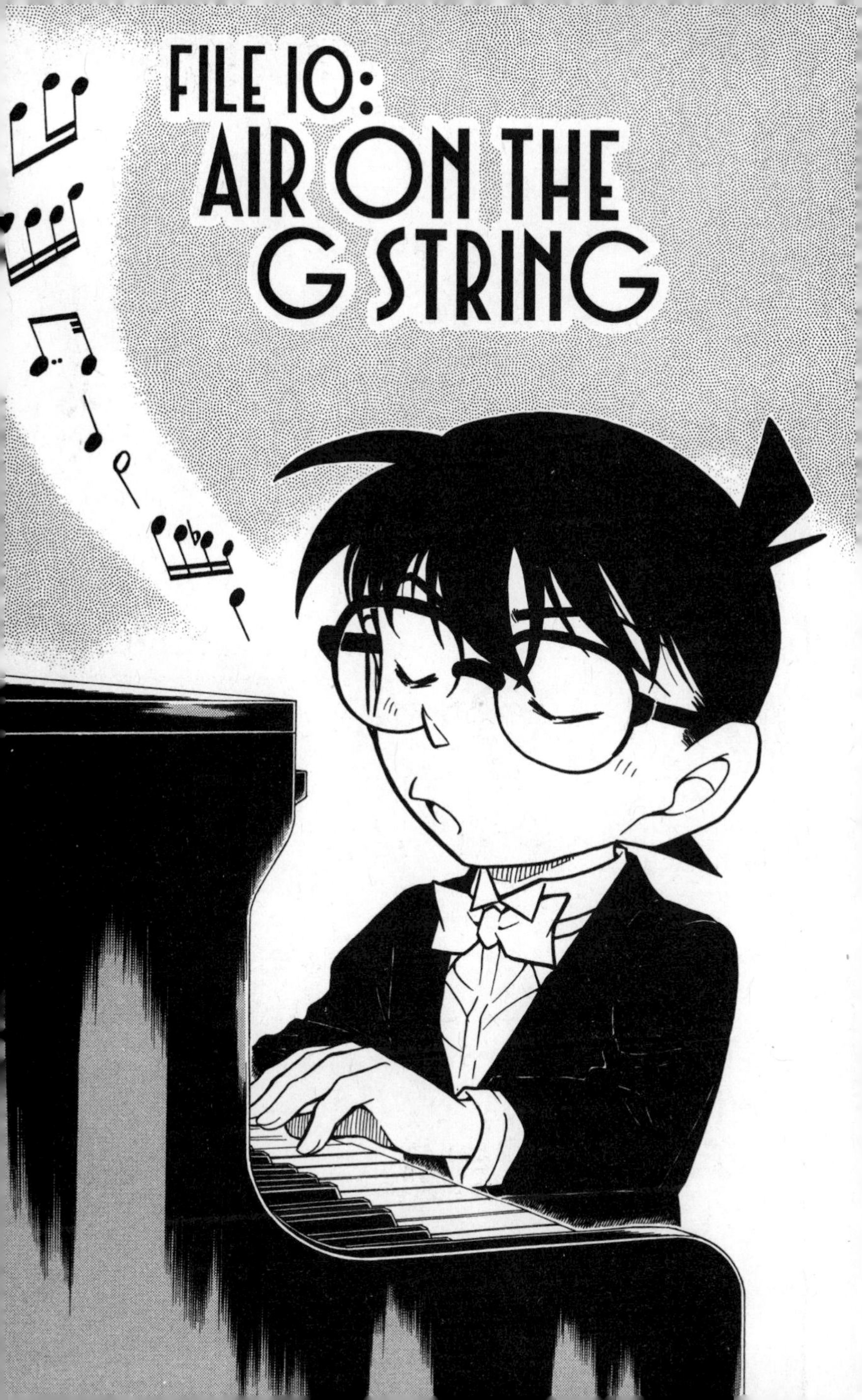
FILE 10:
AIR ON THE
G STRING

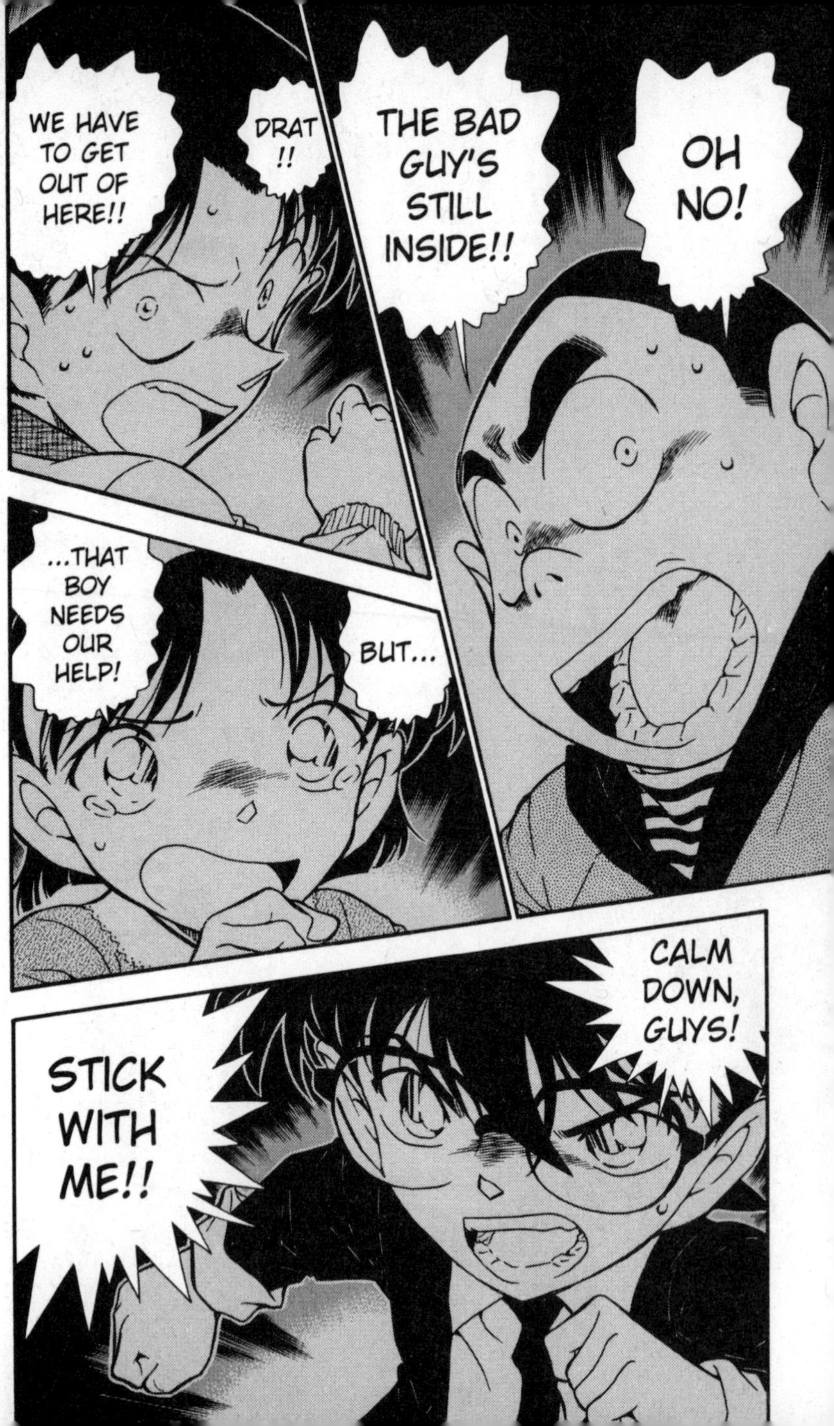
OH NO!
THE BAD GUY'S STILL INSIDE!!
DRAT !!
WE HAVE TO GET OUT OF HERE!!
BUT...
...THAT BOY NEEDS OUR HELP!
CALM DOWN, GUYS!
STICK WITH ME!!

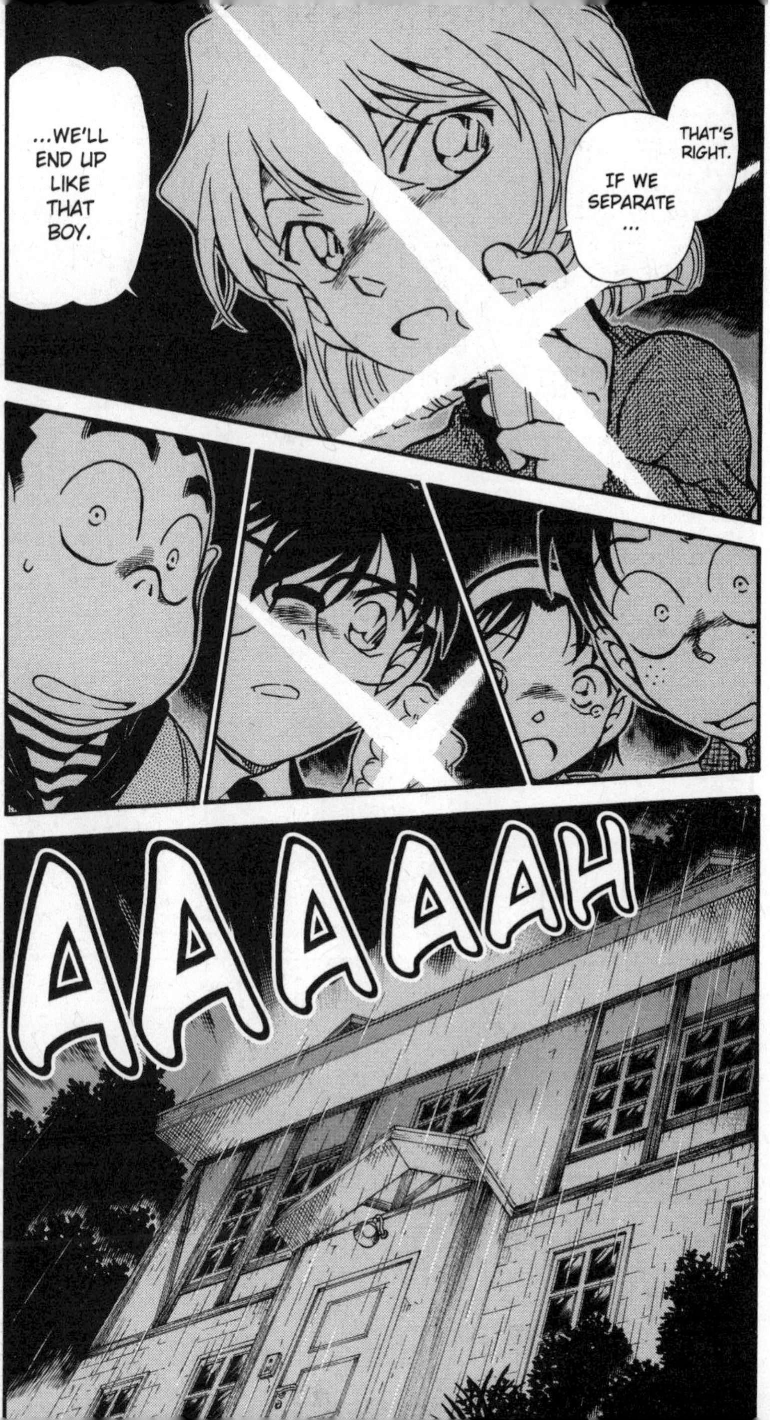
THAT'S RIGHT.
IF WE SEPARATE...
...WE'LL END UP LIKE THAT BOY.
AAAAAH

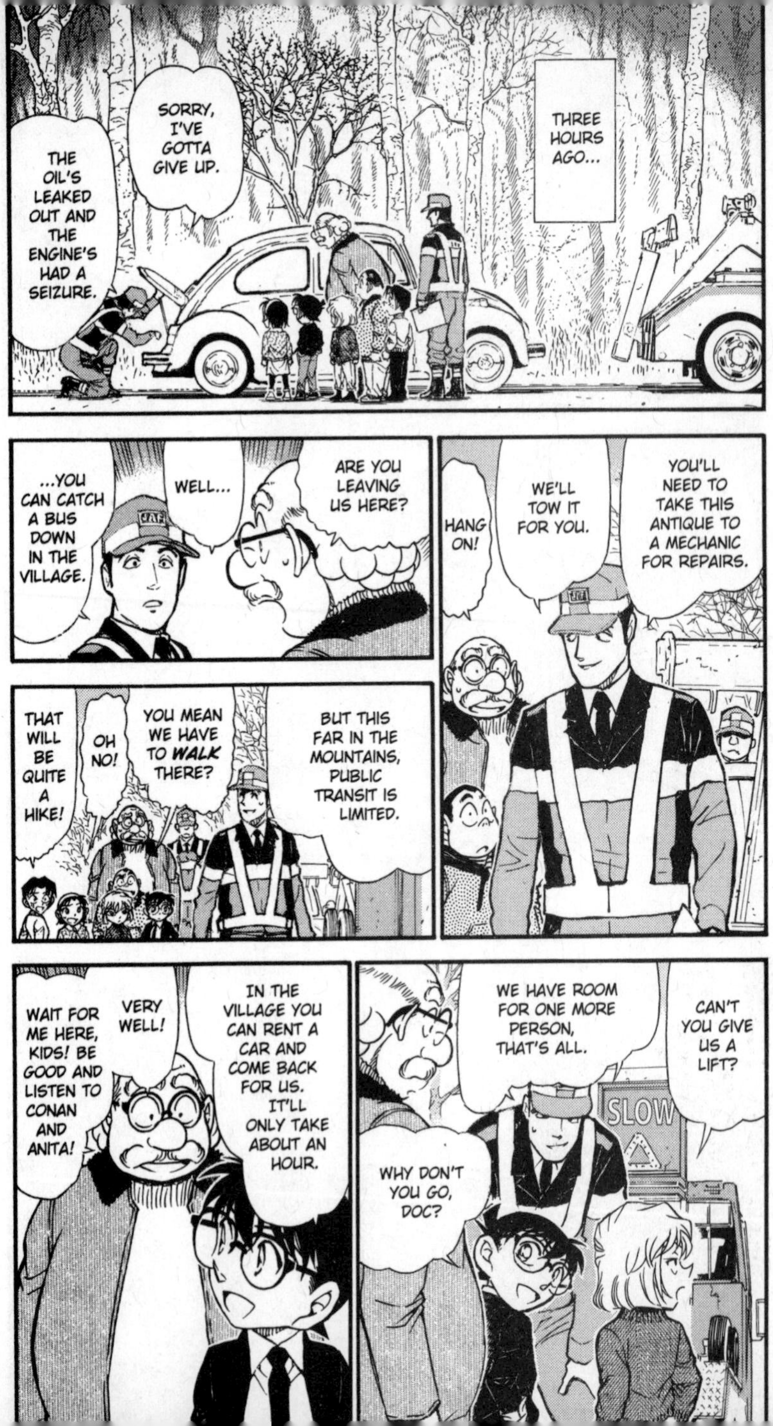
THREE HOURS AGO...
SORRY, I'VE GOTTA GIVE UP.
THE OIL'S LEAKED OUT AND THE ENGINE'S HAD A SEIZURE.
YOU'LL NEED TO TAKE THIS ANTIQUE TO A MECHANIC FOR REPAIRS.
WE'LL TOW IT FOR YOU.
HANG ON!
ARE YOU LEAVING US HERE?
WELL...
...YOU CAN CATCH A BUS DOWN IN THE VILLAGE.
BUT THIS FAR IN THE MOUNTAINS, PUBLIC TRANSIT IS LIMITED.
YOU MEAN WE HAVE TO *WALK* THERE?
OH NO!
THAT WILL BE QUITE A HIKE!
CAN'T YOU GIVE US A LIFT?
WE HAVE ROOM FOR ONE MORE PERSON, THAT'S ALL.
SLOW
WHY DON'T YOU GO, DOC?
IN THE VILLAGE YOU CAN RENT A CAR AND COME BACK FOR US. IT'LL ONLY TAKE ABOUT AN HOUR.
VERY WELL!
WAIT FOR ME HERE, KIDS! BE GOOD AND LISTEN TO CONAN AND ANITA!

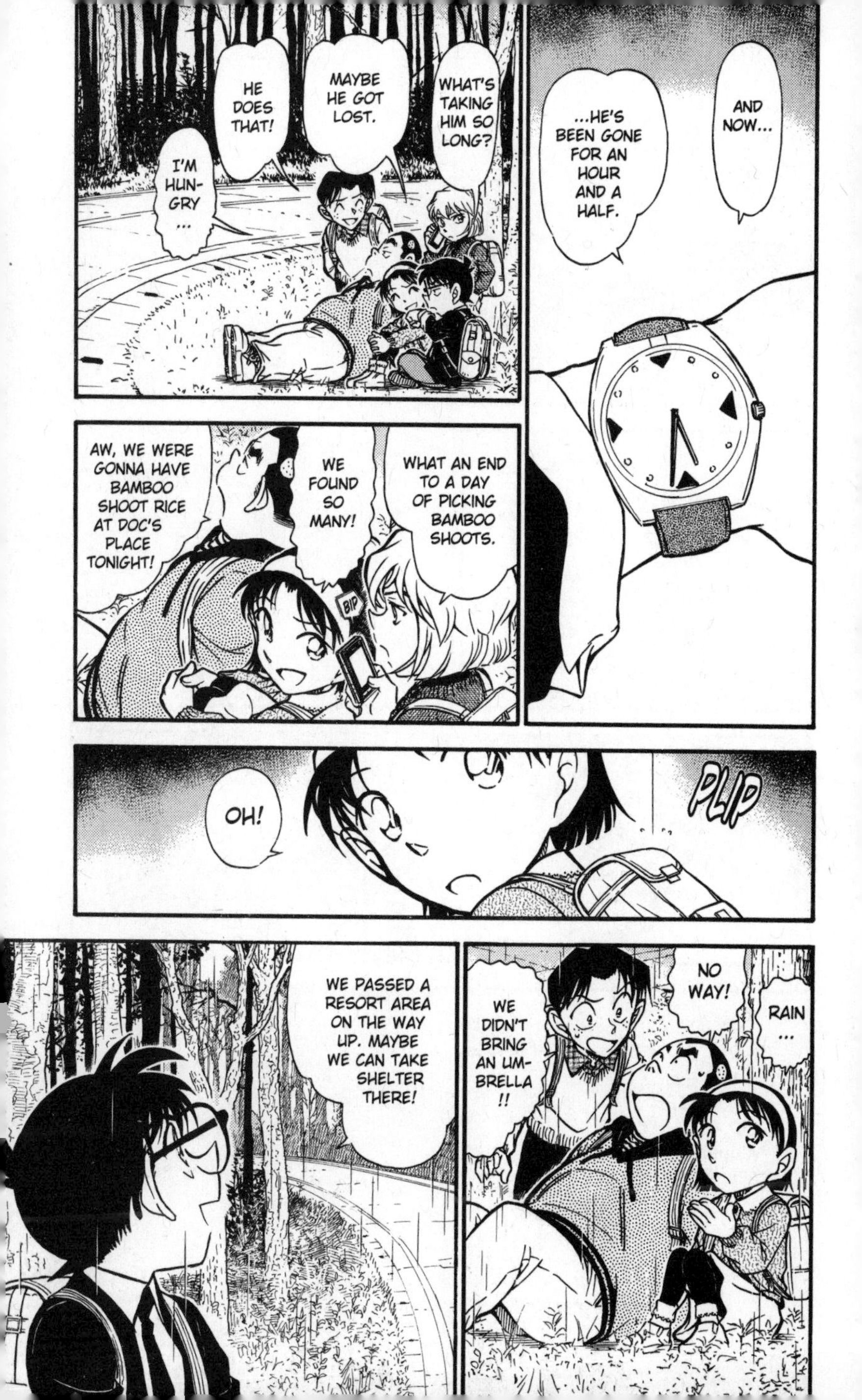
AND NOW...
...HE'S BEEN GONE FOR AN HOUR AND A HALF.
WHAT'S TAKING HIM SO LONG?
MAYBE HE GOT LOST.
HE DOES THAT!
I'M HUN-GRY ...
WHAT AN END TO A DAY OF PICKING BAMBOO SHOOTS.
WE FOUND SO MANY!
AW, WE WERE GONNA HAVE BAMBOO SHOOT RICE AT DOC'S PLACE TONIGHT!
BIP
PLIP
OH!
RAIN ...
NO WAY!
WE DIDN'T BRING AN UM-BRELLA !!
WE PASSED A RESORT AREA ON THE WAY UP. MAYBE WE CAN TAKE SHELTER THERE!

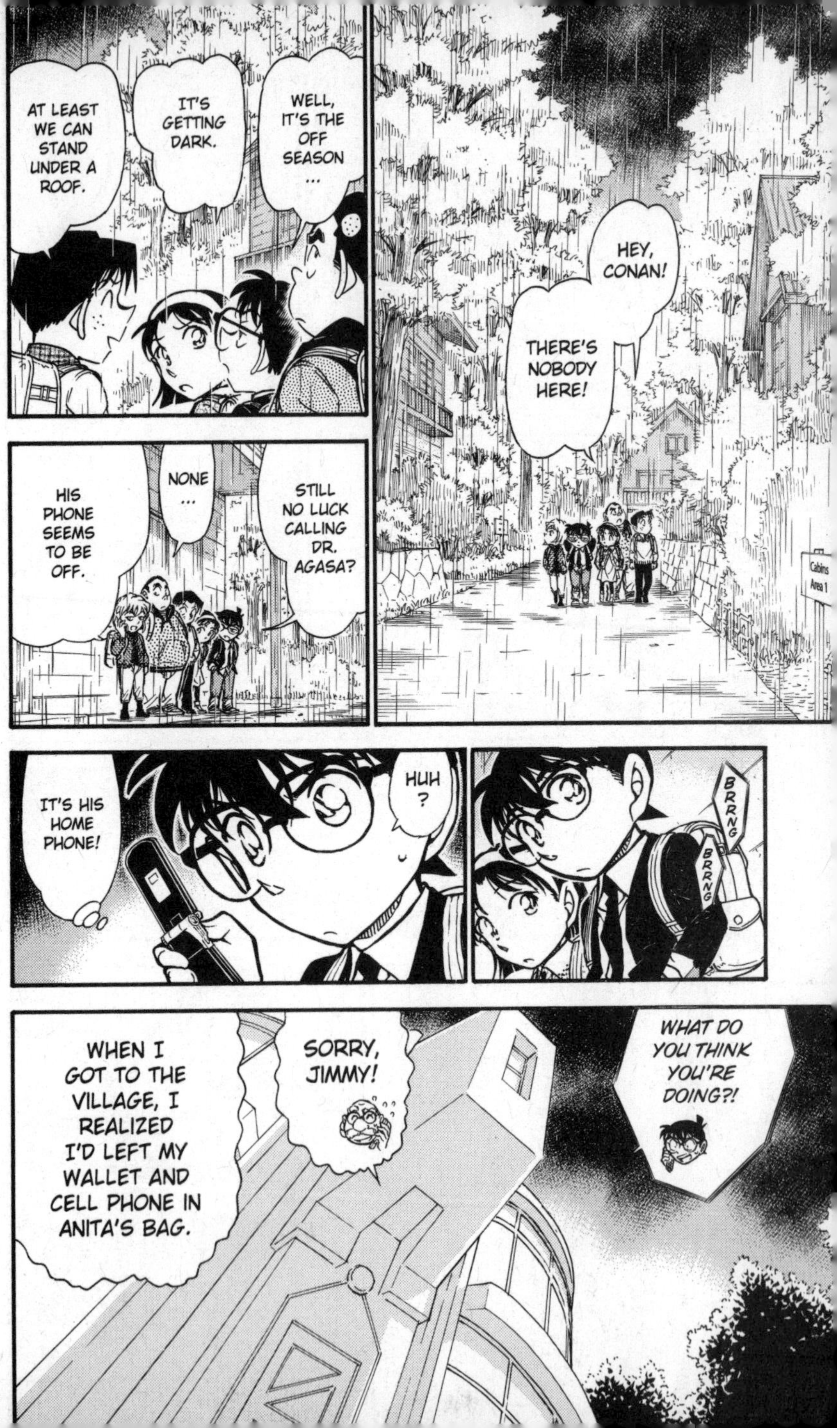
HEY, CONAN!
THERE'S NOBODY HERE!
Cabins Area 1
WELL, IT'S THE OFF SEASON...
IT'S GETTING DARK.
AT LEAST WE CAN STAND UNDER A ROOF.
STILL NO LUCK CALLING DR. AGASA?
NONE...
HIS PHONE SEEMS TO BE OFF.
BRRNG
BRRNG
HUH?
IT'S HIS HOME PHONE!
WHAT DO YOU THINK YOU'RE DOING?!
SORRY, JIMMY!
WHEN I GOT TO THE VILLAGE, I REALIZED I'D LEFT MY WALLET AND CELL PHONE IN ANITA'S BAG.

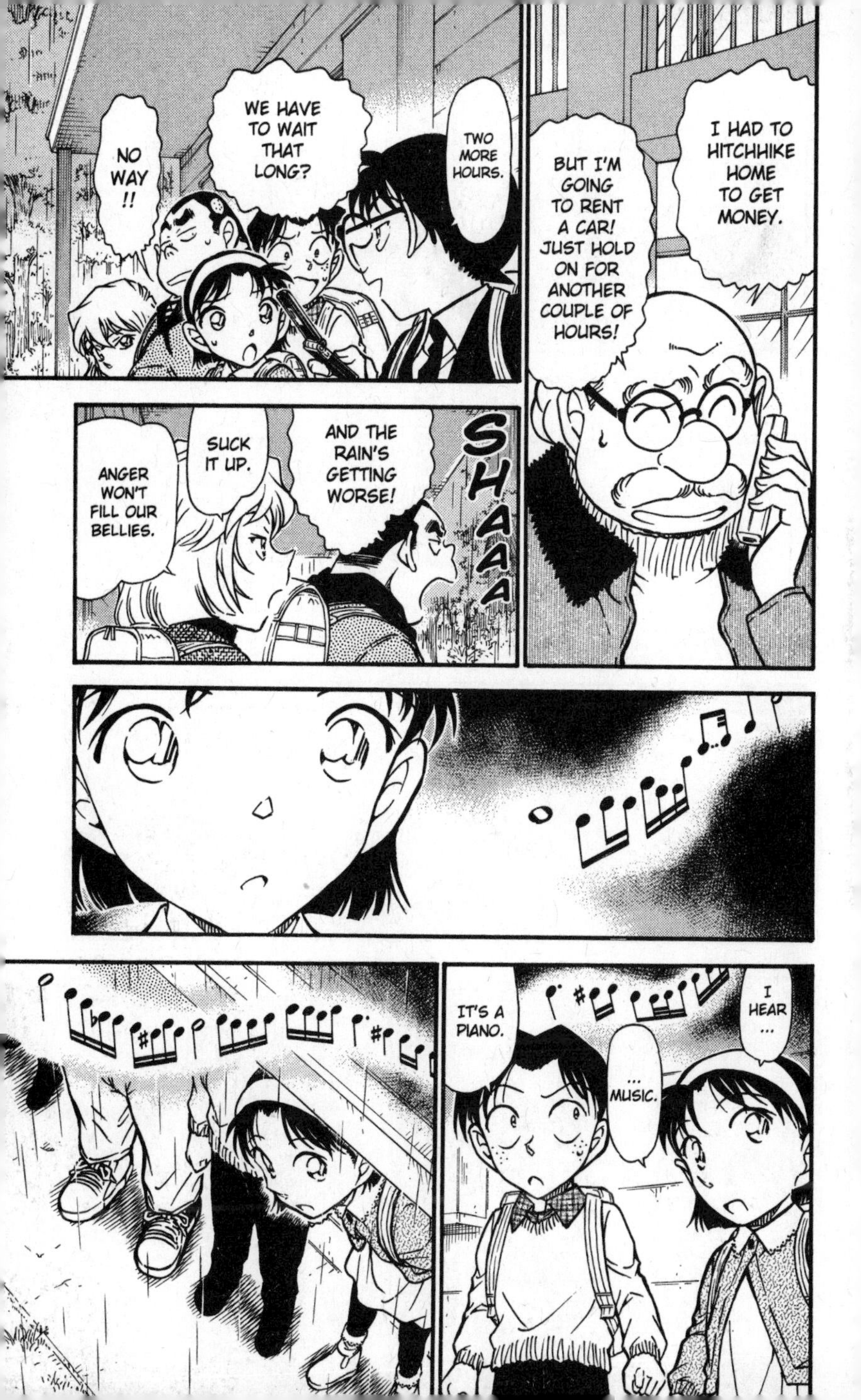
I HAD TO HITCHHIKE HOME TO GET MONEY.
BUT I'M GOING TO RENT A CAR! JUST HOLD ON FOR ANOTHER COUPLE OF HOURS!
TWO MORE HOURS.
WE HAVE TO WAIT THAT LONG?
NO WAY !!
SHAAAA
AND THE RAIN'S GETTING WORSE!
SUCK IT UP.
ANGER WON'T FILL OUR BELLIES.
I HEAR ...
... MUSIC.
IT'S A PIANO.

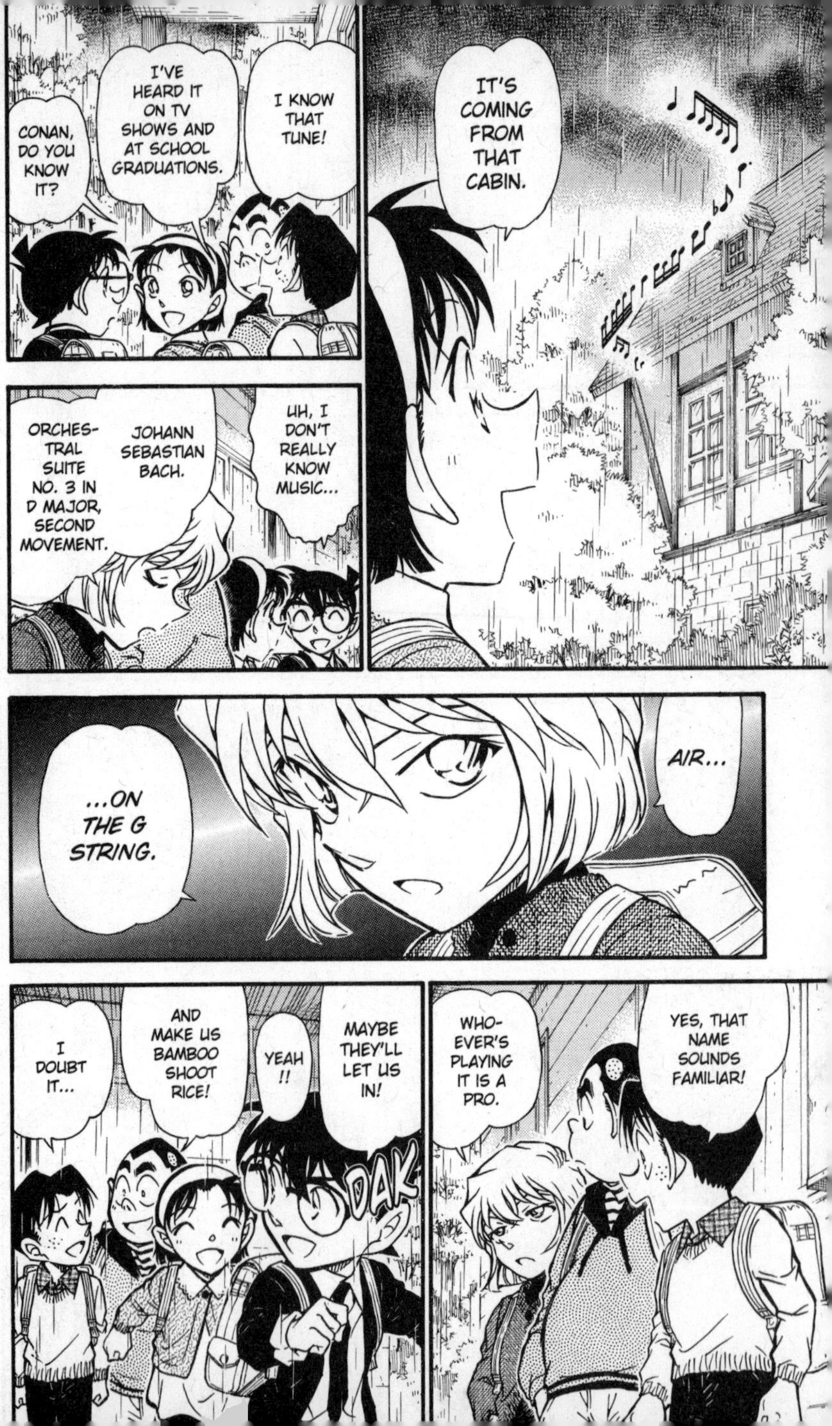

IT'S COMING FROM THAT CABIN.
I KNOW THAT TUNE!
I'VE HEARD IT ON TV SHOWS AND AT SCHOOL GRADUATIONS.
CONAN, DO YOU KNOW IT?
UH, I DON'T REALLY KNOW MUSIC...
JOHANN SEBASTIAN BACH.
ORCHES-TRAL SUITE NO. 3 IN D MAJOR, SECOND MOVEMENT.
AIR...
...ON THE G STRING.
YES, THAT NAME SOUNDS FAMILIAR!
WHO-EVER'S PLAYING IT IS A PRO.
MAYBE THEY'LL LET US IN!
YEAH!!
AND MAKE US BAMBOO SHOOT RICE!
I DOUBT IT...
DAK

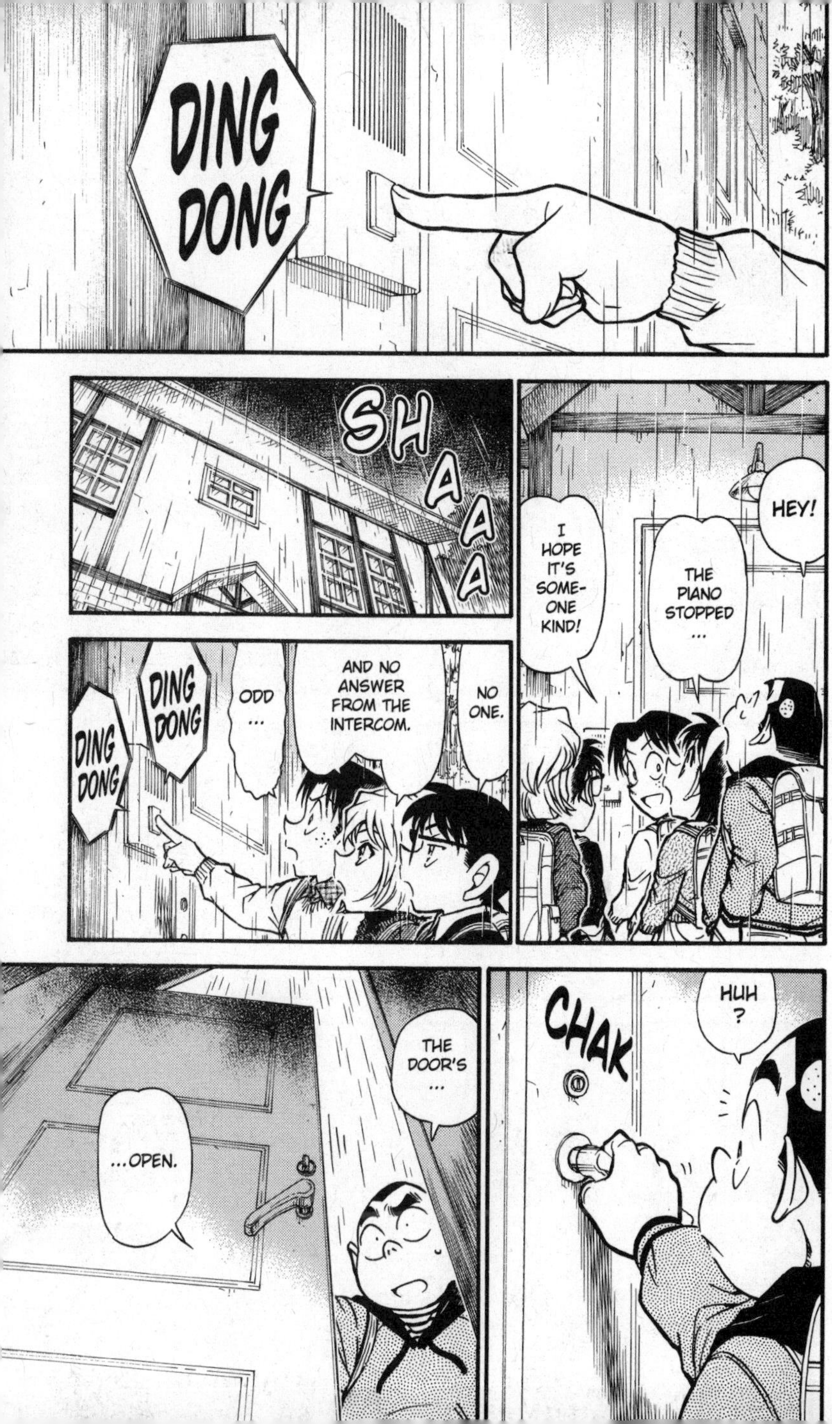
DING DONG
HEY!
THE PIANO STOPPED ...
I HOPE IT'S SOME-ONE KIND!
SHAAAA
NO ONE.
AND NO ANSWER FROM THE INTERCOM.
ODD ...
DING DONG
DING DONG
HUH ?
CHAK
THE DOOR'S ...
...OPEN.

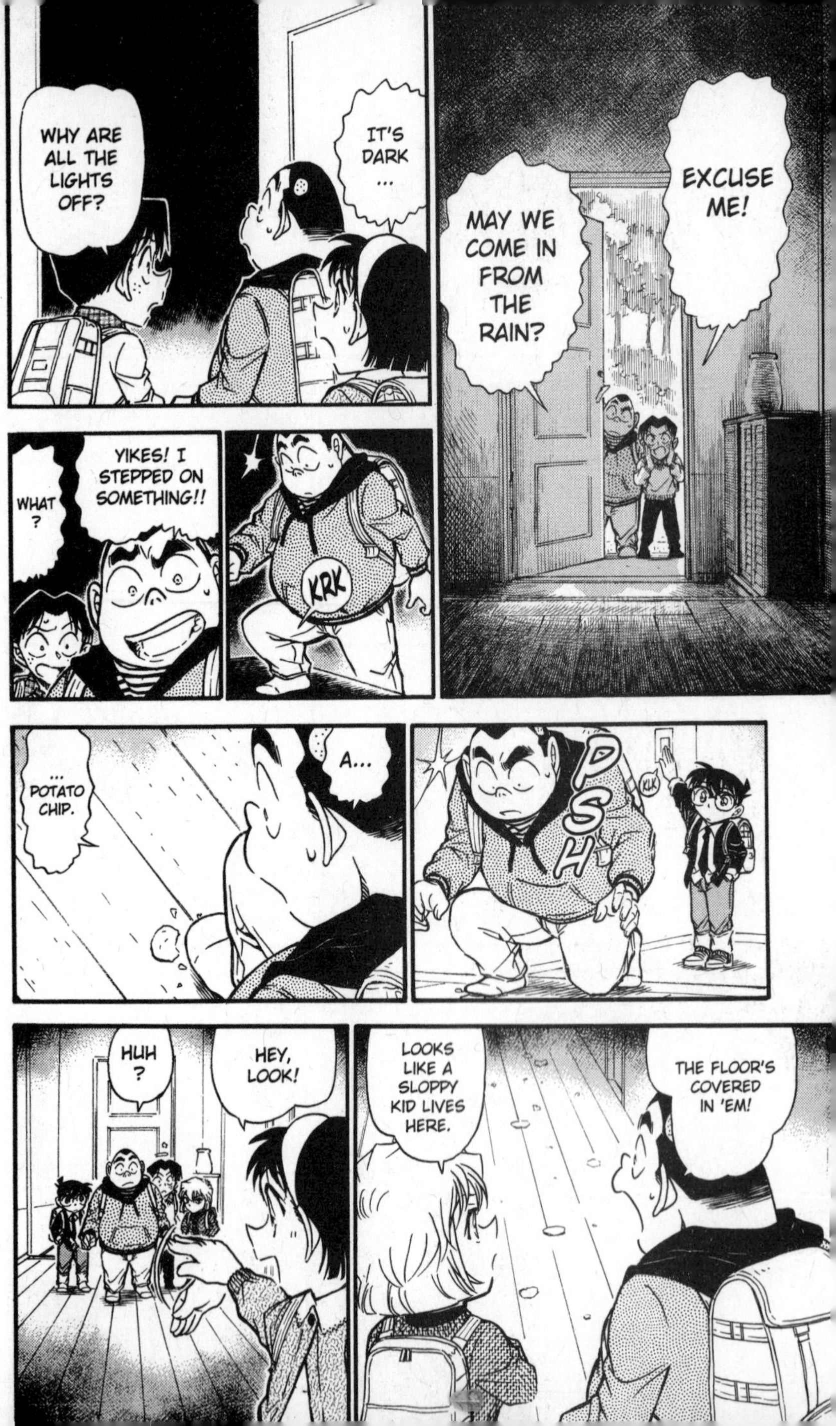
EXCUSE ME!
MAY WE COME IN FROM THE RAIN?
IT'S DARK ...
WHY ARE ALL THE LIGHTS OFF?
KRK
YIKES! I STEPPED ON SOMETHING!!
WHAT ?
PSH
KLK
A...
... POTATO CHIP.
THE FLOOR'S COVERED IN 'EM!
LOOKS LIKE A SLOPPY KID LIVES HERE.
HEY, LOOK!
HUH ?

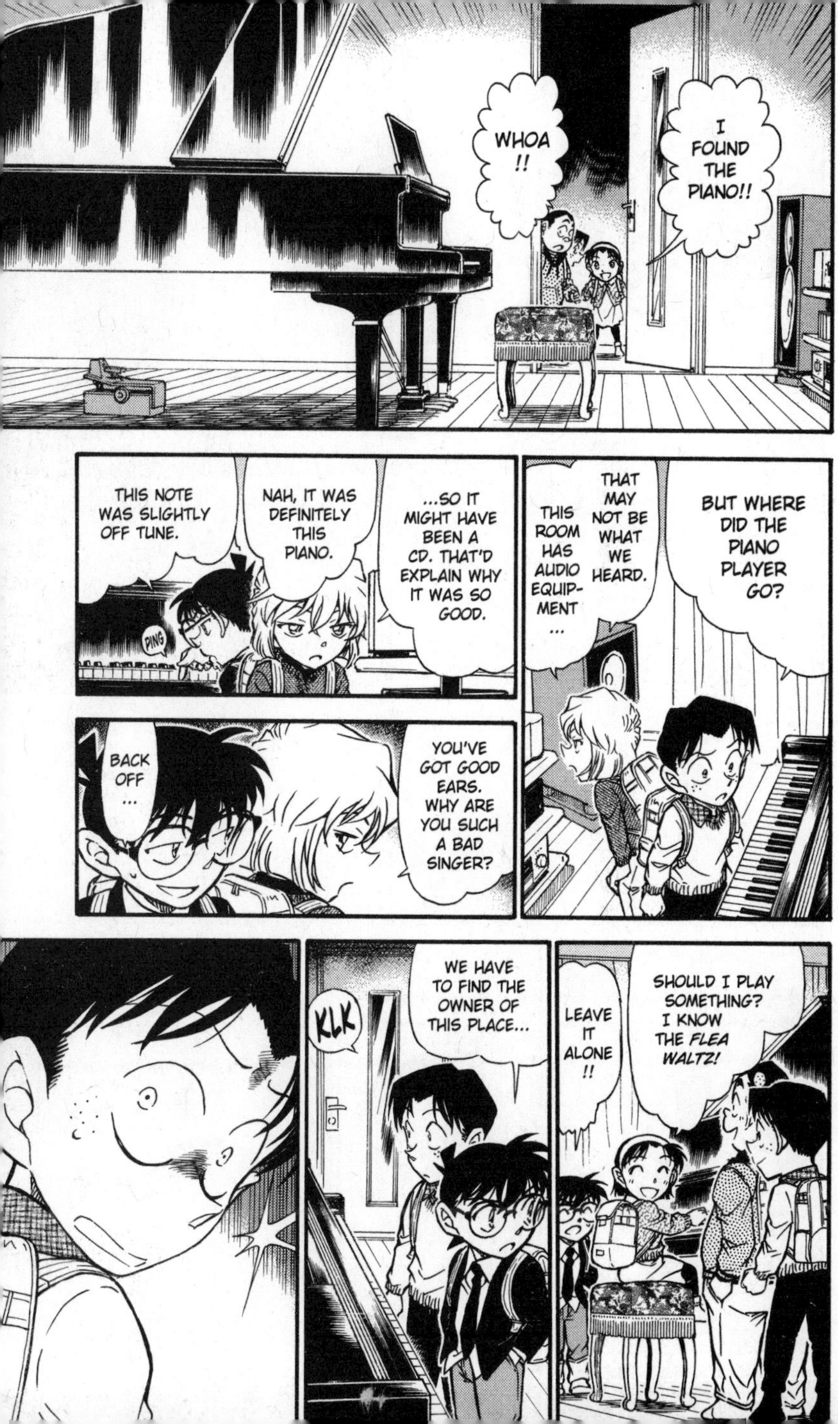
I FOUND THE PIANO!!
WHOA!!
BUT WHERE DID THE PIANO PLAYER GO?
THAT MAY NOT BE WHAT WE HEARD.
THIS ROOM HAS AUDIO EQUIP-MENT...
...SO IT MIGHT HAVE BEEN A CD. THAT'D EXPLAIN WHY IT WAS SO GOOD.
NAH, IT WAS DEFINITELY THIS PIANO.
THIS NOTE WAS SLIGHTLY OFF TUNE.
PING
YOU'VE GOT GOOD EARS. WHY ARE YOU SUCH A BAD SINGER?
BACK OFF...
SHOULD I PLAY SOMETHING? I KNOW THE *FLEA WALTZ!*
LEAVE IT ALONE!!
WE HAVE TO FIND THE OWNER OF THIS PLACE...
KLK

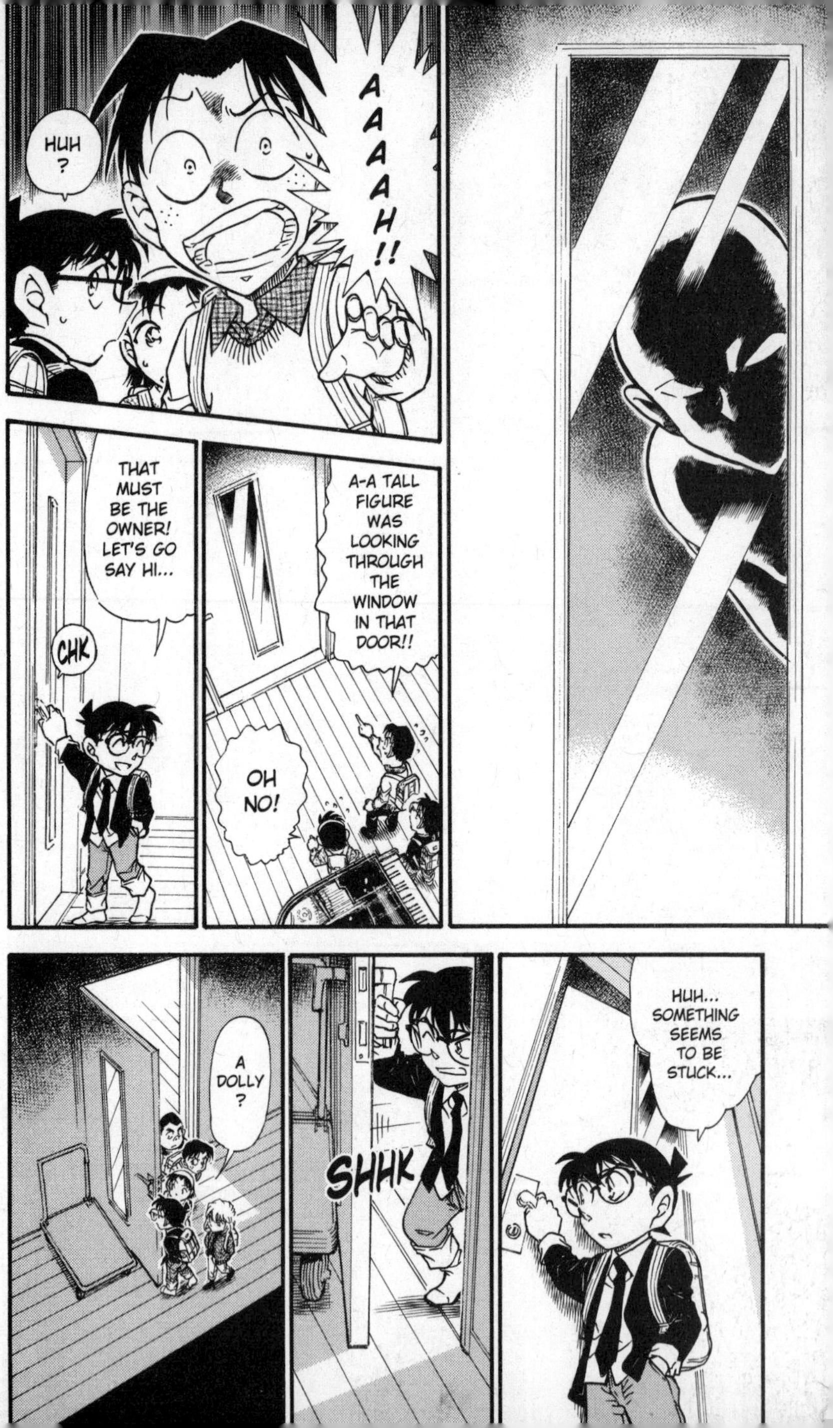
AAAAAH!!
HUH?
A-A TALL FIGURE WAS LOOKING THROUGH THE WINDOW IN THAT DOOR!!
OH NO!
THAT MUST BE THE OWNER! LET'S GO SAY HI...
CHK
HUH... SOMETHING SEEMS TO BE STUCK...
SHHK
A DOLLY?

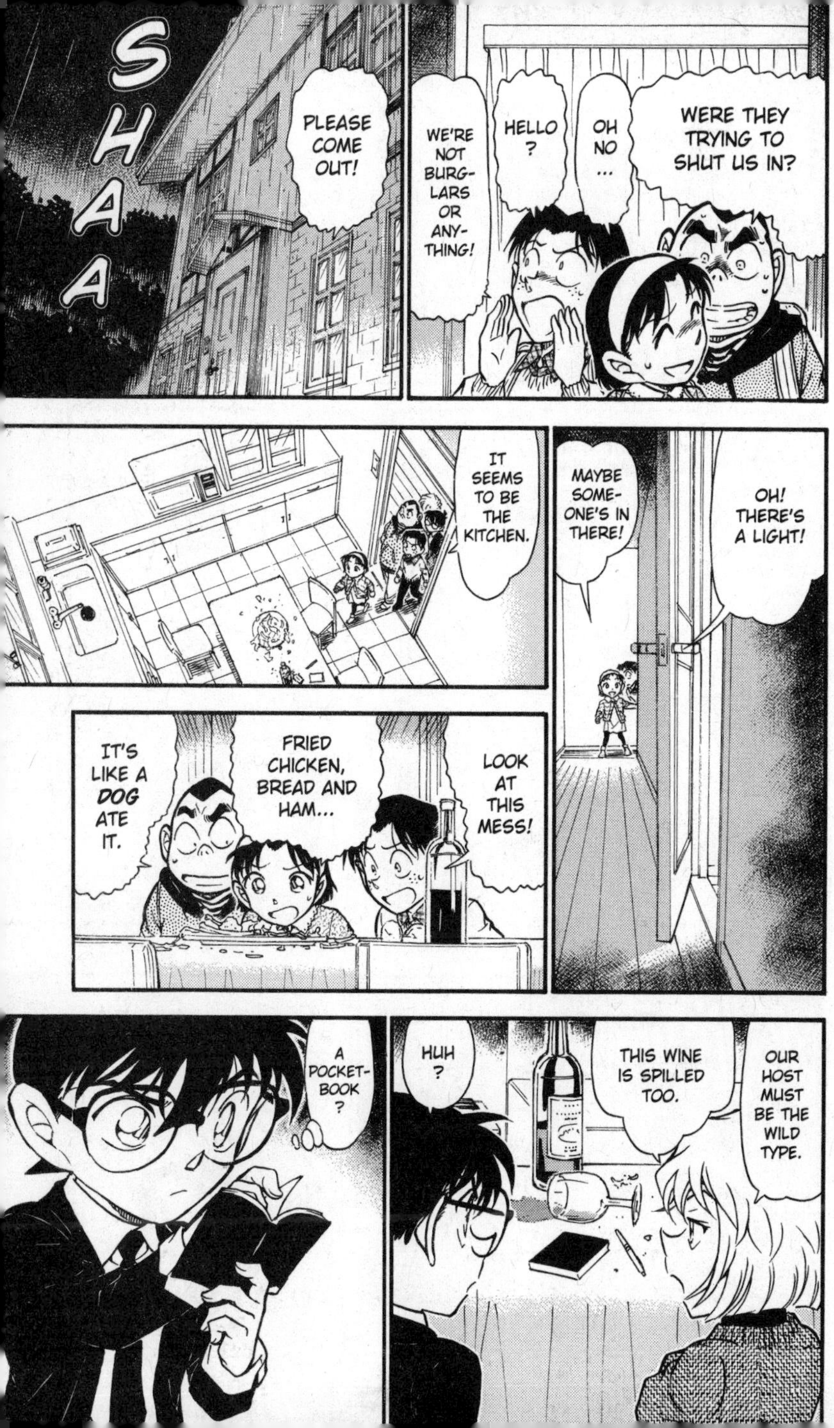
WERE THEY TRYING TO SHUT US IN?
OH NO ...
HELLO ?
WE'RE NOT BURGLARS OR ANYTHING!
PLEASE COME OUT!
SHAAA
OH! THERE'S A LIGHT!
MAYBE SOMEONE'S IN THERE!
IT SEEMS TO BE THE KITCHEN.
LOOK AT THIS MESS!
FRIED CHICKEN, BREAD AND HAM...
IT'S LIKE A *DOG* ATE IT.
OUR HOST MUST BE THE WILD TYPE.
THIS WINE IS SPILLED TOO.
HUH ?
A POCKETBOOK ?

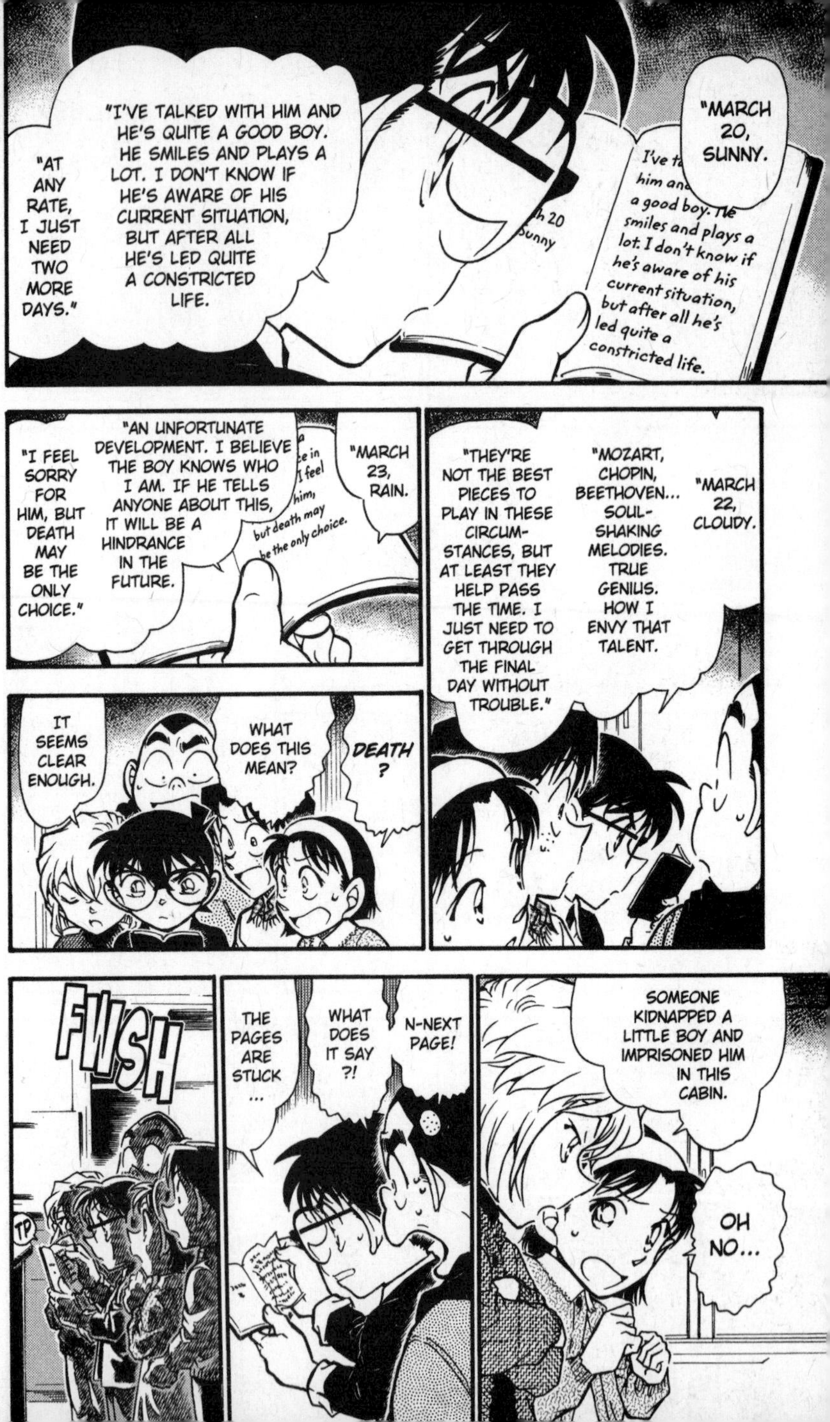
"MARCH 20, SUNNY.
smiles and plays a lot. I don't know if he's aware of his current situation, but after all he's led quite a constricted life.
"I'VE TALKED WITH HIM AND HE'S QUITE A GOOD BOY. HE SMILES AND PLAYS A LOT. I DON'T KNOW IF HE'S AWARE OF HIS CURRENT SITUATION, BUT AFTER ALL HE'S LED QUITE A CONSTRICTED LIFE.
"AT ANY RATE, I JUST NEED TWO MORE DAYS."
"MARCH 22, CLOUDY.
"MOZART, CHOPIN, BEETHOVEN... SOUL-SHAKING MELODIES. TRUE GENIUS. HOW I ENVY THAT TALENT.
"THEY'RE NOT THE BEST PIECES TO PLAY IN THESE CIRCUM-STANCES, BUT AT LEAST THEY HELP PASS THE TIME. I JUST NEED TO GET THROUGH THE FINAL DAY WITHOUT TROUBLE."
"MARCH 23, RAIN.
but death may be the only choice.
"AN UNFORTUNATE DEVELOPMENT. I BELIEVE THE BOY KNOWS WHO I AM. IF HE TELLS ANYONE ABOUT THIS, IT WILL BE A HINDRANCE IN THE FUTURE.
"I FEEL SORRY FOR HIM, BUT DEATH MAY BE THE ONLY CHOICE."
DEATH?
WHAT DOES THIS MEAN?
IT SEEMS CLEAR ENOUGH.
SOMEONE KIDNAPPED A LITTLE BOY AND IMPRISONED HIM IN THIS CABIN.
OH NO...
N-NEXT PAGE!
WHAT DOES IT SAY?!
THE PAGES ARE STUCK...
FWSH
TP

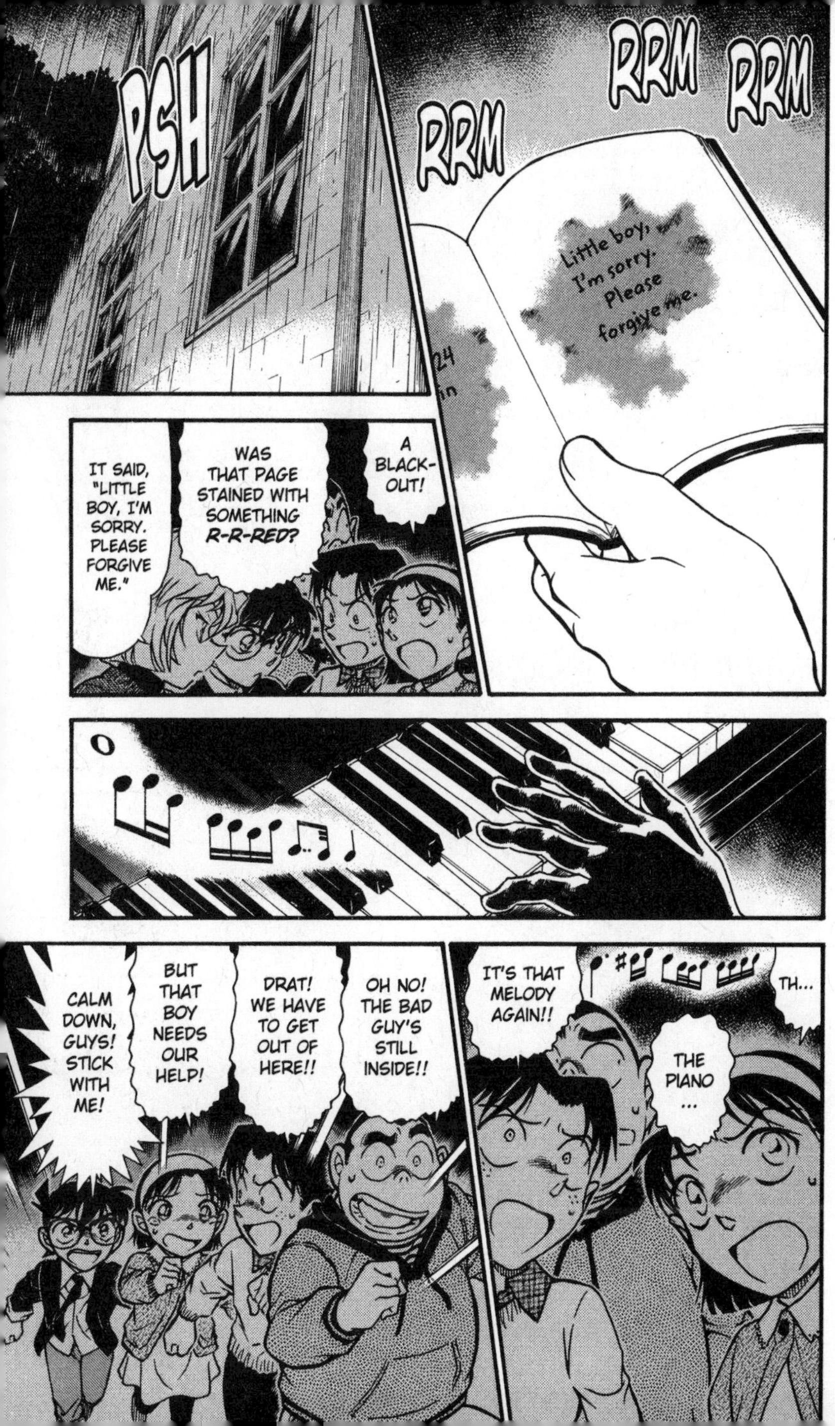
RRM
RRM
RRM
Little boy, I'm sorry. Please forgive me.
PSH
A BLACK-OUT!
WAS THAT PAGE STAINED WITH SOMETHING R-R-RED?
IT SAID, "LITTLE BOY, I'M SORRY. PLEASE FORGIVE ME."
TH...
THE PIANO ...
IT'S THAT MELODY AGAIN!!
OH NO! THE BAD GUY'S STILL INSIDE!!
DRAT! WE HAVE TO GET OUT OF HERE!!
BUT THAT BOY NEEDS OUR HELP!
CALM DOWN, GUYS! STICK WITH ME!

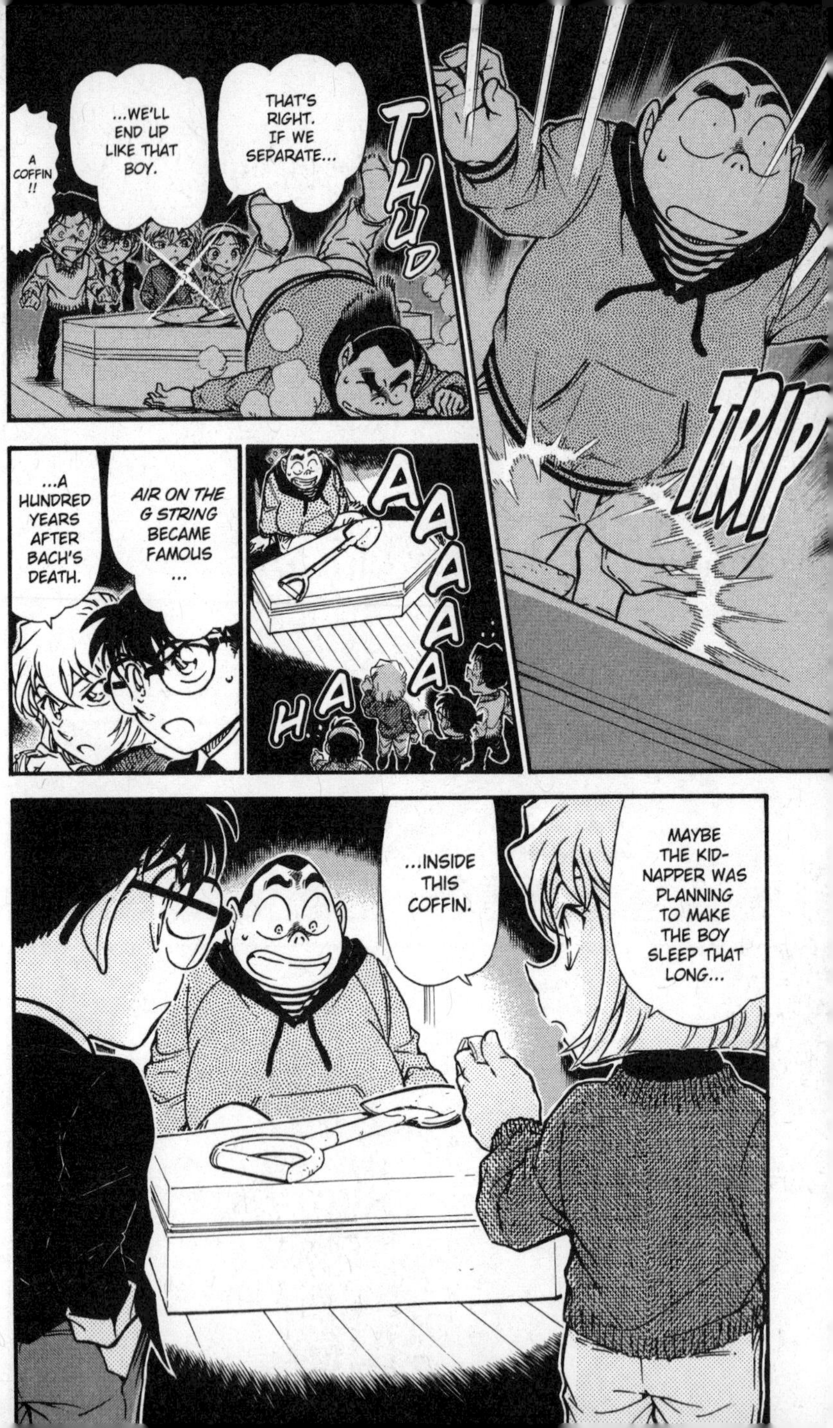
TRIP
THUD
THAT'S RIGHT. IF WE SEPARATE...
...WE'LL END UP LIKE THAT BOY.
A COFFIN !!
AAAAAAAAH
AIR ON THE G STRING BECAME FAMOUS ...
...A HUNDRED YEARS AFTER BACH'S DEATH.
MAYBE THE KID-NAPPER WAS PLANNING TO MAKE THE BOY SLEEP THAT LONG...
...INSIDE THIS COFFIN.

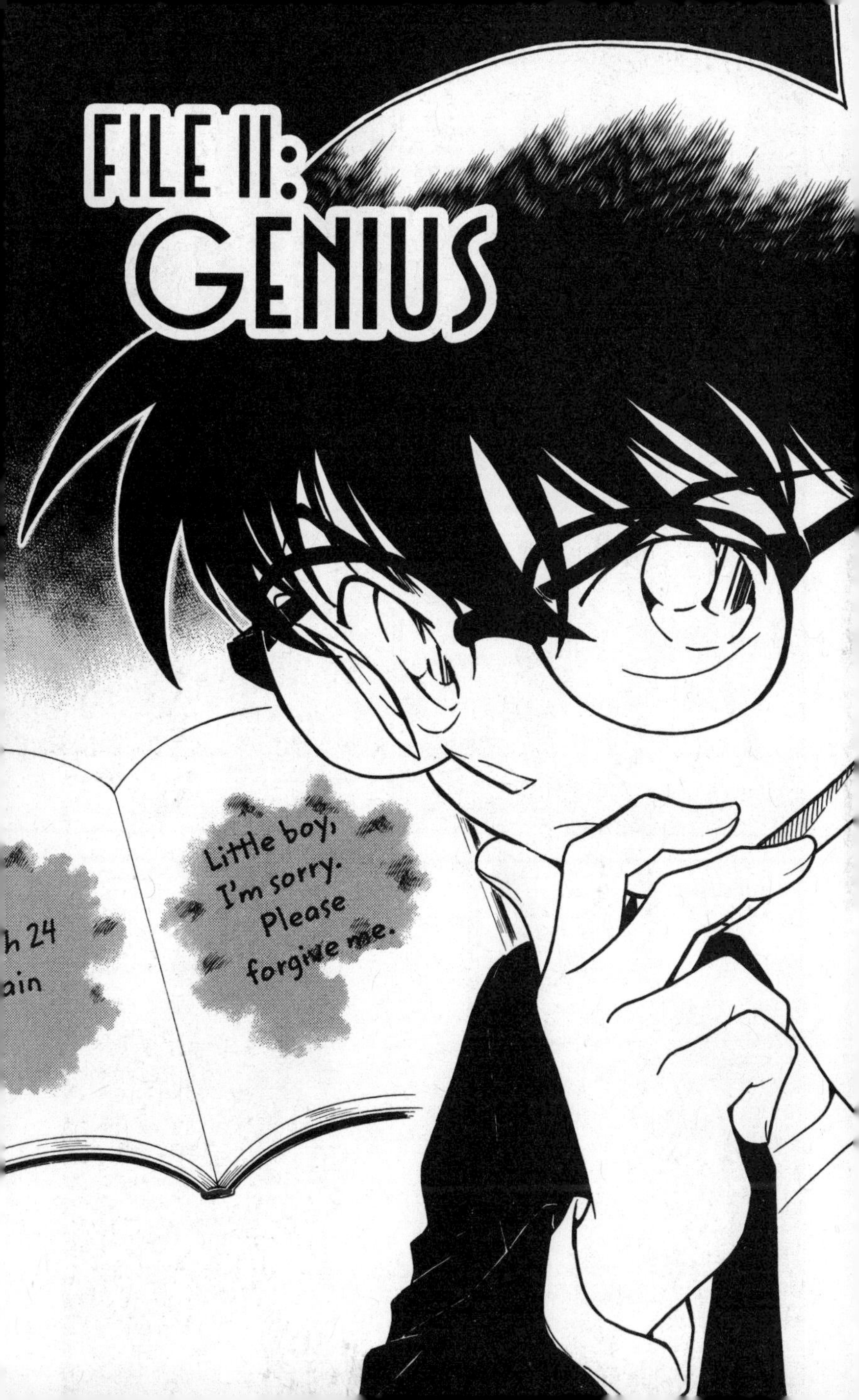
FILE 11: GENIUS
Little boy, I'm sorry. Please forgive me.

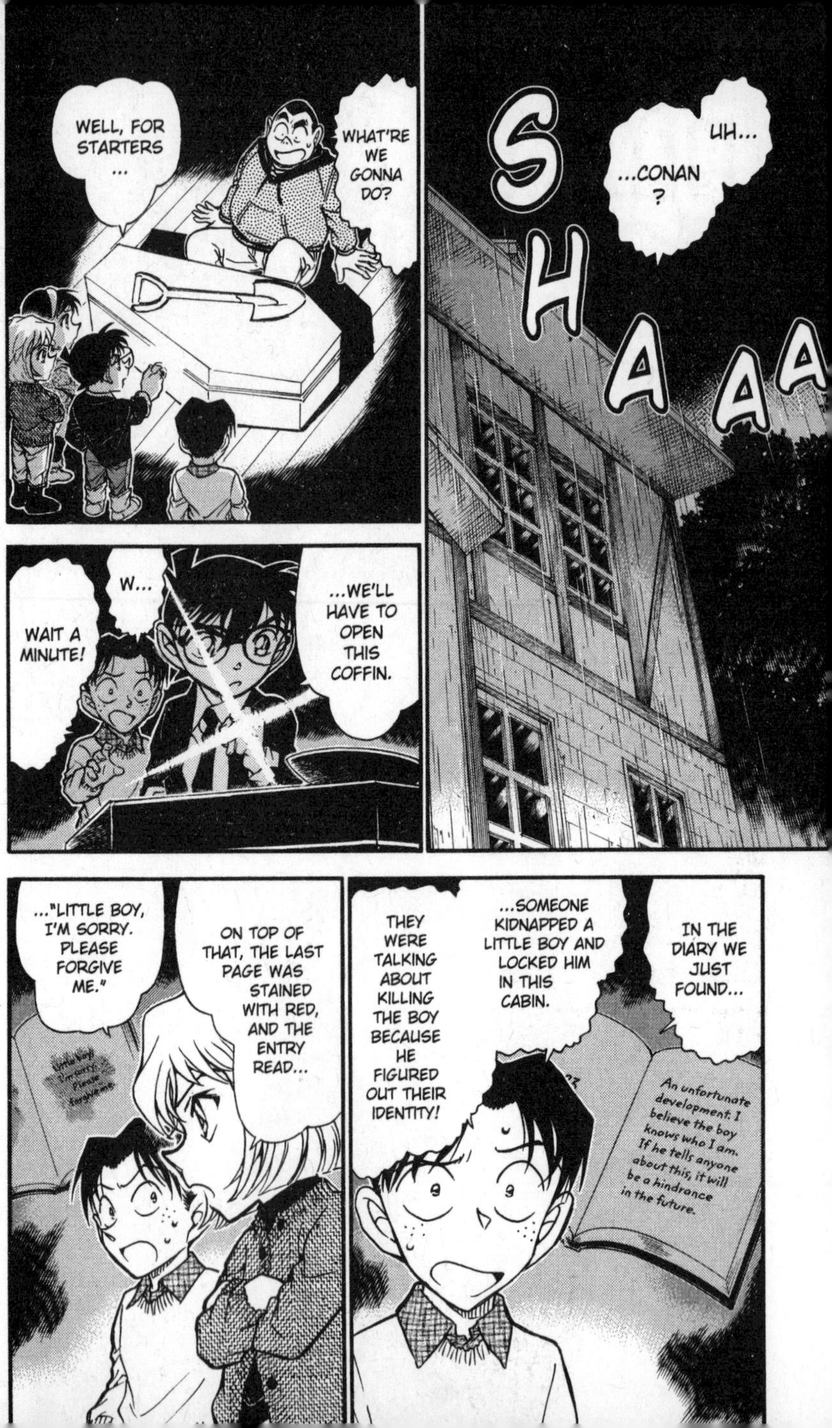
UH...
...CONAN ?
SHAAA
WHAT'RE WE GONNA DO?
WELL, FOR STARTERS ...
...WE'LL HAVE TO OPEN THIS COFFIN.
W...
WAIT A MINUTE!
IN THE DIARY WE JUST FOUND...
...SOMEONE KIDNAPPED A LITTLE BOY AND LOCKED HIM IN THIS CABIN.
THEY WERE TALKING ABOUT KILLING THE BOY BECAUSE HE FIGURED OUT THEIR IDENTITY!
An unfortunate development. I believe the boy knows who I am. If he tells anyone about this, it will be a hindrance in the future.
ON TOP OF THAT, THE LAST PAGE WAS STAINED WITH RED, AND THE ENTRY READ...
..."LITTLE BOY, I'M SORRY. PLEASE FORGIVE ME."

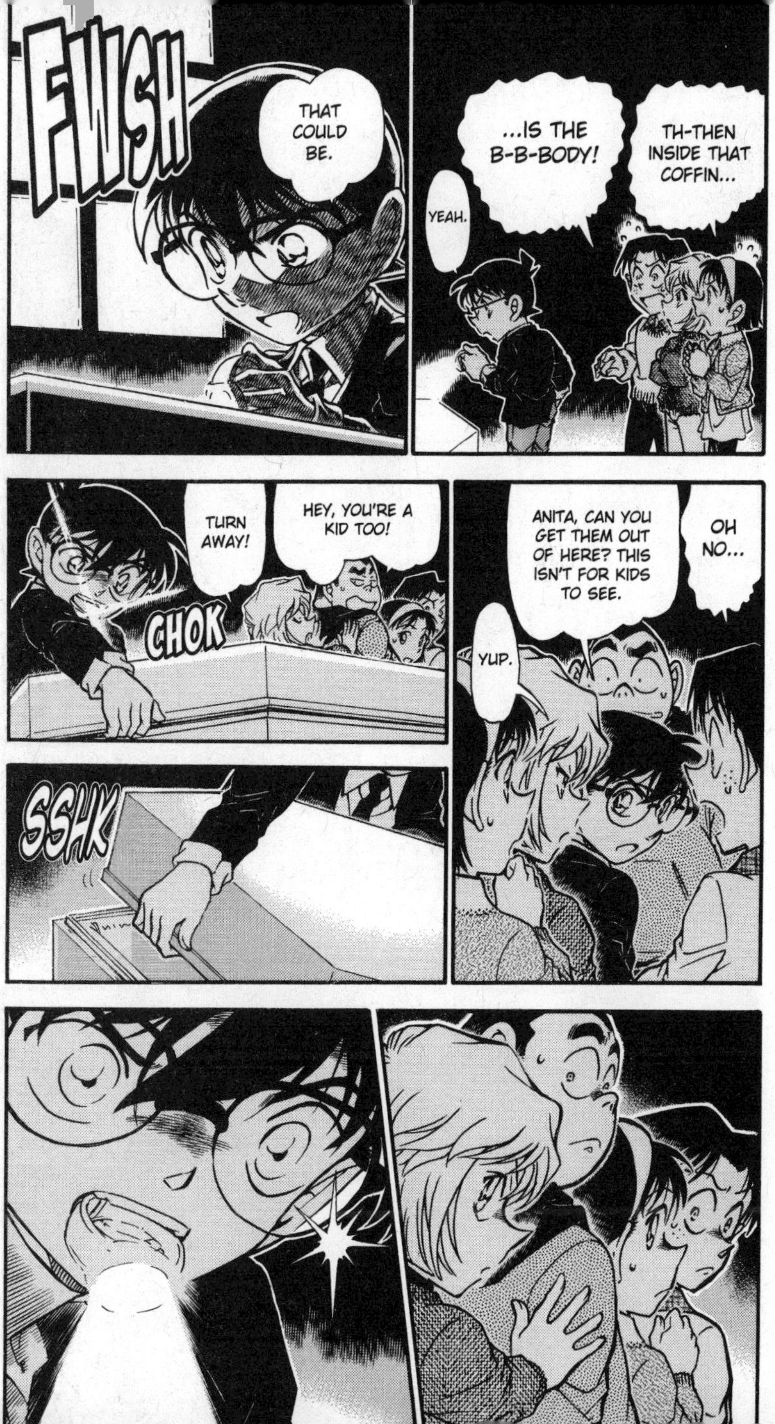
TH-THEN INSIDE THAT COFFIN...
...IS THE B-B-BODY!
YEAH.
THAT COULD BE.
F-WSH
OH NO...
ANITA, CAN YOU GET THEM OUT OF HERE? THIS ISN'T FOR KIDS TO SEE.
YUP.
HEY, YOU'RE A KID TOO!
TURN AWAY!
CHOK
SSHK

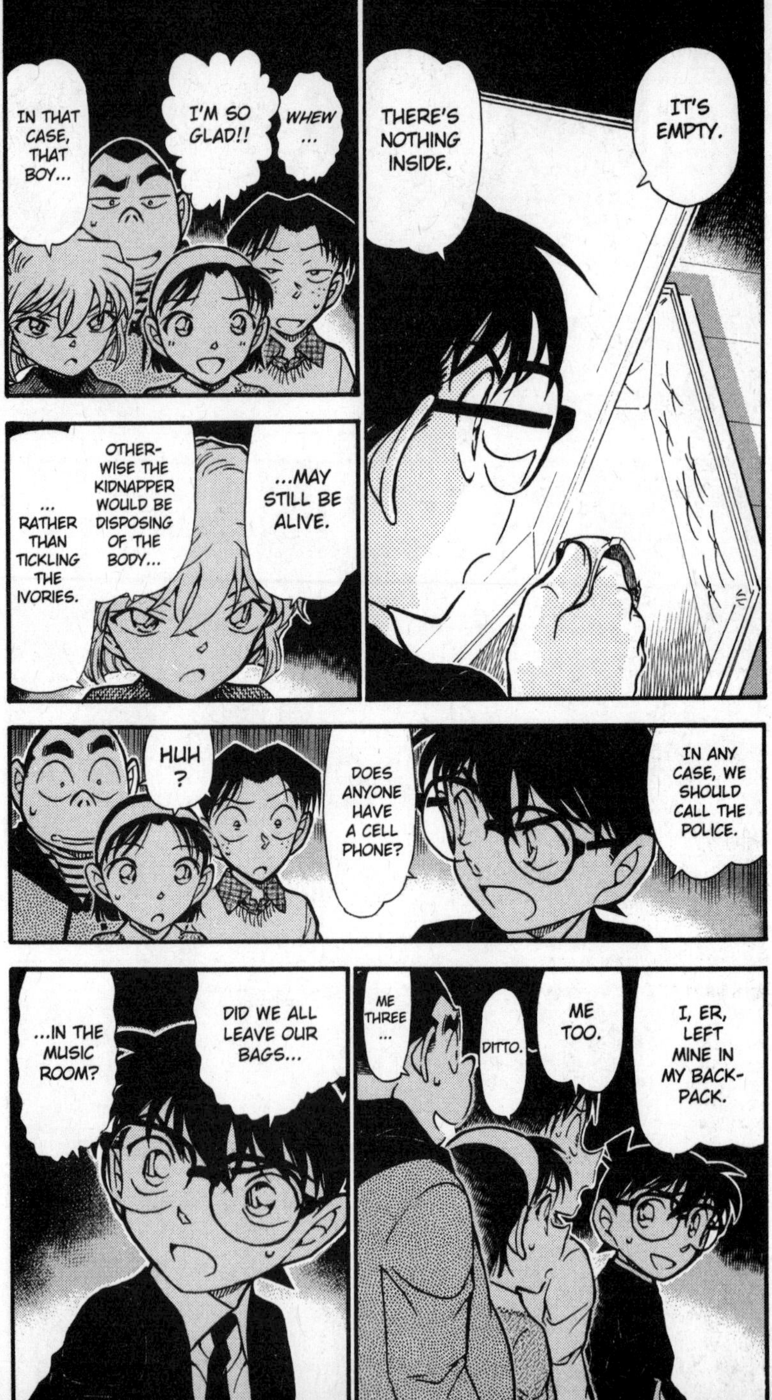
IT'S EMPTY.
THERE'S NOTHING INSIDE.
WHEW...
I'M SO GLAD!!
IN THAT CASE, THAT BOY...
...MAY STILL BE ALIVE.
OTHER-WISE THE KIDNAPPER WOULD BE DISPOSING OF THE BODY...
...RATHER THAN TICKLING THE IVORIES.
IN ANY CASE, WE SHOULD CALL THE POLICE.
DOES ANYONE HAVE A CELL PHONE?
HUH?
I, ER, LEFT MINE IN MY BACK-PACK.
ME TOO.
DITTO.
ME THREE...
DID WE ALL LEAVE OUR BAGS...
...IN THE MUSIC ROOM?

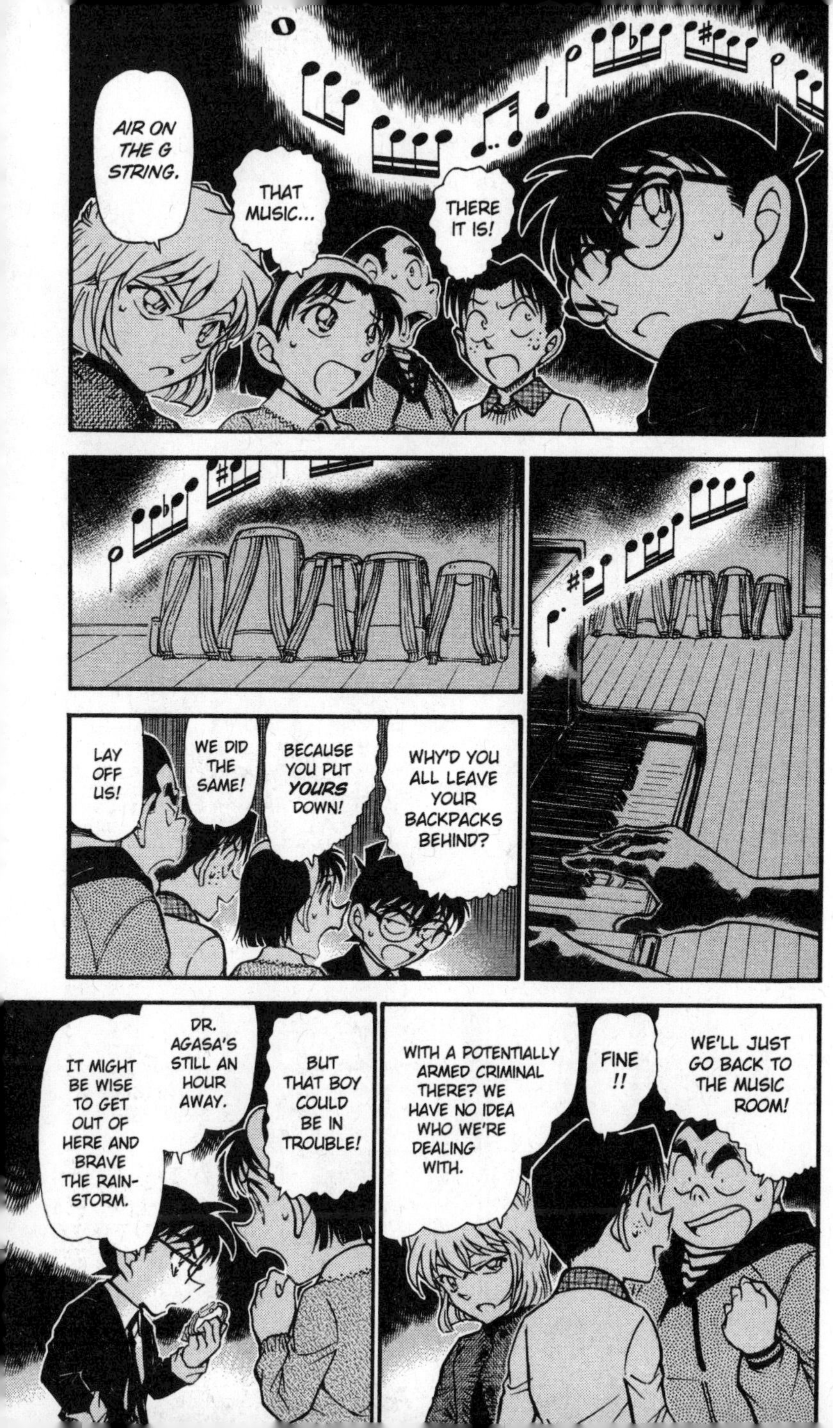
THERE IT IS!
THAT MUSIC...
AIR ON THE G STRING.
WHY'D YOU ALL LEAVE YOUR BACKPACKS BEHIND?
BECAUSE YOU PUT YOURS DOWN!
WE DID THE SAME!
LAY OFF US!
WE'LL JUST GO BACK TO THE MUSIC ROOM!
FINE!!
WITH A POTENTIALLY ARMED CRIMINAL THERE? WE HAVE NO IDEA WHO WE'RE DEALING WITH.
BUT THAT BOY COULD BE IN TROUBLE!
DR. AGASA'S STILL AN HOUR AWAY.
IT MIGHT BE WISE TO GET OUT OF HERE AND BRAVE THE RAINSTORM.

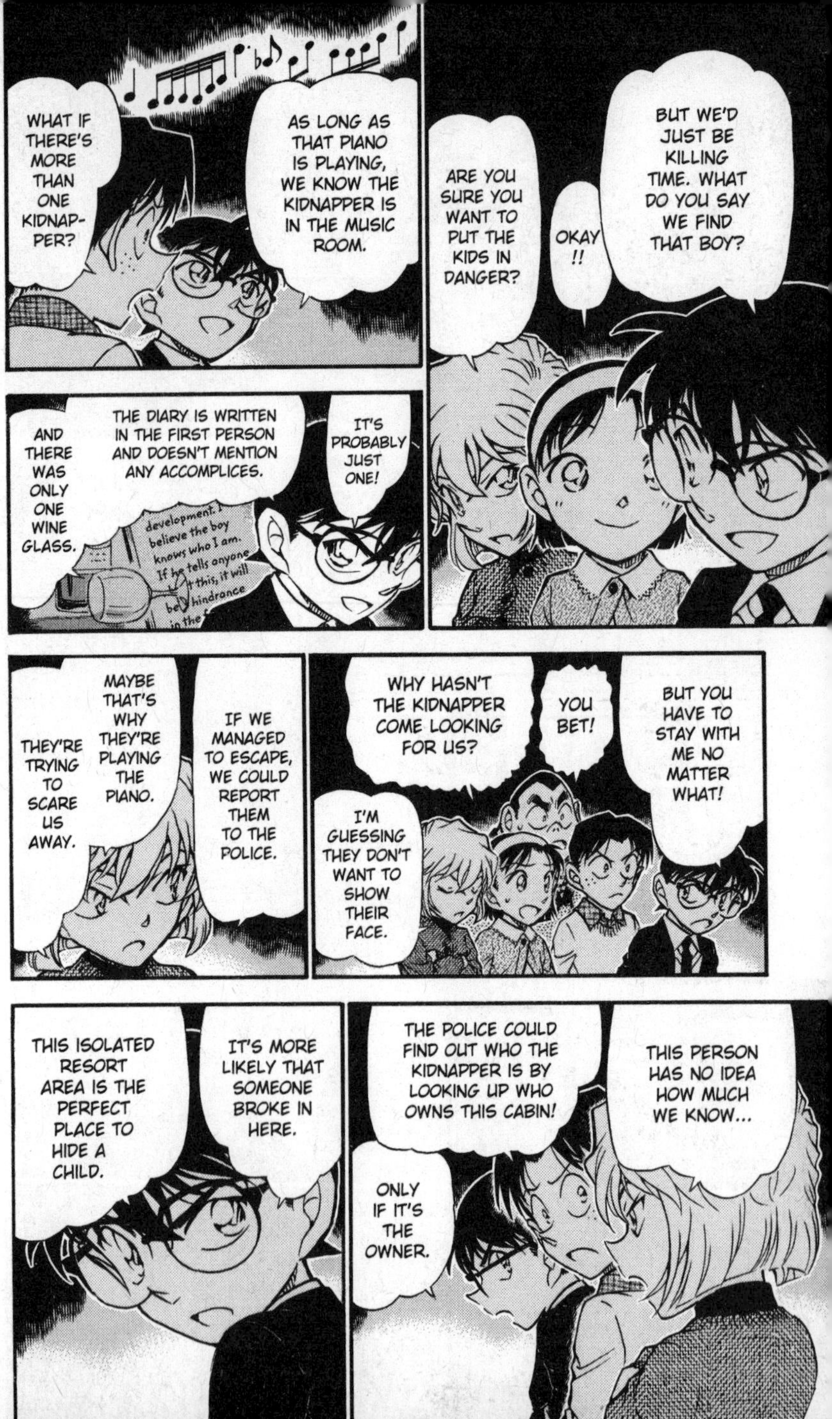
BUT WE'D JUST BE KILLING TIME. WHAT DO YOU SAY WE FIND THAT BOY?
OKAY!!
ARE YOU SURE YOU WANT TO PUT THE KIDS IN DANGER?
AS LONG AS THAT PIANO IS PLAYING, WE KNOW THE KIDNAPPER IS IN THE MUSIC ROOM.
WHAT IF THERE'S MORE THAN ONE KIDNAPPER?
IT'S PROBABLY JUST ONE!
THE DIARY IS WRITTEN IN THE FIRST PERSON AND DOESN'T MENTION ANY ACCOMPLICES.
AND THERE WAS ONLY ONE WINE GLASS.
development. I
believe the boy
knows who I am.
BUT YOU HAVE TO STAY WITH ME NO MATTER WHAT!
YOU BET!
WHY HASN'T THE KIDNAPPER COME LOOKING FOR US?
I'M GUESSING THEY DON'T WANT TO SHOW THEIR FACE.
IF WE MANAGED TO ESCAPE, WE COULD REPORT THEM TO THE POLICE.
MAYBE THAT'S WHY THEY'RE PLAYING THE PIANO.
THEY'RE TRYING TO SCARE US AWAY.
THIS PERSON HAS NO IDEA HOW MUCH WE KNOW...
THE POLICE COULD FIND OUT WHO THE KIDNAPPER IS BY LOOKING UP WHO OWNS THIS CABIN!
ONLY IF IT'S THE OWNER.
IT'S MORE LIKELY THAT SOMEONE BROKE IN HERE.
THIS ISOLATED RESORT AREA IS THE PERFECT PLACE TO HIDE A CHILD.

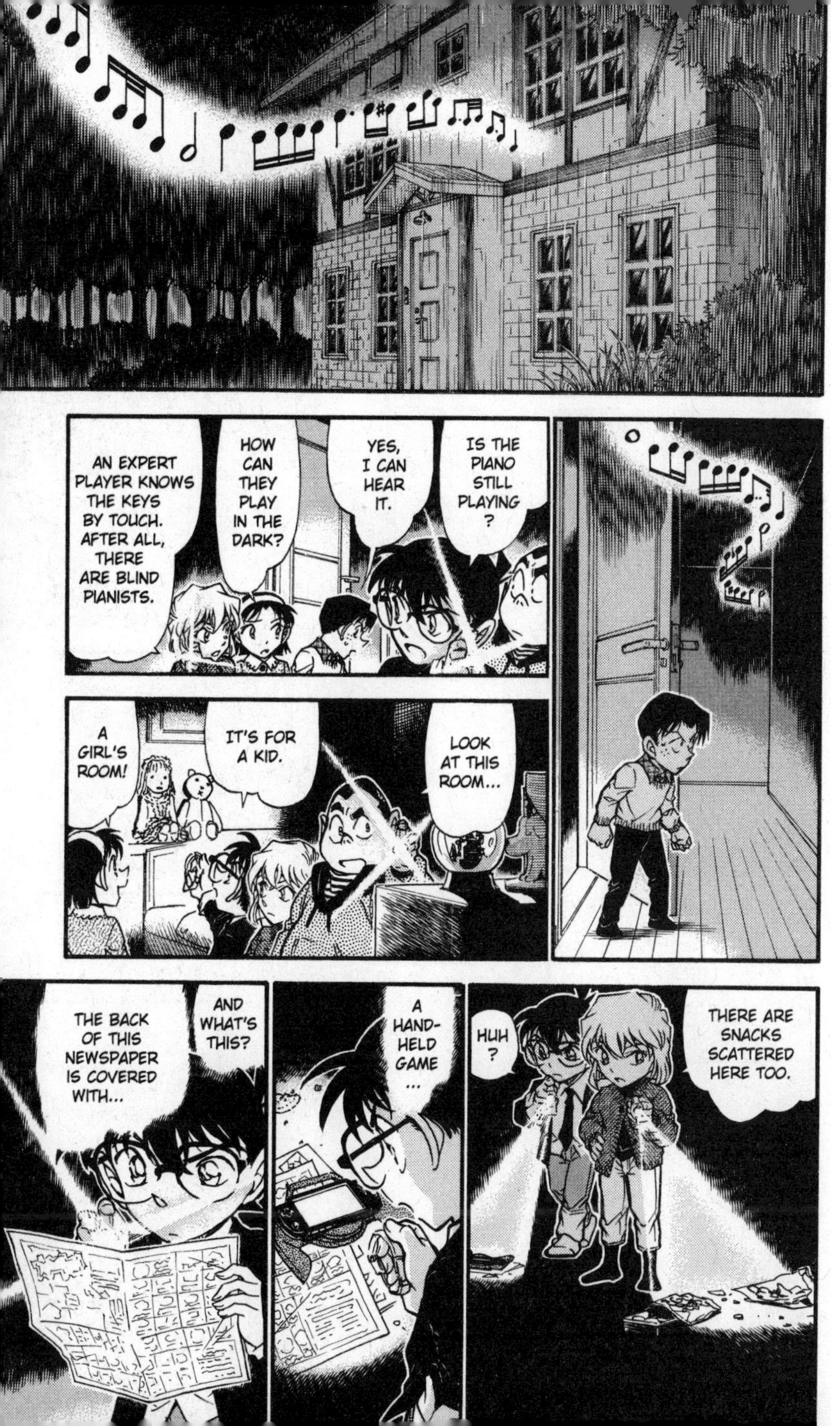
IS THE PIANO STILL PLAYING?
YES, I CAN HEAR IT.
HOW CAN THEY PLAY IN THE DARK?
AN EXPERT PLAYER KNOWS THE KEYS BY TOUCH. AFTER ALL, THERE ARE BLIND PIANISTS.
LOOK AT THIS ROOM...
IT'S FOR A KID.
A GIRL'S ROOM!
THERE ARE SNACKS SCATTERED HERE TOO.
HUH?
A HAND-HELD GAME...
AND WHAT'S THIS?
THE BACK OF THIS NEWSPAPER IS COVERED WITH...

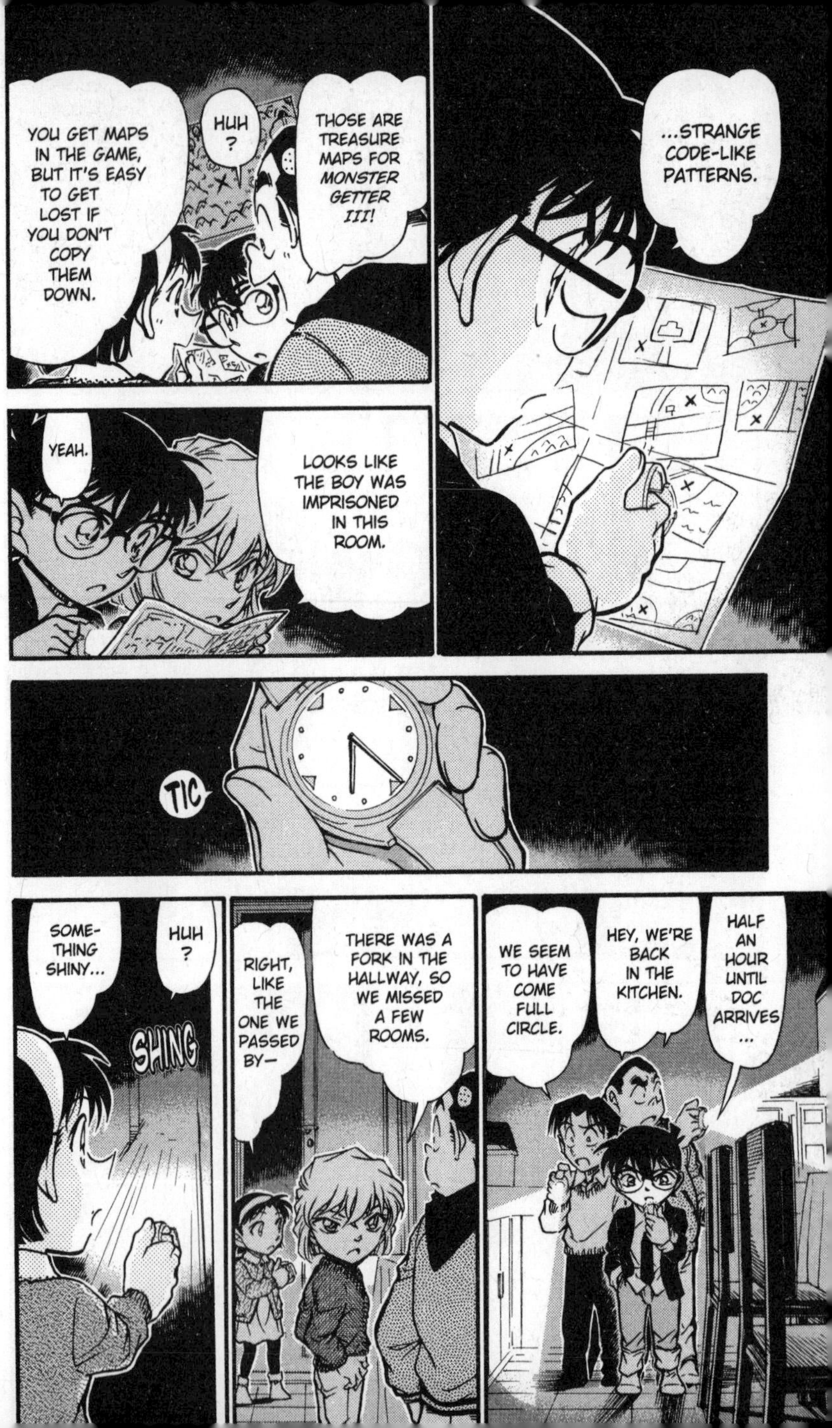
...STRANGE CODE-LIKE PATTERNS.
THOSE ARE TREASURE MAPS FOR MONSTER GETTER III!
HUH?
YOU GET MAPS IN THE GAME, BUT IT'S EASY TO GET LOST IF YOU DON'T COPY THEM DOWN.
LOOKS LIKE THE BOY WAS IMPRISONED IN THIS ROOM.
YEAH.
TIC
HALF AN HOUR UNTIL DOC ARRIVES...
HEY, WE'RE BACK IN THE KITCHEN.
WE SEEM TO HAVE COME FULL CIRCLE.
THERE WAS A FORK IN THE HALLWAY, SO WE MISSED A FEW ROOMS.
RIGHT, LIKE THE ONE WE PASSED BY—
HUH?
SHING
SOME-THING SHINY...

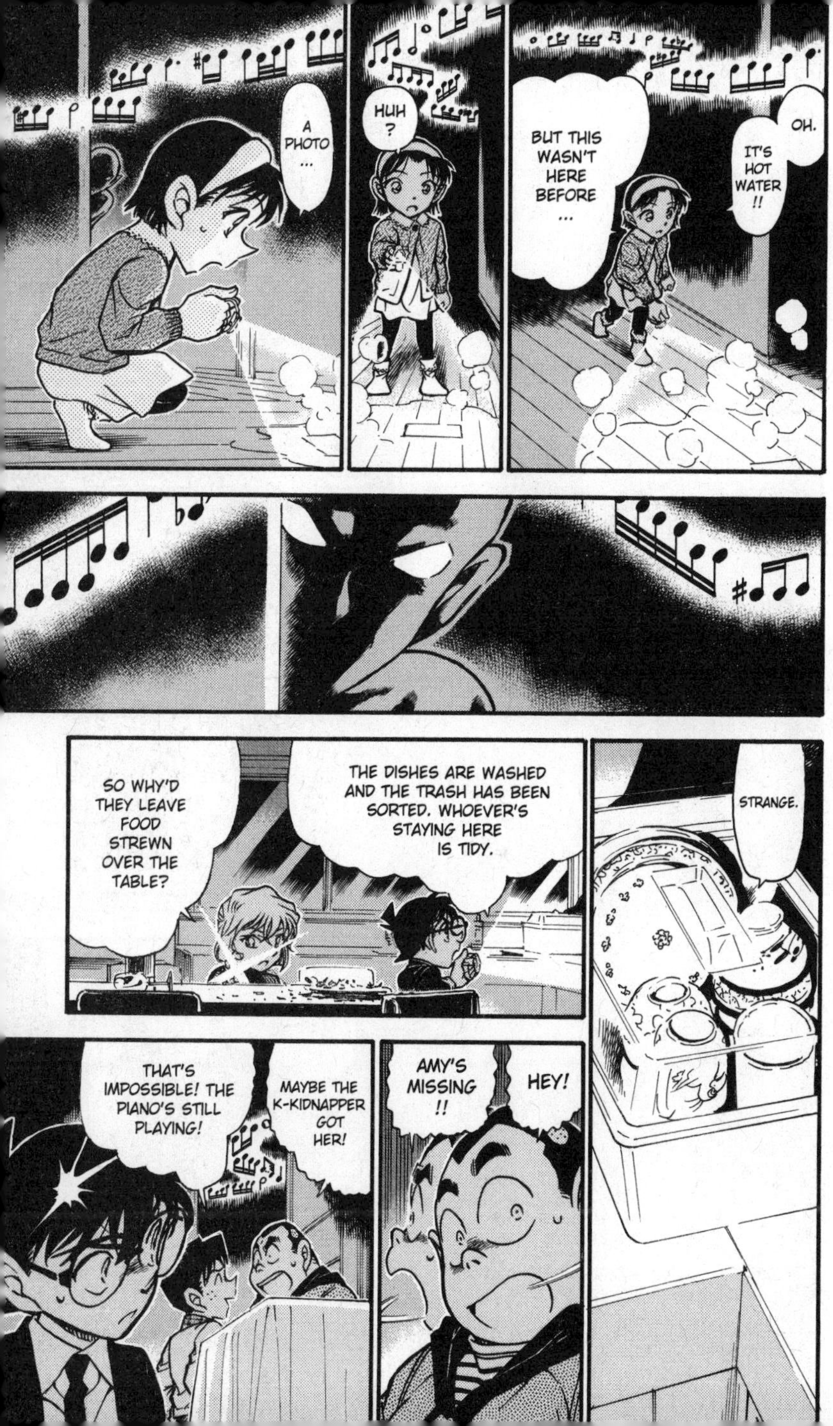
OH.
IT'S HOT WATER!!
BUT THIS WASN'T HERE BEFORE...
HUH?
A PHOTO...
STRANGE.
THE DISHES ARE WASHED AND THE TRASH HAS BEEN SORTED. WHOEVER'S STAYING HERE IS TIDY.
SO WHY'D THEY LEAVE FOOD STREWN OVER THE TABLE?
HEY!
AMY'S MISSING!!
MAYBE THE K-KIDNAPPER GOT HER!
THAT'S IMPOSSIBLE! THE PIANO'S STILL PLAYING!

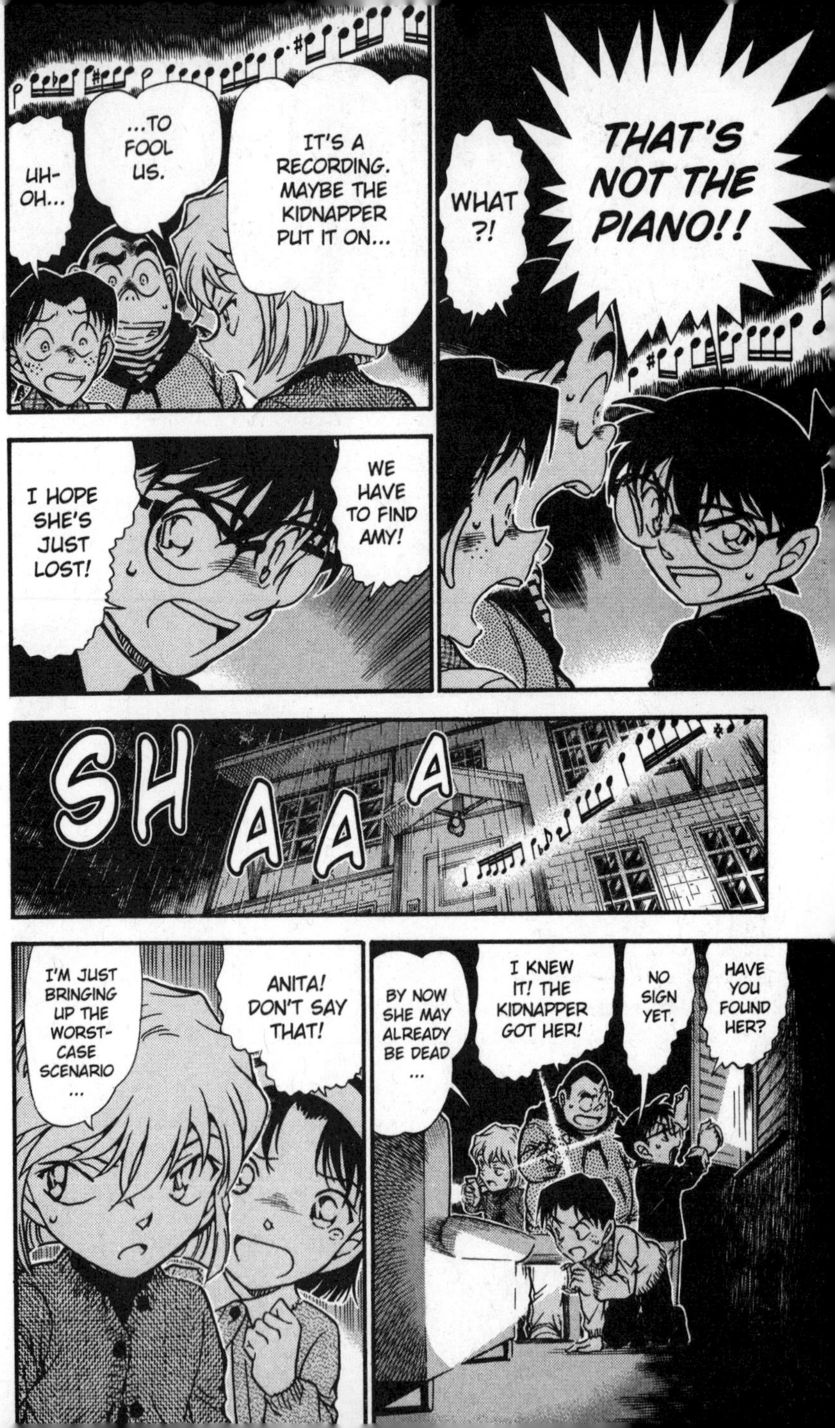
THAT'S NOT THE PIANO!!
WHAT ?!
IT'S A RECORDING. MAYBE THE KIDNAPPER PUT IT ON...
...TO FOOL US.
UH-OH...
WE HAVE TO FIND AMY!
I HOPE SHE'S JUST LOST!
SHAAA
HAVE YOU FOUND HER?
NO SIGN YET.
I KNEW IT! THE KIDNAPPER GOT HER!
BY NOW SHE MAY ALREADY BE DEAD ...
ANITA! DON'T SAY THAT!
I'M JUST BRINGING UP THE WORST-CASE SCENARIO ...

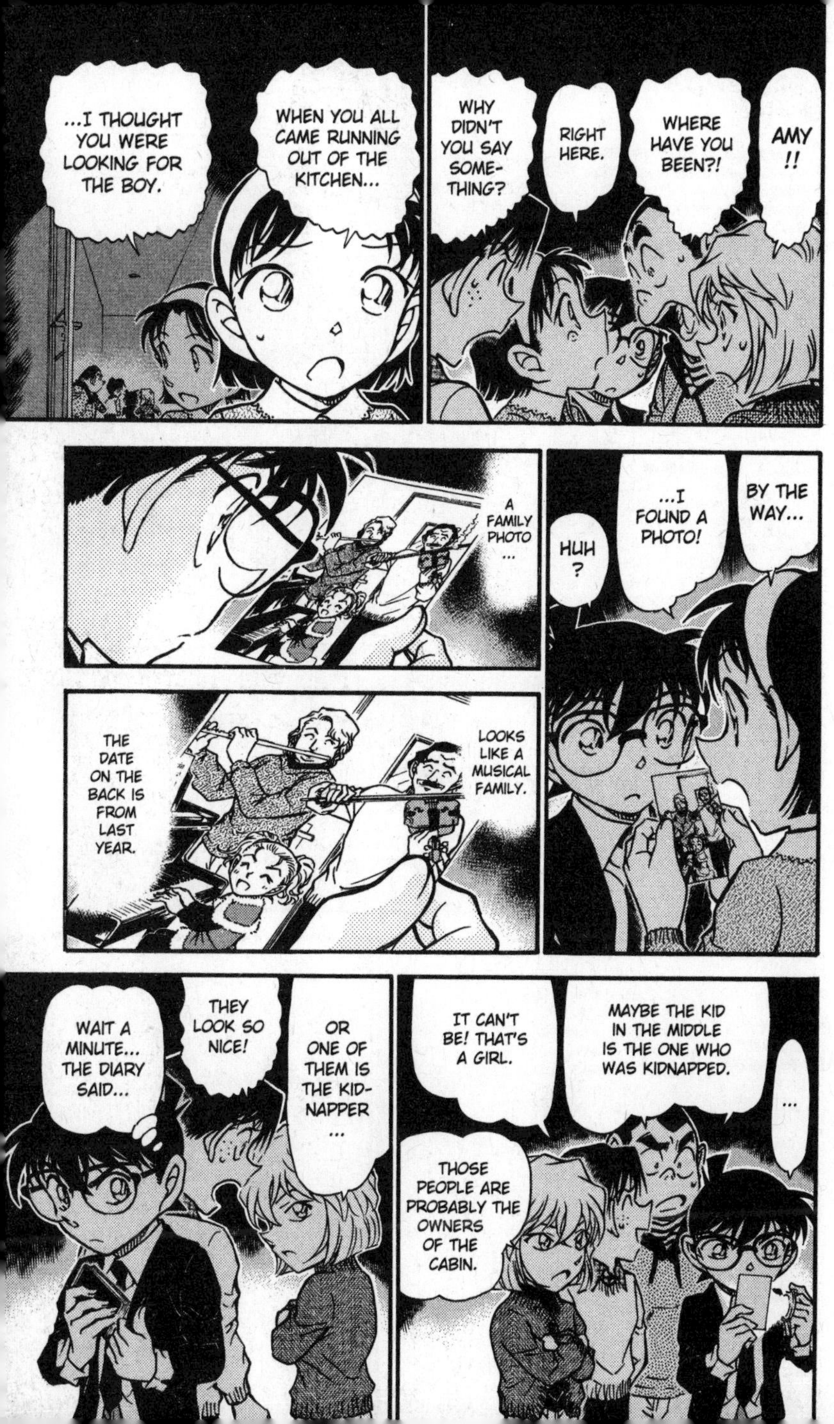
AMY !!
WHERE HAVE YOU BEEN?!
RIGHT HERE.
WHY DIDN'T YOU SAY SOME-THING?
WHEN YOU ALL CAME RUNNING OUT OF THE KITCHEN...
...I THOUGHT YOU WERE LOOKING FOR THE BOY.
BY THE WAY...
...I FOUND A PHOTO!
HUH ?
A FAMILY PHOTO ...
LOOKS LIKE A MUSICAL FAMILY.
THE DATE ON THE BACK IS FROM LAST YEAR.
...
MAYBE THE KID IN THE MIDDLE IS THE ONE WHO WAS KIDNAPPED.
IT CAN'T BE! THAT'S A GIRL.
THOSE PEOPLE ARE PROBABLY THE OWNERS OF THE CABIN.
OR ONE OF THEM IS THE KID-NAPPER ...
THEY LOOK SO NICE!
WAIT A MINUTE... THE DIARY SAID...

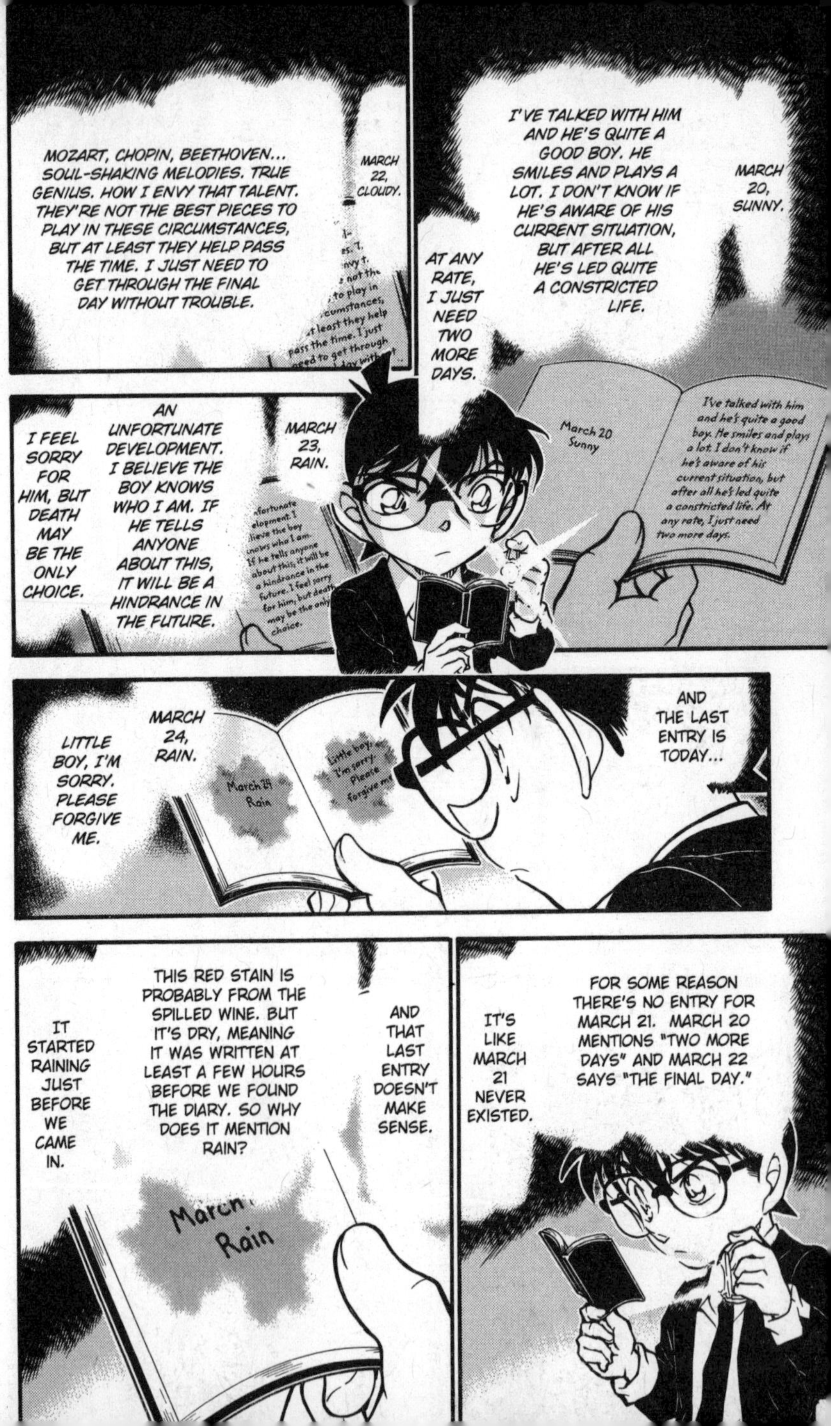
MARCH 20, SUNNY.
I'VE TALKED WITH HIM AND HE'S QUITE A GOOD BOY. HE SMILES AND PLAYS A LOT. I DON'T KNOW IF HE'S AWARE OF HIS CURRENT SITUATION, BUT AFTER ALL HE'S LED QUITE A CONSTRICTED LIFE.
AT ANY RATE, I JUST NEED TWO MORE DAYS.
March 20 Sunny
I've talked with him and he's quite a good boy. He smiles and plays a lot. I don't know if he's aware of his current situation, but after all he's led quite a constricted life. At any rate, I just need two more days.
MARCH 22, CLOUDY.
MOZART, CHOPIN, BEETHOVEN... SOUL-SHAKING MELODIES. TRUE GENIUS. HOW I ENVY THAT TALENT. THEY'RE NOT THE BEST PIECES TO PLAY IN THESE CIRCUMSTANCES, BUT AT LEAST THEY HELP PASS THE TIME. I JUST NEED TO GET THROUGH THE FINAL DAY WITHOUT TROUBLE.
MARCH 23, RAIN.
AN UNFORTUNATE DEVELOPMENT. I BELIEVE THE BOY KNOWS WHO I AM. IF HE TELLS ANYONE ABOUT THIS, IT WILL BE A HINDRANCE IN THE FUTURE.
I FEEL SORRY FOR HIM, BUT DEATH MAY BE THE ONLY CHOICE.
AND THE LAST ENTRY IS TODAY...
MARCH 24, RAIN.
LITTLE BOY, I'M SORRY. PLEASE FORGIVE ME.
March 24 Rain
FOR SOME REASON THERE'S NO ENTRY FOR MARCH 21. MARCH 20 MENTIONS "TWO MORE DAYS" AND MARCH 22 SAYS "THE FINAL DAY."
IT'S LIKE MARCH 21 NEVER EXISTED.
AND THAT LAST ENTRY DOESN'T MAKE SENSE.
THIS RED STAIN IS PROBABLY FROM THE SPILLED WINE. BUT IT'S DRY, MEANING IT WAS WRITTEN AT LEAST A FEW HOURS BEFORE WE FOUND THE DIARY. SO WHY DOES IT MENTION RAIN?
IT STARTED RAINING JUST BEFORE WE CAME IN.
Rain

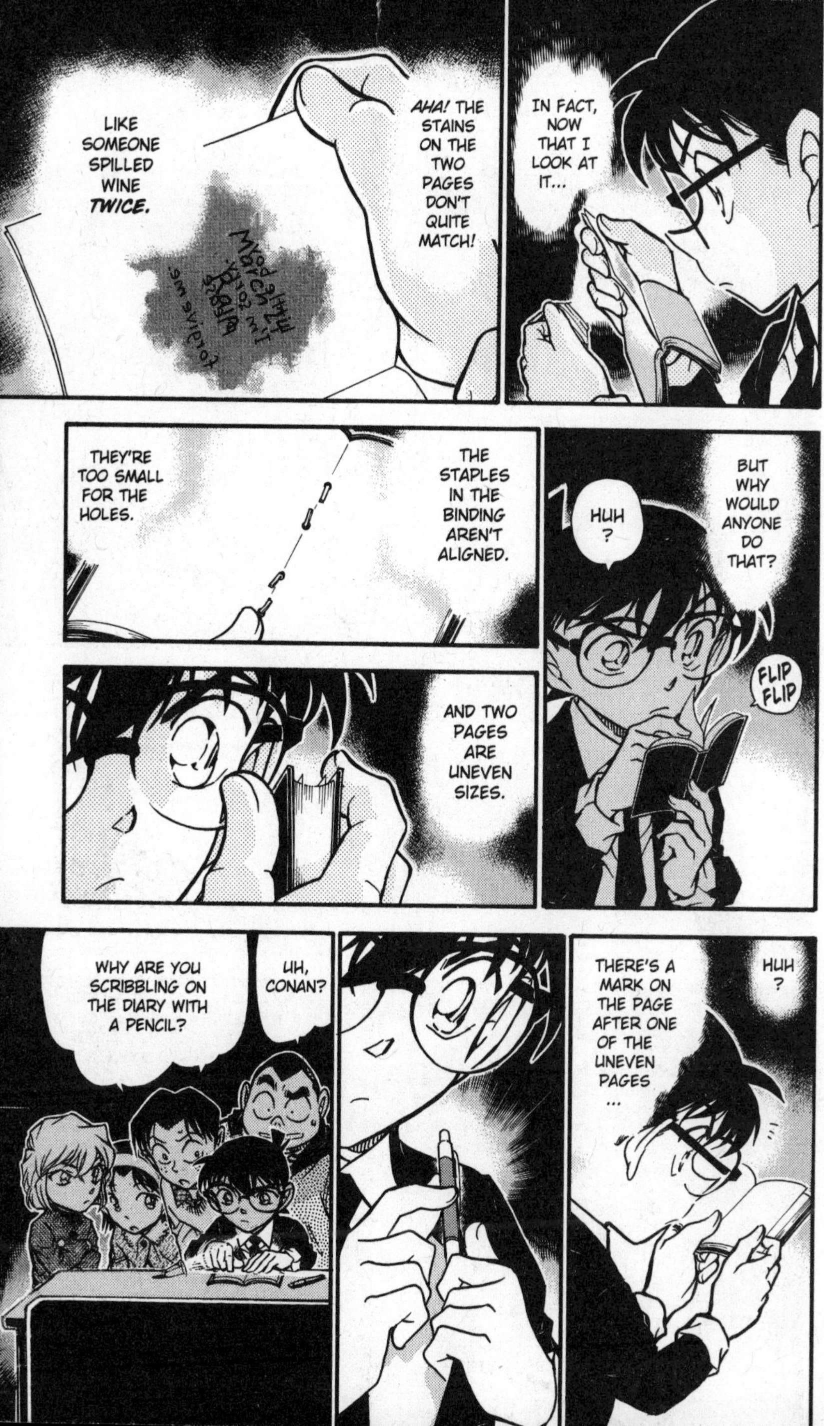
IN FACT, NOW THAT I LOOK AT IT...
AHA! THE STAINS ON THE TWO PAGES DON'T QUITE MATCH!
LIKE SOMEONE SPILLED WINE ***TWICE.***
BUT WHY WOULD ANYONE DO THAT?
HUH?
FLIP FLIP
THE STAPLES IN THE BINDING AREN'T ALIGNED.
THEY'RE TOO SMALL FOR THE HOLES.
AND TWO PAGES ARE UNEVEN SIZES.
HUH?
THERE'S A MARK ON THE PAGE AFTER ONE OF THE UNEVEN PAGES...
UH, CONAN?
WHY ARE YOU SCRIBBLING ON THE DIARY WITH A PENCIL?

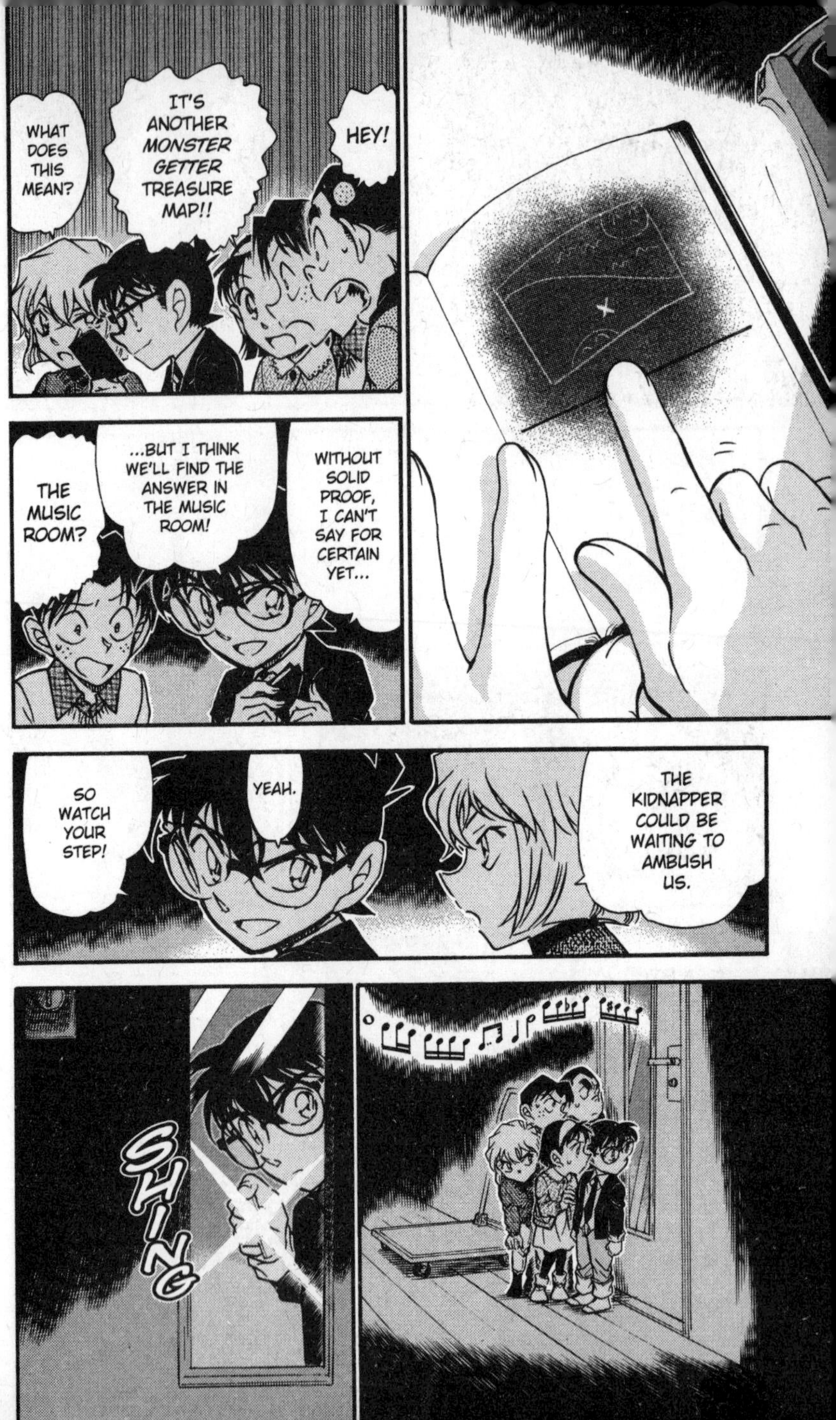
HEY!
IT'S ANOTHER MONSTER GETTER TREASURE MAP!!
WHAT DOES THIS MEAN?
WITHOUT SOLID PROOF, I CAN'T SAY FOR CERTAIN YET...
...BUT I THINK WE'LL FIND THE ANSWER IN THE MUSIC ROOM!
THE MUSIC ROOM?
THE KIDNAPPER COULD BE WAITING TO AMBUSH US.
YEAH.
SO WATCH YOUR STEP!
SHING

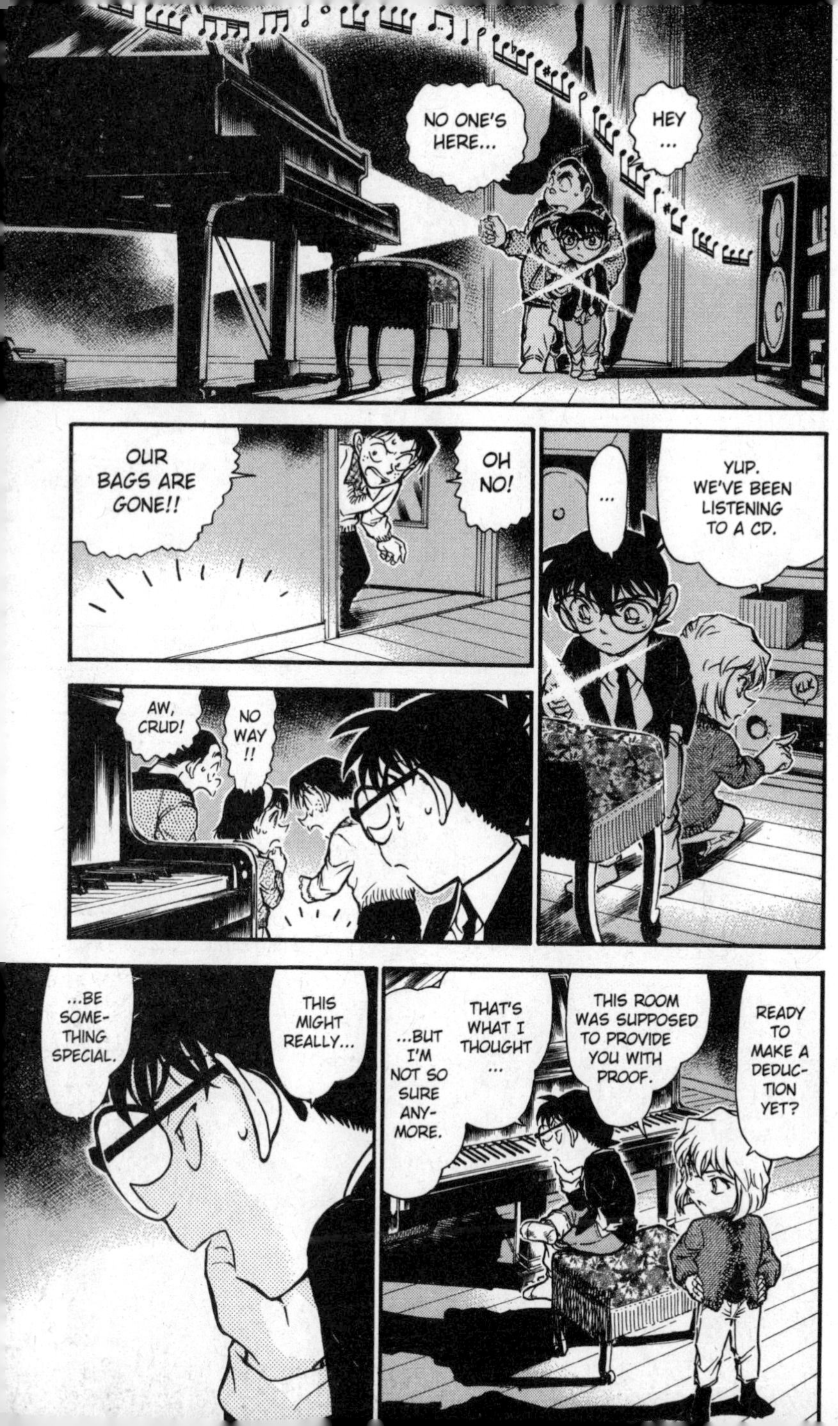
HEY ...
NO ONE'S HERE...
YUP. WE'VE BEEN LISTENING TO A CD.
...
KLK
OH NO!
OUR BAGS ARE GONE!!
NO WAY !!
AW, CRUD!
READY TO MAKE A DEDUCTION YET?
THIS ROOM WAS SUPPOSED TO PROVIDE YOU WITH PROOF.
THAT'S WHAT I THOUGHT ...
...BUT I'M NOT SO SURE ANYMORE.
THIS MIGHT REALLY...
...BE SOMETHING SPECIAL.

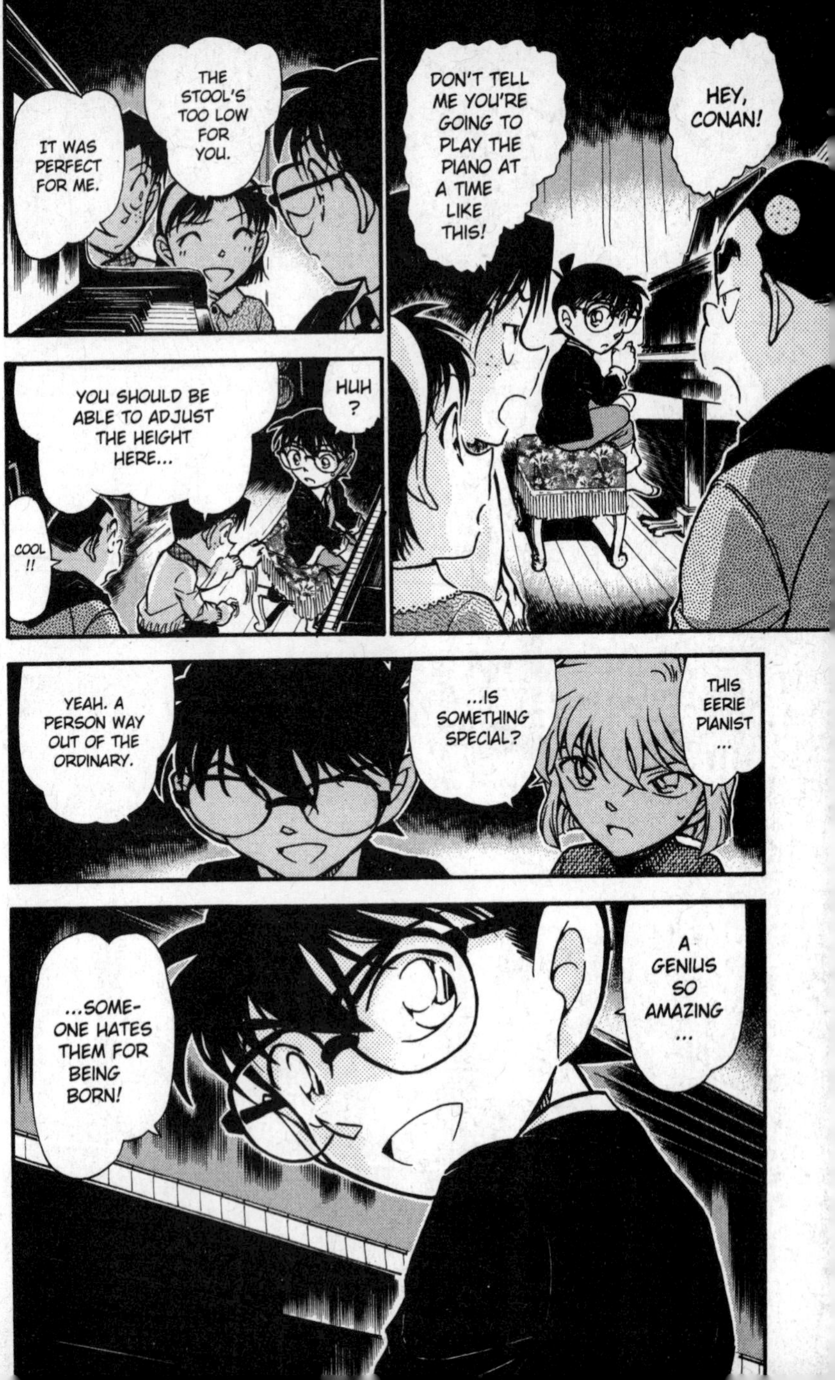
HEY, CONAN!
DON'T TELL ME YOU'RE GOING TO PLAY THE PIANO AT A TIME LIKE THIS!
THE STOOL'S TOO LOW FOR YOU.
IT WAS PERFECT FOR ME.
HUH?
YOU SHOULD BE ABLE TO ADJUST THE HEIGHT HERE...
COOL!!
THIS EERIE PIANIST...
...IS SOMETHING SPECIAL?
YEAH. A PERSON WAY OUT OF THE ORDINARY.
A GENIUS SO AMAZING...
...SOME-ONE HATES THEM FOR BEING BORN!

Hello, Aoyama here!

Did you see it? Of course you did, right? Japan vs. Denmark in the 2010 Soccer World Cup! Two kinds of free kicks, a knuckleball and a spinning ball! An iron-clad defense protecting Japan's goal! And the third fatal goal earned by switching from defense to attack! This match was legendary and inspired me to draw Samurai Blue's Hideo Akagi on the back cover! Sorry he doesn't appear in this volume, though... *Heh.*

Gosho Aoyama's
Mystery Library

69

RICHARD CUFF

If literature's first sleuth is Dupin from "The Murders in the Rue Morgue," who is literature's first police detective? The answer is Sergeant Richard Cuff! All skin and bones with sharp features and dry skin, he looks like a grim reverend or a mortician. No one would ever imagine he's a top detective from Scotland Yard. But his gray eyes see "something more from you than you were aware of yourself" and overlook nothing. He can find the smallest scrap of evidence left behind at the scene of a crime and notice the most trivial contradiction in a testimony. It may come as a surprise that his hobby is gardening and he loves roses.

His author, Wilkie Collins, fell sick while writing this novel but continued to work on it even when he was bedridden. I'd probably just sleep...

I recommend *The Moonstone*.

MAGI

The labyrinth of magic

Story & Art by
SHINOBU OHTAKA

A **fantasy adventure** inspired by
One Thousand and One Nights

Deep within the deserts lie the mysterious Dungeons, vast stores of riches there for the taking by anyone lucky enough to find them and brave enough to venture into the depths from where few have ever returned. Plucky young adventurer **Aladdin** means to find the Dungeons and their riches, but Aladdin may be just as mysterious as the treasures he seeks.